ARMS

ARMS

The Culture and Credo of the Gun

A.J. SOMERSET

BIBLIOASIS
WINDSOR, ONTARIO

FIRST EDITION

Library and Archives Canada Cataloguing in Publication

Somerset, A. J., 1969-, author
        Arms : the culture and credo of the gun / A.J. Somerset.

Includes bibliographical references and index.
Issued in print and electronic formats.

ISBN 978-1-77196-028-1 (pbk.).--ISBN 978-1-77196-029-8 (epub)

        1. Firearms--Social aspects--United States--History.
2. Firearms--Social aspects--Canada--History. 3. Firearms ownership--United States--History. 4. Firearms ownership--Canada--History. 5. Firearms--United States--History.
6. Firearms--Canada--History. I. Title.

HV8059.S63 2015   683.400973   C2014-907927-3
                                             C2014-907928-1

Edited by Martha Sharpe
Copy-edited by Emily Donaldson
Typeset by Chris Andrechek
Cover designed by Kate Hargreaves

Published with the generous assistance of the Canada Council for the Arts and the Ontario Arts Council. Biblioasis also acknowledges the support of the Government of Canada through the Canada Book Fund and the Government of Ontario through the Ontario Book Publishing Tax Credit.

PRINTED AND BOUND IN CANADA

MIX
Paper from
responsible sources
FSC® C004071

ANCIENT FOREST ™
FRIENDLY

Contents

Part III: All Are Punish'd: The Consequences of Never Growing Up

Something about our republic makes us go armed.
—Thomas McGuane

Introduction

I AM FORTY-SIX YEARS OLD, and my ears ring non-stop.

Lying awake in the quiet before dawn, a distant whine fills my ears and I wonder, is this normal? Is it new, or has it been there for years, unnoticed? Or is it perhaps the direct and irreversible result of my recent hobby, trapshooting, hundreds of rounds a week from a 12-gauge, the shotgun bucking in my hands and barking in my ear—in other words, a warning sign that I will soon be deaf?

Common sense suggests the latter. My son, having reached the age where it amuses him to underline his father's advancing decrepitude, tested my hearing with a smartphone app that plays a high-pitched tone, audible only to people under a certain age.

"Can you hear that?"

"Hear what?"

"Are you serious? How can you not hear that?"

He adjusted the phone.

"How about that? Can you hear that?"

"Hear what?"

He collapsed in vales of giggles; it seemed likely he was merely mocking me. There was no sound to hear. I was sure of it.

"You're supposed to be able to hear that, unless you're, like, sixty-five."

I turned to my wife: "Is that thing actually making a sound?"

"Go get your hearing checked."

I envision myself wrinkled and infirm, with a small brass horn held to one ear, hoarse and cranky, answering remarks about the weather: "No, thank you, Miss. I am not into leather."

Accordingly, I have discarded my old ear defenders and replaced them with a heavier set, and now find myself considering a set of custom-moulded plugs to wear under them. I intend to hear music when I die. Of course, I could always quit shooting. But let's not go crazy here.

I LIKE GUNS. That's a difficult admission, as if I were confessing to some kind of perversion, though it ought not to be. People like all kinds of things: cars, sailboats, acoustic guitars, fountain pens, Swiss watches, split-cane fly rods, canoes. Nobody has to justify liking these things, as I am continually asked to justify liking guns. My reason is simple: shooting is fun, just as blasting music is fun, or canoeing, or fly fishing, or driving a powerful car at irresponsible speeds. Nobody thinks you're weird for liking power tools.

But people are likely to think you're weird for liking guns, which is why it's a difficult admission. In their eyes, you become one of those gun nuts. And although I like guns, I do not like gun nuts. I do not like hearing people talk about keeping a gun handy to deal with goblins, or to resist socialism, or to survive the coming collapse. And in the aftermath of some horror show, of a Newtown or an Aurora, I detest the voices that squawk about their right to bear arms in the face of suggestions that, you know, maybe we should make guns just a little bit more difficult for the average homicidal maniac to buy.[1] I like guns, in other words, but I'm uncomfortable with the gun culture.

I've played with a lot of guns. In my short time as an armoured crewman in Canada's armed forces, I fired rifles, pistols, sub-machine guns, machine guns, even the 76mm cannon on the now-obsolete AVGP Cougar armoured car, a vehicle we called a boat for its somewhat questionable amphibious capability.[2] When the main gun fired, the boat bucked like a mustang and the turret filled with smoke and the clang of the spent casing bouncing down into the turret bin. As a crew commander you planted your face in the sight and hugged it before giving the order to fire, because if you left your head floating free in that turret then some piece of cold, recoil-driven steel would split your tender forehead and send you down for stitches. It's said when they test-fired the prototype Cougar, the back

---

1   On December 14, 2012, Adam Lanza shot and killed twenty children and six staff members at Sandy Hook Elementary School in Newtown, Connecticut. On July 20 of that year, James Holmes opened fire in a movie theatre in Aurora, Colorado, killing twelve and wounding seventy.
2   AVGP: Armoured Vehicle General Purpose.

doors blew off the boat, and I believe it. And as the whining extractor fan struggled to clear the smoke, my nostrils filled with the sting of burned powder and hot brass and hydraulic oil, the same thought always was there: this is the most fun you can have with clothes on.

It probably wasn't doing my hearing any good.

That was my biggest gun, if we're keeping score. But they were all fun. A 9mm pistol at a steel plate, swinging around a pole, each shot pushing it around to the other side and in my ears not the report of the pistol but the bullets ringing off the plate with every shot—ting, ting, ting—until the slide locks open on an empty magazine. Blowing hundreds of rounds of excess ammo through the Army's C7 at the end of a range day, a perk of being an instructor, until the barrel smoked. The lesson of full automatic fire on the C7 and on its sub-machine gun predecessor, the Sterling: you make an impressive amount of noise and it sure is fun, but you don't hit a damn thing. Firing the C6 machine gun prone off the shoulder was worse: I couldn't see anything through the dust kicked up by the muzzle blast and had no idea where my tracers were going. So many range days and so many training exercises, as the Cold War fizzled out, none of that training ever put to use. Perhaps I wouldn't think guns were fun if I'd ever shot anyone, or been shot at in turn.

When I left the Army I turned in my uniform and assorted accoutrements and carefully folded my black beret into a closet drawer with my sergeant's rank badges, and I left all that behind. Guns are expensive and the ammo bill soon adds up, and I had no real urge to go shooting anyway. But fifteen years later I got a dog, an idea planted in my mind when doing freelance photography for outdoor magazines. The dog demanded birds. And so I went out and took my mandatory safety course and got my firearms licence and a shotgun, and, having come up through the Army where you never do anything without practicing it first, I found myself on the sixteen-yard line at the St. Thomas Gun Club near London, Ontario, watching a clay pigeon spin away from me unharmed as that familiar burnt-powder smell conjured up all the ghosts of cold and windy ranges past.

What returned most clearly with that scent wasn't the shooting, but the people, because very little of the time spent on ranges is spent shooting. It's spent instead making excuses for missing, knowing everyone sees right through your excuses because they have made all the same excuses, too; in hearing the same old jokes again, the same old stories. There is a difference between war stories and fairy tales, as the joke goes: all fairy tales begin, "Once upon a time," while all war stories begin, "No shit, there we were." St. Thomas Gun Club war stories generally involve coyote or deer hunting in place of midnight recce patrols, but the spirit remains the same. The people and the chatter remain strangely familiar, even after fifteen years in the wilderness. You can count on death, taxes, and repeated complaints of the criminal perfidy of the Liberal Party.

Whether it's from my fifteen-year absence or a contrarian streak I've developed in the interim, I find that I no longer quite fit in. I do not take for granted that Liberal perfidy exceeds that of any other party, or that taxes ought always to be lower regardless of bills that must be paid, or that people who live in Toronto are a special breed of idiots. But something seems off beyond all this, something evident only occasionally here at the gun club, as perhaps when someone declares he will not join this particular club because it is aligned with the Ontario Federation of Anglers and Hunters, whose gun politics are insufficiently hardcore. "They're not gonna stand up for me," he explains, "so why would I give them one thin dime?" Then he goes back to his argument that the most accurate rifle you can buy for the money these days is a Chinese-made copy of the M14. His is tricked out with a black synthetic stock and accessory rails; it looks damn cool, he says, and scares the shit out of the antis. Oh, but it's one of them semi-automatic tactical black rifles, and do you think the OFAH is going to lift a finger to protect that?

On YouTube I find a video released by the Canadian Shooting Sports Association called "The Good, the Bad, and the Ugly." The Good are law-abiding folk just minding their own business and the Bad are violent criminals lurking in the shadows just beyond the porch light. The Ugly are the politicians in Ottawa, who have taken from the Good their God-given right to shoot the Bad dead in self-defence. The solution? Join the CSSA and support its fight to convince the Ugly to allow the Good to go armed.[3] It's not clear just which "shooting sports" had come to include shooting *people*, and thus placed killing within the interests of a shooting sports association, but there it is: Canada's own little NRA, eagerly importing the values of the American gun nut into Canada.

It seemed that in my fifteen years' absence, the gun culture had grown more radical, and less tolerant of any who departed from its

3 This video, which predated the dismantling of Canada's long-gun registry by Bill C-19, has since been removed.

tenets. If you own guns, it is now taken as given that you must believe even the most tentative gun control is at best futile and at worst a step towards the total confiscation of all firearms by a totalitarian state. And of course you are also assumed to hold a set of shared beliefs on any number of subjects completely unrelated to guns—on partisan politics and government and climate change and environmental regulations and religion and whether the war in Iraq was a good idea—as if your gun had come with a free, bonus ideological Family Pack, a ready-made identity. Anyone who breaks ranks is a traitor to the cause. Gun culture, I discovered, is not just about guns.

But what is gun culture? It's all well and good to talk about "the gun culture" in tones of deep disapproval, as people do, but unless we know what we actually mean by gun culture we risk falling prey to what the American poet and novelist Jim Harrison called "the hideously mistaken idea that talking is thinking." And gun culture is a slippery concept.

If you have a gun, are you a member of that gun culture? Here I sit with my Browning pump disassembled on the desk in front of me, yet convinced that I am not of the gun culture. I put the gun back together and lock it away and spend the evening playing *Battlefield: Bad Company*. Fighting my way through the dirty, rubble-strewn streets of Serdaristan, I find myself wondering if even the virtual gun in my virtual hands elects me to membership in a gun culture. Is it the idea of the gun, or the gun itself that matters? What are the core beliefs of the gun culture? What are the shared values of this ill-defined nation? Then I am killed, such thoughts being bad for the gamer's concentration.

"Gun culture" most often denotes that strange and paranoid corner of America represented by the NRA at its most strident. We have on one hand America, a land populated by sane people who believe reasonable things and generally do not shoot each other unless directly threatened, and even then rarely because they do not keep loaded guns handy, and on the other hand we have the gun culture, represented by wackos and weirdos and rednecks, who sit on their front porches stroking the barrels of their shotguns, shooting any animal that moves, and fantasizing about the day some criminal will walk up the wrong garden path where they lie in wait, armed, protecting their Second Amendment rights against their own government. In no time at all, "gun culture" becomes snide shorthand for redneckery.

But the idea of a gun culture originally included us all, even if we experienced guns only through TV, movies, or *Battlefield: Bad Company*. The historian Richard Hofstadter coined the expression in a 1970 essay in the magazine *American Heritage*, in which he contended not that America *has* a gun culture, that America *contains* a gun culture, or that America *tolerates* a gun culture, but that America *is* a gun culture—that the gun as a symbol is so deeply ingrained within the American character as to be inseparable from Mom, apple pie, and all the rest. On the opposite side of the ideological divide, the economist John Lott opens his book *More Guns, Less Crime*—the bible of the concealed-carry movement—with a similar assertion: "American culture is a gun culture—not merely in the sense that in 2009 about 124 million people lived in households that owned a total of about 270 million guns, but in the broader sense that guns pervade our debates on crime and are constantly present in movies and the news." It scarcely matters that 200 million-odd Americans live in households with no guns at all; the gun defines them regardless.

To Hofstadter, a gun culture elevates the gun to a privileged place as a cherished national symbol. America is a gun culture, then, while Canada is not. Canada's foundational myths do not rely on the rifle; in place of the rifle that never seems to leave the Minuteman's hands, the voyageur carries only a canoe paddle. But people in Canada own guns and have attitudes towards guns. Is that not a gun culture of sorts? Blake Brown, in *Arming and Disarming*, his history of gun control in Canada, reminds us that law and culture are the same thing: our culture is our values and attitudes, and the law is our attempt to give those values formal description. If we have laws about guns, then we have a culture about guns, or a gun culture. And from that perspective, every nation has a gun culture, although to say that either Britain or Australia has a gun culture stretches the usage beyond its tensile strength. The concept no longer provides any leverage.

Across the Atlantic, teenaged chavs carry knives under their coats, the better to threaten each other, each shining blade a force multiplier arguing for respect on behalf of the drunken lout that wields it. The problem, the *Telegraph* informs us, is that the courts have "failed to keep pace with the knife culture on Britain's streets."[4] In Australia, a woman breaks up with her boyfriend in a pizzeria, and when the owner tries to kick him out, he pulls out a box-cutter and slashes his ex and

---

4   "'We're out of touch on knife crime,' says top judge." *The Telegraph*, July 9, 2008.

the manager. At trial, the judge proclaims, "Knife culture has to stop."[5] But what is knife culture? And how is knife culture distinct from, say, the culture of drunken louts who hit each other in the head with beer bottles? Is that a broken-beer-bottle culture? Our Australian friend, it turns out, has a history of violent crime. Does anything he does have anything to do with a knife culture, or is a knife simply a convenient, concealable weapon that finds its way into the hands of a violent man?

Any conceptual leverage we get from the idea of a gun culture is illusory if we haven't figured out quite what we mean by it in the first place. You pry at bedrock with a bar of untempered steel that bends as soon as you put your back into it and you imagine you must be tremendously strong, but it is only that your lever is weak. The gun culture is, you know, all those crazy people with guns; it's, you know, all about having a gun and being ready to use it. It's violence—yes!—a culture of violence! And so on and so forth, defining the culture of the Other within our own minds, without examining his actual ideas, which, for obvious reasons, is ordinarily a good place to start.

America is a gun culture, as Richard Hofstadter argued, but America's gun culture is not uniform. American culture forms a battleground, a Passchendaele of mud and slime and half-collapsed trenches across which pro-gun and anti-gun armies writhe, struggling for control and measuring their victories not in yards but in inches. Which faction shall I describe?

Early in 2014, Slide Fire Solutions, a manufacturer of aftermarket gun stocks that in effect make semi-automatic rifles fully automatic, put up billboards in Chicago bearing three images, side by side: a baseball mitt folded around a ball, an apple pie, and an AR-15-style rifle equipped with a Slide Fire stock.[6] Across the bottom of the billboard was a row of symbols: the Statue of Liberty, an ichthys (the Jesus fish), an American flag as stylized for military uniforms, and an oval containing "2A," referring to the Second Amendment. This is what makes America great: God, Liberty, and Guns. Here we find a gun culture

---

5   "'Knife culture' slammed after box cutter attack in Blackburn pizza restaurant." *The Age*, November 22, 2013.

6   See "'Pure American' rifle billboard assaulted." *Chicago Tribune*, February 1, 2014. The Slide Fire stock allows controlled "bump firing" using the recoil of the weapon to rapidly manipulate the trigger. The gun is able to recoil independently of the stock and pistol grip, so that if the shooter pushes forward on the gun's forearm and keeps his trigger finger in position, the cycle of recoil and recovery will repeatedly fire the gun as if it were fully automatic. Since the law defines a machine gun as a weapon that fires repeatedly as long as the trigger is depressed, this design slips through a legal loophole and is considered semi-automatic. The Slide Fire stock is illegal in Canada.

within the broader gun culture that is America, a culture that declares the gun to be as American as Mom and apple pie and as sacred as Jesus himself.[7] This is the gun culture I am after in this book: the weird stuff.

You lift the floorboards to check the bilge and find the bottom of the boat awash with crazy ideas leaking in from someplace. It seems they're always sloshing around under the floorboards, no matter how long you run the pumps: dark, oily stuff with dead things floating in it. Never enough to put you in any danger of sinking, but once you know it's down there, the smell starts to get to you. It's got to be coming from somewhere, and I aim to find out where. I am after the source.

Guns don't kill people; ideas kill people. This is not a book about guns or about gun control, although of course guns and gun control figure in it. Neither is this a work of history, although the search for the source of this dark, oily bilge water will drag us into America's archives. This is a book about ideas that kill people, about the palimpsest of untruth, half-truth, and wishful fabrication that Americans have piled up to paper over their inconvenient truths. It is a book about how American gun activists have come to place their AR-15s alongside apple pie and a boy's well-worn baseball mitt as symbols of Good American Values, and to transform the Second Amendment into a religious text consisting of only four words: Shall Not Be Infringed. It is about why so many Americans count themselves as gun people, and about what it means to be gun people, about how so many people have become convinced they must keep a loaded gun handy *just in case* and hold on to their guns to keep the government at bay, and even to stockpile ammunition in case tomorrow brings the end of the world as we know it. And it is about how these ideas have come across the border and taken hold in Canada, even as the mass of the Canadian public congratulates itself on living where there is no gun culture.

I want to know where these things come from, why people believe monumentally stupid things about guns, and why their beliefs—their faith, because that is what it most resembles—are so immovable. Ponce de Leon hunted wild across the New World, seeking the Fountain of Youth; I am after the Wellspring of Crazy. I am not so foolish as to think that finding it can solve anything. I just want to know why.

---

7   It's not clear why "Mom" is considered an American innovation. This may reflect a failure of sex education in American schools.

PART I

ON THE ORIGIN OF SPECIES
How America Created the Gun Culture

A Nation of Riflemen

A Revolution in Firepower Spawns the American Sniper

The first step—in the direction of preparation to avert war if possible, and to be fit for war if it should come—is to teach men to shoot!

—Theodore Roosevelt

IVAN IS COMING AT ME, with bayonet fixed.

The main thing, in such circumstances, is to control your breathing. Prone on the cold ground with my cheek on the stock of my rifle I breathe slowly in and out, watching the post of my front sight rise and fall on the centre line of Ivan's body. Halfway through the exhale, I hold my breath with the post square in the centre of his torso and then gently tighten my index finger on the trigger. The shot is supposed to come as a surprise, although of course you are not supposed to flinch as the rifle jumps back into the pocket of your shoulder. Flinching would throw off your shot. More importantly, flinching would suggest that you are some kind of pussy. You are supposed to keep your eyes on Ivan. You are supposed to take the recoil like a man and kill Ivan dead. My finger squeezes slowly down on the trigger and the sear lets go of the hammer and the rifle bucks back into my shoulder, the muzzle jumping.

Ivan is still coming at me.

It is the spring of 1989 and the Berlin Wall is still standing and Ivan is the black silhouette of a charging soldier on a cardboard Figure 11 target, the standard target used in Army rifle training. One hundred metres downrange, in the butts, a fellow recruit hauls down the steel frame in which the target is set, Ivan sinking out of sight behind the berm as if caught in quicksand. Then he rises again, a bright orange disc marking the hole I've shot through his sternum.

We are engaged in an exercise called grouping and zeroing, to verify that our sights are properly aligned before we shoot our qualifying test. Given a basic level of skill—something that is far from guaranteed in a recruit firing his rifle for the first time—a group of three shots ought to suggest a point of impact relative to the point of aim. And once you know the point of impact, you can adjust your sights so that the point of impact coincides with whatever you happen to be aiming at. All down the line I can see Ivan's cardboard comrades, each with three orange dots scattered over his body. On my target, target number one, there is only one orange dot. Where my other two shots have gone, I have no idea. I am a numpty.

And there will be no redemption. We are finished. Some other group of recruits now gets to lie on the cold ground for grouping and zeroing. It is our turn down in the butts, steel helmets strapped on our heads, wobbling like strange mushrooms on slender, razor-burned stalks. The NCO in charge gives us no time to sit down.

"Who the fuck was on target one in that last serial?"

My own fearsome section commander, Master Corporal Iorio: five feet and six inches of terror. And the only thought in my mind is that I must have accidentally shot something I shouldn't have. I assume the natural defensive posture of the recruit: standing properly to attention, eyes front and looking my height, mentally in the fetal position.

"I was, Master Corporal."

"You ever shoot a rifle before?"

"Just a .22, Master Corporal."

"Well, fuck, Somerset, we oughta put your ass on a fuckin' sniper course."

Iorio had left the target unpatched so I could see my group: two shots a half-inch apart, with the third an inch-and-a-half away. The rifle was the FNC1, which was already being phased out and replaced by the smaller, lighter C7; the FNs were old, and their barrels were worn, and we were firing over iron sights. For someone who had never before fired a centre-fire rifle, it was fine shooting. It was, in fact, the tightest group

I would ever fire from an FNC1. I reached out and touched the bullet holes in Ivan's chest, lingering on the third, least accurate shot.

"Musta pulled that one, Master Corporal."

"Fuck off, Somerset."

I fucked off, as ordered. But I was hooked.

I had joined the nation of riflemen, a nation in which my rifle and I are defenders of our country, masters of all enemies, and saviours of my own life. Survival on the battlefield is ultimately up to me. My rifle is my only true ally, the only force on which I can confidently depend—and my rifle, of course, depends on me, to keep it in good working order and to aim it true. I am always prepared; I am self-reliant; and I am confident, because I have seen that grouping and I know that I can shoot fly shit out of pepper.[8] I alone am master of my fate, and I will stop Ivan in his tracks, dead.

I know this nation because I have carried its passport on all those windy rifle ranges. Its ideas are well worn and foolish, but we all cling to old and foolish ideas when they suit us. To function as a soldier requires that you buy into the mythology, at some level; the alternative is to look on yourself, perhaps too accurately, as cannon fodder to be tossed into the tactical equivalent of a garburator. It is hardly a winning theme for a motivational speaker. Nowadays, the quixotic mythology of the nation of riflemen belongs only to the military, and even there only to the combat arms, the rest of that institution having figured out that it's far better to have a real job. But at one time, these ideas ran in the mainstream, the stuff of editorials in the newspapers of record. These ideas midwived America's unique relationship to its guns. To understand why, we must return to the nineteenth century, to the revolution in firepower that gave us modern firearms, and to the birth of the NRA. If we're going to find the Wellspring of Crazy, that seems a good place to start.

AMERICA AND THE GUN GREW UP together through their awkward teenaged years: played truth or dare in the darkened basement of the thirteen colonies, had their first, clumsy kiss at Lexington and Concord, groped each other at Gettysburg, went breathlessly all the way in the flickering half-light of a Western movie and got in trouble in Vietnam, a back-alley abortion they prefer not to talk about even now. If you

---

8 Subsequent experience has taught me that fly shit is in no danger from me, most days.

knew them then, pimple-faced and skinny, you would not recognize them today. America grew taller and filled out in the shoulders, spread ever wider at the waist, started driving a minivan and then, in denial, a shining mall assault vehicle with high ground clearance and four-wheel drive. But the gun, the gun blossomed and matured, lost its gangly coltish legs and grew sleek, sexy, stylish. One wonders how on earth this couple is still together, but there's no explaining love.

America's formative years coincided with a remarkable revolution in firepower, and that revolution propelled American expansion as the young nation gobbled up its frontier and pursued the genocide of its native peoples and its wars against Britain and Spain for control of the American continent. No less significantly, this revolution in firepower began just in time for the United States to turn on itself in the Civil War. At the beginning of the nineteenth century the infantryman's weapon was still the flintlock musket, a clumsy and inaccurate weapon that had been in service for two centuries and was little different from the matchlocks, wheel locks, snaplocks and snaphaunces that had served for the two centuries previous. But in scarcely twenty-five years, the rifle replaced the musket and transformed warfare.

Accuracy and rate of fire were the chief problems of the musket era. The musket provided a high rate of fire by the standards of its day: a trained infantryman could load and fire his musket as many as five times a minute. But this rate of fire came at a price. The musket was quick to load because it was a smoothbore weapon firing a relatively loose-fitting ball, which was easy to ram down a dirty barrel. But thanks to that same smoothbore barrel, it was woefully inaccurate except at short range. The prospects of hitting a man at anything more than fifty yards were poor, and became rapidly worse as the billowing white smoke of black powder guns obscured the battlefield. Taking aim was pointless. A massed formation of infantry was simply supposed to throw enough lead in the general direction of the enemy that someone was bound to be hit, which would have been a very silly idea were it not for the fact that everyone cooperated by forming the infantry up in tightly massed ranks, the better to repel cavalry charges.

The early rifle, which reached the peak of its development in the American longrifle of the Revolutionary War era, had the opposite problem. A rifle could hit a target out to two hundred yards, thanks to the stabilizing spin that its rifled barrel put on the ball. But the benefits of rifling depended on a tight fit between ball and bore, and ramming a tight-fitting ball down a barrel fouled by the residue of burning black powder took time. The rifleman was too slow. And as he loaded, he was vulnerable to cavalry, charging with elegance, fashion sense, sabre, and lance. A massed formation of riflemen could easily be routed by a cavalry charge. And so the rifle remained largely a hunter's gun, its use in war limited to snipers and "skirmishers," small units of light infantry sent out ahead of the main body to harass the enemy. The battlefield belonged to the volley fire of massed infantry armed with fast-loading, inaccurate muskets.

What infantry commanders needed was a weapon that combined the accuracy of the rifle with the musket's easy loading. That weapon was the rifled musket, made practical by a Frenchman, Claude-Étienne Minié, who developed the first widely used cylindro-conoidal—that is, bullet-shaped—bullet. Minié's bullet, called the "Minié ball," fit loosely into the barrel like a musket ball, so that a soldier could easily ram it down on the powder charge. But unlike a musket ball, its hollow base deformed as the powder charge ignited, sealing the sides of the bullet against the barrel and allowing the rifling to do its work. The Minié ball appeared in 1849, put an end to four hundred years of the smoothbore musket, and ushered in the age of the rifle just in time for the American Civil War.

The history of warfare is the history of the balance of power between offence and defence, between cavalry and infantry, a balance continually tilted and toppled by technology. For years, that balance had been stable. The massed infantry's bristling hedgehog rows of bayonets and whizzing musket balls kept cavalry at bay; victory waited only on musket and cannon fire to smash holes in those ranks and let the cavalry go to work. The rifled musket now tilted the balance. The accuracy and range of rifled muskets drove infantry into entrenched positions and commenced the decline of cavalry, a decline that would continue until the cavalry finally exchanged its horses for tanks. And the American Civil War consumed the lives of more than 750,000 soldiers on both sides.

But to industrial warfare, 750,000 lives were merely hors d'oeuvres. The revolution in firepower was just getting started. The rifled musket was still a muzzle-loader, and muzzle-loaders, with separate powder charge, wad, and bullet, were just too slow. The answer was the breech-loading rifle, firing a ready-made, one-piece cartridge.

The Snider-Enfield entered British Army service immediately after the Civil War, in 1866. It adapted a breech-loading action invented by an American, Jacob Snider, to the 1853 muzzle-loading Enfield rifle, which had fired a Minié ball. The external hammer, which on the 1853 Enfield had struck a percussion cap, now drove a firing pin into the primer of the .577 cartridge. And although the Snider-Enfield was a single-shot rifle, it allowed a trained rifleman to reload, aim, and fire ten shots a minute. Even so, it was a stopgap weapon, a modification of an existing rifled musket rather than a purpose-built rifle. In 1871, the Martini-Henry, a single-shot, breech-loading lever-action rifle based on a Civil War-era American design, replaced it in the British Army.

As the British Army transitioned from musket to rifle, American know-how was driving ahead, adapting the revolution in firepower to the needs of a young and violent nation intent on taming its frontier, killing its native peoples, and fulfilling its manifest destiny. In the same year the Snider-Enfield entered service, another American innovation had already pointed to the future: the Winchester Model 1866 repeating rifle. Unlike the single-shot rifles used by the world's armies, the Winchester featured a built-in magazine, from which it loaded a fresh cartridge every time the shooter worked the lever action. Improved models quickly followed. A Winchester 1873 chambered in .44-40 could fire fourteen shots without reloading, and the rifleman recharged the magazine simply by pushing fresh rounds into the loading port on the side of the receiver. Against this innovation, the Snider-Enfield's ten shots a minute was comically slow. The future had arrived.[9]

Only twenty-four years had passed since the introduction of the Minié ball ended the four-century reign of the smoothbore musket. Within another twenty-five years, the world would have its first machine guns. The significance of the revolution in firepower is difficult to comprehend today; we are too used to modern guns, too habituated to the way things are. But for the nineteenth-century soldier, warfare had been radically transformed. The whole game had changed. And the consequences of that transformation reached beyond the ranks of the

9 So why, you ask, was the Winchester used only for America's Indian wars? Because it was a carbine—a rifle firing a short-range bullet—and armies at the time were fascinated by the long-range potential of full-bore rifles.

infantry and their unit drill, beyond battlefield tactics, and gripped the national psyche. The invention of the modern rifle was no less significant than the arrival of the Internet and the smartphones that followed.

In Europe and North America, the rifle seized the high ground in the martial imagination that would later be taken over by the aeroplane and the tank. Victory on the battlefield now depended not on the mechanical discipline of well-drilled troops but on the marksmanship of the individual rifleman. A force of trained marksmen would easily defeat troops who had not been instructed in the proper, scientific use of the rifle, in the principles of its use and the technique of estimating range. And since training marksmen takes time, and since in the era of mass warfare you go to war with what you've got, any nation that wished to be taken seriously as a military power would have to turn its farmers, its shopkeepers, and its bankers into marksmen. Every nation would have to become a nation of riflemen.

Canada was born just in time to join the fun. Few Canadians are aware that the first sport to receive federal funding in their fair and peaceful land, almost as soon as Canada became Canada, was rifle shooting.[10] In 1867, the *British North America Act* created Canada; in 1868, motivated by the need to defend peace, order, and good government, Canada became a nation of riflemen through a Militia Act that created a 40,000-man active militia. The federal government was soon funding the newborn Dominion of Canada Rifle Association to the tune of ten thousand dollars a year. Ottawa also provided rifles to all active militia members, bought and rented rifle ranges for the Rifle Association, funded rifle competitions, and provided a supply of cheap ammunition. National defence was an urgent matter. Everyone still remembered the Fenian Raids.[11] With all that money behind them, Canadian shooters were soon winning medals in international rifle matches, and in 1871 at Wimbledon—a venue then known for rifle-shooting, and not for tennis—took prizes in all events they entered.

"In England, and more especially in Canada, the policy of providing ranges of sufficient extent for long-range rifle practice, has developed a

---

10   Blake Brown's *Arming and Disarming: A History of Gun Control in Canada* provides a fascinating review of Canada's nineteenth-century gun culture, and is the source for most of the information in this chapter on the place of guns in Canada before 1900.

11   That was then. Now, nobody recalls the Fenian Raids, a series of cross-border raids between 1866 and 1871 against the British in Canada by Irish-American guerillas, to encourage the British to get out of Ireland.

large and formidable force for national defense," remarked an 1872 editorial in the *New York Times*. "Canada today has 45,000 trained marksmen among her volunteers, England 150,000, while the United States has none." The *Times* even agreed that there was some merit to the common public view of the New York National Guard as a force "terrible only in the eyes of boys and young women; and whose chief victories are won on the floors of ballrooms." This was the best-organized state militia in the United States, yet its members suffered "lamentable ignorance in the proper use of their weapons," and were they to come up against Canada's crack shots … well, America could hardly pretend that losing would not matter, which is one of several ways in which warfare differs from Olympic hockey.[12]

In 1871, dismayed by the poor shooting they had seen among Union recruits in the Civil War, and sharing the popular view that individual marksmanship would settle the fate of nations, General George Wingate and Colonel William C. Church followed the example set by Canada and Britain and founded the NRA to "promote and encourage rifle shooting on a scientific basis." For help, they turned to the experts. The NRA sent emissaries to Canada, Germany, and England to confer with expert marksmen and military thinkers, and Canadian rifle shooters were soon helping to instruct the NRA's members. In 1872, when the NRA started building the first rifle range in the United States at Creedmoor on Long Island, they enlisted the assistance of their Canadian counterparts. Even when it comes to the NRA, we can blame Canada.

In the late-nineteenth century, rifle shooting was a mainstream sport, and the *New York Times* and Toronto's *Globe* newspaper reported the results of shooting matches as they do golf today. Everyone got in on the game. Prominent citizens donated prizes to rifle associations, including cups and gold badges just as Lord Stanley and the Albert Grey, 4th Earl Grey, donated trophies for hockey and football. The *New York Times* published frequent reports on the NRA's plans and on the progress of construction at the Creedmoor range, which opened in June 1873. At the NRA's first annual match at Creedmoor, in October 1873, there was just one long-range shooting event, the Sharpshooter's Championship, at

---

12   "Rifle Practice." *The New York Times*, April 7, 1872. The sentiment was repeated in "Rifle practice. Necessity for a school of marksmanship—what the State Militia should do about target practice." *The New York Times*, May 3, 1873.

800 and 1,000 yards. First prize went to a Canadian.[13] When the British invited the NRA to send American marksmen to compete at Wimbledon that year, the NRA leadership demurred. The United States was not ready. But by 1874, American shooters were winning rifle matches in Canada.[14] The American rifleman had come into his own.

No nations, perhaps, were as susceptible to the myth of the rifleman as Canada and and the United States, young frontier nations primed by the American romanticism of James Fenimore Cooper. Eager to prove themselves still heir to the frontier tradition, middle-class men in the growing cities took to the range to shoot and to the woods to hunt. In 1872, when the United States set aside Yellowstone as its first national park, it was not to preserve natural ecosystems in an undamaged state but to provide an ersatz frontier on which American manhood might prove itself. Theodore Roosevelt, who doubled the size of the national park system during his tenure as president, had grown up a sickly, asthma-ridden child in New York City, and was fully in thrall to the idea that the historian and cultural critic Richard Slotkin has since dubbed "regeneration through violence": that is, the city and the pull of soft domesticity make us weak, unhealthy, and decadent, so we turn to the manly crucible of the frontier where we harden ourselves into men once more.[15]

In the late-nineteenth century, rifle shooting was held to promote all kinds if martial and manly virtues, by the same dubious logic that gave us *mens sana in corpore sano*. "A marksman is already more than half a soldier," as the *New York Times* explained in promoting the NRA's new range at Creedmoor: "He has developed those qualities of quickness, precision, self-reliance, and coolness which are most valuable to the soldier, and without which all the drilling in the world will make but an indifferent imitiation."[16] Behold the benefits gained by lying on the cold ground, shooting at distant targets!

The rifle, that reservoir of "quickness, precision, self-reliance, and coolness," resonated uniquely with the rugged individualism that the

---

13 "The Rifle Association: The national range at Creedmoor. A review of the first season of the New York Rifle Society." *The New York Times*, December 13, 1873.

14 "The Canadian rifle match: Capt. Fullerton makes twenty-eight points." *The New York Times*, August 17, 1874. Also, "The Canadian rifle matches," *The New York Times*, August 19, 1874.

15 Richard Slotkin is Olin Professor of English and American Studies at Wesleyan University, best known for his exhaustive trilogy tracing the development of the American frontier myth, *Regeneration Through Violence, The Fatal Environment*, and *Gunfighter Nation*. Slotkin is also responsible for identifying the frontier hero as "a man who knows Indians."

16 "Police riflemen." *The New York Times*, June 8, 1873.

North American male fancied he saw in the bathroom mirror. The infantry soldier of the musket era had been little more than a robot remotely operated by an officer and kept in working order by the flat of a sergeant's sword, capable of no more initiative than a granule of explosive inside a hand grenade, and his function was much the same: to throw a piece of metal into the air, where it might or might not hit something. This was the European way of war. But the rifleman aims his rifle at a target of his choosing, fights with his wits, his initiative, and his daring, and becomes the master of his fate. The musketeer is the creature of Old Europe; the rifleman belongs to the New World.

Having just endured a divisive and bloody civil war, America cried out for unifying myths. Thus was born the Myth of the American Rifleman. America soon forgot that the NRA had been born from the discovery that Americans could not shoot, and reimagined itself as a nation of natural-born snipers; descended directly from Davy Crockett. Americans were, in the words of the historian Roger McGrath, "men who had grown up using firearms as part and parcel of their daily lives … By the time they were teenagers, these young men were crack shots whom the family depended on to hunt game for food and to repel Indian attacks." The frontiersman's skill with a rifle soon reached mythical proportions. "Most American frontiersmen became deadeyes and could accomplish shooting feats such as snuffing-the-candle [shooting out a candle flame] or driving-the-nail [using bullet as hammer] as a matter of course," at up to seventy paces, McGrath explains. The importance of the rifleman was so great, in McGrath's mind, that he stops just short of crediting a single sharpshooter, Timothy Murphy, with winning the American Revolution.[17]

History is hard to know, as Hunter S. Thompson wrote, because of all the hired bullshit. It matters little that the rifle was largely impractical as a military weapon in the late-eighteenth century, that the Revolutionary War was ultimately about money, that most American colonists were not expert shots, that the militia in the Revolutionary War (and after) were woefully inadequate and poorly armed forces, or

---

17 McGrath's piece was published in the magazine of the John Birch Society, and its credibility ought to be assessed in that light. The notion that American frontiersmen could snuff the candle or drive the nail at seventy yards "as a matter of course" is particularly entertaining. Few could achieve such a feat even with modern rifles, hand-loaded ammunition, and modern rifle scopes. Can you even see the head of a nail at seventy yards? McGrath, Roger D, "The American rifleman in the Revolutionary War." *The New American*, September 13, 2010.

that the colonists experienced little military success until they adopted the standard European tactics of massed formations of infantry armed not with longrifles but with smoothbore muskets. It matters little that the NRA had been created in the first place because America was not, in fact, a nation of riflemen. The image of the American frontiersman and his rifle defeating the hidebound British through a combination of marksmanship, tactical brilliance, and sartorial superiority is so deeply ingrained as to be impossible to dislodge.

THERE IS SOMETHING TO BE SAID for becoming intimate with a patch of mud.

This conclusion arrived while I was in the patch of mud in question, shortly after first light on a wet November morning. I can be more specific: the something-to-be-said was that, in the time I had lain there, the mud had finally warmed to the point that the parts of me that were intimate with the mud had become comfortable, while the rest of me was wet and cold and more than ready to get up off the ground and get on with the task at hand. I had been lying there since before dawn, and my mud (for I had come to think of it as my own) was nice and warm.

My task that morning was to lead my three-man recce patrol through an abandoned orchard and locate any mines or booby traps the enemy had set up with the aim of protecting their position in a ruined farmhouse. With that vital information in hand, the main force could later bring the hammer down. We were going light, for stealth. No web gear, no steel helmets. Just the essentials: a few mags of ammo and our rifles. All that stood between us and success were a few hundred yards of open, grassy slope, the watchful enemy, and the small problem of daylight. It looked like I was going to have to remain intimate with the mud all the way up that slope. But we did have the drizzle in our corner. I was confident.

All of this was a game, of course. The farmhouse and orchard had been abandoned since World War II, when the Canadian government had appropriated this land and set it aside as a military training area. The booby traps and mines in that orchard would be trip flares, which are not exactly safe to be around—they can burn you badly—but much less dangerous than actual mines and booby traps. And the watchful enemy in that ruined farmhouse consisted of a young officer and two soldiers, who turned out not to be very watchful that morning. My patrol was able to squirm up the slope and pick its way past the trip flares without being detected, which was an embarrassment to the enemy force and made the mud and the wet and the cold worthwhile.

I felt invincible. And this is exactly how the Army wanted me to feel. It is part of the purpose of training. Not to make me feel too invincible, of course, which might lead me to be careless, but rather to convince me that invincibility lies in skill. My individual soldier skills would keep me alive, my leadership would keep my men alive, and we would complete our mission.

This is a myth, of course, because as important as individual soldier skills may be, what actually keeps you and your men alive is more often than not a solid dose of good luck. In combat against our Cold War enemy, the Russians, the decisive factor in my survival would have been whether or not an artillery shell fired from beyond the horizon happened to land close enough to kill me regardless of armour, slit trenches, and keeping my head down. Or whether I happened to be in the wrong place at the wrong time when they used nerve gas, or a nuke. And of course I knew this, but all that's a bit of a downer, so I set it aside. I had windmills to kill.

The army's quixotic battalions need their myths, just as nations need their myths. The United States needed the rifleman of the Revolutionary War as a unifying icon in the aftermath of the Civil War, and so it invested itself in the myth of the rifleman, and began to create an entire mythology around its frontier. And I needed to believe, as the Army needed me to believe, that my individual soldier skills were what mattered most. I needed to believe that my rifle marksmanship mattered, even as I knew that artillery, machine guns, and tank cannons would do most of the killing. And I did. I joined the rifle team and shot at photocopies of a dime with more ambition than skill, and I grew to love the feeling of the rifle in my hands. The rifle was a touchstone filled with confidence. The rifle made me invincible.

A BLACK-AND-WHITE PHOTOGRAPH: Calgary public school rifle champions, five boys in khaki uniforms, knee-high boots and wedge caps, standing rigidly at attention with their Ross rifles at the order arms behind a table with silver trophies and crossed rifles. They are the epitome of sporting accomplishment, posing just as a hockey team might, but their uniforms and bearing remind us that rifle shooting was supposed to serve a practical military purpose in ensuring that the sun would never set on the British Empire. The year is 1912. One wonders how many of these downy-cheeked kids would live to see the armistice, just six years later.

In the cool light of history there is something disturbing in these photographs of innocent Boy Scouts and cadets enthralled by a romantic militarism that would soon be shattered by the experience of World War I. There they stand, children ardent for some desperate glory, ready to take up the white man's burden, to be bound to exile in service of the Empire. These were the children of Kipling and Roosevelt, of Baden-Powell's paramilitary Scout movement, which was originally conceived to cultivate martial virtues, and thus to turn boys into men. To be a man was to be a soldier; to be a soldier was to be a man.

Today, it is difficult to conceive of, let alone to understand, the wild enthusiasm with which nations marched off to war in 1914. Naïve expectations met the reality of machine guns and artillery in disillusionment so complete that despite the much greater destructiveness of World War II, it is the Great War that is today remembered as the ultimate military horror show. For the rifleman did not, as it turned out, reign supreme on the battlefield. It was modern machine guns, lighter and more mobile than their carriage-born predecessors—machine guns that had completed the revolution in firepower, appearing only fifty years after the demise of the musket—and quick-firing artillery that ruled the battlefield in the new century.

It all seems so obvious with the benefit of hindsight. It ought to have been clear to the founders of the NRA, close students of the Franco-Prussian War, a war won by a force with inferior rifles, but better artillery and logistics. It ought to have been obvious to officers used to cowing restive colonials with the Maxim gun. But military minds before World War I were caught up in the mythology of the rifle, and somehow convinced themselves that élan, the offensive spirit of the individual infanteer, could somehow carry the day. First-hand knowledge of the effectiveness of machine guns and artillery was less persuasive than a headful of romantic claptrap.

Hundreds of thousands died before the generals of the Great War realized that élan could not win battles, and sought new solutions. They dug in; they brought up the artillery; they dreamed up the tank.

15

Millions more died. They were not stupid men, these generals, whatever we have come to think of them; they simply faced insurmountable problems. And whatever their critics down in the trenches may have felt, the generals were just as disillusioned as their troops. Imagine the dismay of French and British military leaders, then, when the US Army appeared on the scene in 1917 believing that snivelling, cowardly Europeans hiding in their trenches would easily be overwhelmed by the skill and fighting spirit of the American rifleman. French and British leaders tried to disabuse these newbies of their foolish expectations, but the Americans, infused with the can-do spirit of the New World, ignored their warnings. American generals may well have thought that élan was a pastry, but they were nonetheless fully invested in the idea.[18]

America, arriving just in time for the end, suffered no Somme, no Passchendaele, and no Verdun. France lost 1.4 million soldiers, with another 4 million wounded; Britain had almost 900,000 dead and 1.6 million wounded. The United States lost just 116,000 soldiers, with 200,000 wounded. The total dead in France, military and civilian, amounted to four percent of the population, one in twenty-five people. Everybody had lost somebody. But in the United States, hardly anyone lost a family member; total US dead amounted to just one in a thousand.[19] In a global bar fight that saw other nations cut up with broken bottles and straight razors, America came in late and got little more than a bloody nose. And so, as other nations recoiled with horror from the myth of the rifleman, America preserved it.

Canada and Europe dropped the rifleman myth like a cherry bomb with a short fuse. Messing around with .22 rifles, shooting things that probably ought not to be shot, had once been the kind of thing that turned boys into men. But now boys were expected to grow up into peaceful citizens who believed in law, democracy, and the virtues of hard work. Membership in cadet corps and rifle associations shrank; in 1926, the Boys' Brigade, which before the war had dressed boys in military uniforms and held rifle matches, abandoned even the dummy rifles used for close-order drill. But in the United States, military training for high-school boys persisted.

---

18   See Paschall, Rod, *The Defeat of Imperial Germany, 1917-1918*, Boston: Da Capo Press, 1994.
19   Canada suffered about half the war dead of the United States (64,000), out of a much smaller population. In percentage terms, Canada lost just under one percent of its population, almost ten times the casualty rate of the United States.

By 1919, the machinery of myth-making was hard at work, rewriting the history of World War I. Europe had collapsed into the intractable quagmire of trench warfare and bled itself white in a nightmare of attrition. The American doughboys arrived to save the day and in just one year did what the combined weight of the Entente Powers had failed to do, defeating Germany through guts, cheerful can-do, and, of course, marksmanship. And then the boys came home, smiling and victorious and smelling faintly of French women. The myth of the American rifleman remained an essential joist in the structure of national identity. It would crop up again on Omaha Beach, where the US Army rejected the British tactic of landing specialized combat engineering vehicles to breach the German defensive works, relying instead on infantry. It persisted through bitter Korean winters. The myth of the American rifleman finally went missing in Vietnam, where it is believed to have died, but is still honoured in the doctrine of the US Marine Corps, which values the infantryman with his rifle above all. And it lives on in the name of the National Rifle Association's magazine: *American Rifleman*. We never quite let go of anything.

ABOVE THE BACK DOOR of my grandfather's cottage hung a rifle, a .577 Snider-Enfield, the same rifle that armed Canada's militia when the NRA came asking for help. Above the kitchen window was another, which he called his "English poaching rifle." Years later, I recognized that English poaching rifle at auction and identified it as a BSA Martini, a single-shot .22-calibre target rifle with a Martini-Henry falling-block action, which was produced starting in the late-nineteenth century onward until about 1950. Those Calgary public school rifle champions, learning rifle shooting "on a scientific basis" in the years before World War I, would have used this rifle. My grandfather's BSA Martini had been sporterized, which is to say its heavy stock had been slimmed down to lighten it, converting it from a target rifle too heavy to lug around in the woods to a highly accurate small-game rifle. Most of the Lee-Enfield rifles that returned from World War II would likewise be sporterized, making the Lee-Enfield the most popular hunting rifle in Canada.[20] This is how Canada beats its swords into ploughshares.

---

20 That the Lee-Enfield is the most popular hunting rifle in Canada is so often repeated that it seems irrefutable, although no one can say for sure it is true. Nowadays, many have been retired, although they remain popular because they're inexpensive and reliable.

Nobody hangs a rifle over the door anymore. But in that time and place it seemed appropriate. My being ten years old had something to do with it. It's unlikely that on Lake Muskoka in 1979 you would need to grab a rifle on the way out the door to deal with a bear getting after the livestock, and the Snider-Enfield wouldn't be the weapon with which to do it anyway, since by the time I was born it was already a century old. You can still buy copies from gunsmiths in the Khyber Pass, but if you had fired my grandfather's original Snider-Enfield, it probably would have blown up in your face.

To the adults in the family, that rifle was simply part of the decor. But as such, it was heavy with meaning. Decor is never just decor. When we decorate a kitchen in the country style, we declare allegiance to the image of a fresh-baked apple pie cooling on the windowsill, of sunlight filtering through homemade strawberry preserves. We like the idea of these things, the values they represent, even if we buy our pies at the supermarket and have no time to fuss with Mason jars and pectin. And so the rifle over the doorway, antique as it was, lacking ammunition, the soundness of breech and barrel uncertain, remained a rifle. Even if there were no dangers to be repelled, and no ammunition with which to do so, it signified the possibilities inherent in a landscape where one must keep a rifle over the door. And indeed, there was at one point talk of buying ammunition for the English poaching rifle to defend against a marauding possum in my grandmother's geraniums. Perhaps my grandfather still belonged, at some level, to the nation of riflemen.

On the wall of the house where I grew up hung a small oval of rough, grey clay, which bore in pottery glaze the figure of a knight. I loved that knight, the cold, smooth glaze a splash of wild colour in the middle of that rough, porous clay, the brightness of his armour and shield. But he was a shabby figure, this knight, a bit ramshackle, his lance a rough pole, his helmet askew, his long, grey beard jutting from his chin.

"Who's that?" I asked. I was very young.

"That's Don Quixote."

"Was he a real knight?"

"Not a real knight." And my father explained that Don Quixote was not a real knight but an old man who pretended to be a knight, that his helmet was just an old basin and his horse a nag, and that he fought against windmills because there was, and is, no such thing as a giant. He was, in other words, just like me, scrambling to meet inbound Luftwaffe raiders in the street in my bicycle Spitfire: just a make-believe hero in a world possibility had fled. It was a sore disappointment.

I never got over Don Quixote. But then, nobody ever gets over Don Quixote. Quixote becomes a hero in spite of the fact that all his heroic deeds exist only in his own mad imagination, because we cannot reconcile ourselves to a world without romance. There's a reason we keep flocking to theatres to see Hollywood fantasies. A world without possibility, without room for the hero, a world in which you get up and go to work and come home and eat chicken strips and go to bed and rinse lather repeat until the day you pop your clogs in some drear nursing home where the checkers set is always short one red piece: that world seems far more shabby than Quixote's rusty old armour or his makeshift lance or the shaving basin atop his addled head. That world seems worthless and empty.

The rifle hangs over the doorway to remind us of that. But it is easy to forget that it is only a symbol, and to fall into thinking that it is something more, because Quixote stands for something more than a world filled with possibility. He stands also for a world where violence settles matters, where a real man can never back down from a threat. A real man will defend his home and his family with that same rifle he keeps ever ready. And it is here we will turn: from the defence of nations to the defence of home, where we imagine ourselves fearless knights, forever ready to take up the lance.

The Tendency of the American Mind
From the Duty to Retreat to Stand Your Ground

Mercy but murders, pardoning those that kill.
—*Romeo & Juliet*, Act 3, Scene 1

BRIAN KNIGHT AWOKE ON HIS FARM near Tees, Alberta, in the small hours of March 26, 2009, to the thumping and scraping and cursing of three drunks struggling to load his ATV onto the back of their pickup truck. He grabbed the 12-gauge shotgun he kept handy to keep coyotes away from his calves and gave chase, comically attired in rubber boots and boxer shorts. Two of the men, apparently unaware of the long-standing notion of honour among thieves, jumped into their truck and fled, leaving a third, Harold Groening, to his own devices. Groening availed himself of the only other vehicle to hand: Knight's ATV. Knight, pursuing in his car, collided with the quad and forced it into the ditch. Groening picked himself up and ran across an empty field as Knight stepped out of his car, his shotgun in his hands, and fired. Groening fell, wounded, but then got up and started running again. Knight fired a second shot, wounding Groening in "the back and backside areas," as the *Red Deer Advocate* carefully reported. All told, seventeen shotgun pellets found their way into Groening's back and backside areas.[21]

Thus told, it's the stuff of comedy. But somebody was bleeding. The Criminal Code of Canada, a document entirely devoid of jokes and fun,

---

21   "Brian Knight says he didn't mean to shoot ATV thief," *Red Deer Advocate*, January 14, 2011.

disapproves of shooting people. You can claim self-defence, of course, if you were facing death or grievous bodily harm at the time. But Knight had faced neither. He had recovered his now-damaged quad, and the man who had tried to steal it was fleeing, his back turned. And he had shot that fleeing man not once, but twice. Even the police don't get to shoot a fleeing, unarmed man in the back just to arrest him.[22] And so Knight found himself charged with unlawful use of a firearm, pointing a firearm, assault with a weapon, criminal negligence causing injury, unauthorized possession of a firearm, and, because the cops just can't resist putting a cherry on top, dangerous driving.

Yet Knight became a public hero. Bloggers insisted that, whatever the facts of the encounter, he had acted in self-defence. Those strange people, whoever they are, who post comments under online news stories proclaimed that a man has to do what he has to do when the police cannot. To many farmers, men who know full well that by the time the cops show up your quad will be long gone and you'll be eating the deductible again, there was no question that Knight was in the right. The Crown, apparently taken aback by the vehement public reaction, backed off. At trial, all charges save criminal negligence causing injury were dropped. Knight pleaded guilty and was sentenced to ninety days in jail. Groening, the thief, got only thirty days. Knight appealed the sentence. The Crown eventually agreed that seventeen shotgun pellets had somehow struck Groening after Knight had aimed his shotgun "in the general area, well above" the fleeing man and "discharged it in his general direction," with no intent to wound anyone's backside area. Knight was still guilty, but he would not go to jail.

Knight's supporters declared victory. Knight was the good guy, Groening the bad guy, and the Crown attorney himself an officious little pencil-pushing dickhead who had forgotten the difference between right and wrong. Or something like that. The bedrock truth of the matter was that Knight was sympathetic and Groening was not, and no matter the nuances and complexities of self-defence law, and whatever the facts of the encounter, in the popular imagination the limits of legitimate self-defence revolve around one simple question: Who is the good guy in the white hat?

*

---

22 Consequently, fleeing, unarmed men who are shot in the back by police may find that, in a reversal of the normal sequence of events, the police press guns *into* their cold, dead hands.

> *The dull empiricism, the unashamed, cringing worship of the*
> *fact which is so often imaginary, and falsely interpreted at that,*
> *were odious to me. Beyond the facts, I looked for laws.*
>
> —Trotsky

GOOD OLD TROTSKY: DOWN WITH FACTS! Facts, those slippery little animals, too often contradictory, too often inconvenient, lead us nowhere. They live only moments, slither out of our grasping fingers, and then turn around and bite us. Empiricists gaze at their slime trails, inspect fact scat, and find no answers. America, armed and dangerous, needs not facts but principles, bedrock principles on which a man can stand. America demands universal truths.

"Formerly we suffered from crimes," wrote Tacitus. "Now, we suffer from laws." America cries out that it suffers from both. The tribe of the gun yearns to break free of its chains. It demands new laws, laws that know not of nuance, but speak to the universal truth of good guy and bad. Between 1986 and 2011, thirty-two states enacted laws prohibiting the authorities from denying any law-abiding citizen a permit to carry a concealed handgun, ignoring the slithering mass of contradictory facts in favour of the universal truth proposed by economist and gun rights advocate John Lott: more guns, less crime. But the beleaguered concealed-handgun carrier yet complains: should he be forced to use the gun he now has the right to carry, the state may still step in and prosecute him. He demands guarantees. He may claim he'd rather be judged by twelve than carried by six, but the truth of the matter is he'd rather be neither.[23] He must be immune from any prosecution; he must be held harmless. And so, between 2000 and 2010, twenty-three states gave into the relentless lobbying of the concealed-carry movement and passed laws expanding the right to self-defence by creating the assumption that the shooter is a good guy who is entitled to stand his ground.

Renée Lettow Lerner, a law professor at George Washington University, proposes that stand-your-ground laws are not a uniquely American trend, but part of a "worldwide popular revolt against proportionality in

---

23 "I'd rather be judged by twelve than carried by six," an aphorism of gun writer Lieutenant Colonel Jeff Cooper, is an oft-repeated motto of those who keep guns for self-defence: I'd rather shoot the bastard and face a jury than risk the alternative.

self-defense law."[24] People are frustrated by the sense that criminals have more rights than victims, she argues, and therefore sympathize with anyone who fights back, in revolt against the laws that punish us for standing up for ourselves. Bernard Goetz, who in 1984 shot four would-be muggers in the New York subway and was convicted of illegally possessing a handgun, finds his equivalents elsewhere. In Canada, Brian Knight became a cause célèbre. In the UK, in August 1999, Tony Martin shot two burglars with an unlicensed shotgun, killing one, and went to jail. Despite the fact that Martin shot sixteen-year-old Fred Barras in the back, he too became a cause célèbre to the self-defence crowd. High-profile cases such as these—often involving people who had no lawful excuse to act as they did—attract the sympathy of those who fear that there but for the front-door deadbolt go I.

"There is a growing sense of being under siege," writes Lerner. It's a sense that persists in spite of falling crime rates. The police cannot protect us, and so we must be permitted to protect ourselves. Some crack addict breaks into your house looking for something he can turn into quick cash to pay for his next fix. And you know what those people are like: depraved, determined, and desperate. There's no telling what they're capable of. There's no telling what they might do to you, just for kicks. You can't be expected, in the dark of night, to tell if the criminal in your home intends murder, rape, or burglary, or to determine if he is armed. Little matter that avoiding such confrontations is the very reason burglars choose burglary. Down with facts! You need the right to shoot that bastard dead.

But shooting the bastard has nothing to do with fear, nothing to do with the feeling of being under siege. Fear is merely a smokescreen for the deft politicking of our old friend, violence, and his sidekick, honour. In *Rising Up and Rising Down*, his sprawling, half-mad examination of the morality of violence, William T. Vollman creates an ice cream shop with thirty-seven flavours of self-defence, expanding it into defence of property, defence of race, defence of class, defence of honour, defence of this, defence of that—the book is mind-numbing, a trackless wilderness—all to demonstrate that self-defence expands inevitably into justifications for violence that are anything but defensive. Ultimately, in Vollman's moral calculus, violence is justified only when defending oneself or one's loved ones against violence, a conclusion that

24 Renée Lettow Lerner, "The Worldwide Popular Revolt Against Proportionality in Self-Defense Law," *Journal of Law, Economics & Policy* 2 (2006).

ought not to take us through seven whole volumes. But we get those seven volumes, all that exhaustive history and analysis, because violence is forever offering a counterproposal. Violence is a used-car salesman. Give it an angle and it soon seeks to sweeten the deal.

And Vollman gives it the angle it needs, the only angle it will ever need, in his governing principle of "self-sovereignty." Being sovereign, we reserve the right to violence; reserving the right to do violence, we make violence inevitable. Mercutio, reserving the right to violence, will not budge for no man's pleasure; he offers a fight to no one, but will gladly take one if offered. Along comes Tybalt, that rat-catcher, spitting insults; Mercutio must challenge Tybalt in defence of Romeo's honour, but chiefly in hot-headedness; Tybalt must kill him in defence of self, but chiefly in anger; and Romeo must kill Tybalt in defence of some principle or another, but chiefly in revenge. Just as Europe staggered into World War I, each is compelled to defend his principles.

Good old self-defence is always looking to expand its franchise. It's always self-defence. He wasn't attacking me, yer honour, but he *could have* attacked me at any time. I was *afraid he would* attack me, imminently, and do me grievous bodily harm. I *had every right* to grab him when I caught him, and then when he resisted, well, *I had to defend myself.*

What we call self-defence is often more a matter of masculine honour than of self-preservation. A slap in the face is no threat to life or limb, but if I fail to reply, I become a lesser man, a coward. When I respond to your slap by kicking your legs out from under you and laying my boots to you, breaking your jaw and your orbital bone, flattening your nose and knocking out three of your teeth, you may rest assured that I will claim self-defence regardless. *Hey man, he hit me first.* The idea is so fundamental to our sense of justice that every schoolyard rings with it: *But he started it.*

That same defence of honour soon expands to defence of property. The cartoon penis spray-painted on my garage door degrades me. The thief who breaks my car window to steal my sunglasses does not simply cost me money; he insults me, the damage a slap in the face. The B&E artist who trashes my house looking for valuables does not merely violate my sense of safety in my own home, but also demonstrates by his casual destruction of my things a disdain for me as a person. So it goes with the drunks who steal your quad and the teenagers who vandalize your shed. It is not the value of your property that is at issue, but the fact that it *is* your property. It's the principle of the thing, and you're fucked if that little shit is going to get away with it.

At street level, life is solitary, poor, nasty, brutish, and short. All the while, the legal elite coldly theorizes in its ivory tower, constructing laws that require me to carefully balance my actions in the heat of the moment against complex legal codes. What's a poor middle-class home-owner to do? Or so the complaint goes. But this very complaint is the product of that legal elite. Only a nation whose presidents send lawyers in search of loopholes to excuse torturing human beings could mistake the law for an operator's manual, to be hauled out and consulted to dis-cover what we can get away with. The law is not an operator's manual; it is the essay in which we define our shared values. And when it comes to breaking somebody's kneecaps for the pure joy of it, our values are fairly clear.

The revolt against proportionality does not appeal for mercy on behalf of those poor middle-class homeowners who find themselves unable to navigate the complexities of criminal law in the heat of the moment; it simply rejects proportionality as a moral proposition. It rejects the very idea that we ought to put our disputes before the courts and allow cooler heads to decide. Instead of justice, it demands retribu-tion. And how better to get retribution than to take care of it ourselves?

Justice is complex. Retribution is not. The only question retribution asks is, "was this so-called victim a bad person, who deserved what he got?" And so we ask if Trayvon Martin was in fact a delinquent.[25] If he was, then George Zimmerman becomes the agent of retribution, his justification arising not just from self-defence but from a desire to settle accounts for whatever petty crimes we can pin on Trayvon. Some teenaged kid sneaks out of his suburban home at night and comes home drunk to the wrong house, only to be shot full of holes by his next-door neighbour. Well, he was drinking underage, wasn't he? Another of those little punks who spray-paint mailboxes and steal the change out of your car at night. Yeah, cry me a river, you bleeding hearts. Underaged

---

25   On February 26, 2012, the unarmed Trayvon Martin was shot and killed by George Zimmer-man in Sanford, Florida. Martin was seventeen and black; Zimmerman, a Neighborhood Watch volunteer with a history of reported violence, found him suspicious and followed him. Precisely what happened then remains unclear. There has never been any evidence that Martin was doing anything but walking home from a convenience store when Zimmerman spotted him.

drinking is for punks. But homicide, homicide is just fine. Just so long as its agent is a righteous man, because a righteous man always acts in self-defence.

But we didn't always think this way. Once upon a time, we thought a righteous man was wise enough to keep his head, in more than the usual sense.

LET US SUPPOSE YOU ARE A KING, which ought not to be a stretch, given that your home is your castle. It's good work if you can get it, living off the toil of your subjects by dint of divine right, or at the very least by dint of having killed off your rivals. But all is not rosy in your kingdom. Your subjects—social climbers all—keep going around killing off their own rivals, which as the Royal Economist points out is bad for productivity and makes it hard to forecast your GDP. Kings have easy solutions to these problems: you make it against the law to kill people, and when people offend you by ignoring your law, you kill them. There will be no killing, on pain of death, nor robbery, nor burglary, nor shooting the king's pheasants. No one is to disturb the king's peace. I'm trying to watch TV here, people.

As for your subjects, they generally agree that this is the first useful thing you have done as king: it turns out that making it illegal to kill people and steal their stuff makes the kingdom safe for business, and your subjects prosper, at least to the extent that they can prosper while toiling in the muck and dying of childhood diseases and paying your taxes. But one of your subjects goes and confuses things when some guy barges into his house with a big shiny knife, demanding money: he grabs his sword and lops the guy's head off. "Your majesty," says he, "You were just going to have the Royal Executioner lop that guy's head off anyway, right? So this whole deal is kind of a win-win."

Okay, so new rule: no killing people, generally speaking, but if you happen to kill a man in the act of killing someone, robbing someone, stealing someone's horse-drawn minivan, or shooting the king's pheasants, that's okay. We were just going to have to kill that guy anyway, and you've saved us the cost of another execution. In one of your rare articulate moments, you proclaim, "His fault concludes but what the law should end," the life of the offender. And the people of your kingdom seem happy with this one, too, except for the judges.

27

"Your majesty, every time we try a murderer, he always says the other guy started it. And then the widow starts in saying her dead husband never hurt a fly, blah blah blah, and it's all but-he-did-this and but-he-said-that and frankly, that's why I wear this silly wig: I've long since pulled out my hair in frustration."

"No problem," you reply. Kings have answers for everything. "If it was some kind of chance-medley then there's no point worrying about who started it. They're both to blame for disturbing my peace. So fuck 'em. I've got better things to do, and so do you."

"Chance-medley, sire?"

"A casual affray. An ordinary, everyday fight. Don't you speak English?"

Your judicial lickspittle praises this brilliant idea, but he wants to know what to do if the killer really was trying to avoid the whole fight all along. And so you suggest that if he can show that he really did try to get out of the whole thing, for example by trying to run away, and if he really had no choice but to fight, then that would be a valid excuse—but there would still be some kind of penalty for disturbing the king's peace halfway through *The Walking Dead*. Maybe he should forfeit his chattels to the Crown, you suggest, thinking of the new sixty-four-inch plasma TV you've been considering for the keep at your summer place.

It's all getting a bit complicated, but it seems like a good system. And this was the state of the law in thirteenth-century England. Killing someone in the act of a capital offence had justification, because it did the executioner's work for him. But if you killed someone in a fight—"chance-medley," or as eighteenth-century jurist Sir William Blackstone had it, "a casual affray"—the common law wisely assumed that you and your antagonist had history, and that to disentangle who started it and who was at fault was beyond the court's ability or, indeed, the court's interest.[26] Whether or not you meant to kill him, that was manslaughter at least. Only if you had acted in a way that showed you were trying to avoid the fight might you claim the excuse of self-defence and escape execution. Blackstone clarifies:

> ... if the slayer has not begun the fight, or (having begun) endeavours
> to decline any further struggle, and afterwards, being closely pressed by
> his antagonist, kills him to avoid his own destruction, this is homicide

---

26　Blackstone's *Commentaries on the Laws of England* is an essential text for anyone who burns to understand English common law circa 1769, or who suffers from insomnia.

excusable by self-defence. For which reason the law requires that the person who kills another in his own defence should have retreated as far as he conveniently or safely can, to avoid the violence of the assault, before he turns upon his assailant ...

Here is the "duty to retreat," a concept that has utterly vexed American jurisprudence. America chokes on the duty to retreat, for retreat is calm, dishonourable, vile submission, and submission runs counter to the tendency of the American mind. The American mind prefers John Locke, who wrote, "all manner of force without right upon a man's person puts him in a state of war with the aggressor; and, of consequence, that, being in such state of war, he may lawfully kill him that puts him under this unnatural restraint." Shove me and I may kill you, for I am king unto myself, and reserve the right to war—which was more or less the state of things in the Dark Ages, and the very system that English law had disposed of.

Blackstone, ever the apologist for How Things Are, replies, "the king and his courts are the *vindices injuriarum*, and will give to the party wronged all the satisfaction he deserves." Vengeance is mine; I will repay, saith the Lord. The principle is older than Christianity.[27] Peace grows from a shared commitment to submit our disputes to judges, to abandon some degree of self-sovereignty. Among nations, where no law reigns, we still live in the Dark Ages, and reserve the right to settle our differences with rifles, tanks, smart bombs, and the threat of city-killing nukes launched from beyond the horizon, against which no defence is possible. But within nations, we can tolerate no such anarchy. This is not how you want things to be with your neighbour, the one who keeps complaining that your cat keeps crapping in his rosebed. That guy has nukes.

But the United States would not take the counsel of an apologist for How Things Are. Americans saw themselves as a new breed, uniquely infused with the American spirit, the bold civilizers of a new and savage frontier; they were not to submit to kings, nor to judges. Not for them this "public peace." Not for them this business of retreating. A coward retreats; an American is not a coward. The brave new nation preferred Locke. And so, as the nineteenth-century revolution in firepower placed increasingly lethal weapons in the hands of We the People, the United

---

27 *Vindices injurarium*: avengers of injuries. Although "vengeance is mine" is from Romans 12:19, it paraphrases Deuteronomy 32:35: "To me belongeth vengeance, and recompence."

States discarded the common law duty to retreat, discarded the notion that the state and its courts are the *vindices injuriarum*, and entrenched the culture of honour in its criminal law.

In place of the duty to retreat, American judges created their own idea, the True Man Doctrine: "A true man, who is without fault, is not obliged to fly from an assailant, who, by violence or surprise, maliciously seeks to take his life or do him enormous bodily harm." Why should you have to flee if you are honest and just, a righteous man? Retreat to the wall is cowardly.[28] An honourable, upstanding man—as distinct from a juvenile delinquent lurking in an alleyway, armed with a bag of Skittles—cannot be expected to run away. He can stand his ground and shoot that bastard dead.

The True Man Doctrine comes to us from an 1876 Ohio Supreme Court decision, *Erwin v. State*. The facts are unfortunate. James Erwin's son-in-law was a sharecropper on Erwin's land. Erwin wanted to use a shed between their homes to store his tools; his son-in-law wanted to use it for his own purposes. One day, the son-in-law evicted Erwin's tools from the shed. The men argued. According to Erwin's account, his son-in-law then advanced towards him with an axe, whereupon Erwin shot him with his revolver.

This was, of course, chance-medley, exactly as Blackstone had defined it a century before: no one could truly say who had started the fight or who was to blame, least of all the deceased son-in-law. The trial court judge instructed the jury that Erwin had a duty to retreat and avoid the confrontation, but on appeal, the Ohio Supreme Court forgot centuries of legal precedent and ruled that Erwin had no obligation to retreat from any place where he had a right to be, and instead had the right to stand his ground and shoot his daughter's husband dead. As for Erwin's daughter, her views on the killing of her husband seem to have escaped the interest of historians.

A year later, the Indiana Supreme Court took things a step further. John Runyan and Charles Pressnall were neighbours who held opposing political views, Runyan being a Democrat and Pressnall a Republican.

---

28   Most writers on the True Man Doctrine have insisted that in its original context, "true man" held no taint of masculine bravado, but Jeannie Suk, a law professor at Harvard, has convincingly argued otherwise. Whatever the words meant in the narrow context of *Erwin v. State*, they also inherit broader meanings from popular usage. "The tendency of the American mind," a phrase from *Runyan v. State* (discussed later in this chapter), supports Suk's contention: here, the court suggested that retreat is not only cowardly, but also un-American.

On Election Day, when Runyan and two companions went into town to vote, Pressnall and his friends harassed them. Runyan, whose right arm had been crippled in the Civil War, borrowed a pistol to even the odds, and then went to check the election results. Pressnall and company accosted Runyan and company and, in the true spirit of American political discourse, Pressnall struck Runyan. Runyan, continuing the debate by other means, shot Pressnall dead.[29]

Runyan was promptly convicted of killing Pressnall, but Indiana's Supreme Court reversed that conviction. Self-defence, the court declared, is "founded on the law of nature; and is not, nor can be, superseded by any law of society," a remark that is echoed to this day by the NRA and its followers. Runyan had an absolute right to self-defence, in other words, and running away would have been just plain un-American: "Indeed, the tendency of the American mind seems to be very strongly against the enforcement of any rule which requires a person to flee when assailed." Americans, according to the learned justices of Indiana's Supreme Court, stand their ground and shoot the bastard dead.

In 1921, the Supreme Court of the United States stepped in and extended the True Man Doctrine to the common law for the country as a whole. In Beeville, Texas—a state in which the True Man Doctrine already held sway—Robert Brown was convicted of second degree murder after he shot James Hermis over a dispute on a construction site where Brown was foreman. The two men had fought before, and on at least one occasion, Hermis had attacked Brown with a knife. Brown did the reasonable thing, and came to work with a revolver in his coat. Thus fortified, Brown ordered Hermis to move some earth. Hermis pulled out a knife. Brown ran about twenty-five yards, to where he had put his coat, retrieved his revolver, and shot Hermis four times in the chest. This was three more bullets than were strictly necessary, because Hermis fell after the first shot.

Oliver Wendell Holmes Jr., writing the Supreme Court opinion, expressed the same flawed reasoning that would power the revolt against proportionality a century later: "Detached reflection cannot be demanded in the presence of an uplifted knife. Therefore in this Court, at least, it is not a condition of immunity that one in that

---

29 The fact that Americans continue to this day to treat an election as a signal to stock up on arms and ammunition is one of the less salutary indications of American democracy.

situation should pause to consider whether a reasonable man might not think it possible to fly with safety or to disable his assailant rather than to kill him."

But the law had never demanded detached reflection in the presence of an uplifted knife. It imposed no requirement to pause for anything, or to consider anything. Nobody is required to ask himself, in the heat of the moment, what a reasonable man would do. In the heat of the moment, one acts. It is the members of the jury who are asked, after the fact, to consider if the act was that of a reasonable man, or of a violent, murderous impulse. Only a lawyer could confuse *being* a reasonable man with the need to dupe some future jury into mistaking you for one.

But here, as elsewhere, the courts were not allowing cold reason to carry them to their conclusions. Instead, they reasoned their way to conclusions they had already chosen. The true man was not an expression of American reality so much as an idea of what America wanted to be. And the true man, as an ideal, was not born in isolation. On October 26, 1881, five years after the Ohio Supreme Court decided that a true man had no duty to retreat from any place he had the right to be, four years after the Indiana Supreme Court declared that to run from a confrontation ran counter to the tendency of the American mind, and ten years after General George Wingate and Colonel William C. Church pulled the NRA together to make America strong through rifle shooting, Wyatt Earp and his brothers stepped into American legend by shooting down the Clantons at the O.K. Corral. Just two years later, Buffalo Bill Cody would invent the Wild West. And seven years after that, the superintendent of the census would announce that the American frontier had closed, which would lead Frederick Jackson Turner to argue that it was the Darwinian violence of the American frontier that had made America great. America wanted to believe that *Homo americanus* was unique, that the violence of the American West had bred a nation of strong, righteous men. And *Homo americanus* could brook no retreat. He would stand his ground.

FOR A CENTURY, THE TRUE MAN DOCTRINE held across most of the southern states, with the exception of Florida, whose courts never did buy into the idea. But the NRA was determined to correct that omission. What the common law could not provide, statute could, and so the NRA campaigned for a new law, on the usual tired complaint that we cannot demand detached reflection in the presence of a wacked-out crack addict. Marion Hammer, a past president of the NRA and now its tireless Florida lobbyist, complained that prosecutors had been given too much discretion and were running amok, trying to make their political careers over the ruined lives of righteous armed citizens. And so the draft version of the bill provided for damages against police and prosecutors should they prosecute self-defence cases. "Prosecutors are always looking for someone to prosecute and too often it's the victim," said Hammer, neatly ignoring the question of whether the dead guy deserved that title. "They are part of the problem."[30]

It's not just that a righteous man ought to be able to shoot the bastard dead; it's that the justice system should recognize him as righteous, and leave him alone even as the ambulance carts away the body. He ought not to have to explain himself in court, nor to face charges, nor even to suffer the indignity of arrest. He ought to be immune to any liability, for he is righteous. As the sponsor of the NRA's stand-your-ground bill in the state legislature, Durell Peaden, had it, "Why should you have to hire a lawyer to say, 'This guy is innocent?'"

The NRA's poster child for the stand-your-ground law was James Workman, a seventy-seven-year-old retiree whose home had been half-destroyed by Hurricane Ivan in 2004. Workman and his wife were asleep in an RV parked outside their home when they were awakened by the noise of an intruder, who burst in on them. While his wife called 911, Workman grabbed his gun and fired a warning shot, which didn't scare off the intruder. As the intruder tackled him, Workman fired twice, hitting him in the abdomen and the thigh. The shot to the thigh cut the femoral artery, and the man bled to death before police arrived. It was a clear-cut case of self-defence, yet somehow prosecutors left James Workman and his wife Kathryn swinging in the wind for six months before deciding that Workman would not face charges.

Florida's new self-defence law wrote the True Man Doctrine into statute by declaring that you had no duty to retreat from a confrontation in any place you had a right to be. It also provided immunity from prosecution and from civil liability if you shot someone who threatened you. And it kicked off a wave of similar bills that washed over thirty or more states.

---

30 Quoted in "NRA Uses New Florida Gun Law as National Model," by Dan Christensen, *Daily Business Review*, May 17, 2005.

Among our culture's masculine conceits is the notion that only facts, numbers, and measurements matter; anything else is an emotional argument, the territory of silly girls. Any gun control controversy sends social scientists scurrying to their computers. At Texas A&M University, Cheng Cheng and Mark Hoekstra announced that stand-your-ground laws do nothing to deter crime, but did correlate with an 8 percent increase in murder and non-negligent manslaughter.[31] But something was fishy: in half the states Cheng and Hoekstra examined, the True Man Doctrine was already the common law. Nothing had actually changed. If their findings were true, we could simply be looking at an "announcement effect"—not the effect of the law itself, but of the media coverage that went along with it. Or we could be looking at an entirely spurious result, which is to say, a load of bullshit.

Statistical regression is only as strong as its assumptions, and social science, rapt in the glow of computers running endless regression analyses, misses the point. We love to be impartial and empirical, to base our beliefs on the evidence, or at least to imagine we do. But crime arises from complex causes. It rises and falls regardless of our laws. And what matters is not whether we can prove any given law pushed the crime rate up or down. The law is not purely utilitarian. Justice is not found in metrics. Justice is found in values.

A man goes to the car wash where his girlfriend's ex works, starts an argument, and then pulls out a gun and shoots the other man, who is unarmed, dead. When the police arrive, he tells them he was standing his ground: he was in a place where he had a right to be, and gosh, he was afraid for his life. No charges are laid.

A man with a long history of domestic violence threatens his ex-wife with a gun and gets in an argument with her boyfriend. Later, when the boyfriend's car pulls up outside his home, he walks out into the street and pumps fourteen bullets into the car. His lawyer argues that he was standing his ground. The charges are dropped.

Neighbours argue, the latest in a series of confrontations over a pair of dogs; one turns away, and the other shoots him in the back, saying, "I thought he was going for something." When the alarm on a man's shed goes off at 3:30 in the morning, he goes outside, discovers an apparent

---

31   Cheng Cheng and Mark Hoekstra, "Does Strengthening Self-Defense Law Deter Crime or Escalate Violence? Evidence from Expansions to Castle Doctrine," *Journal of Human Resources* 48(3) (2013).

burglar, and shoots him in the back. A man is taking a shower when he hears a commotion. He gets dressed, goes for his gun, and steps outside as two young men run from his house. He shoots one of them in the back. No charges are laid.

Two men, roommates, have a few beers and then go to bed; later, one wakes up and, for reasons unexplained, attacks the other, who shoots him dead. There are no witnesses. Two other men, also roommates, argue in a bar over a pool game; later, one stabs the other to death. There are no witnesses. Another two men, again roommates, also argue. Their dispute leads neighbours to call police; one shoots the other in the chest with a shotgun before police arrive. There are—you guessed it—no witnesses. No charges are laid against any of them.[32]

No charges are laid, no charges are laid, no charges are laid. All of these killers are immune, because each is standing his ground, or at least claims to be. And with no witnesses to tell us otherwise, the word of the survivor stands. You shoot a man and walk free, as long as you make sure he ends up dead and can't tell his side of it. Whose values are these?

All of these examples are real cases, in which Florida's stand-your-ground law protected killers despite the dubious circumstances of their acts. None of these is the clear self-defence scenario the NRA asks us to imagine, in which some violent crack addict assaults a woman and drags her into an alleyway and she must shoot or die. Surely it's better to let one criminal walk free than to jail ten innocent men; but is it better to let ten men bleed to death in the streets than to demand that one innocent man explain himself in court before a jury of his peers? Should the acts of a killer escape judgment? Joseph Beale, a law professor at Harvard, suggested in 1903 that the True Man Doctrine represented "the ethics of the duelist, the German officer, and the buccaneer." We might extend this to describe the values reflected in Florida's stand-your-ground law, but we would first have to apologize to German officers.

Florida, which had been an exception to the True Man Doctrine, now has the most permissive self-defence law in the United States. And the aim of that law is not to ensure that peaceful homeowners can defend themselves so much as to ensure that anyone who kills in

---

32 These examples are all drawn from the *Tampa Bay Times* database of stand your ground cases.

presumed self-defence can escape prosecution entirely. There will be no need to submit yourself to the whims of a jury, nor to negotiate a wily prosecutor's verbal traps. You need not explain yourself in court. You will not have to remortgage your home to keep a law firm in BMWs. And you will certainly not have to linger in some legal limbo, wondering if your life will be ruined, for six months. You will not suffer as James and Kathryn Workman did.

But the story the NRA had told of James and Kathryn Workman was not quite true, as it turns out. It was true that James Workman shot a man named Rodney Cox in self-defence, and it was true that he suffered for some time in a legal limbo before learning that he would not be charged, but the circumstances were far less clear-cut than Marion Hammer, Durell Peaden, or the NRA would have you believe. And that murkiness explains the prosecutor's delay.

Rodney Cox was not a criminal, and it seems unlikely that he ever intended James or Kathryn Workman any harm. He was a FEMA contractor, a temporary worker from North Carolina who had come to Florida to take a job cleaning up after Hurricane Ivan. Earlier that fatal night, he had called police to report a domestic dispute; when the dispatcher asked him to clarify, he answered "violence to myself." When police arrived, they found Cox jumpy and disoriented, perhaps intoxicated. He said someone had tried to break into his trailer, and he packed his things to head to a hotel. Later, he called his mother, and told her he was looking for a place to stay. How he ended up at the Workmans' place isn't clear.

Neither is it clear why, after Kathryn saw him walking towards her ruined home and woke her husband, who availed himself of a .38-calibre revolver and stepped outside and fired a warning shot into the ground, Cox chose not to run away but instead ran into the Workmans' RV, although it is entirely possible that he was simply running for cover. Nor is it clear why, when James Workman pursued Cox into the trailer where the disembodied voice of a 911 operator urged his wife to stop screaming and explain what was happening, Cox turned and enclosed Workman in a bear hug, although it is entirely possible that he was simply trying not to get killed, just as Workman, when he pulled the trigger, had every reason to be in fear for his own life. What is clear, what became clear after Cox had been shot and had bled to death and had made his way to the coroner's cold slab to face the scalpel in naked indignity, was that Cox had suffered a fractured skull earlier that evening, which probably accounted for his confused state.

Nobody was a criminal, a predator stalking through the hurricane's ruins; nobody was an armed loon, looking for an excuse to shoot; nobody was a bad person who deserved punishment in this life or in the next. No one was the Good Guy, and no one was the Bad Guy. Rodney Cox and James Workman were simply two decent men who collided in confusing and frightening circumstances, with fatal results. But politicians need simple stories with sympathetic protagonists and clear villains. So they turned Rodney Cox into a violent home invader, and, while nobody was looking, deftly doubled the time it took the prosecutor to make his decision from three months to six. And they did this with good reason, not because the American public is stupid and needs a simple narrative, but because the American public is smarter than P.T. Barnum thought, and is well capable of wrestling with the slippery facts.

We love to pick on juries. We watch a few segments on the news or read a few stories on the web and convince ourselves not only that we know the facts of a case, but that we know them better than the jurors, who have spent not a few minutes but a few days in court, learning those facts and meeting the actors first-hand. And the thing about juries is that, when twelve reasonable people face the mass of slippery facts, they do not retreat to the high ground of universal principles and simplistic slogans on which we spend so much of our lives. Instead, they reach conclusions, and prove that in spite of politics and in spite of our endless culture wars, we do share similar values. The O.J. Simpson trial notwithstanding, juries prove time and time again that we're smarter than we look.

We share ideas of what is right and what is wrong, what is blameworthy and what is not—we share, in other words, the values of our culture. When asked to rank the relative seriousness of various offences, most people give the same answers, and when asked how much punishment those offences deserve, most people again agree. In one study, participants agreed on exactly when lethal force was justified in self-defence, and also agreed precisely with the centuries-old English common law, including the duty to retreat and the "castle doctrine"—the old principle that the duty to retreat does not apply if you are attacked in your own home.[33]

And so most of us would agree, faced with the facts of James Workman's case, that he was blameless, that after chasing an intruder into the trailer where his wife screamed for help, and being tackled by a much younger intruder, he had every reason to fear for his life, that the time for discussion, for negotiation, for talking the trespasser down, was well past. Most of us would agree, even if we do not own guns and do not approve of shooting people, even if we feel that perhaps he could have done something else, that when James Workman shot Rodney Cox, his act was not criminal. Even if we disapprove of his act, most would agree that he did not deserve to go to jail.

And he did not go to jail; indeed, he did not even face charges. So justice was done. James Workman's only punishment was to spend three months not knowing what the outcome would be, which if you think about it is not such a bad deal, bearing in mind that Rodney Cox, lying cold and shocky in a puddle of his own blood, had only minutes to come to terms with his own outcome.

Why, then, is self-defence so contentious? Not because we disagree on principle, but because we disagree on those slippery, writhing facts. Place one set of facts in front of twelve people, and they will likely reach the same conclusions; give slightly differing facts to six of those twelve, and you will get yourself a hung jury. And the facts of a real-world self-defence case will always be less clear than the facts you present to twelve experimental subjects. Take those unclear facts out into the court of public opinion, where the outcome becomes political, and we will pick and choose whatever we must to arrive at our predetermined conclusions.

Facts suck; they make things complex, and murky, and they confound the simple conclusions we long to reach. We're not stupid; we're just lazy. And so, unless we're forced to consider them, we prefer to set the facts

---

33   Studies of shared values in self-defence cases: Paul H. Robinson and Robert Kurzban, "Concordance and conflict in intuitions of justice," *Minnesota Law Review* 91 (2007). Castle Doctrine: The NRA and its allies have confused the meaning of "castle doctrine." Originally, the castle doctrine, as described by Blackstone, held that you had no duty to retreat if attacked in your home; fringe wingnuts have since worked to expand this meaning to include a right to shoot anyone trespassing on your property after dark, and now nobody is quite sure what the castle doctrine is anymore. Marion Hammer repeatedly referred to Florida's stand-your-ground law as a castle doctrine law, although Florida law in fact reflected the castle doctrine before 2005.

aside and to find a Good Guy and a Bad Guy. You could have guessed the members of the Trayvon Martin camp and the George Zimmerman camp before that shooting even occurred, with complete accuracy. And throughout the whole circus, each camp worked from its own set of facts, according to a script so predictable you might have thought it had been rehearsed. Knowing how we love to read our parts from a script, Florida politicians and the NRA made a few adjustments to the facts of Rodney Cox's death, and politics played out as usual. And so, in Florida today, you can shoot your wife's lover after an argument and have a square chance of getting away with it, if you play your cards right.

That's provided, of course, that your wife's lover ends up too dead to testify, because if he's alive to tell his side of it then the truth may come out. And this points to a fundamental problem with Florida's stand-your-ground law. One of the tests of a law is whether it creates a perverse result—whether it actually rewards acts that offend our values. And the problem with stand your ground is that it creates an incentive to kill. If the cops are going to show up, you'd better be sure the other guy ends up dead, so that nobody can contest your story that you were the Good Guy and he was the Bad Guy and you were standing your ground. Florida's stand-your-ground law isn't a licence to kill. It's an incentive.

There never is a Good Guy and a Bad Guy. Not in the real world. And none of the major cases that established the True Man Doctrine actually involved a Good Guy and a Bad Guy. The facts were murkier. *Erwin v. State* was an argument between a man and his son-in-law that escalated into a shooting for reasons unfathomable from a simple recitation of the facts. *Runyan v. State* was a confrontation between two neighbours over politics, in which the weaker man replied to a blow with a pistol shot—the kind of violence that flies in the face of respect for democracy. And *Brown v. United States* was a fight between two men who had fought before, and who likely would have fought again, had Brown not decided to shoot Hermis four times. These conflicts take place not on the screen where the Good Guy in the white hat always triumphs, but at street level, where life is solitary, poor, nasty, brutish and short. This is the world of chance-medley, in which the history of the conflict is ambiguous and a disinterested court struggles to divine what has truly taken place. Here, everyone is blameworthy, and the English common law recognizes them as such. Centuries of precedent brought the law to this point. But America, a land powered by fiction, fairy tale, and myth, insists on defining conflict in terms of a Good Guy who was blameless and a Bad Guy who threatens his autonomy.

Critics of movie violence complain that all those good guys shooting all those bad guys have taught our kids to see the world in simplistic terms, to believe that justice flows from the barrel of a gun and that violence solves everything.[34] But we did not learn to divide the world into good guys and bad guys from the movies. America writes movies with good guys and bad guys because the tendency of the American mind, if anything, is to imagine the world in these terms. And American courts, struggling to dislodge the bone that English common law had lodged in Americans' throats, imagined their cases playing out with the same old cast of characters on that same old stage. Hollywood merely showed up with a camera, to make a documentary of the national fantasy. And so, if we want to find the lost and secret pathway to the Wellspring of Crazy, it's to Hollywood we must turn next.

---

34   Angela F. Keaton, "Backyard Desperadoes: American Attitudes Concerning Toy Guns in the Early Cold War Era," *Journal of American Culture* 33(3) (2010).

The West is Still Wild

The Frontier Myth, Wish Fulfilment, and a Century of Westerns

This is crazy. I don't even have any guns.
—Marshal Will Kane in *High Noon*

WINDSOR, ONTARIO, IN THE EARLY 1950S: you would not normally see young boys lined up for a dull and dreary event such as this: the opening of a new wing at a local hospital, complete with a ceremonial ribbon-cutting and the posing and posturing of mayors and members of parliament. And not at this pitch of excitement, the line stretching down the street and around the corner, boys all a-chatter, those at the back of the line fretting that they'll miss the main event. Certainly not dressed like this, in cowboy hats and chaps, vests, and gun belts, kerchiefs around their necks. Not, above all, armed like this, with shining chrome six-shooters, every one.

But Roy Rogers is here, to open this new hospital wing. And Roy is dressed as always in his full cowboy paraphernalia: the hat, the kerchief, the embroidered shirt, the chaps, and, of course, the gun. Roy Rogers himself: tall, handsome, clean-cut, and always smiling that broad and boyish smile. The King of the Cowboys, in full colour.

Rogers personally answers every fan letter he receives. The studio will not pay the mailing costs, so he posts his replies at his own expense. And he will visit every kid in this hospital, and sign autographs for every kid in that line, even the last kid, the anxious kid who's sure that by the time he gets to the front Rogers will be gone, that Roy will have bid happy trails to you and made his smiling exit. Roy will still be there when that kid gets to the front of the line, and he will still be smiling.

My father was in that line. Every kid in Windsor was there.

"Is that a real gun?"

"Sure is."

"Can I touch it?"

"Sure can."

My own father touched the ivory grip of Roy Rogers' six-shooter. That was something.

*

I was here in Tombstone on the 26th of October, when a difficulty took place and a shooting occurred between the parties mentioned.

—*Cochise County Sheriff John H. Behan*

THE FRONTIER IS THE ANVIL AGAINST which America hammers its myths, transforming historical events into Western fables in which the good guys win, the bad guys lose, and American Progress triumphs to the benefit of everyone except that tragic figure, the frontier's man, who must move ever on. Law and order win the day, thanks to hard men ready to do violence on our behalf. This is ultimately what the Western was for: it offered to a nation born of violence, a nation that has never quite overcome its attraction to the power of the gun, an auditorium in which to argue its justifications.

Among Hollywood's favourite Western tales is the shootout at the O.K. Corral, a dirty little gunfight that wasn't even known by that name until 1957, when *Gunfight at the O.K. Corral* appeared in theatres and forever transplanted events that actually took place in a vacant lot on Fremont Street in Tombstone, Arizona, to the O.K. Corral, which Hollywood convention had placed on the edge of town. The difficulty on Fremont Street—the name by which these events were known during the Earp brothers' trial—was the climax of an ongoing feud between groups of men who used public office as a lever to advance their business interests, and who fell to violence when manipulating public institutions failed. It was, in other words, a typically sordid tale of American power, which Hollywood has repeatedly rewritten into a heroic tale of law and order's triumph over chaos and crime.

Popular history describes the Earps as a "tight-knit family," but had they arrived at the wrong side of history they might be better remembered as a gang. They shared what might charitably be called an entrepreneurial spirit and a distaste for the honest toil of farming. If they were known as lawmen, it was because they had discovered that money travels with power. Virgil got himself appointed Deputy US Marshal for the Arizona Territory before moving to Tombstone. In the summer of 1880, Wyatt ran against Johnny Behan, the Clantons' man, for the job of county sheriff, but lost. Still, opportunity rewards the patient. After Curly Bill Brocius accidentally shot and killed Tombstone marshal Fred White in October 1880, Virgil became town marshal, which allowed him to make his brothers deputies. Their duty, as well they knew, was to make the town safe for decent folk by suppressing the kind of violence that disturbs the drinkers, the gamblers, and the whores, which is to say, the Earps' customers and employees.

The Clantons and McLaurys, on the other hand, are known to history not as families but as the Cochise County Cowboys. They ranched around Tombstone, and it is said they supplemented their ranch income by cattle rustling, horse theft, and stagecoach robbery. One does what one must to get by. The Cowboys had been in the territory a long time, and they were the existing power in town, with the sheriff in their pocket; the Earps, who arrived with the silver boom in Tombstone, were newcomers. The conflict between the Earps and the Cowboys was the classic conflict of the American West: the new forces out the old, as the body count rises.

October 26, 1881, saw "the difficulty which resulted in the death of Frank McLaury, Thomas McLaury, and Billy Clanton."[35] Early that morning, Virgil Earp had met Ike Clanton, pistol-whipped him, disarmed him, and charged him with carrying a revolver and a Winchester rifle in defiance of Tombstone Ordinance No. 9, which prohibited carrying weapons in town. Exiting the courthouse, Wyatt Earp met Tom McLaury in the street and pistol-whipped him in turn, later claiming that McLaury was armed. By early afternoon, a group of Cowboys had gathered near the O.K. Corral, and were making threats to kill the Earps. The Earps and their friend, Doc Holliday, walked out to meet them.

---

35   As described by the Earps' attorney, Thomas Fitch, in his examination of Virgil Earp.

The parties met in a narrow empty lot on Fremont Street six doors west of the O.K. Corral. Virgil Earp shouted out that he had come to disarm them, as Ordinance No. 9 demanded. Johnny Behan insisted that the first shot was fired from a nickel-plated revolver, thus pinning the deed on Holliday, although all other accounts agreed that Holliday was armed with a coach gun that Virgil had given him. Wyatt testified that he did not know who fired first, he or Billy Clanton. Billy fired at Wyatt, and Wyatt at Frank McLaury, because, as Wyatt later explained, McLaury was "a good shot and a dangerous man." Tom McLaury, it turned out, was unarmed save for a Winchester in its scabbard on the horse beside him; the Winchester remained there even as McLaury fell dead. Thirty seconds later, Ike Clanton and Billy Claiborne had fled, and the McLaury brothers and Billy Clanton were dead. Virgil Earp was shot through the leg, and Morgan Earp and Doc Holliday suffered minor wounds. Only Wyatt emerged unscathed, a lucky stroke that would enlarge his legend.

The Cowboys turned first to the law, but the law declared the Earps innocent, and so the gun became their *vindices injurarium*. Men armed with shotguns ambushed Virgil Earp and riddled his left arm with buckshot, leaving the surgeon no option but to remove the shattered bone and render Virgil a cripple. The following spring, Morgan Earp was shot in the back while playing billiards; he bled to death in forty minutes. Keeping the business of lawing in the family, Wyatt Earp took over Virgil's position as Deputy US Marshal, an office he promptly abused to carry on a personal vendetta of revenge against the Cowboys, hunting them down and killing them one by one in what is now known as the Earp Vendetta Ride.

These are the essential facts. In its retelling, Hollywood bent and squeezed and hammered these facts to fit the framework of the frontier myth and the shape of the nation's mood. Hollywood cast Earp in the role of frontier hero, with Doc Holliday, the man who knows Indians, as his guide. The remaining Earp brothers were relegated to minor roles, chiefly because Wyatt Earp had outlived them and it was Wyatt, through his biographer Stuart Lake, who had provided the story.

The Western argues for justification, and so Hollywood took Wyatt's older brother James, a Civil War veteran who made his living as a saloon keeper and pimp, transformed him into a callow youth named Jimmy, and killed him. In the 1946 film *My Darling Clementine*, Wyatt Earp kneels over his brother's grave, and sets out to civilize the frontier:

"Maybe when we leave this country, kids like you'll be able to grow up and live safe." In *Gunfight at the O.K. Corral* (1957), Jimmy gets to utter Western clichés of his own, remarking, "It's awful quiet, too quiet," and then compounding his error by talking about his girl back in California. A more experienced movie character would have known not to set himself up this way, but he is just a foolish boy, and within minutes, poor Jimmy Earp is dead again. But thanks to Jimmy's sacrifice, the shootout at the O.K. Corral becomes a fully justified showdown between Good Guys and Bad Guys, in which the Good Guys win. And so the gunfight duly occurs, Tombstone is made safe for women and children, and Wyatt moves on, seeking a new frontier.

The mid-1990s saw two new takes on the story.[36] *Tombstone*, which focused on the gunfight and the Earp Vendetta Ride, starred Kurt Russell as Wyatt and Val Kilmer as Doc, and *Wyatt Earp*, which set out to tell the entire story of Earp's life, starred Kevin Costner as Wyatt and Dennis Quaid as Doc. *Tombstone* drags the O.K. Corral into the modern day with an introductory voiceover that explicitly compares the murder rate in Tombstone to that in modern American cities. If crime in Tombstone was as bad as modern-day Detroit or Miami, the film hints, it must have been very bad indeed—a suggestion that invites us to think we live in extremely violent times. Tombstone's problems, the movie posits, were similar to our own. The Cowboys are no longer mere cattle rustlers and thieves, but an organized crime syndicate. Mattie Blaylock, a former prostitute and Earp's common-law wife, is shown taking laudanum. At one point she overdoses in despair over Earp's affair with Josephine Marcus. When Curly Bill Brocius accidentally kills Marshal Fred White, he has just emerged from an opium den. Tombstone, we are given to understand, was not just a town with a crime problem; it was a town with a drug problem.

Hollywood's Production Code had constrained *My Darling Clementine* and *Gunfight at the O.K. Corral*. The Earps could shoot the Clantons down, but only after Jimmy's death and the Clanton's law-breaking put them on the side of the angels. Above all, the Earps had to uphold the law. But by the time *Tombstone* came around, that code had long since

---

36 Both *Tombstone* and *Wyatt Earp* originated from the same project. A difference of opinion led Kevin Costner to split off from *Tombstone* and make his own movie. The appearance of two O.K. Corral movies in two successive years does not, then, reflect a sudden surge of interest in the gunfight so much as it reflects the reach of Hollywood egos.

disappeared. The Earps could now serve a higher power, justice, to which the law is so often a trifling, bureaucratic inconvenience. And so the Earp Vendetta is clearly justified, because the Clantons were the bad guys. As moral justifications go, it's not exactly sophisticated. Each of us thinks he's the good guy. But this is the best the movies are prepared to give us.

The problem with the Western, a genre that exists mainly to explore American justifications for violence, is that it so rarely struggles to find them. It hammers history into myth with glib certainty, discarding the complexity of law in favour of simple justice, under which you need only feel that you're in the right to inherit all the moral authority justice can bestow. Wyatt Earp is forced to violence, but on arriving in that territory he finds no difficulty in proceeding, physically or morally. One suspects he does not have to be forced there at all, but waits only for some justification to allow him to let slip the dogs he wants so badly to run. The desire goes before the need. And this, perhaps, is what the Western genre really has to tell us about the nation that created it. All those hand-wringers, who fret that violence on the screen may inspire us to solve our own problems with violence, have missed the point entirely. We don't watch Westerns and find ourselves inspired to carry guns; we feel inspired to carry guns, and let Western movies justify us.

IT'S A MAN'S WORLD, THIS FRONTIER. Men go out into the world and do active things, settle matters with their fists, use their guns when necessary, and dress up as cowboys. Women stay home, because when they go out into the world where active things are done they stand to be terrorized or to have foolish horse accidents, which will require the usual masculine rescue. If trouble looms, they restrict themselves to loading the menfolk's guns, or make feckless squeaking noises. Any woman who picks up a gun in a Western is like a trained seal; the movie is gosh-awfully impressed and wonders, briefly, if she can also balance a ball on her nose, before it sends its men back to the business of killing. When Amy saves Will Kane at the climax of *High Noon*, the act does not make her a strong woman; rather, it demonstrates that she is really just a silly girl, because by picking up a gun and shooting a man, she is admitting that her husband was right all along. Men know How Things Work.

Men know that you must stand your ground. Give them an inch, and they'll take everything you own. "Let them have the land. It ain't worth it," says Jane Roberts (Myrna Dell) in the forgettable 1943 movie, *Raiders of Red Gap*. A thousand other token women in a thousand other Westerns have said the same, before and since. But Myrna Dell's 1943 audience knew full well how appeasement worked out for Neville Chamberlain. Fortunately, Red Gap has the Lone Rider (Robert Livingston) to save the day.[37] Kevin Costner couldn't answer Jane Roberts, as he had not yet been born, but he does have an answer ready for Josephine Flood some fifty-one years later in *Wyatt Earp*, when she blubbers that she doesn't want to see him shot down in some street fight she doesn't even understand, poor thing. It doesn't matter that the film's Tombstone, Arizona, is little more than an overgrown mining camp. Wyatt Earp and his brothers have put everything they have into Tombstone, their home, and they will not let themselves be run off. Better to die like a lion than live like a mouse. If only Wyatt had been a little more eloquent, he might have declared that to flee would run counter to the tendency of the American mind.

Women belong to the world of soft domesticity, not out here on the hard frontier. We know Will Kane must be finished as a lawman, because *High Noon* (1952) opens with his wedding. "Never marry a Quaker," Kane quips. "She'll turn you into a storekeeper." But storekeeping is inevitable; it stands for the peace and prosperity we all desire. It is this, after all, that America longs to be: a nation of back-slapping salesmen whose boys play baseball under moth-battered lights on lazy summer evenings. The Old West must disappear, and America must grow up into a nation of shopkeepers, a development made concrete in the marriage of Kane, played by fifty-something Cooper, and Amy Fowler, played by a twenty-two-year-old Grace Kelly in a clean white dress. The problem with women is that we like them, and all that westering is hard on your love life.

In early B-Westerns, the hero generally chooses not to light out for the territory, opting instead to settle down with the movie's token female character, invariably the pretty young daughter of some rancher beset by rustlers or land-grabbing schemers from back east. We know this to be the case because the story ends with a smooch and fades rapidly to black, which betokens both happily ever after and the horizontal mambos forbidden by the Hollywood Production Code. This smooch and all it

---

37   *The Lone Rider* was a ripoff of *The Lone Ranger*, created after *The Lone Ranger*'s creator, George Trendle, wrested the rights to the Lone Ranger away from Republic because of Robert Livingston's insistence that he wanted audiences to see his face. (The Lone Ranger, Trendle insisted, was never to appear without a mask.)

implies is perhaps just a cynical concession to the women in the audience, who presumably demand romance, and who are not so in thrall to the whole frontier thing. Westerns pitched unabashedly at seven-year-olds, on the other hand, cleave to the frontier model and inadvertently comment on the insecurities of American masculinity: there will be no icky girls and no icky smooching. Instead, the hero turns and waves back at the camera as he rides off into what we understand by convention would be a sunset but for the expense of filming available darkness. Offstage, the rancher's daughter returns to scrubbing the floors, a Western Cinderella. In careful restorations of these films, we may hear her mutter, "This sucks."

But *Shane* (1953) hints at a different truth: that it was women who civilized the West, that the frontier of young men, drunken shootouts, and whores would be overtaken by towns filled with women, women who demanded safe places in which to raise the children fathered by their steady and reliable husbands, who demanded law and order and got it, forcing the drunken young men to pack up their mayhem and move on to wilder spaces where things were still fun. The Starrett family—Joe, Mary, and young Joey—stand for the future of the West; Shane is a figure out of the violent past. There will be no guns in Mary Starrett's valley, and no nookie for gunslingers. Guns and gunslingers are cast out, and the West grows more peaceful; children go to school and quiet men like Joe Starrett go to church with their pretty young wives. The gun moves from a man's belt to a place over his front door, thence to a gun rack over the hearth. Eventually, we keep our shotguns locked in gun safes beside our writing desks, and our dogs mope six days a week, twitching in dreams of birds, vibrant with their own canine tinnitus. The agent of progress, we euphemize as love.

But in the meantime, our Western Cinderella has to keep on scrubbing the floor and listening to men puffing out their chests and explaining how everything works. It ain't the land, Jane, it's the principle. This is our home, Josie, and I'm not leaving. Not for nothin'. Not even for you. Only a woman would put love above all; Wyatt, wise in the ways of the world, knows that what really matters is pride.

IN THE 1950S, THE COWBOY WAS KING, in the movies and on television. In 1959, thirty competing Western series aired in prime time, thirty-five in total on network television. Fourteen new Western series premiered that year. In the last week of March 1959, eight of the top ten shows in the Nielsen ratings were Westerns, with *Gunsmoke* leading the list. A strange hunger for stories of cowboys and sheriffs, out on the frontier, not quite explained by the greed-driven copycats of network television, all seeking to cash in on what the other guy was doing. But that longing for frontier stories is not difficult to fathom. It was all about wishful thinking, nostalgia for a simpler world that never really existed, a fantasy world in which problems had simple solutions, families stuck together, and good American values trumped all.

The atomic genie was out of the bottle and Kinsey's cat was out of the bag. World War II had brought American women out of the home and into the factory, and they would not easily be shoved back into their erstwhile roles. African Americans, fed up at being shut out of the nation, were rumbling about their long-denied rights. Life was faster, more complicated. Your father had lived in a small town, where he worked on a farm or perhaps sold things to people who worked on farms. But now you found yourself in a big city, working at some factory that churned out cars or airplane parts or radios or them new-fangled television sets, the only remaining sign of your roots being your willingness to use a word like "newfangled" with a straight face. Everywhere you looked, there were new space-age gadgets. Rocketships were maybe not so far away. So America did what we all do when things start changing too fast: America sought solace in memories of simpler times. This is where the culture war begins.[38]

The Western reached back into history, glossed over the nasty bits, and regurgitated a vision of America's past custom-fit to reassure a nation caught up in a worrisome present. The hero of that vision was the cowboy, no longer a grimy, marginally skilled wage slave working a job no one else much wanted, but the epitome of everything America was supposed to be. The cowboy lives clean, free of the complexities of modern life. He doesn't even know what a communist is, but if he met one, he'd know how to fix his little Red wagon, and it would be a simple fix.[39] In the world of the cowboy, direct action solves everything.

---

38 Arguably, it begins a little earlier: Prohibition was a conflict between teetotalling rural Protestants and gin-swilling urban Catholics. But the *casus belli* was no different.

39 In fact, cowboys knew full well what communists were. Cowboys were poorly paid, and American labour history includes more than one cowboy strike—strikes that failed, because cowboys are easy to replace.

No one (except the villain) ever hires a lawyer. Men make their own fates; no one is a pawn, pushed up the chessboard by forces beyond his control. If you don't like your boss, you tell him to take this job and shove it, without worrying about such troublesome details as paying the mortgage.

That the simpler time portrayed in the Western never actually existed was of no importance, just as the paranoia of the Atomic Age and the rumblings of racial unrest are of no importance for those who now idealize *Leave it to Beaver* fantasies of the 1950s. Buffalo Bill Cody had nailed it eighty years previously when he invented "the Wild West." The West, that land of opportunity and rugged individualism, was ripe for American myth-making. No other genre could so powerfully validate the values America wished were its own. The Western was America, and the cowboy way was the American way.

The desire to return to a simpler, rural past shines out of the screen in *Homesteaders of Paradise Valley* (1947), a Red Ryder movie aimed squarely at an audience too young to remember that simpler, rural past.[40] The movie pits happy homesteaders—who wouldn't be happy, living in Paradise Valley?—against money men from nearby Center City who connive to rob them with a fountain pen. The money men want the community's water, and they'll stoop to all manner of skullduggery to get it. Against them stand Red Ryder, his youthful sidekicks, and an entire community of cheerful, brave Americans infused with the can-do spirit.

Our homesteaders speak "plain American" (a language somehow distinct from English) and reject the "legal mumbo-jumbo" of Center City. They get their news from a "genuine community newspaper" rather than the *Center City Gazette*, a propaganda organ of the money men. Red Ryder, a man so obnoxiously decent that he even draws fire to prevent the villain being shot, insists on putting everything to a vote. Everyone, except for one token malcontent, takes only his fair share of the valley's water. Paradise Valley is a mythical America in which we all pull together for the common good and agree to be governed by the will of the majority, where we get along with our neighbours and everyone pitches in.

If the Western is all about rugged individualism, why is Paradise Valley so full of community spirit? Is it simply that this is a cheesy B-movie,

---

40 *Red Ryder* was a highly successful Western comic strip which ran in newspapers for 26 years beginning in 1938, and spawned countless spinoffs, including a series of movies and the Daisy Red Ryder BB gun, which is still available.

aimed at seven-year-olds, stuffed so full of Good American Values that the script bulges at the seams? Well, probably, but the tension between the rugged individualist and tranquil community, between the pull of the wild frontier and the pleasures of soft domesticity, is at the heart of the Western genre. Shane arrives at the Starrett homestead in the opening scene of his own movie, alone and dressed in buckskin leather, a throwback to a mythological past of frontier scouts and Indian fighters, but the yeoman farmers he defends are a community of families, with wives and children and farms and livestock and homes. We know the men Shane must confront are evil, because the first thing they do is trample the Starretts' vegetable garden with their horses. The Starretts, with their little house on the prairie, stand for civilization, and notwithstanding the rifle hanging over their doorway, Shane has no place there. Even if he is a Good Guy, he remains a man of violence. Yet every boy lined up for Roy Rogers longs to wear Shane's buckskins and each of their fathers longs to distract Mary Starrett from her husband, although as Shane rides off into the middle of the screen and we leave the theatre to return to our quiet lives, we all know that that we are just yeoman farmers (or accountants, or high-school English teachers), that everyone settles down, and that the best model we can emulate is steady, reliable Joe Starrett.

Shane in his buckskins is heir to an unbroken lineage of frontier heroes stretching back to James Fenimore Cooper's *Leatherstocking Tales*. He is the frontiersman: a man who moves between worlds, a man who can move from the civilized drawing rooms of domestic America to her violent frontiers, a "man who knows Indians" and can never quite fit in when he returns to civilization.[41] He can quote Shakespeare and he may even read poetry, yet he is equally capable of winning a bar fight by pistol-whipping his assailant, thereafter downing the remainder of his whiskey, tipping the bartender, and apologizing for the mess as he departs. Departing is his métier, the essence of his role. In a never-ending cycle, he seeks a new frontier, civilizes it by force of arms, and then moves on to yet another new frontier. No strawberry socials, no tea parties, no piano recitals for him. He is stiff and uncomfortable in a starched collar.

Behind the frontiersman's distaste for tea parties and frilly clothes lies the reality that he is a throwback to the past, and he must remain in the

---

41 "The man who knows Indians" is Richard Slotkin's label for this particular trope.

past, where he belongs. And the past is out west. America's longitudinal axis is not geographic, but temporal: as one westers, one travels back in time, beyond the reach of law and order, beyond rules and restrictions and petty bureaucrats, out into landscapes of possibility. Time, in the person of the railway conductor and his imperious pocket watch, races to catch up. Shane's days are over, and he knows it. His obsolescence is clear from the opening scene of the movie, when he appears in buckskins. In the end he must move on, westward into possibility, westward towards his own time. Indeed, all cowboys must ride off into the sunset simply because the sun sets in the West and it is westward they must go. The valley is safe and the farmers may farm; rifles hang over their doorways now only to dispatch the possums among the geraniums. It is the same old Western story: the frontier has been conquered, and there is no more room for the frontiersman.

The rugged individualist must give way to community, because community is civilization. We long for Paradise Valley. The need to come together and create that community gives the Western one of its great clichés, one carefully reiterated by a grizzled old miner named Grimby in *The Crooked Trail* (1936): "We gotta take it on ourselves to organize before outlaws and other varmints run us clear off the crick ... we gotta organize for law and order!" We have to pull together. But too often, pulling together just isn't enough: the Bad Guys have guns and ill will, and we need a frontier hero to step out of the past, as Shane does, and save us from outlaws and varmints and crick-runnings-off. And sometimes we fail to recognize the frontier hero living among us, and turn our backs on him even as he steps in, alone and unheralded, to keep our crick safe for whoever might think living on a crick is a fine idea.

And so in *High Noon* Marshal Will Kane faces Frank Miller's gang alone after the townsfolk abandon him. Kane is not a rugged individualist by choice. If you offered him help, he would gladly accept it. Indeed, he spends about half the movie asking the townspeople for help, only to meet a catalogue of excuses. No one comes to his aid, and in the end he throws away his badge in disgust even as the townsfolk thank him. As his badge falls into the dust we know that this soft community is not worth protecting, that America has become a nation of decadent shopkeepers who have let go the torch passed by their frontier forebears. This town, where people cower in their homes and pull the curtains instead of coming to their neighbour's aid, is no longer Paradise Valley; it merely pretends to be, when times are good.

The theme never disappears. Shane westers until he runs out of land, and then civilization catches up. Presumably, he dies in his dotage in some old folks home where nurses condescend: How are we this morning? But Dirty Harry Callahan knows where to find his frontier.[42] The man who knows Indians has become the man who knows the mean streets of San Francisco. In a cheap diner on those mean streets, the cook greets him by name. Harry, whose keen eye has spotted a getaway car idling outside the bank, calmly orders a hot dog and has the cook call for backup. When the shooting starts, Harry strolls out into the street, shrugs off a shotgun blast, and shoots the two (black) bank robbers and their getaway driver, still chewing his hot dog, before delivering the first of his famous "Do you feel lucky?" speeches.

"I know what you're thinking. 'Did he fire six shots, or only five?' Well to tell you the truth, in all this excitement I kind of lost track myself. But being this is a .44 Magnum, the most powerful handgun in the world, and would blow your head clean off, you've got to ask yourself one question: 'Do I feel lucky?' Well, do ya, punk?"

Which is just a long-winded way of saying, "Draw."

Death Wish (1974) finds the answer for America's woes in the same Western tradition. America has become a nation of soft, decadent shopkeepers whose liberal hearts bleed for the Fourth Amendment rights of the underprivileged. We watch as the underprivileged follow Paul Kersey's wife and daughter back to their apartment and burst through the door to rob and rape them, before killing the wife. The grief-stricken Paul westers to Arizona, where he finds sunshine, wide-open spaces, cows, and real-live cowboys wearing real-live cowboy hats. In a Wild West re-enactment staged for tourists, a brave Marshal guns down a gang of bank robbers as the narrator's voice booms from a loudspeaker: "The outlaw life seemed a shortcut to easy money, which could buy liquor, women, and a turn at the gambling table, but there were honest men with dreams who would fight to protect their [inaudible] and who would plant the roots that would grow into a nation." *Death Wish*

---

42 Dirty Harry Callahan is a San Francisco police detective played by Clint Eastwood in a series of movies, best known for pointing his .44 Magnum revolver at criminals and encouraging them to go ahead and make his day.

knows not of Western Union, and delivers its message with all the subtlety of a ball-peen hammer.

How soon America has forgotten the lessons of its history! Unjust laws make outlaws of righteous men. Back in New York, Paul carries a gun as he walks the streets by night, a felony under the Sullivan Act.[43] But shooting punks proves strangely therapeutic, a balm for a broken heart. With each dead body, the grieving Paul becomes steadily more chipper. When the body count hits six, he repaints his apartment: redecoration through violence.

Too long has America mollycoddled its crooks, granted them rights, allowed greasy lawyers to slither through loopholes and get their clients off on technicalities! *Dirty Harry* and *Death Wish* offer America a simple solution to its ills. The answer to violence, same as it ever was, is greater violence. Harry, the lone hero, must not only find and kill Scorpio, the psychotic sniper who terrorizes San Francisco, but also overcome the resistance of his superiors and the courts, who have discarded the lessons of the frontier. Harry hunts Scorpio across the rooftops of San Francisco, his binoculars spying on the nation's bedrooms where they find a catalogue of decadence and depravity: naked women greeting guests at their apartment doors, a wife beating her soft, useless husband. Is this community even worth protecting? Little wonder that when Harry finishes with Scorpio, he follows Will Kane's lead, and throws his badge down in the dust. The community ideal is dead. All that remains is the urban jungle.

BRIGHT CHROME AND STEEL corpuscles stream along Windsor's arteries, here across the river from 1954 Detroit. This year the Detroit Red Wings beat the Montreal Canadiens in the Stanley Cup finals, four games to three, in overtime. Detroit is in its glory days, the metal heart of America young and strong, pumping out cars. Out across that river Bob Seger is just nine years old, has yet to buy his first record. His father works at the Ford Motor Company. And here is Roy Rogers in royal regalia, king of the cowboys, gun gleaming in hip holster. The entrance lobby of this Windsor hospital is far from the open range, and Trigger, for reasons of hospital hygiene, is nowhere to be seen. But Roy Rogers is

---

43 The Sullivan Act is a New York law that makes it a felony to carry a concealed handgun without a licence, or to possess a wide variety of other concealable weapons such as blackjacks, brass knuckles, and flick knives.

still a cowboy, still wears the hat, the shirt, the kerchief, and, of course, the gun.

Historians of the Western pay little attention to Roy Rogers and his ilk. The singing cowboys embarrass the entire genre. But something significant is going on when Roy, clad in cowboy attire, confronts gangsters in fedoras. Roy Rogers steps onto the screen as a walking anachronism, pulled forward in time from the nineteenth century into the mid-twentieth. Standing in the entrance lobby of that hospital in Windsor, Ontario, very much in the present day, Roy Rogers asserts that somewhere in America, the Wild West still exists.

And so it is essential that Rogers is a "real cowboy," a real Western figure who just happens to let a camera follow his adventures from time to time. To be the same cowboy you played in the movies, you needed to own the film cowboy's horse: Roy Rogers had Trigger, and Bob Keene appeared in opening credits "with his famous horse, 'Prince.'" Buck Jones, the most popular B-Western star of his day, was born in Indiana but claimed to have grown up on a ranch in Indian Territory, better known now (and then) as Oklahoma. If the Hollywood cowboy didn't grow up on a ranch, he needed some other qualifications, and he was usually all too eager to prove them. When Hugh O'Brian, who played Wyatt Earp on television, claimed to be the fastest draw in Hollywood, the war-hero-turned-actor Audie Murphy challenged him to a fast-draw shootout, with live ammunition.

In the golden age of the Western, a B-movie star often played a single character in a series, a character who often shared the actor's first name. Or they simply appeared as themselves. Buck Jones appeared again and again as US Marshal Buck Roberts; the character actor George "Gabby" Hayes would always appear as characters named Gabby. The Range Busters were led by the fictional cowboy Ray "Crash" Corrigan, who by some not entirely wild coincidence was played by an actor named Ray Corrigan. Tex Ritter appeared as Tex Haines, Tex Coulter, Tex Terrell, Tex Martin, Tex Rawlings, Tex Reed, Tex Lawton, Tex Roberts, Tex Rockett, Tex Wright, Tex Regan, Tex Wallace, Tex Lowery, Tex Masters, Tex Yancey, Tex Allen, Tex Ramsey, Tex Houston, Tex Newman, Tex Stewart, Tex Lawrence, Tex Collins, Tex Martin, Tex Rand, Tex Archer, Tex Randall, Tex Masters, Tex Malinson, Tex Saunders, Tex Lansing (who in turn used the alias Tex Rawlins), just plain Tex, and "Texas

Ranger Lieutenant Tex Ritter." Roy Rogers kept things simple; born Leonard Franklin Slye, he became a man named Roy Rogers, on and off the screen.

America still wants to believe in its open frontier. America wants to believe that cowboys still ride the range as modern-day knights-errant, living by the cowboy code, that somewhere out there, an American man can still live free with his pony and his rifle. What was true for Wyatt Earp could still hold true for you in the suburbs with your riding lawn-mower. Roy Rogers, the Hollywood cowboy carrying on the Western tradition in the modern world, enacts that very possibility. In *Romance on the Range* (1942), Rogers and the Sons of the Pioneers find them-selves pitted against a gang of trapline thieves. When the ranch owner and her friend Sally are held up, it's up Roy to rescue them, his six-gun in hand. But after Roy saves the day, Sally does not collapse in tears, or shake with nerves, or show any other sign that the experience of being held at gunpoint and then rescued by a man waving a gun was in the least frightening or stressful. Instead, she bounces with excitement in the seat of her car, thrilled, and shouts America's fervent prayer: "The West is still wild, isn't it?"

The Secret History
of the Second Amendment, Part One
A Well-Regulated Militia as an Aid to Settling Irksome Labour Disputes

If I get shot, they can't shoot the union out of me.

—Florence Reece

A WELL-REGULATED MILITIA being essential to the security of a free state, the right of the people to keep and bear arms shall not be infringed.

And be it further enacted, That whenever the laws of the United States shall be opposed or the execution thereof obstructed, in any State, by combinations too powerful to be suppressed by the ordinary course of judicial proceedings, it shall be lawful for the President of the United States to call forth the militia of such state to suppress such combinations, and to cause the laws to be duly executed.[44]

The rights of the people being inalienable, a well-regulated militia bought by railroad money, armed with rifles and bayonets, and backed by federal troops moved on striking railroad workers across the nation in 1877, killing more than a hundred Americans. On May 1, 1886, when the people in Bay View, Wisconsin, marched towards the Milwaukee Iron Company rolling mill to demand an eight-hour workday, a well-regulated militia shot and killed seven of them. When the people of Pullman, Illinois, a town owned entirely by engineer and industrialist George Pullman, embarked on a wildcat strike against the Pullman Palace Car Company on May 11, 1894, twelve thousand US Army troops suppressed such combinations, killing thirteen. On September

---

44 Adapted from the Militia Act, 1792.

10, 1897, near Hazleton, Pennsylvania, a sheriff's posse of 150 deputies faced down four hundred unarmed strikers, and shot nineteen in the back. In 1905, in Chicago, the Teamsters went on strike; twenty-five were killed and 416 wounded. The 1907 San Francisco Streetcar Strike left thirty-one dead. The Pressed Steel Car Company strike of 1909 killed up to twenty-six. And on May 8, 1910, during the Westmoreland County Coal Strike, a group of strikers brazenly mocked sheriff's deputies, who responded to their exercise of the First Amendment by reminding them of the Second, killing one and wounding thirty. The laws of the United States were duly executed.

The grim reality of American freedom is that since the Second Amendment was written, not once has a well-regulated militia been raised for the purpose of resisting the tyranny America so fears. But a well-regulated militia, being so essential to the security of a free state, has repeatedly been used to suppress the right of the people to strike to improve wages and working conditions that no person today would defend.

Call this the secret history of the Second Amendment. It is a history we need to know if we hope to understand why Americans won't give up their guns. For an otherwise law-abiding citizen to insist on keeping guns to fight back against the state seems ridiculous in a modern democracy, an idea straight from the Wellspring of Crazy. But what if we err in assuming that we can trust the courts to settle our disputes? The secret history of the Second Amendment is a story of the weakness of American social capital and the failure of her institutions, of what happens when justice takes off her blindfold and holds out her hand to the highest bidder. The powerful can buy all the justice they need. The weak must fashion their own.

A MIGHTY STAR BURNS OUT OF CONTROL, hydrogen compressed by gravity to such a point that atoms themselves fuse, flinging light and radiation through the void to fall upon some primordial swamp, on ferns and fronds of strange vegetation, a bleary brontosaur lifting its massive head, blinking, oblivious, weed and water trailing from its teeth. The wonder of this star's power, the alchemy by which the energy of the universe itself is ensnared and bound in fertile green growth, escapes the dumb brute. It looks up to watch a meteor trace its burning path across the sky, and continues its repast.

All things pass. Trees fall; ferns sink into the fetid swamp, mud enclosing rotting green mush, methane bubbles wobbling through dark water. Years blend into eons and eons into eras, the dark swamp now compressed deep underground into black rock, the strange shapes of ancient ferns and flowers impressed in its dark clefts and crevices. This is coal: by some mad magic, a rock that burns. Miners break the rock from the ground by the ton to build the wealth of nations.

The power of that ancient star now burning in its belly, the Leviathan heaves and hisses, wheezing, pistons thrusting, steam snorting from metal nostrils; its massive wheels spin and slip and grip the steel rails and it creeps forward, gathering speed. This is progress, this is industry, the world shrinking as steel rails cross continents, telegraph lines singing alongside. Some old farmer blinks, bewildered, as the beast thunders past. Jesse James gallops alongside, gun in hand, fighting a doomed, hopeless rearguard action against the railroad, against the shrinking realm of possibility, against the power of ancient stars. Someday, he knows, we will take granddad's rifle down from its place above the door and sell it at a flea market. Jesse James, too, must pass, dead as the dumb brontosaur. The landscape shrinks and men shrink with it.

Coal fires locomotives, steam hammers, blast furnaces, ships. Steam is the power that cranks the ratchet that tightens the net of steel rails around the earth, squeezing it ever smaller, shrinking the realm of possibility, and the power firing that steam is coal, a humble rock. Coal burns in the Leviathan's belly, lights the red fire of his eyes, drives the steam from his nostrils. He demands coal by the ton, by the truck, by the trainload, always more coal. He has no patience with Jesse James, nor with anyone else who disturbs the steady machinery of production, the toil of his labourers. The Leviathan controls all, his baleful eyes steady on you as you work, ready to slip his dogs. He walks them on a short leash. Throughout the history of American industry, of mines and factories and electrification, we never need look far to find men with guns.

Capital had discovered Darwinism. That labourers were poor was simply the natural order of things. The working man was little more than an animal. And when a dog turns rabid, you put it down. Strikes demanded a swift and brutal response, the decisive answer of the rifle, the sawed-off shotgun, the machine gun. No one chanted, "No war for coal." Instead, thugs shot at strikers and strikers responded in kind, fighting back with rifle bullets. Adam Smith made capital, and Karl Marx made labour, but Samuel Colt made equalizers.

In 1912, the United Mine Workers set out to organize the southern Colorado coal fields around Trinidad. After hired thugs from the Baldwin-Felts detective agency killed union organizer Gerard Lippiatt, the workers voted to strike, laying out seven demands: recognition of the union, a ten-percent wage hike, an eight-hour workday, pay for "dead work," elected checkweighmen, enforcement of laws that the operators had conveniently ignored, and the right to live outside company towns, to see independent doctors, and to shop from independent stores.[45] Today, it is difficult to imagine such demands giving rise to violence. Only the ten-percent wage hike seems unreasonable (although in light of miners' wages, perhaps it was not); the rest are given.

But the mine operators reacted to the strike, set for September 23, 1913, by evicting union miners from company housing, and miners moved into tent colonies like the one at Ludlow, where attacks by company thugs became a part of daily life. Snipers around the camp kept the miners jumpy, and Baldwin-Felts men patrolled the camp perimeter with an armoured car equipped with a Colt-Browning M1895 machine gun, which the miners nicknamed the "Death Special." The miners dug in, protecting their camp with a ring of rifle pits. By night, Baldwin-Felts men shone searchlights down onto the tents from the hillside above the camp, and fired rifle bullets through the canvas without consideration for who might be inside. Mining families were soon sleeping in tented trenches. In 1913, this was collective bargaining.

A well-regulated militia being essential to the security of a free state, on April 20, 1914, the Colorado National Guard set up machine-gun positions overlooking the Ludlow tent colony, and demanded the release of a man whom the strikers were allegedly holding prisoner. Louis Tikas, one of the strike leaders, met with National Guard officers. During that meeting, someone either in the camp or on the hillside above fired a shot, and then everyone began shooting. The National Guard fired

---

45　Miners were paid not by the hour but by the ton. Checkweighmen were responsible for measuring the tonnage of coal extracted by each miner. A natural complaint was that checkweighmen underreported tonnage to keep wages down, and so miners' demands routinely included the right to elect their own trusted checkweighmen, who would record the tonnage accurately. "Dead work" was work that did not contribute to a miner's tonnage but was nonetheless vital, such as shoring up the roof of the mine.

machine gun and rifle bullets into the camp from the hillsides; the miners responded with steady rifle fire. After several hours of fighting, troops advanced into the camp, and tents began to burn. The strikers claimed that the National Guard had poured kerosene on the tent canvas, and torched the camp; others insisted the fire was started when bullets hit boxes of stored ammunition.[46] Tikas was captured and murdered, shot in the back. By the time the fire burned itself out, nineteen were dead: one militiaman, and eighteen members of the Ludlow colony. Eleven of those were women and children, who died in their burning tents.

But the strikers were not defeated. Death was a normal part of their working lives, and they were not shy of risk. These men were miners, and knew how to mine—and how to engineer cave-ins. Throughout April, during what is now called the Ten Days' War, guerillas struck at mine operators across the southern coalfields, killing thirty company men, destroying six coal mines, and razing the company town of Forbes, Colorado. And the fighting might have continued, had not a mass of about a thousand women descended on the governor's mansion, demanding that the governor appeal to the president for federal troops to put a stop to the coalfield war. When the governor protested that he could not meet with the women because his chambers could not accommodate them all, they occupied the legislature and proposed to meet him there. They did not care to take sides, they insisted. They just wanted the fighting stopped.

Governor Elias Ammons called in federal troops, and the miners went home. The Ten Days' War, the bloodiest labour conflict in American history, was over. All this happened in the United States of America, in the land of the brave and the home of the free, in 1913.

ON NOVEMBER 4, 1961, A YOUNG, raw Bob Dylan played the Carnegie Chapter Hall in New York City, and as seems to be the case wherever Bob Dylan goes, somebody was there to tape it. Like most early Dylan bootlegs, the recording is rough and uneven, the volume fading in and out. He jokes about the list of songs he has taped to his guitar: "I went around to

---

46 This explanation of course puts blame on the miners for arming themselves. But it is exceedingly unlikely that bullets striking stored ammunition could have started the fire. The popular notion that ammunition will explode when you shoot it is a myth; normally, firing a bullet into a box of ammunition will only result in a box of wrecked ammunition. The story is plausible only if the ammunition were ignited by tracer bullets fired from the machine guns, but tracers could equally have ignited canvas, bedding, grass, or anything else that would burn.

other guitar players and looked at their lists and copied down the songs on mine. Some a these I don't know so good." Dylan has yet to make his mark as a songwriter, and the songs are reliable old standards: "Pretty Peggy-O," "Gospel Plow," "In the Pines," "Fixin' to Die," and others, but the standout is Dylan's performance of Woody Guthrie's "1913 Massacre."

The song tells the tale of a copper strike in Calumet, Michigan, or, more precisely, of the striking miners' Christmas party. The party was held at the Italian Hall, a building with a poorly marked fire escape and just one other exit, at the bottom of a long flight of stairs. With five hundred people crammed into the hall, someone—presumably, thugs in the pay of the mine operators, although a century later this point remains disputed in a nation that refuses to live up to its own past—raised a false fire alarm. In the rush to escape, seventy-three people were killed, fifty-nine of them children. But like Guthrie's take on the Ludlow Massacre, "1913 Massacre" does not let mere facts get in the way of a good story. Guthrie insists that "copper-boss thug men" not only raised the alarm, but also held the doors shut. All seventy-three victims become children in this retelling, and the thug men laugh as they are trampled and crushed to death. Nuance is not in it.

Guthrie's own recording of "1913 Massacre" is a shambling thing, a lurching limp, a fingerpicked waltz with a man whose left leg is six inches shorter than his right. But in Dylan's performance, the solid driving thump of the bass strings is answered by an insistent strum, a driving and urgent rhythm that pushes ever forward. And where Guthrie's vocal slid and skidded over his loping ground rhythm, losing traction and sliding off in its own directions, Dylan's is grounded in the persistent bass thump of his E-string, joining the guitar's ceaseless demand for forward movement. We take a trip with Bob, in 1913, a nasal ghost of Christmas past, to enjoy the hospitality of good working men and their wives and watch their kids laughing and singing around the Christmas tree. Later, we see those same children, limp and lifeless, carried back up to "their tree." And finally, Dylan breaks out the trick he learned from Woody, the trick that Woody, in turn, had learned from Appalachia, of drawing out a vocal line to build tension. "See," he sings, and leans on it, the ever insistent guitar urging forward as the sustained note holds back, leaning on it still: "what your greed for money has done."

And with that, the song is done, a musical punch between the eyes.

Who listens to Woody Guthrie today? The folk revival is long dead—killed, in part, by Bob Dylan himself, as "folk music" transformed itself from the reiteration and reinvention of traditional songs into the confessional singer-songwriter mode mistaken for folk today. No more strange modal tunes come howling down out of the past, no more mountain sevenths like sour candy, no more floating couplets waiting to be stolen down from the body of Anglo-American tradition and repurposed for another murder. These things persist only in the corners. Woody's idiosyncratic delivery and his rough-hewn sound are now shelved somewhere near the back of the American consciousness, where the dust piles up. Kids learn to sing "This Land is Your Land," but their teachers surely steer them clear of "Jesus Christ," in which Guthrie tells us that good working folks believed Christ's message, but that bankers, preachers, sheriffs and landlords conspired to murder the Messiah.

Yet all of America is in Woody, from sea to sea. Woody wove the strands of American left-wing populism into songs for the working man, songs whose warp and weft is the virtue of hard work, distrust of authority, admiration for the outlaw, and a simple religiosity. The politics of these songs are not practical, but they don't need to be; these are songs about what is fair and decent, not apologies for the intricate machinery of the American economy. Do not speak to us of the wealth of nations, of free markets, of your gross domestic product, of downturns and corrections and productivity. We are good folk here, the Homesteaders of Paradise Valley. You can hie your suited backside back to Center City. Around here, we speak plain American. We're American citizens, and we ain't gonna be treated this way.

And these songs are filled with violence. Woody's violence is not the random violence of crime, but the purposeful violence of class war. The jolly banker is here to help until he comes around to foreclose, his papers backed by the sheriff's guns. Pretty Boy Floyd is not a bank robber and a killer, but a social outlaw, an American Robin Hood fighting the good fight against the bankers who rob you with a fountain pen. Men hang from the hangknot, and Woody asks us just who made the law, but we already know the answer: the banker. In Winston-Salem, everything the common man does is against the bankers' law. What's an honest, hard-working man to do? The buffalo skinners, double-crossed by their duplicitous employer, kill him and leave his bones to bleach on the open prairie. And as the class war moves from the Spanish Civil War's Jarama Valley to the Russian Front, Guthrie gets downright bloodthirsty: "Miss Pavilichenko" celebrates a Soviet sniper's success killing Nazis, its chorus a celebratory chant: "Fell by your gun, fell by your gun, more than three hundred Nazis fell by your gun."

This Woody is not the Woody we teach to schoolchildren. Let Pete Seeger's smarmy banjo surround hate and force it to surrender. This machine kills fascists.

Among Woody Guthrie's great influences was John Steinbeck, who, in *The Grapes of Wrath*, created the lasting novel of the Great Depression. Steinbeck had been freelancing for *The Nation*, where he covered the plight of migratory workers around Salinas, and was appalled to find children starving to death in California, right under the noses of the middle class. He tried to express his anger and disgust in a nasty satire of Salinas called *L'Affaire Lettuceburg*, the manuscript of which he later destroyed, likely at the urging of his first wife, Carol, who was his first and possibly his best editor. *The Grapes of Wrath* took shape only after he realized that the migrant families, rather than the Salinas bourgeoisie, were his proper subject.

Steinbeck, as he finished the final draft, foresaw what would follow. In a letter to his editor, Pascal Covici, he warned, "the fascist crowd will try to sabotage this book because it is revolutionary. They will try to give it the communist angle." And while the critical response to the book was generally positive, American conservatives immediately attacked it as a work of Marxist propaganda. The FBI had begun its investigation of Steinbeck as a subversive before the book even saw print. Rising in Congress, Lyle Boren declared, "I cannot find it possible to let this dirty, lying, filthy manuscript go heralded before the public without a word of challenge or protest ... the painting Steinbeck made in his book is a lie, a damnable lie, a black, infernal creation of a twisted, distorted mind." Threatening letters poured in from cranks. Warned of a plot to frame him on a rape charge, he stopped going out alone. At times, he carried a revolver. In a letter to his friend Carlton Sheffield, written soon after the book was published, Steinbeck reflected, "they can't shoot me now because it would be too obvious."

Today, Steinbeck is beaten up for his sentimentality and his authorial intrusions in the novel, a form he professed never to like, having a dramatist's sensibility. Woody Guthrie, too, could be naïve and impractical, too personally invested in labour conflict, a peddler of simplistic propaganda. But whatever the complaints about these artists, there are no great novels exalting capital, only the poisonous screeds of Ayn Rand. No great American folk song extols the bravery of the Baldwin-Felts men, sniping at the families of strikers. *Of Human Kindness*, Ruth Comfort Mitchell's overwrought and dishonest reply to *The Grapes of Wrath*, is a historical curiosity. Woody and Steinbeck ended up on the right side of history and all the rest of that crap fell away, because we all long to live in Paradise Valley, and not among the Center City money men. As Jim Harrison said, "the people who condescended to John Steinbeck didn't even write *The Grapes of Goofy*."

What people remember about reading Steinbeck is his sympathy for his subjects. But his novels of depression-era California are also marked by violence and by threats of violence. Tom Joad has not yet found his family before we face the first threats of armed resistance, as nameless sharecroppers confronting nameless landlords promise, "We'll get our guns, like Grampa when the Indians came." A tenant meets a man working a tractor—Joe Davis's boy—and promises, "I'll be in the window with a rifle. You even come too close and I'll pot you like a rabbit." But such rebellion is pointless: the tractor operator is only following orders, as was the man who gave the orders, as was the banker whose dictates he in turn followed. Joe Davis' boy knows the score: "Maybe there's nobody to shoot."

And the Oklahoman sharecropper is left standing by the ruins of his home, his family by his side and his impotent rifle in his hand, as the tractor drives on. America's great myth of the gun has been defeated. Just as Martin Luther King, Jr. reminded us that you can't murder murder, you can't shoot the free market. You cannot conquer the Leviathan. All that happens is you end up dead. And you may end up on the right side of history, but that will scarcely satisfy your cold, crumbling bones.

BY 1920, THE AGE OF OIL HAD BEGUN. Coal operators, facing shrinking margins and a declining market, reacted in the way they knew best: by squeezing wages. Miners responded in the way they knew best:

they went out on strike. But when strikers walked off the job in the coalfields of Pennsylvania, mine operators simply filled the declining demand for coal from their mines in Appalachia. The operators planned to hold the line and break the strikes in Pennsylvania with Appalachian coal; the United Mine Workers of America sought to win the strikes in Pennsylvania by organizing the coal miners of West Virginia and paralyzing the Appalachian mines.

Appalachian mines were remote from the markets they served and more costly to operate, and so wages in Appalachia remained low. Even as the rest of the nation entered the boom years of the 1920s, West Virginia mine workers lived in company-owned shacks in company-owned towns patrolled by company-owned police, and bought their goods from company-owned stores with the company scrip they received in place of real money. They were, in effect, company-owned slave labour. Appalachian miners, derided even today as gap-toothed, inbred hillbillies, looked out on America, saw boom times leaving them behind, and simmered with anger.

The miners were ready to kill for better pay, better housing, and simple dignity; the operators would kill to protect their profits. The first victory went to the mine workers' union, which successfully organized a mine three miles from Matewan, a small town in Mingo County, on the Kentucky border. The operators immediately brought in the Baldwin-Felts detective agency, the same agency that had run the Death Special around the Ludlow camp, to break the union. And the detectives were dedicated to their work. They were true believers. Al Felts, the field manager in West Virginia, said that if it took a million dollars and put a hundred men in jail, he would stop the union. It was a bold promise, and it probably helped that the million dollars he pledged was not his own.

But the chief of police in Matewan would not cooperate with the Baldwin-Felts agency. Sid Hatfield had worked in the coal mines from his teens, eventually being promoted out of underground work into a blacksmithing job. He was not a big man, standing only five-foot-six and weighing just 150 pounds, but he had a reputation as a hothead and a fighter. He was also an excellent shot. Mayor Cabell Testerman had appointed Hatfield as chief of police, and had protected Hatfield from legal troubles arising from fights and moonshine. Hatfield's constituency, and Testerman's, was the miners, and both knew it. But Al Felts did not, and when he offered Testerman and Hatfield five hundred dollars to let him put machine gun emplacements on the town's rooftops, Hatfield responded by ordering him out of town.

On May 19, 1920, Al Felts returned with his brother, Lee, and eleven other Baldwin-Felts detectives, armed with rifles, to evict striking miners from company-owned housing. In Matewan, miners reached for their guns. Having discovered that Felts had no authority to evict anyone, Hatfield requested warrants to arrest him and his men. He also had Testerman issue arrest warrants on town authority, for carrying guns in violation of Matewan's ordinances, choosing to turn a blind eye to the miners who were doing the same.

As the Baldwin-Felts men prepared to leave town, Hatfield confronted them on the street in front of Testerman's hardware store. A small crowd gathered, and armed miners took up concealed firing positions along the street. Hatfield declared he had warrants to arrest Felts and his men. Al Felts responded that he had a warrant to arrest Hatfield. As Hatfield faced down the Baldwin-Felts men, someone ran to get Testerman. Testerman hustled out into the street and demanded to see Felts' warrant. Felts held it out, and Testerman, in the middle of a crowd of armed men, said, "This is a bogus warrant."

Within minutes of Testerman's declaration that the warrant was bogus—a declaration later upheld during a Senate hearing during which the warrant was called "void on its face"—nine men were killed and six wounded. First to fall were Testerman himself and Al Felts, Felts with a bullet to the head and Testerman with a shot to the abdomen. Seven of the dead were Baldwin-Felts detectives, and the others unarmed miners caught in the crossfire. One of the Baldwin-Felts men, J.W. Ferguson, tried to shelter in a nearby house, but a group of miners dragged him out into the alley and shot him nine times. Testerman would later die of his wounds, bringing the death toll to ten. The shootout at the O.K. Corral killed only three.

The West Virginia Mine War, also known as the Redneck War for the red bandanas the union miners wore, followed a steady pattern of sniping, guerilla attacks, and intimidation.[47] Baldwin-Felts thugs

---

47 The term "redneck," meaning an ignorant and violent rural person, was then already in wide use, but the union miners were called rednecks because of their informal uniform. Miners had been called rednecks in other labour conflicts. To what extent the two connotations of "redneck" coloured each other is an open question.

ambushed union organizers; union thugs struck at scabs brought in to keep the mines open. West Virginia sent all the state police it could spare to Mingo County, and Kentucky sent its own National Guard to the state border to contain the violence. John Cornwell, the governor of West Virginia, requested federal troops, which arrived in August. By November, the situation seemed calm, and federal troops withdrew. But the guerillas returned to action, and only three weeks later the governor requested federal help again, saying that Mingo County was in a "state of insurrection." Federal troops returned, and in the calm enforced by the 19th Infantry Regiment, Sid Hatfield took over Testerman's hardware store and turned it into a gun shop, supplying arms and ammunition to the strikers in preparation for the next round. Scabs, too, armed themselves, as the state of West Virginia hastily reformed its National Guard. Nothing had been settled. In May 1921, with the situation again calm, the US Army pulled out. Fighting immediately flared up once more, and on May 19, West Virginia again declared martial law, this time under the National Guard.

The National Guard enforced martial law with entirely one-sided zeal. Jails in Mingo County soon overflowed. Prisoners were sent to neighbouring counties, where the jails again filled up. Men were jailed simply for possessing union leaflets, or for speaking out. Under the West Virginia National Guard's martial law, Mingo County was a mineshaft filled with firedamp and coal dust, waiting only for the careless flame of a miner's lamp.

On August 21, 1921, Sid Hatfield and his friend Ed Chambers went, accompanied by their wives, to Welch, West Virginia, to answer charges related to a failed attack on a mine in the town of Mohawk. Hatfield was unarmed. Charlie Lively, who had been working for the Baldwin-Felts agency as a spy in the union ranks, met the pair on the courthouse steps. As the men's wives looked on, Lively and his companions drew their guns and opened fire. Five bullets struck Hatfield, three of them from behind. Chambers was shot seven times. As Chambers lay on the courthouse steps, unconscious or perhaps already dead, Lively leaned over him, pressed the muzzle of his revolver against his ear, and pulled the trigger.

You cannot simply murder men on the front steps of a courthouse, in broad daylight. Not in a liberal democracy. Not in a state governed by the rule of law. Not in the United States of America. And so Lively and his accomplices were promptly charged with murder. And just as promptly, Lively and his accomplices were released on bond.[48]

Redneck miners were enraged: their hero, Sid Hatfield, had been shot down unarmed and in cold blood at the very feet of whatever passed for justice in the rotten state of West Virginia, and his killers had walked free. And so they took up arms, an assortment of rifles and revolvers, donned their old World War I helmets, found bayonets. The owner of a general store in Racine, West Virginia, reported that he had seen one miner carrying a hand grenade. They commandeered trains to move their ragtag army—so many that rail service in the region was soon suspended. Not enough locomotives remained under the railroad's control to pull scheduled trains. By August 23, anywhere from five to thirteen thousand men had gathered with the vague aim of marching on Mingo County and setting things straight.

But to get to Mingo, the miners would have to pass through Logan County, where Sheriff Don Chafin was firmly in the coal operators' pocket. Chafin drew the line: "No armed mob will cross Logan County." He had prepared by hastily organizing the construction of trenches and fortifications along a ten-mile front. Volunteers flooded into Logan County, and the defending force grew to 2,800 men. Chafin had also secured the use of three civilian biplanes, and enlisted the aid of a local chemist in constructing high-explosive and poison-gas bombs. In all of these things, Chafin had the full support of the governor, with only one caveat: Chafin was not permitted to attack the miners' army. All he could do was hold the line.

In Washington, President Harding mobilized two infantry battalions and formally ordered an end to the insurrection. He also ordered a squadron of seventeen US Army Air Force bombers to West Virginia, under the command of General Billy Mitchell, who was eager to prove that air power could decisively end civil unrest by bombing American citizens to pieces.[49]

---

48 Naturally, Charlie Lively and his associates claimed that they had acted in self-defence, and none was convicted, despite the fact that Hatfield was unarmed.

49 Mitchell would miss his opportunity. One-third of his bombers got lost, crashed, or crash-landed en route, and the remainder were used only for reconnaissance. In the end, mechanical failure and accidents disabled half of Mitchell's bomber force, and American air power served chiefly as a curio to be goggled at by excited crowds of boys. Chafin's planes also proved ineffective, as they were unable to drop their bombs accurately or to create sufficient concentrations of gas to cause casualties. The only known gas casualty was a miner who handled an unexploded bomb. The gas was never identified.

What followed is known to history as the Battle of Blair Mountain: ten thousand men fighting along a ten-mile front, the largest battle fought on American soil since the Civil War. Luckily for Chafin, the miners' army had no real organization, no clear chain of command, and no strategy to speak of. No battlefield leadership was available to organize and motivate decisive attacks, and no communications existed with which to coordinate the assault. Fighting was more or less continuous—witnesses recalled non-stop gunfire throughout the battle—but indecisive. On the evening of September 2, the third day of the battle, the first federal troops moved in, with orders to disarm the miners. Most chose to cache their guns and slink away, rather than turn them in and surrender. In the town of Sharples, only six hundred miners had surrendered by September 3, and those six hundred men had turned over only eighty guns. In Blair, four hundred surrendered, turning in two hundred guns. Eighty years after the fact, archeologists were still turning up caches of weapons and ammunition on Blair Mountain.

And so the Battle of Blair Mountain fizzled out in anticlimax. Although some claim that more than a hundred men were killed in the battle, others put the casualty count as low as sixteen. But what is important about the Battle of Blair Mountain is not how many were killed. What is important is that as recently as 1921, the democratic institutions of the United States in West Virginia were so weak, and the police forces so corrupt and partisan, that miners and mine operators chose to settle their differences not by negotiation and not through lawyers, but by taking up arms and fighting a sixteen-month guerilla war interrupted by temporary, forced ceasefires, a war that climaxed with more than ten thousand men shooting at each other and the president sending bombers to kill his own citizens.

AGAIN AND AGAIN, America goes for its guns.

In 1973, coal miners at the Eastover Mining Company's mine at Brookside, Kentucky, voted to bring in the United Mineworkers' Union, but Duke Power, which owned the mine, refused to sign their contract. Harlan County had been through its own labour wars in the 1930s, when it earned the nickname "Bloody Harlan," and old-timers still remembered the fighting, which had inspired Florence Reece to write "Which Side Are You On." They say in Harlan County, there are no neutrals there; you'll either be a union man, or a thug for J.H. Blair. Little had changed in fifty-odd years. Workers at the Brookside mine lived in company housing without running water. In Barbara Kopple's 1976 documentary *Harlan County, USA*, we watch a woman bathing her daughter in a washtub on the kitchen table, promising that when the strike is won, there will be baths with hot running water.[50] Even in 1973, mine operators still housed their employees in company-owned hovels.

At one point in the film, Lois Scott, a leader among the miners' wives, complains that the operators treat them "like we're animals, dogs." And when a dog turns rabid, you put it down. From the start, we see guns, although at first people try to keep them hidden. As trucks carrying scabs push through the miners' picket line early in the strike, a miner points and shouts, "There's the damn guy drawed that gun on me, right there, you sonofabitch you." Lois Scott points out Basil Collins, a "gun thug" whom she accuses of threatening picketers with a gun. Before the film is over, we see him point a revolver at the camera. In another scene, he stalks towards the picket line with a pistol barely concealed in his pocket, backed by scabs armed with truncheons. The miners complain that they can't carry any weapons on the picket line, but the scabs carry guns and clubs. One of the strikers' homes is shot up at night; in the morning, he points out the bullet holes. He is not the only one. Soon the scabs are shooting their way through the picket line. At a meeting of the miners' wives, Lois Scott sets an example by pulling a revolver out of her bra. "It's time for us to stand together and get just as violent as they are," Scott proclaims. "You fight fire with fire." As pickets block the road one more time, we see revolvers, rifles and shotguns openly displayed. A line of men behind their cars level guns at the convoy of scabs; Lois Scott and her band of wives brandish truncheons.

In the end it was guns, not negotiation, that ended the strike after one of the strikers, Lawrence Jones, was shot in the head with a shotgun by Bill Bruner, a mine supervisor.[51] Jones was well liked, had a sixteen-year-old wife and a five-month-old daughter, and Kopple's cameras

---

50 As it happened, Kopple was there with her cameras when the strike began. She had been working on a documentary about internal power struggles within the UMWA, but when the Brookside workers went out on strike, she chose to make a film about their strike instead. The resulting film won the Oscar for Best Documentary Feature in 1977.

51 Bruner claimed that he shot the unarmed Jones in self-defence. A deadlocked grand jury did not indict him.

catch the men debating whether to concentrate on getting the contract Jones died for, or to go after Collins and the company bosses and "put the lead to 'em." One man argues staying the course, recalling a strike in the 1930s in which four men were killed beside him, all for a contract; the miners ought to honour Jones' sacrifice by sticking to their strike and getting that contract. Another man advocates mayhem. But the miners are close to victory. Fearing more violence, and the bad publicity it would bring, the operators cave in.

In a Harlan County courtroom, in 1973, after the judge has already handed down her sentence, a miner's wife insists on standing in court and exercising her right to be heard. "I knew we weren't gonna get any justice. You say the laws were made for us," she says, an unconscious echo of Woody singing *This land was made for you and me*, as the bailiff reaches for her arm, to pull her away. "The laws were not made for the working people in this country … what we did was right and we all know that." The Leviathan offers us a deal: submit to me, and my courts will be your *vindices injurarium*. When we cannot rely on the courts to protect us, when our opponents can buy their own justice, can anyone be surprised that we turn to the gun?

The gun settles accounts that the law will not. Today, in the comfort of the early twenty-first century, we tend to a patronizing view of those who believe guns safeguard their rights. This view, we insist, is the product of a gun lobby that spent the 1970s arguing that guns are the safeguard of constitutional freedom until America fell for it. But for some, the connection between guns and freedom is no abstraction. Not for the descendants of the rednecks fighting on Blair Mountain, and not for anyone who remembers Harlan County in 1973. They will keep their rifles hanging over the doorway, just in case. There's always a next time. And we will reap what we sow: before Americans willingly give up their guns, the machinery of American power must give up on violence and invest in the social capital of democratic institutions. But before that happens, if history is any guide, everyone will get a pet unicorn and a box full of rainbows.

The Secret History
of the Second Amendment, Part Two
From *The Birth of a Nation* to Ferguson: Guns in American Race Relations

The gun is where it's at and about and in.

—Huey Newton

DETROIT, 1967: THE RED WINGS, soon to be dubbed the Dead Wings, lie fifth in a six-team league and the Toronto Maple Leafs take the Stanley Cup. For ten years, the white middle class has been making for the suburbs, and the auto factories and their jobs have followed them. In Detroit, factories are closing down. Black men who try to follow the jobs to the suburbs are told, flat out, they aren't welcome. Back in Detroit, one in four black men is unemployed. And then, in the wee hours of a July Sunday, the cops raid the wrong bar. White cops, black bar, eighty-two people inside, more than they can handle, and then decades of resentment come to a head: resentment over Detroit's informal but effective system of segregation, over black families forced into overcrowded neighbourhoods with substandard housing, over justice based on colour, over African American homes bulldozed to make way for highways. And now windows are breaking all along 12th Street, not enough cops to stop it, not enough cops even to contain it, not enough cops to do anything but watch as the windows break and the buildings burn. On Monday the state police roll in, then the National Guard, almost five hundred fires burning, whole blocks aflame, National Guard troops pinned down in the streets by snipers. The next day, the president orders the 82nd Airborne Division to move in. In the riot zone, the cops beat the shit out of anyone they catch, no matter the circumstances. At the Algiers Motel, they shoot three black men just because. And Roy Rogers has gone west, gone back to his ranch in Paradise Valley, gone like Arthur sailing to Avalon, Excalibur thrown into Lake St. Clair; Roy Quondam, Royque Futurus. Detroit the pulsing metal heart of America, Detroit the blackened battlefield: Murder City, USA.

The Kerner Commission, convened to study the problem of race riots in the aftermath of the summer of 1967, reported that there had been 164 "civil disturbances" across the United States in the first nine months of that year, although 123 of these were relatively insignificant and perhaps got attention only because of the climate of fear that more serious riots had created—an atmosphere that was surely intensified by the fact that most of the unrest occurred during the height of summer. The most serious of all these riots was the 12th Street Riot in Detroit. Americans turned on the evening news to see tanks in the streets of the Motor City, soldiers with M16s and fixed bayonets, entire city blocks destroyed by fire, skeletal ruins. Detroit was in flames. Whither goes Detroit, America follows: the nation was falling apart.

The 1960s were already drawing to a close. Peace and love were dead. Fear and loathing had arrived. Angry men preached black supremacy, Olympic medalists raised their fists in the Black Power salute, and inner cities collapsed in open insurrection. And those inner cities were becoming increasingly dangerous, even at the best of times. On May 8, 1968, Richard Nixon addressed the problem of violent crime using the racially loaded metaphor of the urban jungle, imagining the black inner cities of a segregated America pitted against its white suburbs:

> If the present rate of new crime continues, the number of rapes and robberies and assaults and thefts in the United States today will double by the end of 1972 … That is a prospect America cannot accept. If we allow it to happen, then the city jungle will cease to be a metaphor. It will become a barbaric reality, and the brutal society that now flourishes in the core cities of America will annex the affluent suburbs. This nation will then be what it is fast becoming—an armed camp of two hundred million Americans living in fear.

The United States was not yet an armed camp, but it was already a nation of two hundred million living in fear. Handgun sales were on the rise as

Americans armed themselves against crime, which is really just a way of saying they armed themselves against each other. For more than a decade, whites had been fleeing the urban jungle for the suburbs. And African Americans had much to fear from whites, as proven in Detroit itself when black families faced violent attacks after moving into white neighbourhoods. Rosa Parks' childhood memories included her grandfather standing guard over their rural Alabama home with a shotgun, as she slept in her clothes, the better to run if the Ku Klux Klan came raiding. America's great fear, usually unspoken, is not crime or terrorism but race war. War is, as von Clausewitz famously said, simply a continuation of policy by other means, and racism has been policy far too long to be simply swept aside. This is, perhaps, what the Second Amendment is really for.

RACE WAR IS NOT SOLELY A white preoccupation. African Americans are acutely aware of the nation's ongoing racial cold war. And it was black men who first used the Second Amendment to argue that they had the right to walk about openly armed, in American cities.

In October 1966, Huey Newton and Bobby Seale formed the Black Panther Party for Self-Defense in Oakland, California, with a "ten-point program" that cited the Second Amendment and encouraged black Americans to arm themselves for self-defence. The Panthers wanted self-determination for black Americans. They wanted full employment, decent housing, compensation for slavery, and education. Perhaps most importantly, the Panthers wanted an end to police brutality, an end to police harassment. In the simplest terms, they wanted the cops out of black neighbourhoods. With this end in mind, the Panthers adopted a uniform: blue shirt, black pants, black leather jacket, black beret, and a loaded 12-gauge shotgun. "The gun," Panther literature proclaimed, "is the only thing that will free us."

Newton, who was studying law, had discovered that in California it was completely legal to walk around with a loaded shotgun or rifle provided that you carried it in plain view and did not brandish it, or point it at anyone. Carrying a loaded shotgun made perfect sense in a rural area during hunting season, but no sense at all on the streets of Oakland on a Saturday night.[52] To white Californians, the Panthers were understandably threatening: armed men, many with criminal

---

52　Almost fifty years later, American law has yet to catch up with American reality, as the open carry movement epitomized by the advocacy group Open Carry Texas has recently demonstrated.

records, preaching armed resistance to the police, distributing socialist pamphlets, and openly confronting the police with guns. Talk of killing "the pigs" and blowing up police stations did not go down well in the suburbs. That the armed men in question were angry black activists pushed the needle of the fear meter from "alarmed" to "terrified." The day of reckoning was at hand.

In 1967, California responded with the Mulford Act, a gun-control law proposed by Republican Don Mulford, who represented Oakland. The Mulford Act was not gun control, but black control: by prohibiting anyone from carrying a loaded gun in a California city, it took aim squarely at the Panthers, who were determined not to let it pass. And so on May 2, 1967, the Black Panthers armed themselves with shotguns and rifles, drove to the California legislature in Sacramento, and walked right on in. They had come, they said, to defend their right to bear arms under the Second Amendment.

The Panthers had overreached. Don Mulford called their invasion of the legislature "a direct attempt to coerce me" and "an affront to the people," and promised to toughen his law by making it a felony to carry arms into the legislature. Bill Greene, a black Democrat from Los Angeles, said the Panthers' protest was "not militant, it was senseless. No person black or white can condone this action." Governor Ronald Reagan was equally unimpressed, and made clear the gap between the Panthers' actions and his idea of American values: "Americans don't go around carrying guns with the idea they're using them to influence other Americans ... there's no reason why on the street today a citizen should be carrying loaded weapons."

But citizens reached for their loaded weapons all the same. As President Nixon fretted that the barbaric urban jungle might annex the affluent suburbs, as armed Black Panthers marched into the California legislature, as Detroit burned, America reached for its national security blanket, the gun. From 1964 to 1966, annual handgun sales in the US doubled, from $600,000 to $1.2 million; by 1968, sales had doubled again, to $2.4 million. America's relationship to its guns was rapidly changing, and race was the engine.

RACE WAR HAS LONG BEEN the drunken uncle of American gun culture, the problem that people politely refuse to discuss even as they stockpile their ammo. But gun control in the United States was about race from the start. D.W. Griffiths' 1915 silent film *The Birth of a Nation* is popularly known as both a great achievement in early film-making and an appalling example of American racism, but it is also a dissertation on gun control, and specifically on the perils of allowing blacks to go armed. As the movie has it, the antebellum South is a peaceful place where blacks are happy as slaves and white men have no need of weapons. But then the war frees Southern blacks, who get above their raising. Black men go armed in the streets. White men are forced to salute black officers. Armed blacks turn whites away from polling stations, electing black politicians who make a mockery of the legislature. Worst of all, black men take an interest in white women. All of the usual racist fears are on display.

Only one thing can save the South: guns. An intertitle quotes Woodrow Wilson: "The white men were roused by a mere instinct of self-preservation ... until at last there had sprung into existence a great Ku Klux Klan, a veritable empire of the South, to protect the Southern country." White men spring to the defence of white women by terrorizing and disarming black men. Reconstruction is soon defeated, and the Klan ushers in the Jim Crow era. The movie concludes with the image of black voters being kept away from the polls by armed Klansmen, because this, of course, is how functioning democracies run their elections.

America is terrified of armed black men, and that fear crops up everywhere, even in the worst decision ever made by the Supreme Court of the United States, the Dred Scott decision of 1857. Dred Scott was born a slave, sold by his original owners, and transplanted to Illinois, which was a free state. He sued, on that basis, for his freedom, lost, won at retrial, and then lost on appeal. When the case eventually found its way to the Supreme Court, it was as a complaint of assault against John Sanford, his owner under Missouri law. The court had the opportunity to strike a blow for human rights, but it chickened out by ruling that Scott, as a black man, could not be a US citizen and therefore had no standing to bring the case to begin with. In explaining itself, the Supreme Court proved itself to be deeply concerned with who got to be called a citizen, because if it recognized free African Americans as citizens, then it would give them the right "to keep and carry arms wherever they went,"[53] which

---

53   See *Dred Scott v. Sanford*, 60 U.S. 393.

would only enflame their remaining enslaved brethren and potentially incite slave revolts.

In a racially charged view of American history, guns are all about keeping black people down. Some say the Colt revolver was intended to help southern slave holders better control their slaves, its six-shot capacity being a powerful deterrent to anyone who got it in his head that there is strength in numbers.[54] Some insist that the Second Amendment was added to the constitution chiefly to assuage the fears of southern slave owners. The unfortunately named Carl T. Bogus, Professor of Law at Roger Williams University, argues that Madison added the Second Amendment to mollify southern slave owners and Patrick Henry, who argued that the constitution, as originally proposed, gave the federal government the power to disarm state militias, leaving them vulnerable to slave uprisings.[55]

Anti-gun bloggers love this one, and continually reiterate it, although it looks like a case of projecting present concerns onto the past. It's an attractive argument, lending itself as it does to a favourite use of race in the Great American Gun Kerfuffle: to poison the well. If the Second Amendment was created to preserve slavery, then the Second Amendment becomes a legacy of American shame, and those who support it are actually supporting American racism: shame on them. Second Amendment supporters immediately reverse the charges: since early gun-control laws were enacted to keep southern blacks disarmed and at the mercy of Klan vigilantes, and since black Americans remain most at risk of violence and therefore most in need of guns to defend themselves, gun control itself is an inherently racist proposition and its proponents are, at least unconsciously, racist: shame on *them*.

Everything is racist these days, even your breakfast cereal, because race makes such a good cudgel.[56] Even the Gun Control Act of 1968,

---

54 See, for example, Richard Slotkin's review of Michael Bellesiles' discredited book, *Arming America*, in the Nov., 2000 edition of *The Atlantic Monthly*: "Colt is said to have conceived the repeating pistol to enable a single white man to defend himself against an unruly gang of slaves." Obviously, a repeating pistol would be useful to slave owners, but surely this was not the only need driving its development.

55 Controversy over this proposal has overshadowed Bogus' more important point, that the Second Amendment was not insurrectionist in its intent and was never supposed to give ordinary Americans the right to keep guns with which to overthrow their own governments.

56 An article in *Mother Jones* from March 2015 suggested that "dogmatic adherence" to the American three square meals a day "is anti-science, racist, and might actually be making you sick," apparently on the grounds that European settlers discounted the ancient wisdom of American native peoples when it came to mealtimes.

which passed in the context of assassinations, civil rights, rising crime, and cities riven by race riots, faces charges of racism. As Minister of Information for the Black Panthers, Eldridge Cleaver complained that the new rules "don't name me; they don't say, take the guns away from the niggers ... they have to pass them in a way that will take in everybody." But some of those new rules were aimed squarely at young black men. Among other things, they banned "Saturday Night Specials": small, cheap, usually imported handguns assumed to be favoured by low-income folk living in inner cities—which is to say, young African-American men—and then deployed on Saturday nights in robberies and drunken mayhem. Robert Sherrill, a reporter and the author of *The Saturday Night Special* (1973), noted that the ban was not really gun control, but "black control." The NRA, feeling that black control was something the sportsmen of America could live with, cautiously approved.

And so America blunders into a new century, armed against itself. Nobody except the Black Panthers and perhaps the likes of the Aryan Nation likes to say it out loud, but this is the real reason many Americans still cling to the Second Amendment.

ON MAY 3, 1967, the *Toledo Blade* ran two stories side by side on page 17. The first was a wire story on the Panthers' invasion of the Sacramento legislature. The second concerned a "Cleveland negro group" that was supposedly plotting a revolt. That story, based entirely on the opinion of a police "subversives unit" detective, one Sergeant Ungvary, reads like one of Hunter S. Thompson's parodic news stories from *Fear and Loathing in Las Vegas*, long on paranoia and short on sense. The militants, following the teachings of their "so-called high priest," are convinced that a May 9 solar eclipse will precipitate a war between the United States and "Red China," which will result in National Guard troops being stripped from the interior of the country. They will take advantage of the situation to launch a "black revolution." This is good intelligence. Race war in Cleveland is right around the corner. And if China didn't cooperate by starting a war, Ungvary suggested, the blacks of Cleveland would revolt anyway, just to save face.[57]

---

57 This story, too, went out on the wire and appeared in many newspapers across the country. Although the *Toledo Blade* doesn't report the fact in their version of the story, the stalwart Sergeant Ungvary was testifying before the Senate Internal Security Subcommittee.

History records that May 9 came and went and that the moon eclipsed the sun as expected. But history makes no mention of Cleveland's black revolution. Neither does history record how Sergeant Ungvary saved face.

The threat of a Communist-inspired race war has long been the paranoid wet dream of the American right, a John Birch Society campfire story designed to give back-slapping Chamber of Commerce blowhards a thrilling attack of the willies as they nosh on brats and beer around the backyard barbecue. For the paranoid right, this is the perfect storm: Reds collaborating with blacks to overturn the established order and redistribute the wealth of whites. And the Sergeant Ungvarys of this world are always on hand to make it seem halfway plausible.

The basic features of this campfire story are laid out in *The Turner Diaries*, published by American neo-Nazi leader William Luther Pierce in 1978: an international conspiracy to enslave the United States under a Zionist Occupation Government, ZOG, African Americans acting as foot soldiers of the Jews, and the persecution of white Christians. And since you cannot enslave armed men, the story imagines that the first goal of a Zionist Occupation Government must be to disarm Americans.

In *The Turner Diaries*, ZOG has enacted "the Cohen Act," which bans all private gun ownership, and has followed up with "the Gun Raids," during which armed blacks deputized by "Human Relations Councils" confiscate everyone's guns. The Gun Raids themselves are facilitated by sales records that ZOG laws had required gun sellers to keep—an idea borrowed directly from the NRA's mantra, "registration leads to confiscation," and alluding directly to the 1968 Gun Control Act, which imposed just that requirement on American gun dealers. But so many patriots have defied the Cohen Act that the government can't jail them all. Instead, they take their guns away and turn them loose. Earl Turner, the man who keeps this diary, among them.

The Turner Diaries rings with disdain for those soft, weak, lazy people who have failed to recognize the need to prepare themselves for the great struggle for freedom. The weak, the stupid, and the unprepared get their comeuppance; we hate to say we told them so, but we did in fact tell them so, and having failed to make their beds they must now sleep on the cold, hard ground and succumb to hypothermia. America is plunged into race war and a vicious neo-Nazi campaign of extermination begins, directed not only against Jews, blacks, and all other visible minorities, but also against whites who failed to recognize the righteousness of the cause. Not only does Pierce's neo-Nazi fantasy cleanse the world of all non-white ethnicities, but it also purges the white race of all other points of view, because of course there's nothing more obnoxious to an extremist than a dissenting point of view.

It's tough making common cause with neo-Nazis these days. Being overtly racist is out of fashion. But this doesn't mean that racism is dead. It simply means that we preface our racist remarks with "Now, I'm not a racist, but ..." Or, that's not prejudice, as someone once said to me about Hispanics, that's experience. And the close correspondence between the virulent American fascism of *The Turner Diaries* and the everyday rhetoric of America's right-wing fringe is eerie. It is not only fascists who believe our guns keep us free, that registration must lead to confiscation, that liberals are essentially feminine and dangerously out of touch with reality, that civilization is only held together by men brave enough to take up the sword, or that American freedom is threatened by shadowy international elites bent on global domination. These ideas are staples of mainstream pro-gun activism, of the NRA and the Gun Owners of America—the organization you join when you realize the NRA is too soft—and the Oath Keepers and the legions of followers who swallow their ideas then regurgitate them undigested.

And it is not only fascists who believe that we can thwart gun control by simply owning guns and refusing to turn them in; this idea is the motivating force behind the surging sales of guns and ammunition that followed the December 2012 Sandy Hook massacre. With a black Democrat in the White House and a resurgent gun control movement, Americans responded by emptying store shelves of guns and ammo. The shortage of rimfire ammunition was particularly severe; some were willing to drive to the next town for a single brick of .22-calibre ammo. And when the gun stores ran out of guns and ammunition, Americans snapped up the reloading supplies, the powder and bullets and primers you use to make your own ammunition from spent casings, so that it was two full years after Sandy Hook before smokeless powder supplies finally began returning to normal. Where were all these guns and ammo, all this powder? In the basements of men convinced that the shortage was not created by their own panicked buying, but by the government itself, which had engineered the shortage for its own unexplained ends.[58]

America's paranoid right-wing fringe may not actually be fascist, but it certainly has no problem with a lot of fascist ideas. The virulent racism of *The Turner Diaries* lets us pat ourselves on the back and assure ourselves that there's no real problem here. As long as a few fringe loonies remain, as long as we see news stories about some mouth-breathing skinhead in Idaho who wants to name his kid after Adolf Hitler, we reassure ourselves that the beast is all but dead. That isn't us; that isn't anyone we know. Those people ranting about their political opponents being traitors? They're merely "ultra-conservative." That they keep repeating most American crime is the work of a single racial group doesn't matter. That the best place to buy a copy of *The Turner Diaries* is at a gun show attended by thousands of ordinary patriots doesn't matter. That the same ordinary patriots rush out to buy guns and ammunition on the election of a black president does not matter.[59] And that talk about eliminating liberals? Just folks blowing off steam. Never mind all those people who keep loaded guns handy because anything could happen, at any time, and spend every day living in armed camps. There's nothing to see here. Nobody here is afraid of some looming race war. All those ideas belong to somebody else.

EVERYBODY KNOWS THIS STORY: on a February evening, a black teenager walks down to the 7-11 to buy iced tea and candy. On his way home, he attracts the attention of an overzealous white—oops, *Hispanic*—Neighbourhood Watch volunteer. George Zimmerman is armed with

---

58 Fears that Barack Obama would bring in new gun control laws drove up sales of guns and ammo following his election in 2008. Between 2007 and 2012, excise taxes collected on ammo sales almost doubled, from $108 to $207 million. Following the Sandy Hook massacre, 2013 excise taxes on ammunition rose to $255 million, a 23 percent increase on a commodity already in short supply. Ammo makers responded by adding shifts at their factories, and reported they were working around the clock to fill demand. By early 2015, empty ammo shelves seemed to be a thing of the past, although a shortage of rimfire ammunition persisted, prompting a May 18, 2015 news story in Canada's *National Post*.

59 Did Americans really rush out to buy guns on the election of a black president? As previously noted, ammo sales almost doubled during Obama's first term. Gun sales followed the same trend. It might be argued that this was simply a response to potential gun control measures, and that it had nothing to do with Obama's race, or the wacky rumours that he was a foreign-born Muslim. Heck, you can even argue that those wacky rumours had nothing to do with race, if you like. But the fact remains that the buying spree kicked off by the election of the nation's first black president was a unique phenomenon.

a Kel-Tec PF-9, a 9mm sub-compact pistol. Trayvon Martin is armed with a bag of Skittles.

And everybody knows this story: when no charges are forthcoming against George Zimmerman, Martin's family is aghast. They call in a civil rights lawyer. The police make excuses. Soon, the Reverend Al Sharpton makes an appearance. Florida's governor appoints a special taskforce to re-examine the state's controversial self-defence laws. The President of the United States makes a carefully balanced speech.

And of course, everyone knows this story, too: supporters of Florida's stand-your-ground law jump in to side with George Zimmerman on the assumption that the shooting was legitimate self-defence. They go online to find photos of Martin that make him look like a scary black man. They repeat that he was suspended from school for possession of trace amounts of marijuana, and for writing graffiti on a door, and that in the second incident a search of his backpack found women's jewelry, which might have been stolen. They make sure to mention his tattoos, his supposed fighting, his profane remarks on Twitter, and the photo in which he gives the camera the finger. They have proven that he was a big, black, menacing criminal—although of course they have proven this to no one save themselves. But no matter. The true aim of all their rhetoric is merely to reassure themselves that the unanswered death of Trayvon Martin is not the perverse outcome of a bad law, but a just and righteous judgment on the bad guy.

And at the risk of repeating myself, everyone knows *this* story: at the end of all that, not a damn thing changed. But if everybody knows all these stories, why do we insist on pretending that this whole race problem belongs to someone else?

No, don't tell me. Because everyone knows that one, too. One side complains that black men are simply *assumed* to be criminals, and are treated as such until (and perhaps after) proven otherwise. The other side complains that black men *actually statistically are* criminals, and so they can't complain when people treat them that way until (and perhaps after) proven otherwise. That's not prejudice, they say; that's experience. The crime problem has a colour, and that colour is black.

But do our statistics actually, statistically, hold water? It is true that black men are convicted of crimes at a higher rate than whites. And it is also true that victimization surveys suggest this is not simply a problem with the police and the justice system. But it is also true that the high rate of crimes by young black men is the work of a small subset of young black men, just as crime by white men is the work of a small subset of young white men, an observation borne out by repeated research showing that the people most victimized by crime are, in fact, other criminals. And it is also true that white criminals more than make up for any discrepancy in crime rates by dint of their greater numbers. You are more likely to be mugged, assaulted, robbed, beaten or raped by a white man. So if crime has a colour, that colour is white.[60]

Regardless, to recite statistics is to miss the point: that African Americans feel they are treated differently, and that they *are* treated differently, if not always in the courts then in the court of public opinion, in the media and in the attitudes we encounter when concealed-carry activists set out to reassure themselves that the white man standing his ground actually *is* the good guy. Trayvon Martin was deemed a thug not because anyone could show he had committed any crime, but because of poses he struck for a camera and the language that he used, because he adopted a gangsta persona, the persona of the scary black man. It did not matter that a teenager's online persona is as much as anything a matter of role-playing. It did not matter that, quite possibly, his tongue had been jammed firmly in his cheek all the while. Trayvon Martin became a thug because a thug was what people expected to see, and that expectation was the product of racial prejudice.

60   The FBI's Uniform Crime Reporting (UCR) Program provides annual crime statistics for the United States that include crime rates by race. Although African Americans account for only about 12 percent of the total US population, more than one quarter of all crime and almost 40 percent of violent crime is attributed to them. It is possible, of course, that this reflects higher conviction rates for African Americans accused of crime, yet it is backed up by another source, the National Crime Victimization Survey, conducted bianually by the Bureau of Justice Statistics. Since the NCVS is a victimization survey, it collects crime statistics regardless of whether crimes are reported to police or whether anyone is convicted. And although it is possible that white crime victims might ascribe crimes to blacks where race is not, in fact, known, it is notable that black crime victims also report being victimized disproportionately by black criminals. That violent crime is the territory of a small subset of African-American men (or, indeed, of any recognizable group) is neatly borne out by a social network analysis by Andrew Papachristos and Christopher Wildeman, published in the *American Journal of Public Health*, which found that the risk of being shot and killed in a predominantly black Chicago neighbourhood was dramatically higher among people who had earlier been convicted of committing crimes alongside others who had also been shot and killed. Almost half of all killings involved only 4 percent of the population, and association with other violent criminals predicted homicide more accurately than race. (Andrew V. Papachristos and Christopher Wildeman, "Network Exposure and Homicide Victimization in an African American Community," *American Journal of Public Health* 104(1)(2014).) It is important to bear in mind that almost three-quarters of all crime—most crime, in other words—is the work of white criminals.

But that's just the story of one black kid. We can always hide behind specifics and pretend any given incident has nothing to do with race, that the whole racism problem belongs to someone else. You have to consider this, we say; you have to consider that. So if this whole racism thing still seems somehow to belong to someone else, let's forget how individual people react to one black kid and instead look at how a whole crowd of people reacts to a whole crowd of angry African Americans. We won't have to look far. Everybody knows this story, too.

August 9, 2014, Ferguson, Missouri. Darren Wilson, a white police officer, shoots Michael Brown, an unarmed black teenager. It looks bad: there are fifty-three cops on the local force, and only four are black. And it gets worse: the police promptly demonstrate their racial sensitivity by reacting to the inevitable protests as if facing Sergeant Ungvary's long-overdue black revolution. Predictably, things get violent. But this is not the point. The familiar story that plays out on the nightly news is only the soundtrack to the real story.

As the grand jury deliberated whether to indict Wilson, area residents grew nervous. What if there was no indictment? There would certainly be riots. And apparently people feared those riots would spread outside Ferguson, which is predominantly African American, into nearby suburbs, where more than 80 percent of the population is white—although of course, riots seldom do. It was time for ordinary God-fearing American white folk to protect their lives and property. In St. Charles, fifteen miles distant, and in Bridgeton, halfway to St. Charles, gun sales increased tenfold. Steven King, a Bridgeton gun-shop owner, told CNN that people were coming into his shop with fear in their eyes, saying they needed guns to protect their homes. People were breaking into their piggy banks, spending their savings, buying guns on credit. Most of these people were first-time buyers, because those who already had guns had only to stock up on ammo, which was also flying off the shelves. Applications for gun permits in St. Louis doubled.

Everybody knows this story, too: none of those people was racist, and none of them feared a race war. None of those people thought for a moment that the nation had come to resemble an armed camp, prepared for war with itself. Yet here we are, continuing our 150-year racial cold war, and perhaps our greatest shame is to have made Richard Nixon look prescient, as the United States increasingly looks like an armed camp of three hundred million Americans living in fear, each armed against the other and clinging to the Second Amendment as a martyr clings to his crucifix.

But this is not the whole story of the Second Amendment. One part of its secret history remains to be told: which is how, as crime began rising in the 1960s and 1970s, a nation intent on controlling guns accidentally transformed the Second Amendment from a two-hundred-year-old historical artifact into a living force in American politics. For the Second Amendment had been essentially dormant for centuries, irrelevant. Even the gun lobby hadn't paid it much mind. To understand how it came back to life, we must turn to another secret history: that of the NRA.

An Uncertain History

How Gun Control Created the Gun Lobby

*I own about a dozen guns, but as far as I'm concerned the NRA
is blowing my gig. That waterhead president (Orth?) doesn't
speak for me.*

—Hunter S. Thompson

ON THE KITCHEN CALENDAR a firm red pencil draws an X through yesterday and the world shrinks smaller yet. With the clatter and bang of the Model-T Ford, distance collapses in on itself, far-off towns draw closer, and the open spaces of the West close in. The telegraph jangles our nerves with news of another robbery, electrons singing their secret music through the wires. Bonnie and Clyde career from one state to the next, clouds of dust roiling in the wake of their jalopy, a trunk full of guns and ammo and stolen licence plates, one step ahead of the law. This is a stick-up, says Pretty Boy Floyd, Machine Gun Kelly, Baby Face Nelson: now is the hour of the Tommy gun, the fractured patchwork of American law enforcement forever out of its jurisdiction, unable to keep pace with automobile-powered interstate crime. But all will meet sticky ends at the hands of G-men armed with revolvers and submachine guns, their black-and-white mug shots crossed out firmly one by one by that same red pencil. One-hundred-and-seven bullet holes riddle the death car of Bonnie and Clyde and better than fifty of those bullets found their way into Bonnie. Lights out.

By the 1920s the revolution in firepower had reached its logical conclusion. The Thompson sub-machine gun came on the market in 1921 and completed the development the Minié ball had commenced in 1849: in place of the clumsy and inaccurate musket with its five shots per minute, you could now tote a Tommy gun that could fire 850 rounds per minute. Weapons technology had made enormous strides, but the law had not kept up. There were no laws controlling who could buy a gun, or what kinds of guns you could buy. The only thing keeping the Tommy gun out of reach was its price tag.[61] Governments developed a pressing interest in gun control and that interest created the gun lobby. The history of the gun lobby changes according to who is doing the telling, but one thing is clear, as we shall see: gun control created the gun lobby, with Newtonian certainty. Exert pressure on one body, and it will push back with equal and opposite force.

Before the Tommy gun, the US government had shown little interest in gun control. Regulating guns was a policing matter, and policing lay outside the federal government's power, for the constitution reserved police powers to the states. The result, inevitably, was a confusing patchwork of laws that differed from one state to the next. The American Bar Association recognized the problem, and had been working to create uniform state gun laws. So had an organization with a surprisingly healthy interest in gun control: the NRA. Karl T. Frederick, a lawyer and the NRA's president, had in the 1920s drafted a Uniform Firearms Act, borrowing from a Revolver Act promoted earlier by the US Revolver Association, where Frederick had also been president. The idea was to get all the states to bring in the same law, the law that the NRA had helpfully provided.

But the NRA's proposed gun-control law was not as toothless as one might cynically expect. It did not, for example, propose arming schoolteachers, bank tellers, and telegraph operators, with the suggestion that the only thing that stops a bad guy with a gun is an armed citizen. Under the NRA's Uniform Firearms Act, you would need a licence to carry a concealed handgun, a licence you could get only if you could show a good reason for needing it. Dealers would have to keep records of all handgun sales, and there would be a two-day waiting period every time you wanted to buy a gun. Committing any violent crime while armed would bring additional penalties, regardless of whether you actually used your gun, penalties that grew steeply with each additional offence. Convicted criminals would not be allowed to own guns, and

---

61   The Thompson sub-machine gun sold for $200, the equivalent of about $2,600 today.

knowingly selling a gun to a minor, a felon, a person "not of sound mind," or a drug addict would be an offence. Regardless of its source, this was a genuine gun-control law.

Why was the NRA promoting a gun-control law? For the NRA, this gun-control law made sense: one law, in all states, affecting all NRA members equally, which would still allow law-abiding citizens to own guns. A cynic might suggest that the NRA's commitment to gun control in the form of the Uniform Firearms Act may have been nothing more than an attempt to head off more laws like New York's restrictive Sullivan Act. But the Uniform Firearms Act also represented a different NRA, an NRA whose members stood for law and order, who stood for the status quo, for peaceful communities where no one felt the need to go armed with a Kel-Tec P-3AT concealed in an inside-waistband holster. The NRA had formed, a half-century before, to train men to fight America's wars. It stood with the state and its police and if it insisted that private citizens had the right to keep and bear arms, that right existed so that they could stand alongside the forces of law and order. The NRA stood onside with the Leviathan.

But the Leviathan had its eyes on the NRA's guns, and soon everything would change.

SEVEN MEN MEET IN AN UNHEATED garage on an ordinary Thursday morning in February. One is there to fix a truck. Two others will drive out of town to pick up a load of stolen Canadian whiskey, for Prohibition is still in full swing, the Nineteenth Amendment proof that the constitution of the United States is not, in fact, graven in stone. Four others are there to meet the boss, but the boss has slept in and has yet to arrive. So they are standing around, smoking and shooting the breeze, when the police burst in.

They know the drill, these men. This is not their first police raid. And there is no booze here anyway, nothing to incriminate them, nothing to tie them to any crime. They drop their cigarettes and raise their hands above their heads. The mechanic, he's just there to fix the truck, and he does as he is told, lines up with the others, facing the whitewashed garage wall. "Go ahead and search," says one. "You ain't gonna find nothin'." But the cops don't search. They open fire, with two Tommy guns, a shotgun, and a revolver, the garage a staccato cacophony of gunshots, blood spattering the whitewash as the seven men fall, each of them hit at least a dozen times, their blood pooling on the garage floor. The cop with the shotgun shoots the mechanic in the face, just to make sure. Only one man survives, but he's taken fifteen bullets and he ain't gonna make it. It is February 14, 1929, in Chicago: Valentine's Day.

Five-hundred-and-ninety-five miles to the east, the rattle of gunshots disturbs the snoozing Leviathan. The beast snorts and stirs, one eyelid lifting to reveal its red and baleful eye. A claw twitches, tightening, and pulls its net of steel rails tighter. In 1934, Washington answers the St. Valentine's Day Massacre by passing the National Firearms Act to go after "gangster weapons."

The National Firearms Act got around the constitutional problem of police powers by disguising itself as a tax measure: rather than trying to prohibit the manufacture, sale, or transfer of short-barreled shotguns and machine guns outright, it simply taxed them to the tune of two-hundred-dollars a pop, which at the time was much more than the price of the gun itself. You could buy a shotgun for just five bucks, and the tax neatly doubled the already steep price of the Thompson. And the better to collect that two hundred dollars, the law required that those guns be registered, and prohibited transporting them across state lines unless they were. Ordinary people could no longer afford a Thompson sub-machine gun, and gangsters naturally preferred not to register their guns. The taxman had priced the gangster's machine gun into oblivion.

In its original form, the National Firearms Act would have done the same to handguns, but the NRA objected—not by squawking that Americans had a right to keep and bear arms, or that Americans needed handguns to protect all their other rights—but complaining that taxing handguns would hurt hardware stores from coast to coast.[62] According to Frederick, after Pennsylvania's version of the Uniform Firearms Act imposed a ten-dollar annual fee on handgun dealers, many hardware stores simply stopped selling handguns because they couldn't justify the cost. And driving hardware stores out of the handgun business would

---

62　The NRA was openly admitting what today it carefully omits: the chief reason to oppose gun control is that a lot of American livelihoods depend on guns. And although gun-control advocates today like to claim that the NRA exists to protect the profits of gun makers, a "big gun" to rival Big Tobacco, radical opposition to gun control seems to originate most powerfully from thousands of much smaller businesses: gun shops, accessory manufacturers, private shooting ranges, and instructors. It makes perfect sense: just as only fishing nuts become fly-fishing guides, you don't choose to make a hand-to-mouth living in the world of guns unless you really, really like guns.

"destroy the opportunity for self-defence of the ordinary man in the small community, where police forces are not adequate."

But the NRA of 1934 was just fine with the rest of the National Firearms Act, although it did want to help clean up a few little details. For example, the bill's authors had, for their own obscure reasons, defined a machine gun as a firearm capable of discharging twelve or more shots, automatically or semi-automatically without reloading—a bizarre definition that would have made the lever-action Model 73 Winchester rifle into a machine gun, which it assuredly is not. And, as Frederick pointed out, the Browning Automatic Rifle—a light machine gun developed for use in World War I—would remain a rifle because of its limited magazine capacity. But Frederick apparently felt that the BAR ought to be restricted anyway, and proposed that a machine gun is actually "any firearm ... which shoots automatically more than one shot without manual reloading, by a single function of the trigger."[63]

As for the good old Second Amendment, it seemed not to be too high among Karl Frederick's concerns. He never once brought it up. The Ways and Means Committee of the House of Representatives even went out of its way to ask Frederick if he thought the National Firearms Act might violate the right to keep and bear arms. His reply was astonishing: "I have not given it any study from that point of view."

A sardonic Soviet-era joke held that the Soviet Union was the only nation in the world with an uncertain history. There in a photograph stand Lenin and Trotsky, in Red Square for the second anniversary of the revolution; a few years pass, and there in the self-same photograph stands Lenin, alone. The NRA's own official history claims that the organization has defended the right to keep and bear arms against repeated attacks since the beginning of time, or at least since 1871. The NRA's critics, on the other hand, love to quote selectively from Frederick's testimony, to prove that the NRA didn't even think of the Second Amendment until sometime in the 1970s. Neither view survives a careful examination of the retouching marks on the surviving photographs.

It wasn't that Frederick didn't think the Second Amendment mattered. But when he appeared before the Ways and Means Committee, Frederick found himself commenting on a bill he had seen for the first time only that morning. Gun control had never before been a federal

---

63 Thus, the NRA helpfully supplied the definition of "machine gun" that is used today not only in American gun laws, but in Canada's Criminal Code.

problem, but now the game had changed, and Frederick was unprepared. As the committee pressed him, he conceded, "I do think it is a subject which deserves serious thought." And the NRA was sufficiently worried by the National Firearms Act that it promptly formed its Legislative Affairs Division, the forerunner of today's Institute for Legislative Action, to give the Second Amendment the serious thought it deserved.

Still, there is no disputing that the NRA of 1934 was a far more moderate organization than the NRA we know today. The NRA had originally formed not to protect Americans' supposed right to keep guns for the purpose of resisting their own government, but to train American riflemen so that same government could put them to work as soldiers in times of crisis. It was closely aligned with Washington and with the army. It stood with Don Chafin's ragtag militia, determined that no armed mob would cross Logan County, and with the militia raining bullets down on the Ludlow camp. It stood also with armed southerners determined to maintain the stable, Jim Crow status quo. In 1934, the NRA above all stood for law and order, for How Things Are.

Karl Frederick was certain that gun ownership deterred criminals, and declared that "the great mass of unorganized citizens" ought to be able to own handguns to form a kind of national immune system against crime. While he had "never believed in the general practice of carrying weapons," and did not "believe in the general promiscuous toting of guns," Frederick argued also that regulations "should not impose undue hardships on the law-abiding citizens and that they should not obstruct him in the right of self-defense." Writing in *The American Journal of Police Science*, he declared, "I am as much against the gangster as any man, but I do not believe that we should burn down the barn in order to destroy the rats." Frederick believed every law-abiding American ought to be allowed to own a handgun. Yet at the same time, he raised no objections to restricting machine guns and sawed-off shotguns, and even helped Congress to craft a more effective definition of the machine guns it sought to restrict. To the NRA of 1934, no right was absolute.

It was almost as if the NRA were *reasonable*.

JACK MILLER WAS A PETTY CROOK, a 240-pound thug who specialized in armed robbery, although he probably could have coerced his victims using little more than his bulk and a sweet, murderous smile. By age twenty-one he had a criminal record; by twenty-four he had killed a man in a fist fight. In 1934, Miller joined up with the O'Malley gang, who had carried off a dozen bank robberies across the Midwest, as a lookout and getaway driver. But the age of the gangster was already ending, and one by one, the gang members were captured. When Miller's turn came, he gave state's evidence in exchange for immunity from prosecution. That's what you get for trusting the new guy.

On April 18, 1938, Jack Miller and another man, Frank Layton, were stopped by police in Arkansas, en route from Oklahoma. In their car was a sawed-off Stevens shotgun. The police decided that two men with a sawed-off shotgun, one a known bank robber, were in all likelihood up to no good, and arrested them both. And so Miller and Layton found themselves charged under the National Firearms Act with transporting an unregistered short-barrelled shotgun across state lines.

The Man had them dead to rights, and Miller and Layton pleaded guilty. But in an unusual move, the district court refused the guilty plea and appointed defence counsel for them.[64] Their court-appointed lawyer promptly raised a Second Amendment defence, and the District Court just as promptly struck down the relevant section of the National Firearms Act, without providing reasons. The prosecution, in turn, appealed to the Supreme Court. But Miller and Layton would never see the Supreme Court. Neither would their lawyer. None of them could afford the trip. Besides, Miller had a prior engagement: on April 3, 1939, he met with two colleagues who helped him carry out an armed robbery, and then shot and killed him. And so the government submitted its arguments to the Supreme Court, but the defence never got to present its side.[65]

The government won. But that fact is less important than the reason they won: the Supreme Court declared that the National Firearms Act didn't infringe anything by restricting sawed-off shotguns, because sawed-off shotguns weren't military weapons. The "obvious purpose" of the Second Amendment was to preserve the effectiveness of the militia,

---

64 The right to have state-appointed counsel in a criminal trial at that time existed only in capital cases. It would be extended to include all cases later, in 1938.

65 The unusual circumstances of Miller and Layton's trial and appeal, and the fact that Miller was already a stool pigeon, have led conspiracy theorists to argue that the entire thing was orchestrated for the purpose of finding the National Firearms Act constitutional. See, for example, Brian L. Frye, "The peculiar story of *United States v. Miller,*" *NYU Journal of Law & Liberty* 3 (2008).

to which end the United States had passed any number of supplementary militia acts.[66] Justice McReynolds' decision rambles through a cook's tour of those acts and related references, noting who was allowed (or alternatively, required) to serve in the militia, with what they were to be armed, how often they would train, and so on, and then abruptly remarks that among all the various provisions the states have made with respect to keeping and bearing arms, none supported striking down the law: "In the absence of any evidence tending to show that possession or use of a 'shotgun having a barrel of less than eighteen inches in length' at this time has some reasonable relationship to the preservation or efficiency of a well regulated militia, we cannot say that the Second Amendment guarantees the right to keep and bear such an instrument."

If you want to argue that the Second Amendment protects a sawed-off shotgun, in other words, you have to come to court prepared to prove that your sawed-off shotgun has something to do with a well-regulated militia. And the defence hadn't, of course, because they weren't there in the first place, but it probably wouldn't have mattered if they were.

In the Great American Gun Kerfuffle, credibility hinges on the struggle to appear neutral. And the conventional neutral comment on *United States v. Miller* is that it is a muddled ruling that supports both sides.[67] But this only exemplifies the middle ground fallacy. The ruling is not nearly as muddled as it appears: McReynolds clearly ruled that the Second Amendment is about militia, militia, and militia, and the guns it protects are those suited to militia service. We might well interpret this today to mean Americans have the right to own machine guns and perhaps anti-aircraft missile launchers, but not single-shot shotguns meant for trap shooting. And if that seems absurd, which it is, then that is what *United States v. Miller* is to the Second Amendment: *reductio ad absurdum*.

Inadvertently or otherwise, McReynolds' strange ruling simply demonstrates how obsolete the Second Amendment had already become. In all the ruling's catalogue of militia equipment and training, its descriptions of muskets, "carrying an ounce ball, and three feet

---

66   *United States v. Miller:* "With obvious purpose to assure the continuation and render possible the effectiveness of such forces [i.e., the militia], the declaration and guarantee of the Second Amendment were made. It must be interpreted and applied with that end in view."

67   It is said to support the pro-gun side by recognizing a right to own weapons for militia service, and to support the anti-gun side by declaring a limit on gun ownership constitutional.

eight inches long in the barrel," or perhaps "not less than three feet, nine inches, nor more than four feet three inches in length," and of the necessity of a "Pouch with a Box therein to contain not less than Twenty-four Cartridges suited to the Bore of his Musket," there is not one reference to what equipment might be required to properly accoutre the militiaman of 1939—because the militia as conceived by the framers of the constitution was by that time an anachronism; no such requirement existed. If the Second Amendment existed for the purpose of maintaining a well-regulated militia, but no regulations then existed for the equipment and training of such a militia, then perhaps the Second Amendment had already become a nullity, a historical curio.[68]

Former Supreme Court Chief Justice Warren Burger's oft-repeated remark that the NRA's interpretation of the Second Amendment was a fraud on the American public has some merit.[69] The right to keep and bear arms had been treated as a historical relic and largely ignored up until the 1960s, having been dusted off only briefly in the unsuccessful defence of a pair of petty thugs to whom no one today would extend the right to carry a gun. It would remain a dead issue until the spectre of federal gun control encouraged the NRA to resuscitate it and set it lurching through the cultural landscape like a zombie, hungering to chew on the great American brain.

SIX THOUSAND GATHERED BEFORE City Hall, the largest crowd it has ever seen, and a restless crowd at that. The mayor steps forward, determined: these goddamned Bolshies will never win their demands. A chorus of

---

68 The National Guard is not a militia as conceived in the constitution. Its arms are provided by the state, which only serves to further illustrate how the revolution in firepower and the professionalization of soldiering has made the Second Amendment obsolete.

69 "If I were writing the Bill of Rights now there wouldn't be any such thing as the Second Amendment ... This has been the subject of one of the greatest pieces of fraud, I repeat the word 'fraud,' on the American public by special interest groups that I have ever seen in my lifetime. Now just look at those words. There are only three lines in that amendment. A well regulated militia—if the militia, which was going to be the state army, was going to be well regulated, why shouldn't 16 and 17 and 18 or any other age persons be regulated in the use of arms the way an automobile is regulated? It's got to be registered, that you can't just deal with at will ... I don't want to get sued for slander, but I repeat that they [the NRA] ... have had far too much influence on the Congress of the United States than as a citizen I would like to see—and I am a gun man. I have guns. I have been a hunter ever since I was a boy." Burger, quoted in William G. Merkel, "*The District of Columbia v. Heller* and Antonin Scalia's Perverse Sense of Originalism." *Lewis & Clark Law Review* 13(2), (2009).

hoots and catcalls as he starts to read from a single sheet of paper, at first in a tremulous voice but then with growing confidence and volume.

"Our Sovereign Lord the King … Our Sovereign Lord the King chargeth and commandeth all persons, being assembled, immediately to disperse themselves, and peaceably to depart to their habitations, or to their lawful business, upon the pains contained in the act made in the first year of King George, for preventing tumults and riotous assemblies." He lowers his sheet of paper and then shouts the last line: "God Save the King!"

More hoots, more catcalls, and with that the North-West Mounted Police ride into the crowd, swinging truncheons, firing their revolvers, as men turn and scatter and fall before them. Two men are killed and over thirty wounded. By the end of the day, the army will patrol the streets with machine guns. It is June 21, 1919, in Winnipeg: Bloody Saturday.

Thousands of soldiers returning from the front found thousands of new immigrants competing for what few low-wage jobs there were. The trade union movement swelled, pressing the usual radical demands: recognition of trade unions, a living wage, and an eight-hour workday. Everyone knew these were dangerous subversives. In Russia, a general strike in Petrograd had spun out of control and snowballed into the Russian Revolution, and it was well known that the trade union movement was full of shifty foreigners from Eastern Europe, most of them Bolshevik agitators and anarchists, people with funny accents, a penchant for radical politics, and none of the English decency that they might have learned at a respectable school such as Upper Canada College. These bloody foreigners were known for carrying weapons, including revolvers. Could there be any greater threat to peace, order, and good government than a mass of swarthy Bolshies with guns in their pockets and Marx on their minds?

Fiery trade-union speeches and the cheers they rouse from crowds of working men penetrate the Leviathan's slumbering mind and muddle its anxious dreams. It twitches in its sleep. It suddenly seems important to do something about guns.

Arthur Meighen, Prime Minister Robert Borden's justice minister— the same man who had declared that Winnipeg's general strike was merely a cloak for a conspiracy to overthrow the government, and then ordered in the army—announced that too many revolvers were now in the hands of too many "aliens," and presented to Parliament a bill that proposed gun licences, not for loyal subjects, but for aliens—which of course provoked objections that the law ought to apply equally to all. Meighen countered that by committing crimes, aliens forfeited their right to equal treatment under the law, a remarkable argument that today would provoke howls of derision and an inevitable rebuke from the Supreme Court when the law was challenged—but his bill passed nonetheless. And in 1934, Canada took a further step and created a handgun registry, which persists to this day. It took up to six years to register all the guns, but the registry enjoyed wide public support and, unlike the long-gun registry created sixty years later by Jean Chretien's government, faced little protest.

Britain had almost entirely ignored the revolution in firepower, probably because the working man wasn't likely to own a gun anyway. Guns belonged to landowners and the social elite, who trotted them out to shoot pheasants and dispose of unwanted pests; gentlemen might own revolvers, but were unlikely to shoot anyone save themselves. But many guns had come home as war souvenirs, and were now in the hands of veterans who had been exposed to dangerous political ideas, not to mention too much shelling, and whose mental wiring might not be strictly up to code. Shifty continental Bolshies and the Irish provided all the motive Britain's Parliament needed for their 1920 Firearms Act, which proposed to keep guns away from the "anarchist or 'intellectual' malcontent of the great cities, whose weapon is the bomb and the automatic pistol" by requiring permits, banning pawnbrokers from selling guns, and making dealers keep records of their sales.[70]

The revolution in firepower had finally prompted lawmakers to react. The Rifleman was dead, buried in some muddy trench by an artillery barrage, and in his place were crooks, wise guys and shifty-eyed Bolshies. The last thing any good, upstanding citizen wanted was to see guns in the hands of criminals, trade unionists, and foreigners. And for now, good, upstanding citizens didn't mind gun control, because for now, their own guns were safe.

FOR NOW, THE SECOND AMENDMENT remained dead and in its grave. Nobody much worried about gun control, and when they did, the

---

70 The Blackwell Committee, convened in 1918 to study the problem of controlling firearms after the war's end, apparently did not feel that Marxists were true intellectuals, and so adorned the word with what today we call scare quotes.

NRA wasn't too militant about the question. In 1938, Congress passed another gun-control law, the Federal Firearms Act, which the NRA endorsed—as well it might have, given that the NRA itself had drafted it.[71] An article in the *St. John's Law Review* called the Federal Firearms Act "sensible and desirable," although in practice it proved difficult to enforce.[72] But no one clamoured to make it more effective. Gun control was simply not a hot issue.

Then came the 1960s. An Italian Carcano rifle in the hands of an ex-Marine who had defected to the Soviet Union, a rifle that had been bought by mail order for just $19.95 (plus shipping and handling) from an ad in the NRA's *American Rifleman* magazine, kills the president. Bobby Kennedy falls to a bullet from a .22-calibre revolver in the hands of a Palestinian activist incensed by Kennedy's support of Israel. Armed Black Panthers march into the California legislature, and riots burn in the hearts of American cities. The noise rouses the Leviathan. The beast lifts its head, smells burning gasoline and spent powder, snorts and flexes its claws. Who dares challenge its power?

The problem was no longer just the gangster's Tommy gun and the hold-up artist's sawed-off 12-gauge, but ordinary rifles and pistols in the hands of people who appeared to be ordinary citizens. The problem was all those traditional guns, and perhaps even the tradition itself. It was time to do something about guns in general.

The Gun Control Act was five years in the making, and the version Lyndon B. Johnson eventually signed was a watered-down compromise. The first draft demanded licensing for all gun owners, and registration of all guns. But the NRA shouted that registration leads to confiscation, a simple slogan that has since become the gun nut's shibboleth, and those provisions disappeared. In 1968, not even the assassinations of Martin Luther King, Jr. and Robert Kennedy could create enough political momentum to get Congress to bring in licensing and registration. Nothing ever has.

The Gun Control Act continued the same old theme of countless gun control laws, banning sales to criminals and the mentally ill. It also restricted mail-order sales to dealers holding a Federal Firearms License.

---

71   The Federal Firearms Act, among other things, introduced the requirement for any dealer or manufacturer in firearms to hold a Federal Firearms License, or FFL. This law still stands.

72   That article was Alfred M. Ascione, "The Federal Firearms Act," *St. John's Law Review* 13 (1939).

Import restrictions on military surplus guns, like Lee Harvey Oswald's mail-order Carcano rifle, demanded that they have a "valid sporting purpose." The same applied to foreign-made pistols, a measure aimed at Saturday Night Specials. And all firearms manufactured in or imported into the United States would have to be marked with a unique serial number; previously, .22-calibre rifles and some shotguns had been exempt.

In the public eye, the criterion of success for any gun control law is dead simple: either crime falls, or it doesn't.[73] And after 1968, it didn't. Markets adapt. When the Gun Control Act made importing small, cheap handguns difficult, manufacturing small, cheap handguns became a growth industry. And cheap handguns weren't really the problem anyway. "Handguns retailing for under $50 are a major public safety problem," as the prominent criminologist Franklin Zimring pointed out, "but so are those retailing for over $50."[74] As a landmark survey of convicts discovered, criminals actually prefer large, powerful handguns, and since they often carry stolen handguns anyway, price is no object.[75] If you need a gun, you need one that hits hard.

And the Gun Control Act had important loopholes and shortcomings. In place of licensing, it relied on background checks, which allow anyone to buy a gun unless he is provably ineligible. No background checks were required for private sales—the "gun show loophole." A private seller could sell a gun to a person prohibited from buying one, and could ship a gun across state lines, with little risk of ever being caught. Furthermore, sales records would not be centralized for ease of searching—a deliberate concession to the gun lobby's cry of "registration leads to confiscation." Instead, the police would have to go to the store where the gun had been sold to check the records, which would be kept entirely on paper.[76]

---

73 This is actually a strikingly silly way of thinking about laws. If murder rates don't fall when we ban murder, does this mean that outlawing murder is futile? The debate has been framed incorrectly from the start.

74 Franklin E. Zimring, "Firearms and Federal Law: The Gun Control Act of 1968," *J. Legal Stud.* 4(1975).

75 The survey in question was by James Wright and Peter Rossi, and is covered by their book, *Armed and Considered Dangerous: A Survey of Felons and Their Firearms.* Their findings suggest that stolen guns are a serious problem. In the absence of registration, many stolen guns probably circulate through gun shows, private sales, and even legitimate dealers: if the serial number doesn't happen to show up as stolen, there is no way to trace the gun. An effective system of registration makes it far more difficult to sell a stolen gun through legitimate channels.

76 When Stephen Harper's government abolished Canada's long-gun registry, the chief firearms officers in several provinces (including Ontario) required licensed dealers to continue keeping paper

The apparent failure of the Gun Control Act only bolstered the gun owner's long-standing objection to gun control: it makes life difficult for the law-abiding, but leaves the criminal, who ignores the law anyway, to pursue his trade unmolested. And if gun control is ineffective in controlling crime, something else has to be done. The gun lobby, looking for a counter to gun control, hit upon the obvious: deterrence. The solution was more guns.

TODAY, THE NRA VOWS TO GIVE not one inch, and proudly proclaims it has been defending the Second Amendment from day one. But in January 1968, when Robert Kennedy accused the organization of opposing "any legislation to try and control the misuse of rifles and pistols in this country," *The American Rifleman* published a pained rebuttal, citing the NRA's support for the Uniform Firearms Act, National Firearms Act, Federal Firearms Act, and other efforts.[77] "The National Rifle Association has been in support of workable, enforceable gun control legislation since its very inception, in 1871," said Franklin L. Orth, then the NRA's executive vice president, carefully leaving himself room to oppose any measure he thought unworkable or unenforceable, which of course might just apply to anything.

The old NRA had always stood for law and order, and until the federal government tried to regulate mail-order sales of guns to potentially shady characters, it was opposed to them. "Mail-order dealers in pistols are generally not people of repute and standing," Karl Frederick had written, "but rather fly-by-night concerns which exist largely for the purpose of supplying the underworld."[78] Mail order, to Frederick, was the primary sales avenue for Saturday Night Specials, and "pistols of this type are of little or no value to legitimate users. No military man, no policeman, no bank guard, no target-shooter or sportsman would think of buying such a gun because it is such a poor—almost worthless— piece of hardware that he would be ashamed to own it."

records of all sales. Protests from gun activists that this amounted to a "back-door registry" and that the records could be used to create a new long-gun registry led the federal government to enact a regulation prohibiting CFOs from requiring any such records—a regulation that gun activists promptly misinterpreted to mean that all record-keeping had been banned. Thus, the United States now has more rigorous measures for tracking firearms sales than does Canada. The mind reels.

77   Alan C. Webber, "Where the NRA Stands on Gun Legislation." *The American Rifleman*, March, 1968.

78   Karl T. Frederick, "Pistol Regulation: Its Principles and History," *The American Journal of Political Science* 3(1932).

But by 1968, the NRA's position had changed. Orth backed President Johnson's call to control mail-order sales—but only so long as there was no real control on mail order sales. Rather than banning mail order outright, Orth said Congress should somehow craft "legislation that will keep undesirables, including criminals, drug addicts, and persons adjudged mentally irresponsible or alcoholic, or juveniles from obtaining firearms through the mails." This proposal was, of course, unworkable and unenforceable, unless you could somehow make mailing a letter too difficult for criminals, drug addicts, persons judged mentally irresponsible, and juveniles to handle. The NRA wanted to play it both ways. But behind Orth's careful doublespeak was a growing schism in his organization.

The law-and-order NRA was losing ground to a hardline movement that wasn't necessarily interested in law and order. The old NRA had been an essentially conservative organization that stood for the status quo. But the same forces that operated on America as a whole naturally operated on the NRA itself. Nobody trusted the Man anymore. And now, the NRA members increasingly saw themselves not as loyal militiamen, but as rednecks and rebels, ready to take up arms against the powers that be. For the NRA's leadership, who were struggling to reconcile the schism between the old guard and the hardliners, to back a sweeping ban on mail order sales was out of the question. But standing up for the right of Lee Harvey Oswald to buy his Carcano through the mail (via an ad in their very own magazine, no less) was equally unthinkable. An entirely impractical and unworkable suggestion to magically prevent mail-order sales to alcoholics and drug addicts hoped to satisfy everyone—even alcoholics and drug addicts.

Hunter S. Thompson, who in 1965 had renewed his membership with the remark that he was "concerned about the possible passage of illogical firearms laws," received an assignment in 1968 for a piece on the NRA. Thompson was a member, but had never fit easily into the organization. He was as concerned as any other member about his firearms rights, but his counterculture politics were strongly at odds with those of the rural, conservative squares who formed the old guard— the probable reason he lied to his agent, Lynn Nesbit, about being a long-time member. In a long, rambling letter, Thompson proposed a piece called "Why I Quit the NRA," that would suggest the organization was using, rather than representing, its membership; that is, taking membership dues and doing nothing with them except pay executive salaries. Orth was a "waterhead"—one of Thompson's favoured epithets at the time, slang for a person suffering from hydrocephalus, which causes declining cognitive ability—and *The American Rifleman* "one of the dullest and least informative screeds in the history of printing." By October, with a tentative deal from *Esquire* for the piece, Thompson proposed that "the NRA is a harmless swindle, a massive con job, a rich and well-publicized lobby that isn't doing a fucking thing either for or against anybody except the handful of people on the NRA payroll."[79]

Thompson had correctly perceived that the fuss about Saturday Night Specials was partly motivated by domestic manufacturers' complaints about cheap foreign imports. (Karl Frederick remarked in 1932 that mail order was the territory of "Belgian and Spanish revolvers and automatics of the cheapest kind which have frequently been flagrant imitations of more expensive guns of domestic manufacture.") But when it came to the NRA leadership, his perception faltered. The NRA was indeed doing things with his money; they just weren't doing things that interested him. He simply could not comprehend the gulf between his counterculture views and the rural conservatism of the NRA's old guard. The NRA's growing militant constituency probably felt much the same. Their own organization was siding with the enemy.

As gun control moved on from "gangster weapons" to the rifles and pistols everyone owned, the schism widened. The Gun Control Act of 1968, the creation of the Bureau of Alcohol, Tobacco and Firearms in 1972, and Washington, DC's 1976 handgun ban alarmed hardliners, although these measures had little practical effect on most gun owners. In protest against the DC handgun ban, the NRA moved its annual convention from DC to Cincinnati, and also announced plans to relocate its headquarters to Colorado Springs. To the hardliners, this looked like retreat.

At the 1977 convention in Cincinnati, the hardliners rose up and deposed their leadership, and the NRA took a sharp turn to the right. The new executive vice-president of the NRA was Harlon Carter, a hardliner's hardliner who felt that even tiny derringer pistols ought to be protected by

---

79 Thompson's piece on the NRA, "My Gun Problem, and Theirs," was never published, and although the manuscript apparently survives, it is now located in a cruel and shallow money trench, a long plastic hallway where thieves and pimps run free and good men die like dogs. When I contacted Douglas Brinkley, the editor of Thompson's collected letters, to ask if he knew anything about the manuscript, he did not respond; he did, however, put me on his mailing list and offer to sell me his book on Walter Cronkite.

the Second Amendment, as children could use them for self-defence. To Carter, the body count in the streets was simply the price of freedom. And, whatever the old guard's support for law and order, Carter was a killer. At the age of seventeen, he had taken a shotgun and gone to track down a fifteen-year-old Hispanic teenager named Ramon Casiano, because he thought Casiano knew something about who had stolen the Carter family car. Carter found him, and, mistaking himself for a police officer, he ordered Casiano at gunpoint to come back to his house for questioning. Casiano invited him to pound salt. When Carter pressed the matter, Casiano pulled out a knife. Carter pointed the shotgun at Casiano. Casiano pushed the muzzle aside, stepped back, and laughed. So Carter shot him.

A jury convicted Carter of murder, but an appeal judge overturned the conviction, citing an error in the trial judge's instructions to the jury. Thanks to what Dirty Harry would have called a technicality, the NRA was now led by exactly the kind of man who wasn't supposed to be able to get a gun. And as its rhetoric hardened, its membership tripled.

CANADA IS SUBJECT TO ALL THE social and political forces that operate south of the border, but with a maple flavour. Forever in lockstep with American trends, Canada experienced its own turmoil in the 1960s. The United States had race riots and rising crime; Canada had the merry bombers of the FLQ and rising crime. We should hardly be surprised to find Canada reacting just as the United States did, by turning to gun control. And we should hardly be surprised to find Canada reaching for just the same measures, seeking to keep guns away from the criminals and the crazies, while leaving ordinary hunters and target shooters alone. There were, after all, a lot of guns in Canada, a country that, in geographic terms at least, consists mostly of remote areas where people hunt to eat. But in population terms, Canada consists mostly of cities smeared along the southern border, where people simultaneously embrace the United States and cling to a uniquely Canadian identity by rejecting all things American. And this gives gun control in Canada its unique maple flavour: guns and gun ownership are an American problem that must not be allowed to take root in Canada. Gun control in Canada is not just about controlling guns; it's about who gets to call themselves true Canadians.

The great national beaver pond, fed by dozens of swampy seeps, lacks a unifying national mythology. Each drop of pond water on the microscope slide teems with bizarre creatures; the more carefully one attempts to describe them, the more complex the droplet becomes. The problem, to cultural nationalists, was that the pond water was insufficiently pure, and so they set out to purify it according to their vision of Canada. Anything that didn't fit—anything that smacked of the British Empire or, worse, of the United States—was just plain un-Canadian.[80] To this day, knee-jerk nationalism twitches with the same reflex. The easiest way to find something distinctly Canadian is to find anything distinctly American, and jump on its opposite.

The nation could not be trusted to define itself. It was to be shaped into perfect Canadianness. And guns were deemed un-Canadian, if only because America was a gun culture: individualist, gun-obsessed, violent. The NRA and its American ideas had to be stopped at the border. And the most prominent of those American ideas was, of course, the right to keep and bear arms. In 1885, Liberal MP David Mills, who would later sit on the Supreme Court of Canada, had risen in the House of Commons to argue that Canadians enjoyed a right to own firearms, and that the Second Amendment was in fact merely an American copy of a right that Canadians, as British subjects, already enjoyed. But in the 1970s, the right to keep and bear arms was seen as an unfortunate anachronism promoted by wingnuts addicted to violence, an anachronism that had come to define America. And since owning a gun was American, it sure as hell couldn't be Canadian.

It scarcely mattered that Canadians owned a lot of guns, as befits a frontier nation where, in remote areas, you either eat what you hunt or pay through the nose for food flown in on aircraft of dubious reliability. Canada's cultural nationalists hauled hunting before the House Committee on Un-Canadian Activities, on the grounds of it having something to do with something American; to wit, guns. Hunting itself was now deemed un-Canadian.

Margaret Atwood laid out the case in 1972 in *Survival: A Thematic Guide to Canadian Literature.* "The central symbol for Canada ... is undoubtedly Survival, la Survivance"—her use of the French a shameless

---

80   For a striking example of this, see Margaret Atwood on the poetry of Irving Layton: "Much of the time he accepts the Victor/Victim game, but makes the un-Canadian choice of identifying with the victors rather than the victims." *Survival*, 64. How is the writing of a Canadian poet held to be un-Canadian? Or is this question itself un-Canadian? Shall I now report to a re-education centre to learn the error of my ways?

attempt to make common cause with Quebec and invent a unified Canadian culture where none, in fact, existed or exists. Canadians do not tame the frontier, as Americans do. They endure it. The central theme of Canada's history—literary culture being inseparable from history and the broader culture of the nation—is Putting Up With It. The land is so harsh and the winter so extreme that mere survival is the best one can hope for. The survivor, the true Canadian, can have no victory except to escape with his life, just as in that great, uniquely Canadian novel *Moby-Dick*: "And I alone am escaped to tell thee."

Hunting is American; to die at the wrong end of the rifle is the true Canadian way, because the hunter comes off as the winner, and Canadians are not allowed to win. And so, while American animal stories are hunting stories, Canadian animal stories must sympathize with the hunted animal. *Survival* cites Dave Godfrey's short-story collection *Death Goes Better with Coca-Cola* and the crude stereotypes of hunters painted in Graeme Gibson's *Five Legs* as examples of true Canadian attitudes. In *Survival*'s selective view, the animal stories of Ernest Thompson Seton are canonical, but Roderick Haig-Brown, one of North America's most notable writers on conservation, is not even mentioned—although he, too, wrote animal stories, such as *Silver, Return to the River*, and *Panther*. His failure to cleave to the Animal Victim orthodoxy seems to have excluded him from *Survival*'s Canadian canon.[81]

Defining what is Canadian and what is un-Canadian has become a default rhetorical strategy of Canadian politics. In Ottawa, "American-style" is regularly trotted out as a general-purpose pejorative. It cropped up in June 2013, when Green Party leader Elizabeth May said that Prime Minister Stephen Harper "isn't really Canadian." It is prominent, forty years after *Survival*, in Noah Richler's polemical *What We Talk About When We Talk About War*. A more careful investigation of the national beaver pond might well declare that the unifying thread in *Lament for a Nation, Death Goes Better with Coca-Cola, Five Legs*, and the rest is not "Survival, *la Survivance*" but anti-Americanism, *l'anti-americanisme*,

---

81 Today, *Death Goes Better with Coca-Cola* is out of print; Roderick Haig-Brown's numerous books continue to sell, both within Canada and elsewhere. It does not matter which of these you think has greater literary merit: the culture is what it is, not what you wish it to be. There is also precisely one more provincial park in Canada named for Roderick Haig-Brown than there is for the rest of *Survival*'s canon combined, a fact that may interest those readers who are unafraid that keeping score reflects an un-Canadian desire to win. (True Canadians don't try to win; they just hope to endure the game until the buzzer goes. Ask any hockey player.)

one of the few traits in the national character that genuinely bridges our two solitudes.[82]

So guns and the gun culture were un-Canadian: American ills against which Canada would need to immunize itself. The Liberal Party under Pearson had brought Canada a new flag, and Pierre Trudeau was an energetic nationalist. Gun control was a natural position for his government. In 1969, Liberal MP John Turner, then minister of justice, took the first hesitant steps with a law that—surprise!—strove to keep guns away from criminals and the mentally ill while leaving hunters and sports shooters alone. Turner faced little opposition. In some ways, gun control in Canada actually remained looser than in the United States—as the *Globe and Mail* pointed out in an editorial, Canadians faced more restrictions when buying a bottle of wine than when buying a gun. Sawed-off shotguns and machine guns remained restricted, rather than prohibited.[83] But the three classes of firearms created by Turner's bill—unrestricted, restricted, and prohibited—would form the basis of future Canadian gun control.[84] Although only one model of gun had been prohibited by 1975, the list would expand by the end of the century to include sawed-off shotguns, machine guns, compact handguns, and many specific firearms, including one design—the advanced Heckler & Koch G11 rifle—that was prohibited even though it was never actually manufactured.[85]

In 1975, a rash of school shootings shocked Canadians and gave greater impetus to the gun control movement. The guns used in those shootings were rifles and shotguns, one of them a .22 rimfire rifle, the kind of rifle that had long been considered almost harmless. A boy's first .22 rifle, like his first driver's licence and his first pimples, was traditionally

---

82 Even anti-Americanism is hardly unifying, as there is strong pro-American sentiment among some Quebecers, just as there is a strong pro-American sentiment among English-Canadian conservatives.

83 Canada had imposed a registry on machine guns in 1951, but made no move to prohibit them.

84 Ineffective measures such as Canada's 1969 Criminal Code amendments or the American 1938 Federal Firearms Act have often created structures that future laws have exploited to greater effect.

85 The Heckler & Koch G11 was designed to use a unique, caseless round consisting of a primer, a solid, cuboid propellant block, and a bullet. The cuboid shape of the round used magazine space more efficiently than standard, cylindrical brass cases. The G11 was designed for military applications, but was never selected for use by any military and consequently became an interesting footnote to the history of firearms design. That the G11 was prohibited before it ever entered production is often cited by Canadian gun activists as evidence that the government prohibits guns based purely upon their scary appearance; on the other hand, it is difficult to argue that the G11 would have any legitimate civilian use.

seen as a hallmark of adolescence. I first fired a .22 as a Boy Scout. Just as America had initially concerned itself only with "gangster weapons," Canadian gun control had long concerned itself only with handguns. Now suddenly, *all* guns were potentially dangerous weapons.

In 1976, the Liberals proposed a full licensing system. Your licence application, like your passport application, would need to be countersigned by two guarantors, and Ottawa reserved the right to refuse anyone whom it deemed unsuitable. The Liberals enjoyed a comfortable majority, public support for gun control was running high, and Canada had no gun lobby to speak of. They expected their bill to sail through Parliament. They ought to have known better. South of the border, resistance to gun control had steadily hardened as the focus shifted from gangster weapons to the same guns that everyone owned, and the Liberals were now proposing that everyone who owned a gun would have to apply for a licence to keep it—an application the government might choose to refuse.

And just like that, Pierre Trudeau inadvertently midwived Canada's gun lobby. Before 1976, Canada had none. The Dominion of Canada Rifle Association, unlike the NRA, had stuck firmly to its mandate of promoting competitive rifle shooting and largely confined itself to organizing matches. It ignored handguns, because handgun shooters had clubs of their own. Canada also had a hunter's lobby, the Canadian Wildlife Federation (CWF), which represented provincial organizations such as the Ontario Federation of Anglers and Hunters and the Alberta Fish and Game Association, but these organizations were mostly concerned with wildlife conservation. There were associations of gun collectors, and of course the First Nation peoples, for whom firearms remained a matter of putting food on the table. But there was no single gun lobby, because there had been no reason for one to exist.

Forging a gun lobby out of these diverse interests would not be easy. Hunters were numerous, but a hunter might well ask, "Well, why *not* regulate handguns?" First Nations groups would likely share that view, but hunters and First Nations had long been at odds over hunting rights and regulations and were scarcely eager to cooperate. Handgunners distrusted hunters: all those hunters were fellow gun owners, yet they didn't seem to get it, that gun owners needed to stand together. What would they do, down the road, when the government decided to take away their rifles, and no one remained to stand with them?[86] Most isolated of all were the collectors, whose collections might well include war relics such as machine guns. They felt, justifiably, that nobody else could be relied on to stand up for them.

Gun control doesn't much matter, until they come after *your* gun. Faced with universal licensing, Canada's gun owners struggled to unify. But the vanguard of unity is always the guy who feels most threatened, the guy with the most radical views, who struggles to attract moderate followers. In Alberta, a group called FARO (Firearms and Responsible Ownership) arose to represent a united front for all gun owners, but it attracted only twenty thousand members out of perhaps five million gun owners. Later, the CWF, the Shooting Federation of Canada, and FARO banded together to form the Canadian Association for Sensible Arms Legislation (CASAL). Canadian gun owners finally had a truly united national lobby, an equivalent to the NRA. It helped that CASAL's spokesman, Leonard Nicholson, was an RCMP officer: if you want people to think you're responsible, law-abiding people, line up behind a cop.

CASAL got busy, telling its members to get actively involved in politics. Don't stop at contacting your member of parliament. Join a political party—your choice, buddy, the more the merrier—and get active in your local riding association. Make your views known and let the bastards know that they can forget about winning if they back this bill; even the privilege of running in the next election might just depend on the support of gun owners. We're not giving up and we're not going away.

But CASAL was born with radical DNA, and fringe rumblings hinted at troubles to come. Handgunners tried to convince hunters that licensing was the cusp of a slippery slope. Hardliners warned that only their guns stood between Canada and despotism. Hitler, whose eternal punishments include being continually resurrected in the arguments of idiots, made a routine cameo appearance. Gun control was a Communist plot. One group, RAGO (Responsible Alberta Gun Owners) even warned Canadian hunters that they were facing their "last enjoyable hunting season," in the great tradition of catastrophizing political debate: when gun control came in, it would all be over.

---

86   It's a persistent but stupid argument. In fact, handgun owners are so few relative to long-gun owners that whether or not they disappear is of no political import. But handgun owners don't see it that way, and will forever beat the drum of gun owner solidarity.

The Liberals, taken aback by the vehement response to the bill and facing disappointing polls, allowed it to die quietly on the order paper before coming back with a more moderate proposal. Anyone wishing to buy a gun would henceforth require not a licence but a Firearms Acquisition Certificate (FAC), which would be much easier to get. If you already had a gun, you didn't need to do anything. But then they issued an Order in Council that reclassified the AR-15 rifle, the semi-automatic civilian variant of the M16, as a prohibited firearm. Moderates were happy, and saw a victory; hardliners were alarmed by what had happened to the AR-15. CASAL's fragile alliance came under increasing strain.

Behind closed doors, CASAL hammered out a compromise. But in June 1977, in front of the Parliamentary Justice and Legal Affairs Committee, their spokesman Michael Martinoff went on a rant, decrying the reclassification of the AR-15 and declaring his intent to disobey the law. The committee used him as a verbal punching bag. CASAL's credibility was ruined, and the CWF—representing the moderate mass of its support—promptly distanced itself from the hardliners. Canada's nascent gun lobby had collapsed. But for any gun control activist to celebrate its demise would be premature: it fell apart only because, for most Canadian gun owners, the threat had disappeared when Liberal licensing proposals died on the order paper. Twenty years later, when the government again proposed sweeping gun controls, the lobby would return, stronger and more militant than ever.

ON MARCH 16, 1975, two men broke into the Washington, DC, home where Carolyn Warren, Joan Taliaferro, and Miriam Douglas lived with Douglas's four-year-old daughter. Warren and Taliaferro hid in an upstairs room and called police as the two men raped Douglas. A police dispatcher recorded the call as a burglary in progress. Officers drove past the house without stopping; one knocked on the front door but left when there was no answer. The women again called police. This time, the dispatcher simply logged the call and didn't bother sending anyone to investigate. Soon, believing police had finally arrived, Warren and Taliaferro shouted out that they were upstairs. The rapists then kidnapped, robbed, and repeatedly assaulted the women. In the aftermath, Warren, Taliaferro, and Douglas did what Americans do: they sued the police, and with good reason.

You would think they had some kind of case, that the police had some kind of duty of care that would require them to perform their jobs competently, but you would think wrong. In 1981, the DC Court of Appeals ruled that the police have no obligation to provide protection to any individual citizen, and dismissed their lawsuit. It was, strangely, a significant victory for the gun lobby: even the courts had now come right out and said that *your* safety and security is *your* problem. And that, of course, means that keeping a loaded gun handy is just common sense. Richard Stevens, a DC lawyer, turned the women's ordeal into the centerpiece of a book, *Dial 911 and Die*. Gun writers touted the need to be prepared—not only for your own good, but for the good of your neighbours. Keeping a loaded gun handy was no longer just a desirable option, nor even a necessity for survival. It was, gun activists now argued, a civic duty.

But not in Washington, DC, where the courts had made their ruling. In 1976, the District of Columbia had passed the Firearms Control Regulations Act, which required Washington gun owners to lock up or disassemble their guns. Except for a small number of reasons, just getting your gun out was against the law. And that small number of reasons did not include self-defence. Even if you had an armed intruder in your home, you were not allowed to unlock your shotgun for the purpose of petitioning him to leave. As for handguns, the same law banned them outright.

For NRA hardliners, the DC handgun ban lent special urgency to their fight against gun control. They needed a way to stop the next handgun ban, to throw a spanner into the gears of gun control and forever preserve their guns. That spanner was the Second Amendment, which they reconceived to omit that inconvenient bit about a well-regulated militia: "the right of the people to keep and bear arms shall not be infringed." If the DC handgun ban was the shape of the future, the NRA intended to stop gun control in its tracks, permanently, through the constitution. One small problem confronted their project: outside of the NRA and its followers, nobody much cared about the Second Amendment. So the NRA set out to raise the zombie from its grave.

"To put it mildly, the Second Amendment is not at the forefront of constitutional discussion," wrote Sanford Levinson in his 1989 essay, "The Embarrassing Second Amendment."[87] The right to keep and

---

87 Historian and journalist Gary Wills described this essay as "frivolous but influential." That the Second Amendment had received little attention until the 1980s, however, seems indisputable.

bear arms was a constitutional curio, he wrote, much like the Third Amendment (which prohibits billeting troops in private homes), or the bits dealing with letters of marque and reprisal. The Second Amendment, in the words of the law professor Lewis Larue, was "not taken seriously by most scholars."

It was going to be hard to make headway on this. What's dead tends to remain so, and so the NRA turned to all manner of strange voodoo to get the job done.

The first step was to reinvent the Second Amendment as the single most important sentence in the entire Bill of Rights. Through *The American Rifleman*, the NRA billed the Second Amendment as "America's first freedom," usurping the place formerly held by freedom of religion. By guaranteeing the people's right to bear arms as a defence against government tyranny, the Second Amendment preserved all other rights; it was the only right that really mattered. The message spread from gun writers to outdoor magazines and to the wide community of gun owners. In turn, the same message repeated itself in letters to the editor and flowed from the mouths of politicians.

But the campaign didn't stop at promoting the Second Amendment's importance; the gun lobby also sought to redefine its meaning. "The right of the people to keep and bear arms shall not be infringed" became the whole of it, the question of militia service forgotten. And since the security of a free state is the security of its people, this right would extend to include keeping guns for self-defence against crime. And this right would also be absolute: "shall not be infringed" would mean exactly that. In the game of American democracy, the Second Amendment would become a "Get Out of Compromise Free" card.

Beginning in the 1980s, the NRA and its allies began putting a scholarly shine on the newly interpreted right to bear arms. Don Kates, a lawyer, wrote several articles for law journals promoting the idea that the Second Amendment was about individual rights. Another lawyer, Stephen Halbrook, published his book *That Every Man be Armed* in 1984, arguing that the founders had intended, well, that every man be armed. Joyce Lee Malcolm, whose 1983 paper in the *Hastings Constitutional Law Quarterly* was followed in 1994 by a book, *To Keep and Bear Arms: The Origins of an Anglo-American Right*, worked from the English common law to promote the view that a right to keep and bear arms already existed and that the founding fathers had simply codified it in the Constitution—which, interestingly, is more or less what David Mills had said in Canada's House of Commons, back in 1885.[88]

Outside the gun lobby, the Second Amendment had long been viewed as essentially irrelevant, an artifact of the militia model that had become obsolete when the United States organized a standing army. It was there to provide a militia for the president to call on to ensure the security of a free state from external and internal threats—in other words, to protect the nascent governments of these United States following the Revolutionary War. The militia model went hand in hand with a sense of civic republicanism, of the duty of the individual to his nation; the libertarianism of its modern proponents would have baffled and angered the founders. The Second Amendment was not, and had never been, a right of insurrection. But the new consensus held that the Second Amendment guaranteed an individual the right to bear arms regardless of militia service. Joyce Lee Malcolm insisted that it derived from England's 1689 Bill of Rights, which recognized a right to possess weapons for individual defence—and which, in the context of the Glorious Revolution of 1688, was surely intended also to defend Englishmen against the Crown. The founders intended ordinary Americans to have the power to defend themselves and even to overthrow their own government, if necessary. Every American had the right to own a gun.

It took twenty-five years, give or take, but as the new Second Amendment consensus gathered momentum, gun activists set their sights on an obvious target: DC's handgun ban. It was the nation's most restrictive gun control law, and since DC was not a state, but a federal conclave, there would be no messy questions of whether the Second Amendment might apply to the individual states. But that challenge would not come from the NRA. The NRA would actually oppose the lawsuit, attempt to derail it, and then attempt to take it over with the aim of letting it die. And for good reason: nothing would cripple the NRA more seriously than coming out on the losing end of a court battle, except perhaps coming out on the winning end, preserving the right

---

88   Joyce Lee Malcolm is Patrick Henry Professor of Constitutional Law and the Second Amendment at the George Mason University School of Law. It seems strange that you could have "constitutional law" as one subject, and "the Second Amendment" as separate subject of equal importance, but I guess that just goes to show how important the Second Amendment really is, right?

to keep and bear arms forever, and losing the sense of crisis it had always relied on for fundraising. But the lawsuit against the DC handgun ban went ahead in spite of the NRA's best efforts to stop it. The NRA had lost its grip on the zombie's leash, and now it was running free, following its own disordered agenda.

DC v. Heller was conceived in November 2002 by Clark Neily, a lawyer at the libertarian Institute for Justice. Neily felt that the time was right: the zombie had already half-eaten the great American brain, libertarianism was surging, and following 9/11, America was again in love with the gun and all it stood for. More importantly, George W. Bush would soon appoint a new Supreme Court justice, and tilt the court to the right. Funding for the lawsuit would come from the Cato Institute, a libertarian think-tank. All the challenge needed was litigants—some ordinary people for Neily's chosen lawyer, Alan Gura, to represent. He didn't want another Jack Miller. His litigants had to be decent, law-abiding people who would properly represent the idea that Americans needed guns to keep themselves safe from crime.

One of the group they collected, and the man whose name would end up on the Supreme Court's decision, was Dick Heller, a security guard at a federal building in DC. But although his name is on the docket, *DC v. Heller* is not about Dick Heller, who was never anything more than a cardboard cutout, the Ordinary Citizen under whose name the Institute for Justice and the Cato Institute set out to reshape American law. The resulting court decision was not about Heller or his co-litigants, or their desire to keep themselves safe; it was about American mythology and the text of the Constitution.[89]

"Undoubtedly some think that the Second Amendment is outmoded in a society where our standing army is the pride of our Nation, where well-trained police forces provide personal security and where gun violence is a serious problem," wrote Justice Antonin Scalia in the decision's majority opinion. "That is perhaps debatable, but what is not debatable is that it is not the role of this Court to pronounce the Second Amendment extinct."[90] And so, on June 26, 2008, the Supreme Court

---

89 As if to underscore the point, at time of writing, the Wikipedia page for "District of Columbia v. Heller" had a photograph of the Cato Institute's Robert Levy standing with Alan Gura, but no photograph of Dick Heller himself, or any of the other plaintiffs whose complaints were ostensibly the subject of deliberations.

90 The proper role of the court is, in fact, debatable, regardless of Scalia's declaration to the contrary.

of the United States ruled in *DC v. Heller* that the Second Amendment to the Constitution of the United States guaranteed an individual the right to possess firearms for self-defence in the home.

At issue was what the words of the Second Amendment actually mean: "a well regulated militia being essential to the security of a free state, the right of the people to keep and bear arms shall not be infringed." To readers with any kind of grammatical sense, this simply says that, given the need for a militia to protect the nation, people have the right to keep and bear arms—whatever "arms" are. But Scalia declared that the first part—"a well regulated militia being essential to the security of a free state"—was simply a "prefatory clause," a kind of ornamental flourish that had little bearing on anything. It wasn't so much that you had the right to own a gun so that you could serve in a militia, or that you had a right to own a gun because the state needed a militia. Rather, with a disingenuous nod to the *Miller* ruling, you had the right to own any kind of weapon as long as that weapon *wasn't inconsistent with* service in a militia. And the militia in question was not an organized militia, regardless of the requirement it be "well regulated"; it simply meant all men of military age.[91] And by "the security of a free state," the founders had also clearly meant the personal security of each and every individual citizen thereof. By this sleight of mind, Scalia neatly disposed of the notion that the Second Amendment was somehow related to formal military service.

He similarly dispensed with the idiomatic meaning of "bear arms," and even with the military connotations of "arms." The word "arms," he insisted with tautological certainty, meant only "weapons to be used in a confrontation"—which potentially places baseball bats, three-inch knives, pepper spray, and brass knuckles under the protection of the Second Amendment, perhaps along with rolled-up newspapers, ballpoint pens, and fabulous pumps with three-inch heels. A weapon is, after all, anything you use in a confrontation.

But extending the Second Amendment to cover all weapons, for everyone, introduced an obvious problem: any form of gun control

---

91   10 U.S. Code § 311 defines the "unorganized militia" as all male citizens (and prospective citizens) between the ages of seventeen and forty-five who are not members of the National Guard or Naval Militia. All this really means is that the government has the right to call these men up to active service. Arguably, the Second Amendment guarantees them the right to be armed for that potential service, but the conflict between "a well regulated militia" and "the unorganized militia," and the fact that no previous militia act has required the unorganized militia to provide its own arms and equipment argues otherwise.

could now be unconstitutional, including a ban on, say, the likes of Timothy McVeigh carrying a machine gun into the Supreme Court itself. So winning over a majority of the court took a bit of conceptual horse-trading, some sense of which is evident in Scalia's written decision. Scalia carefully noted that the Second Amendment was still not "a right to keep and carry any weapon whatsoever in any manner whatsoever and for whatever purpose." The court's decision would not automatically overturn existing bans on carrying concealed weapons, or the long-standing laws against convicted criminals and the mentally ill owning guns. It wouldn't overturn any controls on selling a gun. And it certainly wouldn't allow people to carry a gun into a school, a legislature, or the Supreme Court.

There was another obvious problem: fully automatic weapons are clearly consistent with militia service, which suggested that the National Firearms Act might now be unconstitutional. And the court obviously didn't want to come out and declare that every American had the right to own a machine gun. So Scalia deftly reversed the sense of McReynolds' 1939 decision on Jack Miller. Ignoring McReynolds' cook's tour of militia acts, which explicitly defined which weapons were suitable for militia service, he seized on a single phrase and declared that *Miller* had extended the protection of the Second Amendment to any weapon "in common use at the time."[92] So howitzers, anti-aircraft missiles, and machine guns do not fall under the Second Amendment, although they are clearly consistent with militia service, by dint of the fact that your neighbour is unlikely to own one. That it is the National Firearms Act itself that makes your neighbour unlikely to own a machine gun, he simply ignored, showing an unusual tolerance for circular logic.

The gun lobby was delighted. Scalia had entrenched their entire belief system in the law. Everyone now had the right to own a gun. The door was open to countless future court challenges. Joyce Lee Malcolm's work had been cited several times in Scalia's opinion, and, in a shameless display of academic narcissism, she immediately wrote a paper about what a smart guy Scalia was.[93] The Second Amendment

---

92 *Miller* does no such thing. The reference to weapons "in common use at the time" is made in passing, and in the context of references to several militia acts that defined what weapons were to be used. It is clear that the weapons in common military use were not those in common civilian use, which is why the militia acts included such provisions.

93 I refer to Joyce Lee Malcolm, "The Supreme Court and the Uses of History: *District of Columbia v. Heller*," in *UCLA Law Review,* 56(2009). "In this case all nine justices used an originalist

was terribly ambiguous, she wrote, and "In light of this ambiguity, the justices necessarily employed an originalist approach in order to recapture the intent of the Founders and the understanding of 'the people' whose right it was meant to protect. History is essential to revealing that meaning ... The majority opinion is a model of rigorous historical inquiry, while the dissents fall short."

But to conservative critics of the decision, that same ambiguity called for judicial restraint, and ought to have encouraged the Court to pass the torch back to legislators by letting the law stand. Criticism of the *Heller* decision, from conservatives and liberals alike, was savage. On the conservative side, Sanford Levinson attacked both Scalia's opinion and the dissent as "the worst kind of 'law-office history,'" in which each side engages in shamelessly (and shamefully) selective readings of the historical record in order to support what one strongly suspects are pre-determined positions." From the other corner, William Merkel called the *Heller* decision not "a model of rigorous historical inquiry," but "an act of (self?)-deception or conscious fraud" that requires "misreading, misunderstanding, or ignoring the bulk of relevant evidence" and proceeds from "the faith-based assumption that the framers must have intended to protect a private right to gun possession, and then manipulates outlying evidence to dress up [its] claim in ill-fitting pseudo academic garb."[94] Scalia had written "a decidedly disingenuous and unprincipled opinion" that amounted to little more than "results-oriented historical fiction."

But whatever the complaints against *Heller*, the decision is now a fact. The Supreme Court of the United States was asked the meaning of the Second Amendment and ruled that it protects an individual's right to own a gun for self-defence. For the gun lobby, it was a triumph. They had won their case, and had the right of every law-abiding American to keep and bear arms was now settled law. The zombie the NRA had resurrected, having consumed the great American brain in toto, now stalked the nation's streets, its chin dribbling gore, hungering for more. But this was not entirely the gun lobby's doing: that zombie was midwived by the movement for gun control, and in particular by misguided

approach and tried their hands at historical investigation," Malcom wrote, declaring that this would "gladden the heart of a legal historian." Yet its effect on any number of legal historians' hearts appears to have been somewhat the opposite.

94   Merkel is an associate professor of law at the Charleston School of Law. Among his research interests are the history of the militia and the Second Amendment.

laws like the DC handgun ban. Gun control created the gun lobby and, in Newtonian synchrony, transformed the NRA from an organization that had once opposed "the general promiscuous toting of guns" into a hardline lobby, led by a killer, that celebrated the unlimited right to own guns, and argued for the right to carry them just about anywhere. The hardliners are like the nightmare beasts of science fiction: the harder you fight them, the stronger they get.

The same dynamic operated in Canada, whatever the Canadian gun lobby's disarray. As Jean Chretien's Liberal Government introduced new gun control measures in the mid-1990s, Canadian gun owners looked south, wishing they had a constitutional amendment or two of their own. Having no constitutional right to keep and bear arms, they dug into the same body of scholarship on which America's rejuvenated Second Amendment rested, and invented one, just as if God did not exist, it would be necessary to invent him. But Canada's gun activists never made it to the Supreme Court. They never made it past the Ontario Court of Appeal. It's to that story we will turn next. It begins in Ontario's smallest city, a northwestern Ontario pulp and paper town called Dryden.

Judged By Twelve

Fighting Back Against the Long-Gun Registry

I'd rather be judged by twelve than carried by six.
—Lieutenant Colonel Jeff Cooper

IN 1991, BRUCE AND DONNA MONTAGUE moved their family from the heart of southern Ontario to the small northwestern Ontario town of Dryden, to escape the smog, the traffic, and the workaday grind. Dryden, a town of 6,500 people, lies west of Lake Superior, near the Manitoba border. In the unorganized townships around Dryden there was not only no smog, and no traffic, but furthermore no municipal government: no cheap-jack, small-town businessmen posing as politicians, no petty by-laws enacted because they can, no permits required just to cut down the tree in your front yard. In Dryden, there was freedom.

Bruce bought land in Eton-Rugby Township, outside Dryden, and he and his family began building a log home. This was no rough-hewn log cabin. Bruce, an engineer and a meticulous and careful workman, dug a basement, poured a concrete foundation, and bored a well. He cut a stand of red pine and hauled the trees to his property, where he rigged an ingenious derrick to lift them into position. That derrick would later act as a roof support for the finished two-storey home. The family moved from Dryden into the home's finished basement in 1996, while Bruce continued work on the house itself. A 1998 *Dryden Observer* story on the construction of the Montague home—in a place like Dryden, such things are news—describes his plans to become self-sufficient by installing an electricity-generating windmill. "All this work will take time," the reporter wrote, "but if the old saying, a man's home is his castle, applies to this situation, then Bruce Montague is surely on his way to becoming 'King of the Hill' in Eton-Rugby township."

Two photographs accompany that newspaper story. The first shows Bruce Montague standing beside the home: a slender, bearded man, confident and smiling, his hand resting on an outer wall that has reached shoulder height. The second shows his castle-in-progress, the derrick in place, and three courses of logs laid. In front of the house, at the bottom of the frame, is a small sign. The print on the sign is illegible, but the silhouettes of two revolvers are obvious.

Bruce Montague was a gunsmith.

Now, taking a car in to a mechanic is one thing; any fool can fix a car. But gun owners are picky about gunsmiths. Reaming the fixed chokes of an old full-over-mod Browning Superposed to make the gun a functional, I/C-and-mod upland gun is a tricky job.[95] Screw it up, and the gun won't shoot straight, or it will put the pattern of the top barrel twelve inches above that of the lower barrel. If that was Dad's gun, and worth thousands besides, you wouldn't take it to just anyone. You would take it to a man who knew what he was doing, a man who took pride in his work. You would take it to a guy like Bruce Montague.

Bruce Montague quickly became well known in the local hunting and shooting communities—and the hunting and shooting community, in a place like Dryden, is not small. He was an active target shooter and a qualified IPSC range officer, and had built a five-hundred-metre rifle range on his property, where he organized IPSC matches and long-range rifle competitions.[96] Monty's Gunsmithing was the go-to gunsmith in the

---

95 Shotgun choke is a restriction of the bore at the muzzle, which serves to tighten the spread of pellets and thus increase the effective range of the gun. Older double shotguns are typically choked to full over mod (modified), meaning that the upper barrel has a full choke (a restriction of 0.035 inches) and the lower, modified choke (0.020 inches). Modern shotgun shells have been improved so tight chokes are no longer necessary, and so a more popular configuration in an upland gun is now modified choke in the upper barrel and improved cylinder (a restriction of 0.010 inches) in the lower barrel. Modern shotguns also typically have interchangeable, screw-in choke tubes, allowing the shooter to change the choke of his gun as required, where older guns have fixed chokes.
96 IPSC is the International Practical Shooting Confederation. In IPSC matches, the shooter must move, reload, and fire at cardboard silhouette targets, to finish a course of fire against the clock. The sport grew out of police training.

Kenora district for local hunters and target shooters, for the police departments in Dryden and Kenora, and for the Ontario Provincial Police.

Bruce was also widely respected outside the shooting community. His son's ambitious teacher had staged a school production of *Peter Pan*, and wanted trapezes so that Peter and the children could fly. But to bring in a qualified contractor from Toronto was cost-prohibitive. Bruce stepped in, obtained the necessary training and certifications at his own expense, installed the equipment, and rigged and operated the trapezes. He also led youth groups for the Lutheran church and worked with the community theatre. To his friends and neighbours, Bruce was a man of integrity, valuable in the community. As Judith Hamilton, the teacher who staged *Peter Pan*, put it at the time, "he is worthy of respect, and gets great respect."

Bruce had escaped the rat race and taken his family far from the pollution and traffic of southern Ontario. He was respected and well liked in his community, and he was working at a job he loved. He was building his own self-sufficient home, beyond the reach of petty bureaucrats and their building permits. But Bruce Montague's position as king of his own small hill in Eton-Rugby Township would not last. Almost 1,800 kilometres to the east, in Ottawa, Jean Chretien's government was passing Bill C-68.

AT TEN MINUTES AFTER FIVE ON the afternoon of December 6, 1989, Marc Lépine walked into room C-230.4 at the Université de Montréal's École Polytechnique carrying a Ruger Mini-14 Ranch Rifle, fired a shot into the ceiling, and transformed the politics of Canadian gun control. Lépine's murder of fourteen women for no better reason than that they were women and he was a rank loser horrified the nation and galvanized a determined response. Where in the 1970s no gun lobby existed until one was formed to resist Trudeau's gun-control efforts, there existed in Canada previous to the 1990s no meaningful gun-control lobby. Survivors of the shooting joined together with other activists to form the Coalition for Gun Control, which would eventually become Canada's most powerful gun-control lobby.

To the gun owners who found themselves facing a new, energetic, and expressly feminist anti-gun lobby, the Montreal Massacre was the isolated act of a madman that cynical opportunists were seeking to exploit for political ends. Even men who shared Lépine's knee-jerk anti-feminist complaints were horrified by the shootings; they but were equally horrified by feminist rhetoric that suggested they were Lépine's fellow travellers, secretly nodding that he'd done a good job. Canadian gun owners immediately distanced themselves from Lépine.[97] Marc Lépine, they asserted, has nothing to do with us. To the Canadian gun activist, Lépine was and remains He-Who-Shall-Not-Be-Named: they are resistant to his memory, resistant to the very mention of his name.

Canada's new culture war over guns pitted an organized, urban, progressive, and feminist anti-gun movement against a discordant and disorganized gaggle of reactionary pro-gun groups with a mostly rural constituency. Gun control quickly became a gendered battleground. Gun control was suddenly a women's issue, and men who supported it were unmanly. Pro-gun arguments took a condescending line: women, being "over-emotional," by nature, were overreacting to an isolated event by lashing out at all guns, while any rational, logical (read "male") person could see that gun control was not the answer.

It didn't help that some of the requirements of the new Firearms Act were particularly emasculating. When you applied for a firearms licence, your wife would have to sign your application—a requirement that was supposed to keep guns from being used in domestic violence.[98] To many gun owners, this was disturbingly like getting a permission slip. Instead of facing the reality of guns and domestic violence, Canadian gun owners grumbled about feminists and looked the other way.

Canada's new Firearms Act was the work of Allan Rock, who was elected as member of parliament for Etobicoke-Centre in 1993 and became minister of justice and attorney-general in Jean Chretien's government. Rock came to Ottawa, he said, "with the firm belief that the only people in Canada who should have firearms are police officers and the military." In 1991, Kim Campbell had introduced Bill C-17, which amended the Criminal Code to require a safety course and a background check before a Firearms Acquisition Certificate, or FAC, was issued. But you only needed an FAC to *buy* guns; no licence was needed to own one. Rock was determined to introduce a full licensing system and a universal gun registry.

---

97 In recent years, Canadian gun activists have even insisted on calling Marc Lépine by his Algerian birth name, Gamil Gharbi, which serves the dual aims of demonizing Muslims and disputing whether Lépine was in any way connected to Canadian attitudes.

98 The application includes a phone number people can call if they are afraid not to sign, although this is of questionable utility. In one study, women seemed not to be aware that they could call the Canadian Firearms Centre to report concerns with a licence application, probably because they had not read the fine print.

Rock visited firing ranges and fired guns for the first time in his life, apparently expecting this to lend him credibility among gun owners. He talked to the fragmented collection of interests that formed Canada's gun lobby. He spent so much time consulting gun owners that he was dubbed "Minister of Consultation" within his own party. But if C-68 was the product of months of consultation, it didn't show. Among his bill's most disturbing features was a provision that would allow a police officer to enter and search the home of any registered gun owner, at any time during daylight hours, without warrant. Refusal would give police automatic grounds to return with a search warrant.

The FAC would be replaced by a Possession and Acquisition Licence (PAL).[99] Registration, which was already in place for handguns and other restricted or prohibited firearms, would now cover all firearms, including rifles and shotguns.[100] The goal was to better track guns so they could be kept out of the wrong hands. But the lasting impression given by forcing people to register guns they had owned for years and by threatening to search their homes without warrants was that the government viewed all gun owners as incipient criminals, or worse, that the government was laying the groundwork for the eventual confiscation of every gun in the country. Gun activists were quick to pick up on a quirk of the new law's organization: it was a criminal offence to own a gun, they said, to which holding a licence was a defence.[101] Overnight, they shouted, the law would turn every gun owner into a criminal.

Failing to register a firearm would result in criminal charges, a provision that provoked a long game of chicken between the government and the gun lobby, in which the government continually blinked by extending amnesties. An expired licence, likewise, could lead to a criminal charge—which the gun lobby exploited to fire up opposition, suggesting that forgetting to

---

99   It would also create the POL, or Possession Only Licence, for those existing gun owners who refused to take the firearms safety course; they could continue to own their guns under the POL, but could not buy any more. In 2014, Stephen Harper's government introduced a bill to phase out the POL by allowing POL holders to get PALs without taking the course.

100   For various reasons, what the Criminal Code of Canada calls a "prohibited" firearm is not truly prohibited at all. This is perhaps the most confusing area of Canada's firearms laws. In making a given firearm or class of firearms prohibited, the government may either confiscate them outright or grandfather existing owners. Grandfathered owners of some types of prohibited firearms may continue to own and shoot their guns, and sell them to other grandfathered owners.

101   This view of the law is now deeply entrenched among gun owners, but it isn't really true. It is only an offence to own a gun if you do not have a licence. To say that holding a licence is a defence to the offence of owning a gun is like saying it is illegal to drive a car, but you can get off the charge if you have a driver's licence.

file your paperwork on time would send you to jail without passing Go.[102] And the political rhetoric surrounding the bill did little to calm gun owners' fears. Continual talk of "holding gun owners accountable" supported the impression that, in the government's eyes, gun owners were irresponsible at best. Instead of holding thieves to account for stealing, gun activists declared, police would soon be holding gun owners responsible for being stolen from—no sooner would you report a theft, as the law required, than you would find yourself charged with unsafe storage.[103] Gun owners complained that the registry treated ordinary hunters and farmers as common criminals—a complaint manifested in the assertion by the Canadian Advisory Council on the Status of Women that gun owners ought to be treated like drug addicts, and given no say in the debate.

Nothing in Bill C-68 was good politics, and it was accompanied by any number of equally tone-deaf remarks from Liberal members of Parliament, among them Allan Rock's own admission that he saw no reason for anyone to own a gun. Canadian gun owners quickly imported the familiar argument that registration leads to confiscation, a slogan that had mobilized the NRA to neuter the Gun Control Act. Attempts to reassure Canadian gun owners that confiscation wasn't in the cards fell on stony ground.

When Allan Rock first tabled Bill C-68, Canada had no organized gun lobby to speak of. CASAL had rattled apart under the centrifugal pressure of competing interests, and there was no organization in Canada comparable to the NRA. The National Firearms Association, which had appeared after the demise of FARO, had incompetent leadership and few members. But in response to Rock's bill, new organizations sprang up. Among the first to appear were the Law-Abiding Unregistered Firearms Association (LUFA), whose members swore they would refuse to register their guns, and the Canadian Unlicensed Firearms Owners Association (CUFOA), who vowed to not even get licences. Even these small groups could not agree on a common agenda.

But it was not only Canada's disorganized and fractious gun lobby that objected to Rock's sweeping measures. The Canadian Bar

---

102 Arguably, it could not. This would be a *mens rea* offence—that is, it would require evidence of knowledge or intent—and so forgetting to file your paperwork on time would not automatically put you in jail. But this did not prevent gun activists from winding people up by suggesting it would.

103 Also demonstrably untrue. The requirements of the safe storage regulations did not demand that guns be secure from thieves.

Association had attacked the search provisions as blatantly unconstitutional, a rebuke that surprised and disappointed Rock, himself a lawyer. Representatives of the Canadian Medical Association, which might be expected to support any gun control legislation, criticized the emphasis on guns themselves, suggesting that the bill needed to deal with guns in the context of overall violence. But the greatest blow was that twenty-nine Liberal back-benchers stood up for their rural constituents and opposed the bill. One of them, John O'Reilly, summed up the problem neatly. "People say he didn't consult," said O'Reilly. "Well, he consulted, but he didn't pay any attention."

"We cannot stop governing just because it makes some people angry," Rock retorted, ignoring the fact that in a representative democracy, making enough people angry is a proven way to stop governing. But Rock was not a politician; Rock was a lawyer, and he seemed to believe that the public possessed the impartial reasonableness of a judge. Writing in *Maclean's* magazine in 1995, Anthony Wilson-Smith speculated—correctly, as it turned out—that Rock, who had once been touted as a potential replacement for Jean Chretien, might wreck his political future by alienating both rural Canada and his own party in pushing his pet bill through Parliament. But Rock seemed unconcerned with the politics of the matter. He believed he was right, and he was a man of principle, stubborn to a fault.

NEAR DRYDEN, AN EQUALLY STUBBORN MAN of principle was fitting logs together to build his family's home. Regulation of all kinds was one of the things Bruce Montague had gone north to avoid, and he was particularly leery of gun control. He had grudgingly complied with Trudeau's 1977 gun-control law, and then with Kim Campbell's, but his attitude hardened when one of his guns was prohibited and confiscated without compensation by bureaucratic fiat. Bill C-68 was the final provocation. Like many other Canadian gun owners, Bruce became convinced that the Liberal Party had a hidden agenda. The Liberals would, by creeping regulation, steadily restrict gun ownership in Canada until nobody could own a gun at all. And the long-gun registry, which would tell them who owned guns, and how many, would be the tool they would use to do the job.

Bruce had read Joyce Lee Malcolm and had spoken to like-minded gun owners, and he had convinced himself that Canadians had the right to keep and bear arms. His belief gained a gloss of legitimacy from Ted Morton, a conservative political scientist at the University of Calgary, who published a detailed argument that the Firearms Act was unconstitutional.[104] Section 26 of the Charter of Rights and Freedoms said that just because a right wasn't listed in the Charter didn't mean it wasn't protected by the Charter. And the 1689 Bill of Rights, which Joyce Lee Malcolm had brought to everyone's attention, said you had the right to have arms for your defence. John A. MacDonald himself had cited it, asserting that Canadians had the right to keep and bear arms. So, thanks to Section 26, Trudeau's constitution created a right to arms that could not simply be overruled by an act of Parliament. This meant that Bill C-68 was illegal. The registry was illegal. Licensing was illegal. The Firearms Act was entirely without force—and all Canadian firearms laws were in question.

It was a terminal case of wishful thinking.

In the ongoing game of chicken between government and gun owners, the government's final blink extended the deadline for registration to January 1, 2004. Although many gun owners eventually registered their guns, vocal opponents continued their protests for nine years. Bruce Montague was among them. Bruce made no secret of his views. He joined the Canadian Unlicensed Firearms Owners Association and appeared at their demonstrations around the country. He ostentatiously exchanged guns with other CUFOA members in blatant, unregistered transactions. He became a fixture at gun shows, with a .22-calibre Cooey rifle slung over his shoulder and a sign advertising the gun as unregistered and offering it for sale. Bruce made every effort to get arrested, in the hopes of challenging the law in court, but the state unkindly demurred.

Bruce Montague's protests had become so routine that nobody expected anything to come of them. He still held an FAC, which sufficed as a licence until its expiry. At that point, the law required Bruce to replace it with either a POL or a PAL. He did neither. He allowed his gunsmith's licence, which required annual renewal, to expire in 2002. In November 2003, his FAC followed. In June 2004, Donna Montague's FAC expired too. No one in the Montague home had a licence to own a gun.

Somewhere in Miramichi, New Brunswick, a cold computer took note that Monty's Gunsmithing, in Eton-Rugby Township, Ontario,

---

104   While some of Morton's views regarding the constitutionality of Bill C-68 had merit, others of his arguments were simply bad—and unfortunately, it was upon these arguments that Bruce Montague would rely.

held registrations for eleven handguns, and Bruce Montague held registrations for twenty more, all sans licence.[105] The computer's report went to Ontario's chief firearms officer, in Orillia, who in turn emailed Detective Staff Sergeant Doug Carlson, the area firearms officer for the Kenora District. The machinery of the state creaked into motion like a disused steam hammer, and under the piston of that hammer walked an unsuspecting Bruce Montague.

SEPTEMBER 11, 2004: BRUCE MONTAGUE and his twelve-year-old daughter, Katey, drove to the Dryden Agricultural Society fairgrounds to help their neighbour, Dan Landrie, set up a gun-show booth, where he would be selling military surplus gear. Bruce brought his usual prop, the Cooey rifle with its "For Sale" sign. After helping Landrie set up, Bruce and Katey wandered the aisles of the show. A gun show is rather like a giant garage sale, only with guns. Bruce and Katey took advantage of their early arrival to see what was on offer.

Squat, unmarked cars rolled down Dryden's streets under an overcast sky. Shortly after 8:30, Detective Constable Randy Belluz arrived at the Agricultural Society building with three other OPP officers and a warrant for Bruce's arrest. They hoped to intercept Bruce outside the building and arrest him without making a scene, but although his van was in the parking lot, Bruce was already inside. As Belluz entered the building, Bruce Montague was buying a saddle for his daughter. Many of the vendors were still setting up their tables.

Belluz asked Bruce to step outside, into the parking lot. He was still hoping to make the arrest without creating a public spectacle. Bruce replied that he would buy the saddle first, and put his hand in his pocket, perhaps to get his wallet—not the best course of action during an arrest. Belluz grabbed Bruce by the arm, told him he was under arrest, and called for two other OPP officers to assist him. Katey, in a panic, ran crying to Landrie for help as the police led Bruce out of the building. Landrie was helpless dealing with the hysterical child. "I had part of an Egg McMuffin that we had stopped and got," he would explain in court. "It's not very appropriate but I asked her if she'd have something to eat and sit down and settle down."

105 Although Bruce had refused to register his rifles and shotguns, as required by the new Firearms Act, his handguns were already registered under previous gun-control laws.

But Katey was inconsolable. Landrie himself did not fully understand what had happened until two OPP officers arrived to explain. One of them was Detective Sergeant Wade Meeks, who had led the investigation. The sight of more police officers, no matter their insistence that everything would be okay, did nothing to calm Katey.

It was now just after nine o'clock in the morning, and Donna Montague was at home, making manicotti.

THE LOCAL OPP KNEW DONNA MONTAGUE well. She had worked at the station for several years before taking a job at the Dryden mill, and it was a strange and humiliating experience for her to find herself at the station again, this time on the other side of the law. Donna suffered from essential tremors, a neurological condition that leads to progressively more severe tremors of the hands and head, and was visibly shaking. In the boardroom of the Dryden OPP station, the police asked the Montague children, Michael and Katey, to leave before telling Donna that she, too, was under arrest.

"I was questioned by Mr. Belluz," Donna testified, "asking me if there were booby traps in my home, and I was horrified. This is my home. We're a Christian family. We don't have booby traps." Donna and Bruce had discussed his possible arrest, and they had made plans. They believed they had a right to inspect the warrant before allowing a search, and that they had the right to videotape that search. This was the first of several points of law on which the Montagues had unfortunately been misinformed. Donna could not return home, even to get clothes for the kids. Helpless, she asked an OPP constable to make sure that the ground beef she had put out to thaw was put away, and to feed the family dog.

Just as the ears ring following a gunshot, the mind reels in the upheaval of crisis. There is a sense, in reading the transcripts of the Montague trial, that time stopped for the Montagues on September 11, 2004. Donna, in her court testimony, had difficulty with dates following the search, and Bruce continually referred to the events of 2003 as "last year," although the trial was held in 2007. According to newspaper reports, Bruce stopped eating for three days following his arrest. But he tried to stay positive, telling reporters that he been trying to get arrested for almost two years and was looking forward to his day in court.

The Montagues hired a lawyer named Ed Burlew to represent them. Burlew was born in New Jersey, where his father was active in the NRA, and began hunting and shooting as a pre-teen before his family moved to Canada. Up until 1995, he practiced general criminal law, but after the passage of Bill C-68 he began working almost exclusively on firearms cases. Citing "a need to maintain a high level of credibility," he refused to represent people involved in gang activity or violent crime. Instead, Ed Burlew made his living representing ordinary gun owners who found themselves charged with various offences under the Firearms Act. The Montagues had chosen their lawyer well.

Public opinion was on Bruce's side. As the Montagues told it, the police had abandoned a child in their rush to arrest her father, and had treated a respected member of the community like a violent criminal over a paperwork problem. Ed Hudson of CUFOA used Bruce's standing in the community to further the cause by suggesting that police had ample opportunity to arrest Montague at various protests, but chose instead to arrest him at a gun show in his local community, in front of his daughter, so as to embarrass him and to intimidate other gun owners. "This is nothing but cowardly and blatant intimidation," Hudson told the local newspaper. "A mere anonymous tip concerning suspicion of a firearm in your home, and this could happen to you."

The OPP searched the Montague home, loaded their evidence into boxes, and carried it away. But Miramachi's computer was still not satisfied. The OPP were not finished with Bruce Montague's house.

IT ISN'T CLEAR HOW POLICE BECAME convinced that Bruce had built a secret room in his home, but on September 20, 2004, Burlew told Donna that the OPP were planning to drill holes in the walls and floors to try to find it. There was some suggestion, also, that police had threatened to take the place apart with a bulldozer, although the OPP deny it. In any case, shortly after Burlew spoke to Donna, Bruce revealed that he did, indeed, have a secret room—he called it his "secure vault"—and told police how to get into it.

Bruce's secret room lay behind the wall of the basement bathroom, its door lined with pieces of old conveyor belt so that anyone tapping on the wall would not hear a hollow sound. The door opened by means of a nail inserted into an inconspicuous knothole, which lifted a metal plate to release the latch. It was, like everything else Bruce Montague had built, ingenious. Inside, police found more than 130 guns. There was a loaded AR-15 rifle with a laser and flashlight attached; Bruce had converted it to fully automatic fire, ground off the serial numbers, and fitted it with a suppressor. There was a loaded SIG Sauer P226 pistol in a shoulder holster. There was an Uzi with a drilled-out serial number, which Bruce had also converted to fully automatic fire. There were two loaded revolvers. There was a .22-calibre pistol, also with its serial number removed, which Bruce had fitted with a suppressor. There was a fully functional Sten sub-machine gun. There was a Ruger 10/22 rifle and a Chinese-made AK-47 clone, again without serial numbers, which Bruce had converted to fully automatic fire. There were illegal magazines, holding more than the five rounds permitted by Bill C-68. There were more than twenty-thousand rounds of ammunition. There was a roll of det cord and a jar filled with detonators.[106] There were even several guns, which, according to handgun registry records, Bruce no longer owned. And finally, there were a number of books that raised police eyebrows, including military tactics manuals, books on improvised explosives, and a neat little tome entitled *Anarchy for Fun and Profit*.

Bruce Montague, it seemed, had been living a double life.

In the years following the passage of Bill C-68, Bruce Montague had been up to more than mere protests. First, he had decided to hide his guns: he took guns he feared would soon be prohibited and, after removing their serial numbers so they couldn't be traced, he buried them in a watertight container on Crown land. If Bruce couldn't have them, he'd make damn sure that the government couldn't have them, either. But as a man of principle, he later said, this bothered him. He didn't want to be sneaky. So he dug them up again, brought them home, and began openly defying the law.

Having convinced himself that the Firearms Act was unconstitutional, he also began tinkering. Inside the guts of a gun, the bolt pushes a round into the chamber and then locks closed so that the pressure created by firing won't blow the bolt open again. Among the problems one typically encounters converting a semi-automatic into a full auto is controlling the hammer so that it doesn't fall until the bolt is locked. And meddling with

106 Det cord: detonating cord, a hollow plastic cord filled with explosive, used as a fuse or detonator for high explosives.

the sear—the part of the trigger mechanism that holds the hammer back—can allow the gun to fire without pulling the trigger, or to run away, firing uncontrollably. Converting a semi-automatic rifle into a machine gun is a technical challenge, and Bruce Montague loved a technical challenge.

He started by figuring out how to convert his semi-automatic Uzi to fully automatic fire. The Uzi never worked to his satisfaction, but his other conversions—the AR-15, the Ruger 10/22, and the Chinese AK—were more successful. Jean-Paul Menard of Toronto's Centre of Forensic Sciences, who examined and tested Bruce's guns, testified at trial that even the conversion of the Uzi was among the best he had seen; the Ruger, Menard said, was the best .22 calibre full auto conversion he had ever examined. The AR-15, the Ruger, and the AK-47, Menard said, were as good as guns straight from the factory.

His tinkering didn't stop with full auto conversions. In June 2003, Bruce had been hired to repair a ring blaster at the Dryden pulp mill—essentially the equivalent of a large-bore gun firing an 8-gauge shotgun slug that the mill used to blast lime deposits out of kilns. The gun was misfiring, and its suppressor—what most people would call a silencer—was deteriorating. Working on the ring blaster piqued Bruce's curiosity, and he made three suppressors of his own, and fitted them to his Ruger Mark II .22-calibre pistol, his AR-15, and his Ruger 10/22. While the suppressors on the pistol and the Ruger 10/22 were essentially simple tubes filled with fibrous material—"possibly fiberglass insulation," as the ever-precise Menard suggested—the suppressor on the AR-15 relied on an expansion chamber and a series of internal baffles. It was, Menard testified, "very effective."

In the popular imagination informed by television and movies, screwing a silencer onto the barrel of a pistol eliminates the sound of the gun almost completely, so that instead of a bang, the gun emits only a soft "feep." In reality, as any shooter's hearing damage will attest, guns are mercilessly loud. The muzzle blast is loudest, but the bullet itself makes a bang as it passes through the air at supersonic speed. On a semi-automatic, there's also the sound of the action cycling to eject the spent casing and chamber the next round. Consequently, except in the case of a .22 firing subsonic ammunition, there's no hiding the bang of a gun going off. A sound suppressor, which reduces the muzzle blast, merely tones it down. With the suppressor, Bruce Montague's AR-15 would be no louder than a .22 rifle.

There was also the matter of several handguns, which, according to the registry, Bruce Montague no longer owned, including a World War I Luger brought back by his grandfather as a war souvenir. Worried that these guns might be confiscated following some future bureaucrat's decision, Bruce decided to hide them from the government. He claimed he had sold them to American buyers, filled out the necessary paperwork, but then kept them.

Bruce had set out to get himself charged, but he hadn't bargained on getting in this deep. He now faced some fifty-three criminal charges, the most serious being seven counts of possessing a weapon for a purpose dangerous to the public peace, an offence that carries a maximum penalty of ten-years' imprisonment. Donna faced three charges, of possessing a firearm without a licence and unsafe storage. Many of the charges were essentially indefensible. And Ed Burlew was no longer on the case—because, Bruce explained, "he's very busy."

Bruce Montague's only hope was to win a constitutional challenge and have the Firearms Act struck down, and for that Bruce needed the courts to agree that Canadians had the right to keep and bear arms for their own defence.

"LIKE MY GOOD BUDDY THERE," says Fred, apropos of nothing, it being unclear what his buddy is like, or why we should consider him. The friend of a neighbour of an in-law, Fred is in his seventies, white-haired and stoop-shouldered, with hands gnarled by physical labour. Like many men in their seventies he's not shy to share opinions conditioned heavily by talk radio. He has lived in this small village all his life, and he knows how things work. "My buddy's got about a half a dozen guns all squirrelled away where nobody'll ever find 'em. He looks at this new law and says: No. Way. Brother. Says I'm keepin' my guns, case anything happens to one a my daughters."

He pauses, to take a pull on his beer.

"These laws anymore, there's no sense to 'em."

Fred himself has a gun squirrelled away, a .22 rifle, probably a Cooey. Everyone and his brother at one point had a Cooey. Fred never registered that Cooey and he never got a licence for it, the gun having been stashed in the attic long before Bill C-68 and Fred's FAC having expired ages ago. He doesn't hunt and hasn't shot since the 1970s. He doesn't know the new law and doesn't much care about it, hangs onto the rifle just because it's his. And for just in case. Somewhere around the place he might have a box of .22 Long Rifle ammo for it, mixed in with all his rusting tools.

How many rifles across Canada—just like Fred's—disused and slowly rusting, stashed in attics and garages and closets by men who never use them, are kept just because? No one knows. Many more, kept by people who still hunt and shoot, were never registered. Rural Canada has no shortage of men who don't like new rules, and who don't like being told what to do. Bruce Montague had a natural constituency.

As a gunsmith, Bruce Montague made about $25,000 a year, and his constitutional challenge was expected to cost $300,000 or more, so in 2005, having convinced the courts to relax the original bail conditions that prevented him from travelling outside northwest Ontario, he embarked on a coast-to-coast tour of Canada to sound the alarm over the Firearms Act and drum up support for his cause. He put some spin on the story. Newspaper accounts of his appearances mention charges of possessing unregistered guns, or possessing guns without a licence, but never mention fully automatic weapons, explosives, silencers, or defaced serial numbers. He portrayed himself as the innocent victim of a government obsessed with paperwork, an outlaw to bureaucrats alone, his offences mere paper crimes.

"I have been charged by government as a criminal for refusing to register my firearms," Bruce complained—although in fact, not one of the charges against Bruce or Donna Montague actually related to registration. He regurgitated arguments advanced by Joyce Lee Malcolm and John Lott, claiming that crime had risen in the UK and Australia after those countries banned handguns: we needed guns to keep ourselves safe from criminals, yet our government was set on disarming us.[107] And he repeatedly wrapped himself in the flag, suggesting that he stood for the freedoms Canadian soldiers had fought and died for.

"This has nothing to do with firearms at all," he declared, addressing a crowd on the anniversary of the Dieppe Raid. "It's about one thing—our rights. Our God-given, fundamental human rights that were bought and paid for by the blood of the fallen men and women. Lest we forget. How could we have forgotten so soon?"

107 In fact, crime had not risen in the UK after handguns were banned. The apparent rise in crime was due to changes in the way violent crime was reported.

His campaign also used a website to attack the "draconian" conduct of the OPP and the Crown. Press releases complained that six cops had dragged Bruce from the gun show in front of his bawling daughter, whom the OPP had then abandoned; at trial, the defence would labour without success to demonstrate that Constable Belluz had so much as twisted his arm. Katey, too, got in on the act. Coached by Christopher di Armani, a former editor of the National Firearms Association's member magazine who organized Bruce's public relations campaign and wrote his press releases, she began making a series of YouTube videos called "Katey's Firearms Facts" in which she regurgitated well-worn progun arguments, proclaiming that these things were so obvious that even a teenaged girl could understand them. Why were liberals so dumb?

In April 2006, the Montagues formally filed their challenge under the Charter of Rights and Freedoms. Their argument was twofold. First, they argued that the right to keep weapons for self-defence created in the 1689 Bill of Rights had become Canadian law through the British North America Act, and then a constitutional right by virtue of Section 26 of the Charter of Rights and Freedoms, which warns that existing rights not mentioned in the Charter nevertheless remain rights. Secondly, they argued that the Firearms Act violated the right to security of the person protected by Section 7 of the Charter, because it could prevent Canadians from defending themselves. The right to life was sacrosanct; the right to defend your life was therefore sacrosanct also. And consequently, the right to own a firearm with which to defend your life somehow became inviolable.

These arguments seem to have originated from Ted Morton, who had written a brief for pro-gun groups in Alberta, British Columbia, and Saskatchewan in 2002, in which he identified a dozen or more reasons the Firearms Act was unconstitutional. Morton drew on John Lott's *More Guns, Less Crime* and on Joyce Lee Malcolm's books *Guns and Violence: The English Experience* and *To Keep and Bear Arms* to back up his arguments, which he fleshed out with tenuously related Canadian legal precedents. Although many of his arguments, such as the complaint that gun control violated the right to freedom of expression, were sketchy, they were nonetheless embraced by LUFA and CUFOA. Now those arguments would be put to the test.

The Montagues' new lawyer, Calvin Martin, argued the case before Justice John dePencier Wright of the Ontario Superior Court on March

19, 2007. It was a hopeless challenge: Bruce Montague wanted the courts to throw out laws that, in one case, dated back over a century to a time when the common-law right to arms was still taken very seriously. No court was going to throw it all out and set the clock back to 1892. Justice Wright made the practical problems clear from the beginning. "If we strike down this legislation," he warned, "then tomorrow every thug on the streets of Toronto can go out and get a gun."

"I would submit every thug on the streets of Toronto already has a gun," said Martin. But he would have little opportunity to argue the point. The following day, Montague fired him, delaying the hearing by four months.

Lawyers specializing in firearms law are a rare breed in Canada. You can count them without removing your mittens, and Montague had already gone through two. To replace Calvin Martin, he hired a lawyer with little experience in firearms cases, but no shortage of experience with Charter challenges: Douglas Christie.

Christie enjoyed a reputation as Canada's most hated lawyer. During the 1980s, he had been the attorney of choice for Holocaust deniers and neo-Nazis charged under Canada's hate speech laws, including James Keegstra, the Alberta schoolteacher who was charged for teaching his students that the Holocaust was a fraud, and Terry Long, a one-time leader of the Aryan Nation's Canadian branch. He represented the infamous British historian David Irving at an immigration hearing that would see Irving kicked out of Canada.[108] He defended the Holocaust-denier Ernst Zundel, taking Zundel's case to the Supreme Court, where he ultimately succeeded in having Section 181 of the Criminal Code, the "false news" law, ruled unconstitutional. He also defended accused Nazi war criminal Imre Finta in Canada's only war crimes trial, and he won.

Many believed Christie himself was a neo-Nazi or anti-Semite, a charge he denied. Vandals had painted swastikas on his office windows, windows that he eventually boarded up, after growing tired of sweeping up broken glass at the start of each working day. The Law Society of Upper Canada declined to discipline him, but the society's discipline

---

108 Irving had been deported from Germany after he denounced accounts of mass extermi-nations at Auschwitz as a myth. Canadian authorities denied his entry into Canada on grounds that he was likely to do the same there, but he was permitted to enter Canada and remain for the purpose of appealing the decision.

chair, Harvey Strosberg, was scathing. "He has crossed the line separating counsel from client: he has made common cause with a small, lunatic, anti-Semitic fringe element in our society. We know who Mr. Christie is," wrote Strosberg. "Suffering Mr. Christie's words and opinions is part of the price one pays for upholding and cherishing freedom of speech in a free and democratic society."[109]

But Christie insisted he was doing nothing more than to uphold and cherish freedom of speech; he was a libertarian, and a man of principle.[110] "I believe law is the front line between the growing and insatiable appetite of the state for money, power, and prestige on the one hand and the rights and freedoms of the individual on the other," he wrote, decrying those lawyers who see the practice of law as "essentially a game played by lawyers to see who is the most clever."[111]

Douglas Christie, defender of the indefensible, was now Bruce Montague's lawyer.

In October, Bruce was back in court, with Christie covering familiar ground: the 1689 Bill of Rights, Blackstone's *Commentaries on the Laws of England*, the natural right of self-defence. He submitted, too, a copy of one of Joyce Lee Malcolm's papers on the history of the right to bear arms. Historically, he argued, the law had never controlled the possession of firearms, but only their use or abuse. In early Canada, many politicians believed in a right to bear arms. Indeed, as Justice Wright pointed out, John A. Macdonald had fiercely upheld the common-law right to arms. Macdonald had argued that because of the Fenian threat and the exigencies of living in a wild country, Canadians ought to enjoy a wider right to own firearms than men in England.

"Few people would ever dare, in 1867, say you have no right to keep a gun," Christie declared. "But now, in 2007 it seems ... it's considered passé. Well, I'm here to maintain that these inherent rights cannot be lightly and for transient causes taken away."

---

109   On February 23, 1993, the Law Society of Upper Canada decided not to discipline Christie over his conduct during the Finta and Zundel trials. Strosberg wrote the Society's 37-page decision.

110   Whatever his true principles were, Christie showed enormous tolerance for anti-Semitism, and did not distance himself from anti-Semites outside his legal practice. Among the candidates running in 2001 for the Western Block Party, a political party he organized and led, was Paul Fromm, one of Canada's best known white supremacists. Christie died in 2013.

111   See "Guiding Principles" outlined by Christie on his website: http://www.douglaschristie.com/guiding-principles/

Christie even argued that fear itself justifies the right to go armed. The courts had recently extended the right to security of the person to include a right to *feel* secure, by identifying psychological stress as a threat to that security. Section 7 of the Charter, Christie submitted, "gives us the right to protect our physical integrity and maybe even our psychological integrity ... Am I not entitled to protect myself from psychological fear and physical violence by the possession of a firearm?"

Wright was unimpressed. "If the government opened up the laws with respect to firearms, is it more likely that you would then walk down the street in fear of being shot by a criminal, or fear of being shot by some damn fool who should never be allowed to be near a gun?"

In reply, Christie cited John Lott's claim that right-to-carry laws—laws that require states to issue concealed weapons permits for the asking—had reduced murder, rape, assault, and robbery across the United States. The news that Lott's work had been discredited had yet to penetrate the consciousness of pro-gun pundits.[112] Christie also cited the research of Simon Fraser University professor Gary Mauser in his claim that firearms bans cost more lives than they save—a conclusion that is not actually supported by Mauser's work.[113]

The faces of the actors change, but the play remains the same. Not one of the arguments presented in the Montagues' constitutional challenge was original, save the uniquely Canadian argument revolving around Section 26 of the Charter. The idea that arming the public will stop mass shootings, the claim that banning guns will cost more lives than it saves, the "more guns, less crime" hypothesis, the argument that the police exist only to serve, and not to protect, the argument that the right to be safe and feel safe trumps everything: all these had been

---

112   The Washington-based National Academy of Sciences had, in 2004, exhaustively reviewed the work of Lott and others, and found no credible evidence that right-to-carry laws reduce crime. Given Lott's argument that the great weight of his evidence—thousands of regression analyses—unequivocally and without exception support his claims, that reply ought to have ended the matter. A decade later, it still hasn't. Lott's book, *More Guns, Less Crime* is in its third edition, the jacket copy still proudly proclaiming that no one has yet proven it wrong.

113   Mauser, in his paper "Armed Self-Defence: The Canadian Case," the paper on which Christie relied, speculates that if firearms saved lives in only 5 percent of incidents, assuming the accuracy of his survey data, 3,300 lives would be saved annually. But with no hard data to indicate how many lives were actually saved, Mauser cannot conclude that a firearms ban would cost more lives than it would save, and finally concludes only that "additional firearms legislation may not act to save lives as claimed, but it may actually cost lives by rendering it too difficult to obtain a firearm when one is needed."

around for years, were lifted directly from the playbook of the American gun lobby.

"Even Blackstone noted that at Common Law the right to possess firearms was not an absolute right but an auxiliary right," replied Justice Wright in his reasons for judgment. The common law right to arms had indeed been received into Canadian law, in Wright's view, and Canadians did have the right of self-defence. But the 1689 Bill of Rights specified that the right to keep arms was "as allowed by law," a proviso on which the House of Lords had cautiously insisted, which meant that it had always been subordinate to the authority of Parliament. The Supreme Court of Canada had previously upheld laws allowing for the confiscation of firearms and mandatory firearms bans for those convicted of crimes against the person. Indeed, in the 2005 case *R. v. Wiles*, the Supreme Court had specifically stated that Canadians enjoyed no constitutional right to keep and bear arms, and that firearms ownership was a privilege—although Wright rebuked the Supreme Court for casually dismissing the possibility.

"Now one might quibble with the language used," Wright wrote. "It seems to suggest that the only rights Canadians have are the fundamental rights guaranteed by the Charter. Surely this is not the case. [Section] 26 stands for that. The casual downgrading of a right held dear by many right thinking Canadians to a 'privilege' without any principled analysis of the situation has done much to heat the debate before me. However, as much as I might deplore that wording, the fact still remains that this right is not guaranteed under the Charter and it remains subject to the power of Parliament to regulate it."

The Montagues' challenge was dismissed.

"I've got a funny feeling that things aren't really stacked in my favour," said Bruce, noting that the same judge who had denied his Charter challenge would also preside over his trial. It was a glorious understatement. The Montagues faced fifty-six criminal charges, many of them slam-dunks for the Crown. There was no question that he had possessed firearms without a licence, that he had converted firearms to fully automatic fire, that he had built sound suppressors, that he had violated safe-storage laws, or that he had defaced serial numbers. That Bruce could be acquitted of all charges was inconceivable.

However, Bruce's complaint that Justice Wright or the justice system in general was biased against gun ownership was not true. Indeed, what is striking in the transcripts of the various Montague court proceedings is just how many of the people involved are shooters. Many of the police officers involved in the investigation were recreational shooters, as was the Crown's technical expert, Jean-Paul Menard. Some of the police witnesses had even had their guns fixed by Bruce Montague. Even Justice Wright, himself a shooter, remarked during the constitutional challenge that he had been forced to give up his own suppressor: "It used to be that the onus was upon you to show that you had it for a legitimate purpose, but you could have it ... But then they switched and said 'can't have it' ... And I didn't get any compensation."[114]

Indeed, it was Justice Wright who clarified for the jury one of the more arcane points of firearms lore: the formal definition of shotgun gauge. The gauge of a shotgun is the number of lead balls of the same diameter as the barrel that make up one pound of lead. It takes twenty 20-gauge balls to make a pound of lead, for example, and twelve 12-gauge balls.[115]

The trial, which was scheduled for two weeks, actually took four. With a total of fifty-six charges to deal with and hundreds of exhibits, it was a complex proceeding. The defence, having little recourse to the facts, threw up red herrings. Christie repeatedly suggested that the OPP had stolen money during the second search, an allegation for which there was no evidence.[116] Bruce tried to muddy the waters by suggesting that the rules of the FAC system, under which he was entitled to keep his guns for life without a licence, somehow still applied, and that his gunsmith's licence entitled him to experiment with suppressors and automatic weapons. But all this was to little avail.

The most serious charges, and the most contentious, were seven counts of possessing a weapon for a purpose dangerous to the public peace, a charge that carries a maximum sentence of ten years' imprisonment. Exactly what makes a weapon dangerous to the public peace is tricky. The Criminal Code of Canada does not ban possessing weapons,

114   While Hollywood has firmly implanted in the North American mind the idea that suppressors are the tools of assassins, they are, in fact, required by law on rifles in parts of Europe to reduce noise. Shooters' ears would benefit significantly if the law in Canada were changed to allow suppressors on centre-fire rifles.

115   "I'm surprised you're that educated in it," said Bruce from the witness stand, "but that's exactly what 'gauge' means, yes." Christie then said to his client, "Diplomacy was never your forte, I take it."

116   The fact that this money was never mentioned in Donna Montague's journals or raised as an issue before trial strongly suggests it never existed.

in general, but it does ban possessing a weapon with the intent to use it to commit a crime or otherwise to make trouble. This is a crime of intent. As evidence of Bruce's fell purposes, the Crown pointed to the vast quantity of manuals on improvised explosives, military tactics, and other such topics that he kept stashed in his secret room, not to mention the converted AR-15 and similar weapons, and the existence of the secret room itself. Bruce didn't help his case by repeatedly speculating that guns like his AR-15 would be useful in the event of war or terrorist attack. His fears that the government ultimately intended to confiscate all firearms, and his remark that firearms confiscation was a prelude to genocide, were similarly unhelpful. The Crown argued that Bruce had tired of peaceful protest and was preparing for armed resistance.

"I felt at times, when I'd come into this court and hearing some of Mr. Montague's testimony, like Alice in Wonderland," said Peter Keen, the Crown attorney, addressing the jury. "I don't know if you know the story, but Alice gets stuck down a rabbit hole and people doing all these crazy and bizarre things around her and acting like it's completely normal, and I felt like that when I was listening to Mr. Montague testify. I want to suggest a reality check to you here, ladies and gentlemen. It's not normal to be building secret rooms. It's not normal to be building fully automatic weapons and hiding them in a secret room. It's not normal to be going and filing serial numbers off guns and burying them in the bush because you're worried somebody might dig them up from the middle of the bush and track them back to you. That mindset suggests that Mr. Montague has some fairly disturbed views of reality."

Christie responded that Bruce Montague was a curious man, who simply wanted to know how things worked, that his illegal firearms tinkering was motivated by the technical challenge and not by any intent to actually use an assault rifle against anyone. He bought and sold box lots of books and manuals through gun shows, and had never read much of the material that alarmed the police. Regardless of whether he had taken the jury down the rabbit hole with his testimony, it was inconceivable that a man like Bruce, who had given up hundreds of hours of volunteer labour to help the school put on an appropriately spectacular *Peter Pan*, who helped stage productions for his church and the community theatre, who led church groups and helped his neighbours, could intend any ill towards his own community. Bruce Montague was not an insurgent. He was a decent man whose views were at odds with the times, and who had allowed what he most wanted to believe to betray him.

The jury took less than a day to decide fifty-six criminal charges. Donna shook as the jury found Bruce Montague guilty on twenty-six counts, but not guilty of possessing a weapon for a dangerous purpose. He received eighteen months in prison, ninety days of it to be served in the community, followed by one year's probation. Donna was convicted of one count, possession of a firearm without a licence, and was sentenced to six months' probation.

Bruce Montague took his case to the Ontario Court of Appeal, but received no satisfaction. The appeal court was, if anything, even less receptive to his arguments than Justice Wright, suggesting that the clauses of the 1689 Bill of Rights cannot be imported into the constitution except by specific reference, and that the right to arms created in 1689 did not exist in Canada—a view that Sir John A. Macdonald would surely have disputed. But even if Sir John A. were right, the court said, "The impugned firearms legislation does not prohibit the right to possess and use firearms for self-defence—in the home or elsewhere. Rather, it simply regulates the circumstances under which such possession and use are permissible.

"Finally, we note that the trial judge considered in detail the Montagues' constitutional challenge … His reasons in support of his ruling dismissing that challenge are thoughtful and comprehensive. He essentially held that there is no protected constitutional right in Canada to possess or use firearms. We agree with this conclusion and see no basis on which to interfere with his ruling."

The court's final words left little hope for further appeal. On September 16, 2010, just over six years after the whole mess started, the Supreme Court of Canada dismissed the Montagues' application for leave to appeal. Their case would not be heard.

Try as he might, Doug Christie could not move the right to arms out of the common law and into the constitution. And the simple reason was that no matter how badly Bruce Montague and his fellow travellers wanted to see it there, it never existed. Indeed, if anything in the Montague case lay down the rabbit hole in a secret room where normal people don't go, it was this idea: that a musty old English law pulled out of a book by an American historian could somehow create a constitutional right to keep and bear arms in Canada, the existence of which no one had hitherto suspected.

The case of Bruce Montague is of little legal significance. His appeal never reached the Supreme Court, and no important precedent was set. Neither was it historically important. The radical fringe of Canadian gun culture did not take it as a correction to their ideas; instead, they have taken it as evidence that a court system full of Liberal appointees has simply ignored the law of the land. Ted Morton's arguments continue to be passed around as if the courts had not dismissed them out of hand. But Montague's story does tell us how completely the ideas of America's gun lobby have been imported into Canada. All of Bruce Montague's arguments originated in the United States—even the argument surrounding Section 26 of the Charter, which relied on a book by American Joyce Lee Malcolm.

If you don't like your reality, you can always import a new mythology.

A Woman's Right
Gun Culture's Appropriation of Feminism

At core, men are afraid women will laugh at them, while at core, women are afraid that men will kill them.

—Gavin de Becker

As BRUCE MONTAGUE'S CONSTITUTIONAL hearing approached, his public relations campaign took to YouTube with a series of short videos in which Katey touted the need for women—and in particular, young, attractive women—to carry handguns for self-defence. The videos, about thirty seconds in length, were crafted as advertisements, each ending with the message, "self-defence is every woman's right," before plugging Bruce's "court challenge for liberty and rights." That Bruce's case had absolutely nothing to do with the rights of women didn't much matter. What was needed was a message that would strike directly against the feminist tenor of Bill C-68, and convince gun owners to open their wallets in support of Bruce Montague's defence. And who better to deliver that message than Katey?

Following Marc Lépine's murder of fourteen women at the École Polytechnique in Montreal, a newly energized gun control movement was quick to suggest that Lépine's rampage was simply an extension of the everyday experience of women, a continuation of policy by other means. Katey Montague's videos responded directly with a doomed frontal attack on the moral high ground. But the gurgling idiocy of the videos had little appeal beyond their existing constituency of white, middle-aged male gun owners. These were videos for men, not videos for women. In a feminist age, the only thing the pro-gun movement likes better than guns is women with guns—provided those women cooperatively play their assigned roles.

"Being an independent woman means it is my duty to have the means and the training to fend for myself," says Katey in one video, brandishing a handgun. "Learn to use the tools that can save your life." Strong women own guns, she insists; bimbos don't. And conversely, women who don't own guns are bimbos. Oh, you may *think* you're a strong, independent woman, young lady, but you lack the means and the training to fend for yourself. The independent woman has a duty to arm herself, presumably so as not to burden the rest of us by having foolish horse accidents or getting tied to the railroad tracks, thus necessitating the usual masculine rescue. The big, bad world is full of lurking predators who wait for those feckless girls who venture beyond our protection. In a longer video, we watch as a rapist in a balaclava ambushes a young woman, who desperately attempts to dial 911 on her cell phone before he drags her out of the frame. Then we see the alternate ending: the young woman pulls out a handgun and her would-be attacker flees. "Your daughter," suggests a subtitle. "Which option?"

Gun activists have responded to changing times by becoming feminists, of a sort—the sort who detect no paradox in juxtaposing the idea that guns are the resort of a strong, independent woman with the blatantly patriarchal suggestion that a strong, independent woman's father ought to decide that his daughter should carry a gun. This is a special form of feminism, in which men are still in charge, and strong, independent women stand up for the things men like, such as guns.

South of the border, the NRA plugs its "Refuse to Be a Victim" program—which trains women to carry concealed handguns—by telling tales of women raped on university campuses where guns are banned. If only women could carry guns on campus, they'd be safe! The Internet produces an endless stream of photos of attractive young women with guns, with slogans like "This is my rape whistle. Because I shouldn't have to blow anything for a rapist," and "My arm strength may be lacking but bearing arms makes up for that." (This may have seemed witty to its author at the time.) One features a city map, with one arrow pointing to "Your Daughter" and another, just around the corner and up the street, to a "Crack Addict Rapist with AIDS." The self-defence message is pitched also at the soccer mom: a woman with an AR-15 and a holstered handgun advises us that although 11,500 soldiers and 4,000 cops will be assigned to protect President Obama's inauguration, no one is assigned to protect her family—except her. It's all very inspiring, but of course none of this has anything to do with women. It seeks instead to justify laws that allow men to carry guns, because it's men who want to.

None of this actually appeals to women's fears; it appeals instead to men's. What will happen to your daughter when she steps out from under your protection? What will happen to your wife when you're not around to protect her? The world is a threatening place, but the threat is always out there in the dark, beyond the family circle. The threat is the Crack Addict Rapist With AIDS hiding in some alley. But what women fears is more pragmatic. They know where the true threats lie.

The true threat to women's safety is not in the park, where imaginary balaclava-clad rapists lurk; it's in the home, and it calls you "Honey." In 2010, the police-reported sexual assault rate in Canada was sixty-four per 100,000 population, with about three-quarters of assaults committed by family members or people known to the victim.[117] The family violence rate—which accounts for all violent crime, including sexual assaults, committed within the family—was 363 per 100,000, and accounted for one-quarter of all violent crime reported to police. As much as one-eighth of all police-reported violent crime in Canada is spousal assault.[118] And this is to say nothing of the spousal assaults that go unreported. Neither do rapists typically lurk in parks or alleyways. The Paul Bernardos of this world are the exception. Your rapist will be someone you know and trust.

But domestic violence remains invisible to the self-defence culture, particularly in Canada, where gun control's explicitly feminist rhetoric has spawned wilful blindness among those gun owners who have come to view feminism as their greatest enemy. And the gun culture is built

---

117 Sexual assault and domestic violence statistics are a tricky area, because both categories are stigmatized crimes, which victims are often reluctant to report. Police-reported crime significantly undercounts both. Attempts to measure the reporting rate using victimization surveys are confounded by the same victim reluctance to report the crime, so it is difficult even to say what proportion of crime goes unreported. With that in mind, depending on the estimate, from 80 to 90 percent of sexual assaults are not reported to police, and perhaps 72 percent of domestic violence is unreported. According to a 2004 estimate, as many as 7 percent of Canadian women had been the victims of spousal assault in the previous five years.

118 In 2007, 12 percent of police-related crime was spousal assault according to Statistics Canada.

entirely on masculine archetypes. The frontiersman is the frontier's man; the soft domesticity he longs for cannot contain his masculine nature and finds its archetype in a civilized woman. He westers to escape not only the decadence of modern civilization but also the pull of domestic life, just as Calvin in Bill Watterson's *Calvin and Hobbes* resists Susie's intrusions into his club, GROSS (Get Rid of Slimy Girls). Nothing is as debilitating to manly vigour as a table set for tea. And even when the table is set for tea, the gun culture insists that the domesticated man's role is to provide for and protect his family, with his rifle hanging over the doorway. The threat is always outside.

Battered women simply do not exist in such a worldview, even with the lamentably recent recognition that beating your wife is a crime rather than a family matter, which accounts for the clumsy and contradictory way gun culture has absorbed feminism. Your daughter is a strong, independent young woman, which is why you must decide for her that she needs to carry a gun to protect her from the dangers that lurk outside the home that you protect. She is a strong woman, and a strong woman has a duty to learn to use the tools that can save her life, because no one else will be around to save it for her; women are weak, delicate creatures who cannot function independently without some kind of help. Even as they take up arms, women must play their feminine roles. In short, you better carry a gun, honey, because you're the weaker sex.

ON THE MORNING OF MARCH 8, 2010, Ontario Provincial Police Constable Vu Pham passed a white Dodge pickup truck on a back road near the town of Seaforth, in Huron County, and turned around to pull it over. Pham was searching for Fred Preston. Earlier that day, Preston had gone to his sister-in-law's house with a rifle. He called his daughters, and threatened to kill his sister-in-law unless they told him where he could find his wife, Barb, who had fled to a women's shelter. Naturally, his daughters called the police. As Pham switched on his emergency lights, the white Dodge pickup pulled to the side of the road, and Preston got out.

Constable Del Mercey arrived just in time to see Preston open his rear door and reach for his rifle. Preston's first bullet struck Pham's sidearm and disintegrated, shedding a fragment that hit Pham in the forehead and killed him. Preston then turned his attention to Mercey, who bailed out of his truck into the ditch, where he used the tires of his SUV as concealment, continually shifting his position so that Preston would have to change his aim. Mercey fired nineteen rounds at Preston, hitting him six times before finally incapacitating him. Preston died three days later, in hospital.

Commenting on the coroner's inquest into the shooting, OPP Deputy Commissioner Chris Lewis said that he doubted the inquest would lead to recommendations that might prevent such a shooting from occurring in future. Everything that could have been done had been done, but events were too unpredictable to foresee. And it would be easy to agree with Lewis, were it not for the facts that Preston had a thirty-year history of domestic violence, that his wife had recently left him, and that he had previously threatened to kill her sister unless she returned. Neither Pham nor Mercey, nor the dispatcher who sent them to find Preston, were aware of these facts, but in their cold light it is hard to agree that the events leading to the deaths of Vu Pham and Fred Preston were anything but sadly predictable.

Preston had first lashed out at Barb thirty years earlier, when he told her to shoo the cat off the table and she told him to do it himself. Instead of shooing the cat, he grabbed her and choked her. In 2009, when she finally announced she was leaving him, Fred threatened to kill her, and then to kill himself. For twenty years, Barb Preston had been having an affair with one of Fred's best friends, an affair she finally admitted in the hopes that Fred would understand their marriage was over and go his own way. But Fred discovered, to his shame and anger, that he was the last person in the village of Sundridge, Ontario (population 985), to know the truth.

On March 3, Fred broke down Barb's door, found where she was hiding, and throttled her while delivering a three-pronged ultimatum: either he would kill her and then kill himself, or he would torture and kill someone she loved, or she could come back to him. Her choice. Naturally, Barb agreed to return, but as soon as Fred left, she took a taxi to a women's shelter in North Bay. For days, Fred went from one daughter to the next, demanding to know where Barb was hiding, but getting no answers. Everyone feared what he might do next, yet nobody called the police. One daughter told the inquest that she was in denial, another that she felt sure the family could handle it themselves. Although two of Fred Preston's family members had been trained to counsel victims of domestic violence, they simply expected things to work themselves out.

But eventually Fred took a rifle and drove south to find his sister-in-law.

The risk factors for domestic homicide are no mystery, and Fred Preston was a four-alarm fire. He had a history of domestic violence and a controlling personality. Barb was afraid of him. He had made death and suicide threats. He had access to firearms. And the incident that tips years or even decades of abuse into murder is usually the victim's attempt to leave. These were the circumstances that OPP Deputy Commissioner Chris Lewis called too unpredictable to foresee.

We never think it can happen to us. Domestic violence rarely tips over into murder, and the tiny numbers of domestic shootings comfort us into thinking that things will work out, that a murder is always somebody else's problem.[119] They lull us into believing that all those duck guns and deer rifles really are as harmless as the Canadian Shooting Sports Association insists. They have convinced many gun owners that all this domestic violence the Coalition for Gun Control keeps going on about is really just made up, a tiny problem inflated into a crisis by gun-hating antis who just want to register guns so they can take them away. Ask anyone: most of those domestic violence complaints are just some bitch trying to get back at her ex, right? The instructor of my firearms safety course suggested to us that the most important thing to remember is not to get in fights with your wife—and that if anything happens, if you have a spat or a breakup or anything that might cause problems—you should give all your guns to a buddy so that the cops can't confiscate them, and then get them back when it all blows over.[120] And of course your buddy will cooperate, because the flip side of "it can't happen to me" is "my buddy would never be that guy." It's always somebody else.

---

119   In a 2010 review of domestic homicide, the Office of the Chief Coroner for Ontario counted just twenty-four domestic homicides in a province with a population of about twelve million people. Only six of those homicides were shootings.

120   This is nonsense, of course. If I give you my gun, I remain in possession of it and as such must be licensed to possess it, even if it is not in my home or under my control. My intent to have control of it and my ownership establish possession in the eyes of the law. If the cops have a prohibition order and your buddy is keeping your guns, he's aiding and abetting your criminal offence: possession of a firearm without a licence. This is why you should never take legal advice from a firearms safety instructor.

And as for those real cases of abuse, those things that can't happen to you or to anyone you know? Well, wouldn't those women be a lot safer if they owned guns? The guy wouldn't mess with her if she had a gun—not twice, anyway. And so we see, in the United States, laws that protect abused women by guaranteeing them concealed-carry permits, laws made by people who fail to grasp that a handgun is probably the last thing a woman fleeing to a shelter can afford with her limited funds. The gun lobby fully backs these laws, even as it resists attempts to take away guns from men accused of battering their wives unless they're actually convicted of felony assault. The solution is not to take guns away from abusive men; it's to give them to abused women.

But one other detail deserves mention, before we move on, another case of the real world raising its hand with a polite cough: one of the reasons Fred Preston's actions were "too unpredictable to foresee" was that all of his guns were accounted for, securely locked up at home in his safe. The rifle that killed Constable Vu Pham belonged to Barb.

APPARENTLY, WOMEN OWN A LOT OF GUNS. Indeed, the media tell us that American women are buying guns like crazy. According to a February 2013 story in the *Christian Science Monitor*, 15 percent of American women own guns, up from 12 percent in 2007. Anecdotal evidence from various sources backs up the claim, in article after article. Range operators, gun shop owners, and self-defence instructors continually tell us they're seeing more women with guns than ever before. "The argument that women need guns for personal safety and home defense resonates with many women," the *Christian Science Monitor* insisted, which may well be true, depending on how you define "many"; it's said the Saxons, too witless to consider their thumbs, counted any number above four as "many." In winter, bemittened Canada struggles to count as high as six, and then only by including her feet. How many women is many?

NBC picked up the story and reported two days later on the evening news that women were suddenly buying guns not like crazy, but like even-crazier: according to Gallup only 13 percent of women owned guns in 2005, but by 2011, that number had grown to a remarkable 23 percent. For some reason, NBC had waited until 2013 to report a poll published two years before. Had they compared the 2011 Gallup numbers to other, more recent polls, they might have concluded that women were in fact *selling* guns like crazy, ownership having declined from 23 to just 12 percent between 2011 and 2013.[121] Why the selective reporting? Several explanations present themselves, but let's go with the obvious. You should never let mere facts stand in the way of a good story. And women with guns is always a good story.

It has ever been so. In 1998, *More Guns, Less Crime* informed us that one-in-four American women owned a gun, about half the number of male gun owners, and that women were buying guns like crazy, based on exit poll data. From the early 1980s on, American newspapers have repeatedly asserted that women are buying guns like crazy. In the late 1980s, the gunmaker Smith & Wesson commissioned Gallup to poll American gun owners, and reported that women were buying guns like crazy: the number of women owning guns had grown 53 percent between 1983 and 1986, making women the fastest-growing group of gun owners. Furthermore, lots of women planned to buy even more guns. Women have always been buying guns like crazy. But that's women: they just love to shop.

"It is a truth universally acknowledged that a single woman in possession of a trailer has a gun," quipped Thomas McGuane in his 2010 novel, *Driving on the Rim*. And this is the story the news media push: the women who buy guns are single, live alone, and buy their guns for self-defence—although the media cautiously avoid suggesting that gun ownership relates in any way to trailer park habitation. But the General Social Survey tells a different tale entirely.

The General Social Survey is a periodic sociological survey of Americans, run since 1972 by the National Opinion Research Center (NORC) at the University of Chicago. Among the many trends the survey tracks is gun ownership. Tom Smith, a senior fellow at NORC, has long disputed the story that women are buying guns for self-defence. Comparing the General Social Survey with Smith & Wesson's claim, he found no significant changes in gun ownership among either men or women in the 1980s. And the women who did own guns often owned long guns for hunting or target shooting, not handguns for self-defence. They were more likely to be married and to live in small cities or rural

---

121 Based on Pew Research Center's polling. Many observers have suggested the 2011 Gallup number is an outlier, and in 2013 Gallup estimated women's gun ownership at 15 percent, based on an aggregate of previous polls, rather than relying on the 2011 poll.

areas. Most started shooting because their husbands were shooters. In spite of what Smith & Wesson and the media kept telling us, they were not single women living in the urban jungle.

So where are all these women we keep hearing about, the ones who buy guns like crazy and take concealed handgun courses? If history is hard to know, the present is equally murky, and hired bullshit equally prevalent. Look at who pushes the story that more and more women are buying guns for self-defence—Smith & Wesson, for example, and the NRA—and you'll find yourself a vested interest. Look who feeds the media all that anecdotal evidence: gun shop owners, range owners, self-defence instructors offering special classes for women only. Again and again, the American media takes dictation from a man with a marketing plan.

In fact, there is no clear evidence that women are buying guns like crazy. Gallup routinely polls Americans on whether they own guns, among other things, and the results fluctuate up and down by about 5 percent. The *Christian Science Monitor* had wrapped an entire article around a supposed trend that was probably nothing more than statistical noise. And the 2011 Gallup poll, which NBC had used to make their story more compelling, appears to be an outlier. It found an apparent jump in gun ownership among women and Democrats, which disappeared in more recent polls.

One thing does seem clear: the overall number of gun owners is shrinking. Since the early 1990s, the percentage of Americans who own guns has steadily declined, even as the civilian gun stock has steadily grown. There are a lot of guns out there to go around. And guns are durable, much more durable than cars or other consumer goods. On any trip to the range you may well see guns fifty years old or more. The market is flooded with used guns.

Even as they post record sales, American gunmakers fret about hard times being right around the corner. If Americans stopped buying guns—if they decided they had enough guns, which they surely do, or if a generation of young Americans lost interest—the market for new guns would swiftly collapse. This prospect is the stuff of nightmares that jolt the CEOs of America's firearms industry from their sleep. There, there, coos the blubbering executive's wife, as she rubs his heaving shoulders and hands him a cup of warm milk: I'll always love your guns. In the darkness above our executive's head, a light bulb snaps on: Women are the answer. Perhaps ... pink handgrips?

There is no shortage of pink handgrips on the market, nor of pink rifle stocks and pink camouflage. Women hunters are expected to wear form-fitting camo outfits with pink trim while their husbands and boyfriends slouch along in shapeless old jackets. The female hosts of TV hunting shows are universally blonde and ponytailed, and never appear without perfect makeup. The marketing tells us that women who shoot are expected to be perky and cute while doing it. And apparently a lot of them want to be, which suggests that the General Social Survey is right about women and guns, and that most women with guns own their guns because well-meaning husbands and boyfriends bought them as gifts, that shooting is something they do together with their partners. The supposedly booming women's gun market seems to revolve, as usual, around men.

That the various popular ideas about women with guns exist chiefly in the minds of men with guns is never more obvious than in a brief dive into *Guns & Ammo* magazine. The image of the armed soccer mom, so beloved of gun bloggers, does not appear here. Neither does our young, single woman, armed against rapists and home invaders. When women appear in the pages of *Guns & Ammo*, they're in ads, where they clutch AK-47s while wearing bikinis, or cast seductive eyes at the reader with compact pistols concealed in their exposed stockings. A bikini would be impractical shooting wear, I think, although I hasten to add that I have never shot in one and therefore am not qualified to judge. Neither am I inclined to research the matter. In any case, these ads do not seem to be pitched at soccer moms or young women off at college. They are aimed at the man whose peculiarly limited awareness somehow fails to register that the bikini-clad, AK-47-toting chick was thinking, "The next time my agent calls with a cheeseball job like this I'm gonna tell him to get stuffed," at approximately the instant the shutter released. As usual, this idea of women with guns is pitched entirely to men. It's just that this time the bikinis make it obvious.

And this, of course, is why women who host TV hunting shows have blonde, ponytailed hair, perfect makeup, and form-fitting camo with pink trim. The ideal of a woman with a gun is not threateningly feminist, but traditionally feminine: she needs help from masculine "experts," wears lipstick in a duck blind, and is easy on the eyes. She accepts that men know best, and she doesn't try to figure out anything for herself. This woman is a walking, talking validation of the masculinity of the gun culture, a reply to all that female skepticism directed at men and their guns, who are otherwise at best goofy, and at worst downright frightening. And so the gun culture claps its hands, absorbs the idea of women with guns, and declares that it is now feminist. It thinks women should be encouraged to do everything men do.

That new-found feminism is suddenly forgotten, however, when gun activists confront women who don't like guns, and whose idea of doing everything men do includes involving themselves in politics and expressing their views. When Canada's Coalition for Gun Control made gun control an explicitly feminist issue in the 1990s, things got downright nasty. The same has happened in the United States in the wake of the Sandy Hook massacre, which spawned Moms Demand Action for Gun Sense in America. The moms in question have been stalked, threatened with rape, and in one memorable case, spat on. In November 2013, as Moms Demand Action and Open Carry Texas engaged in a round of protest and counter-protest, a group of open-carry activists used a topless female mannequin, its arms raised in surrender and its pants around its ankles, as a target for a "mad minute," a minute-long rapid-fire practice that left the mannequin riddled with bullets. C.J. Grisham, the founder of Open Carry Texas, once called Moms Demand Action "thugs with jugs," although he later said the expression was "in jest," as if this somehow excused it. One widely circulated photo showed Watts photoshopped to look like a zombie with a machete stuck in her skull. Another depicted a woman in a short, tight skirt—clearly a prostitute—leaning against a lamp post with the MDA logo and the slogan, "We're back!" Men slapping women, men spanking women, men putting women in their place: this is the persistent theme in the mildest of supposed gags targeting Moms Demand Action.

How have we created a culture so defective that people respond to any perceived threat to their guns with insults, threats, and even with violence? For "defective" is certainly the appropriate word. Something here is operating well outside its specified parameters, if it is operating at all. These are not functioning adults. I'm tempted to write that if this keeps up, somebody is going to get killed, but in fact somebody already has been. It's well past time that gun owners who are functioning adults—and there are many of us—stood up to say, "You do not speak for me," but somehow, that never seems to happen. I know where the gun culture comes from. I have met the True Man and I know the secret history of the Second Amendment. But what I want to know is, what are these goddamn animals? It's time to turn from history to taxonomy. It's time to face the enemy.

PART II

A BESTIARY
Being an Incomplete Taxonomy of Gun Owners

Fudds

The Redneckization of the North-American Hunter

In the woods you suddenly become the chief law-giver to yourself.

—David Adams Richards

JUST NORTH OF CALGARY ON HIGHWAY 2 you'll find Crossiron Mills, a sprawling shopping mall surrounded by a vast parking lot and not much else. And at the southernmost end of Crossiron Mills you'll find the northernmost outpost of Bass Pro Shops Outdoor World. Bass Pro Shops is one of the anchor stores of Crossiron Mills, a colourful, fluo-rescent-lit retail paradise divided into "neighbourhoods" and apparently laid out to prevent the unfortunate shopper from ever again locating his automobile, dooming him instead to forever wander the mall's antiseptic halls like a ghost ship with glowing credit cards for sails. Externally, Crossiron Mills is a jumble of long, low, undistinguished boxes, but Bass Pro is built to look like an Alaskan fishing lodge—or at least, what an Alaskan fishing lodge would look like if it had 130,000 square feet of retail floor space and had been grafted onto the end of a shopping mall on the shore of a lake covered with asphalt and teeming with huge, shining, metallic fish.

Hunters imagine themselves heir to a tradition of calm, older men who hand down their well-worn rifles and shotguns from one generation to the next and hone their age-burnished knives on Arkansas stones hollowed by use. But hunting is big business, a business that sells bright, shiny new guns and electric knife sharpeners and just about anything else you could ever conceivably want. What's most surprising about Bass Pro Shops is not the sheer number and variety of products aimed at today's outdoorsman (and woman), but those few items that have nothing whatsoever do to with the outdoors. A tin sign, for example, bearing the image of a Colt 1911 pistol and a warning: We Don't Dial 911. All the usual nonsense, just as in the range shack where I can reliably expect complaints that the Liberal Party is a crime organization. Do we all buy our belief systems at Costco, in some kind of family pack? This has to go with that? I don't actually like all the things in this bottomless grab bag, but I get to pay for them anyway. Perhaps if I dig to the bottom, I'll find the Wellspring of Crazy. Or at least a clue.

So here I am, at the shores of this concrete lake: a man with a mission. Behind its huge, faux-rustic doors, Bass Pro brings Alaskan lodge decor to big-box retail. This isn't just Bass Pro Shops, a retail outlet; it is Bass Pro Shops *Outdoor World*, a kind of retail theme park filled with the deferred adventure of new fly rods, upland shooting vests, and hunting boots. A replica of a de Havilland DHC-2 Beaver, with a canoe strapped to one float, hangs from the ceiling. The antlers of what were surely hundreds of deer decorate the walls. In the hunting department, you will find stuffed ducks, grouse, pheasants, and deer. Moving from Outdoor World into the bright light of Crossiron Mills, you pass two bull moose engaged in a permanent taxidermized dominance struggle. The gun over the mantle symbolizes possibility; the float plane hanging over Bass Pro's wandering shoppers stands for a dream of outdoor adventure on the northern frontier, a dream packaged and sold by an industry that began selling The Wilderness Experience™ even before Buffalo Bill Cody invented the Wild West.

But beyond dreams, Bass Pro also sells identity. The clothes make the man, as Elmer Fudd discovers when a truck carrying hats spills its load in an old Looney Tunes cartoon: each hat that finds its way onto Elmer's head, replacing the hunting cap in which he pursues Bugs Bunny, completely changes his personality. So the hunter, sucked into the commercial vortex of that outdoor dream, dons his camouflage and becomes himself. He sticks a Browning Buckmark logo—the outline of a deer's head and antlers, stylized into the letter B, a trademark of the gunmaker Browning—in the back window of his truck. He wears a Winchester or Federal ammunition ball cap. If he's really far gone, he decorates his home with camouflage bedspread, camouflage curtains, camouflage wallpaper. In the most extreme cases, his wife logs onto cabelas.com and orders up a camouflage teddy with matching panties, which in the end plays hell with his sex life because she blends right into her surroundings—which of course may have been her plan all along.

And he calls himself a redneck, even if he's actually a dentist from Montreal. Call it redneckization: the process by which people glom onto a good-old-boy identity, packaged and sold at retail, in reaction against the cosmopolitan, intellectual progressive who increasingly looks on hunting as uncouth and cruel. Redneckization is not simply a matter of adopting an identity; it's a gleeful embrace of redneck stereotypes by the people to whom those stereotypes are (however inaccurately) applied, a raised middle finger to the supposed elites who apply it. Our redneck need not even be a hunter. Thanks in part to the success of the reality show *Duck Dynasty*'s success at marketing some stereotypical "redneck" lifestyle there's no shortage of men who wear ball caps indoors, who don camouflage jackets to go grocery shopping, and who stick Buckmark logos in the back windows of their trucks, even if they own no guns and have never held a hunting licence. They just want to get in on that redneck cachet.

Bass Pro has become a destination in itself, a kind of tourist draw. Come and see the redneck nation, the redneck mecca! At the grand opening of the Bass Pro Outpost in Niagara-on-the-Lake, Ontario—an "Outpost" being smaller, as you might expect, than an entire Outdoor World—I navigate aisles clogged with tire-kickers and tourists in my search for a knife with a bird hook and a lightweight blaze orange toque, neither of which Bass Pro sells, apparently.[122] An Asian woman lifts a turkey call from the shelf, cranks it, and giggles: what on earth is this? Her husband, bemused, can only shrug. In the next aisle, teenaged boys fondle crossbows they lack the strength to draw. And then some goof starts honking on a duck call, endless rounds of feeding chuckles, on and on, drawing a crowd. Crowds irritate me; I want to smack the call out of his hand. But he honks on and on, as if to demonstrate that he

---

122   I eventually found my bird hook knife in a hardware store in Houston, Texas.

truly belongs here, that he is One of Us, that he is not a tourist. We all long to declare our allegiance, to don our camouflage jackets and ball caps for grocery shopping or yard work, to slip into the camouflage uniform of our Camouflage Nation.

THE DULL THUMP OF SHOTGUNS out over the marsh half an hour before sunrise announces legal shooting light, enough light for the waterfowlers to tell duck from drake. Colour paints the landscape in pastel tones muted by frost. Sadie, my Welsh springer, dances on her front paws, tail thumping the floor of her crate. Alert as a runner in the blocks, she hits the ground at a run, nose down, when I open the gate. We wade the frost-soaked grass under drifts of morning birdsong. In a tight band of aspens she puts up a woodcock, a sudden peeping flutter of wings, and as the bird levels off my shot splits the morning peace, a nail hammered through bone china, ears ringing in the quiet as Sadie picks the bird.

No one much complains at this assault on peace and quiet, unless he's just moved out here from the suburbs. You might as well complain about roosters, tractors, or the smell of manure. Hunting is a part of rural life. Trudge the banks of the Bayfield River with a fly rod on any given October morning in search of steelhead, and you'll hear shotguns. Statistics tell us that rural Americans are about twice as likely to own guns as city-dwellers, a pattern that is perhaps even more pronounced in Canada where hunting, rather than personal protection, is the leading reason people own guns. You'll find as many gun shops in a small Ontario town like Tillsonburg or Delhi as you will in the entire city of Toronto.[123]

But for years, the number of hunters has been shrinking. As the years go by, you get out less. Sitting in a frosty duck blind with a runny nose and cold feet becomes less appealing as the joints get stiffer. Your kids, meanwhile, head for the cities, find themselves jobs in Toronto or Calgary. My father, who taught at the University of Western Ontario, used to ask his first-year classes for a show of hands: how many came from small-town, rural Ontario? And how many intended to return to Exeter, or Mitchell, or Port Burwell, after finishing their degrees? Precious few. Hunters hunt because their parents hunted, because they were raised in a context where hunting was accepted simply as something men did, because they read hunting stories and hook-and-bullet

123 At present, Toronto proper has just one. There are several more out in Mississauga, Vaughan, and other satellite areas.

magazines as they grew up and lived in places where they could go hunting without having to drive for miles and knock on doors and ask permission. The story of the twentieth century is that we moved to the cities and left our old ways behind.

As the numbers of hunters has shrunk, those that remain have become self-conscious. We hardly think of the things we do when everyone else does them, too, but as those things start to set us apart, we become aware of our otherness. A driver's licence is a rite of passage and a ticket to freedom, yet we are all drivers, so the idea that there's a car culture escapes us even as we tap our feet to the Beach Boys having fun, fun, fun 'til her Daddy takes the T-Bird away. Your average Canadian does not notice his Canadian "eh" or the way he says "about," and will probably even deny such things exist until he opens his mouth in South Carolina. In that instant, he becomes in his own mind The Canadian. To the hunter who increasingly feels himself an outsider, likewise, hunting becomes his identity. And that identity is increasingly under fire.

"Whether it is from compassion for Bambi or an association with Elmer Fudd," writes Steven Pinker in *The Better Angels of Our Nature*, "fewer Americans shoot animals for fun." Pinker's remark is a catalogue of unverified assumptions, assumptions that give the hunter good reason to consider himself misunderstood. It is urbanization, not compassion or a sense that they are as ridiculous as Elmer Fudd, that has led Americans to put away their deer rifles. But it is this notion that hunters shoot animals "for fun," a notion dearly held among people who know nothing about hunters or hunting, that sounds the trumpets and demands we choose sides. Find any news story on a fatal hunting accident and check the comments left by online readers; inevitably, at least one commenter will declare that the hunter deserved it. Someone, fancying himself a wit, proposes that hunting can only be called a sport if the deer could shoot back. You can buy T-shirts with slogans like, "There's no such thing as hunting accidents. It's called karma." Presumably, the people who find these T-shirts amusing never expect to explain their slogan to the victim's mother. It would be a short conversation.

Hunters are quick to protest that it isn't killing that makes the hunt compelling. "I loved the hunt," writes David Adams Richards in *Facing the Hunter*, "but I never thrilled at the killing." In *A Hunter's Confession*, writer David Carpenter recounts his most memorable hunt, an elk-hunting trip on which he fired not one shot. "Killing has a place in hunting, if only a small one," wrote Roderick Haig-Brown in *Measure of the Year*. "I see it as a rite, a sacrifice, an acknowledgment of the sport's origin that gives meaning to what has gone before." Or, as the Spanish philosopher José Ortega y Gasset put it, "One does not hunt in order to kill; on the contrary, one kills in order to have hunted"—which seems almost to suggest that a ruffed grouse must die for no other reason than to prevent my December jaunt with dog and shotgun from seeming pointless and silly. But game ends up on the table and gives meaning to all that has gone before: not killing, but taking food from the Earth that sustains us.

The moralist demands consistency, that hobgoblin of small minds, but humans are inconsistent creatures. My daughters' pet rabbit is lovingly cared for, but between October and January you may find me skinning and gutting rabbits in the backyard. The rabbit wants to live but the coyote has to live, too, as parents explain to their small children. Anyone who feels boneless chicken breasts wrapped in plastic are a more ethical choice than a freshly shot pheasant ought to look at that package on the supermarket shelf and see if he can perceive his footprint. The body of a pheasant in your hand has the dead weight of consequences, the limp neck and lolling head, the cold, dead skin against your fingers, slightly sticky, as you pluck its feathers. When you have seen that bird burst from over, heard its wild cackle, tail streaming behind in early morning light, you understand more clearly that the meat in the freezer is dead and that your every step makes a mark on the earth. As the writer and film-maker Guy de la Valdène wrote, "the consequences of carrying a gun is measured in the silence of the birds I have shot."

And as the writer and conservationist Aldo Leopold points out in *A Sand County Almanac*, "the hunter ordinarily has no gallery to applaud or disapprove of his conduct. Whatever his acts, they are dictated by his own conscience, rather than by a mob of onlookers." But a mob of onlookers has much to say about killing Bambi and skulking through the woods like Elmer Fudd, and hunters have become increasingly sensitive to criticism both real and imagined. The antis—those people who feel that hunting is immoral, and want to put a stop to it—are suddenly everywhere. And just as gun control created the gun lobby and strengthened its extremists, the antis have had a predictable effect, too.

To Camouflage Nation, those who live in cities and call hunting cruel are "citiots" who must think meat is manufactured, harmlessly, behind the scenes in the supermarket. It's not necessary to understand the antis, or their views; they're just antis. And so we can never find common ground. Any sign of moderation is probably a nefarious plot devised by antis to lull us into a false sense of security. Hunters need friends, and the only people they can trust are their fellow outsiders. All for one and one for all is their cry.

Naturally, our fellow outsiders are ready to welcome us into the fold, just so long as we support them. In the Bass Pro Outpost in Niagara-on-the-Lake I found tin signs for sale proclaiming "What Makes America Great," with stars and stripes (they must have taken a wrong turn at Albuquerque), "I'm All for Gun Control (I Use Both Hands)," "Due To The Rising Cost of Ammo Do Not Expect a Warning Shot," "If You're Found Here at Night You'll Be Found Here in the Morning." All the bullshit sloganeering was there. Camouflage Nation finds itself allied, in an uncomfortable marriage of convenience, with urban handgun owners obsessed with self-defence. We rednecks have to stick together.

A MARRIAGE OF CONVENIENCE IS NEVER an entirely loving arrangement, and the marriage between Camouflage Nation and city folk is not without its domestic spats—domestic spats that, like most domestic spats, have their roots in long-standing slights and jealousies.

For years, hunting was the main reason that Americans owned guns. Handgun ownership didn't really take off until the crime wave of the 1960s, and the concealed-carry movement is a recent phenomenon. But it is urban gun owners, people who own handguns and black rifles (a general name for the AR-15 and its ilk) and who are increasingly likely to hold hardline views, who feel most threatened by gun control.[124] Out comes the good old slippery slope: if handguns (or assault rifles, or large-capacity magazines) are banned or regulated, lawmakers will find it that much easier to do the same to rifles and shotguns and then hunting will be over for good, and we will live out our days in a wasteland of soy lattes and veggie burgers and tofu. For gun owners, it must be all for one

---

124 I simplify. Of course, many hunters also own handguns. But hunters are *less likely* to own handguns, and people who own handguns only are rarely hunters. Despite the overlap, there is a real division between the two groups; the existence of the overlap helps the slippery-slope argument stick.

and one for all, and woe betide he who fails to stand in solidarity with his brothers and sisters. He is a traitor to his brethren, and will be cast out.

Take the unfortunate case of Jim Zumbo. Zumbo is a career outdoor writer, who started writing for outdoor magazines in 1962. *Outdoor Life* and *Field & Stream*, the two biggest outdoor magazines in North America, reach a readership of millions; every outdoor writer wants his byline in their pages, for both pay and prestige. In 2007, Zumbo, as hunting editor of *Outdoor Life*, was not only on the inside, but firmly there. But then Jim Zumbo made a mistake.

On February 16, 2007, Zumbo went on a coyote hunt with a guide who mentioned that large numbers of his clients now hunted prairie dogs with AR-15-style rifles, which were growing popular following the expiry of the Clinton-era assault-weapons ban in 2004. But whatever its growing popularity, not everyone loved the AR-15. A man toting a rifle derived from the M16, with a thirty-round magazine, a rifle that allows him to shoot and shoot and shoot until he finally manages to hit something, seems the ultimate slob hunter. Zumbo, put off by that image, posted an entry in the hunting blog at *Outdoor Life*'s website.

I call them "assault" rifles, which may upset some people. Excuse me, maybe I'm a traditionalist, but I see no place for these weapons among our hunting fraternity. I'll go so far as to call them "terrorist" rifles. They tell me that some companies are producing rifles that are "tackdrivers."[125]

Sorry, folks, in my humble opinion, these things have no place in hunting. We don't need to be lumped into the group of people who terrorize the world with them, which is an obvious concern. I've always been comfortable with the statement that hunters don't use assault rifles. We've always been proud of our "sporting firearms."

This really has me concerned. As hunters, we don't need the image of walking around the woods carrying one of these weapons. To most of the public, an assault rifle is a terrifying thing. Let's divorce ourselves from them. I say game departments should ban them from the prairies and woods.

The backlash was immediate. Naturally, hunters who used AR-15-style rifles objected to Zumbo's condemnation. But Zumbo had not

---

125 Tack driver: a highly accurate rifle, i.e. one capable of repeatedly hitting the head of a tack. This sentence is something of a non sequitur.

anticipated the response his post would provoke from gun activists, from the gun lobby, and from gun manufacturers eager to rebrand "assault rifles"—with their obvious image problems—as "modern sporting rifles" suitable for hunting.[126] His legitimate concern about the public image projected by hunters carrying modern military-style rifles was lost in the shouting. Zumbo, realizing that he had misjudged the popularity of the AR-15 among his readers, apologized. But by then nobody cared what he said. Zumbo had become a Fudd.

In a savage attack on Zumbo on the self-defence-obsessed website "The Martialist," the writer Phil Elmore (who has contributed to such men's adventure series as *Mack Bolan* and *The Executioner*) imaginatively defined what a Fudd is:

> A Fudd is an ignorant hunter who sees no connection between his "sporting firearms"—his hunting tools—and his firearms rights. He is not a Second Amendment supporter; he may even be a Democrat. He loves to hunt, for whatever reason, but he has no respect and no use for "non-traditional" shooters. He can't imagine a rifle stock made of plastic being good for anything; he can't see a need or a "legitimate sporting purpose" for any weapon cosmetically similar to a military arm. He is, in short, an elitist who doesn't wish to associate with those gun owners he considers beneath him.

Elmore's terms of opprobrium are peculiarly American. Fudds are elitist, cosmopolitan snobs far removed from the practical concerns of everyday Americans. These people speak legal mumbo-jumbo, not plain American. They probably eat things you've never heard of and drop foreign words into conversation just to show off. *They may even be Democrats.* They think they're better than you!

Zumbo was partly right: to the wider American public, the notion of hunters going after prairie dogs with assault rifles is offensive, particularly given the assumption that those assault rifles are equipped with thirty-round magazines with which to spray said prairie dogs, and the

---

126 Strictly speaking, an assault rifle is a selective fire weapon: that is, it is a weapon that is capable of both semiautomatic and fully automatic fire. The AR-15 is semiautomatic, so by that definition, it is not an assault rifle. But before "assault rifles" became leading targets of gun control advocates, the AR-15 and other semiautomatic rifles were often marketed as "assault rifles." The industry's image problem is thus partly of its own making.

surrounding terrain, with bullets. And there is no real need for such rifles, because traditional hunting rifles kill groundhogs just fine. But Zumbo was also partly wrong, because there is really no functional difference between an AR-15 with a five-round magazine and any of the numerous semi-automatic rifles already used by hunters—rifles which, because of their wood stocks, traditional design, and small magazine capacity, scarcely raise an eyebrow. Whatever people may assume, those AR-15-equipped prairie-dog hunters are not spraying the landscape with bullets from thirty-round magazines. They're taking single, aimed shots, just like anyone else.

The AR-15 is popular for a reason: whatever its image problems, it's a good design. The attraction is its versatility. The design is essentially modular: if you want a shorter barrel, or a longer barrel, or even a different calibre, you can change out the upper receiver. You can also change out stocks, sights, and hand grips with little effort. A hunter can stick a five-round magazine in an AR-15 and have a rifle little different, for hunting purposes, from any other—but it offers much more because it can be several rifles in one. The "modern sporting rifle" is a solution without a problem in that existing hunting rifles work just fine for the same purpose, but it is a very good solution nonetheless.

If outdoor writing were a functioning, effective form of journalism, Zumbo's blog post would have kicked off a lively debate. If outdoor writing were a functional and effective form of journalism, outdoor writers might freely question the strategies of the lobby groups that solicit their readers' money, and the attempts of the commercial industry surrounding hunting and fishing to invent new ways of lightening their readers' wallets. They might well ask if the modern sporting rifle is a solution without a problem, or if gun manufacturers are pushing new guns as a means of keeping themselves afloat in a saturated market. They might ask some questions that their readers might not entirely like, as well they should. A writer ought to discomfit his audience; his job is not to soothe, but to wake the reader from his comfortable snooze and ask him to think. But any conversation Zumbo might have initiated was stillborn, and those who stepped up to defend him soon back-pedalled, because outdoor writing is rarely permitted to be a functioning, effective form of journalism. The outdoor writer is too close to his magazine's advertisers, and his audience is defensive and reactionary.

The first rule of Camouflage Nation is "no one questions Camouflage Nation." We cannot ask questions or indulge debate. We cannot think. As soon as we think, the antis win.

"In light of comments made by Jim Zumbo in his February 16, 2007 blog posting on the magazine's website, Mr. Zumbo has offered to terminate his association with *Outdoor Life*, and the magazine has accepted his offer." With those words, *Outdoor Life*'s editor, Todd W. Smith, shot Jim Zumbo in the leg and left him to the ravening zombies. Smith insisted that resigning was Zumbo's own idea, and declined to comment on what the magazine might have done if Zumbo hadn't taken the initiative. But the magazine had received six thousand complaints in just three days, and although it is not clear how many of those complaints came from bona-fide subscribers, or even from hunters, something had to be done. The Outdoor Channel, similarly, took Zumbo's show off the air indefinitely. Noting that Zumbo's sponsors included the gunmaker Remington, the mob called for a boycott; Remington, mindful of previous gun-owner boycotts of Ruger and Smith & Wesson, cut Zumbo loose.[127]

Zumbo had been a member of the NRA for forty years, yet the NRA helped to organize the destruction of his career, and then celebrated his downfall *pour encourager les autres*. There would be no divide-and-conquer, even if the divisions came from within. Dissent would not be tolerated. Nobody would be made to think for himself. Camouflage Nation would have to fall in line; the Fudds would be cast out. The gun nuts were in charge.

---

127 Ruger suffered a boycott when William Ruger, the company president, advocated a limit on high-capacity magazines as a practical and more effective alternative to an assault-weapons ban; Smith & Wesson suffered a boycott for cooperating with Clinton-era gun-control efforts.

Collateral Damage
The Militarization of the Suburban Male

Arms, my only ornament. My only rest, the fight.
—Don Quixote

I LIKE THE GUN, as Roderick Haig-Brown confessed; it is a familiar thing, full of associations. The C5 machine gun—the Canadian Army version of the Browning M1919, still in service with reserve units through the early 1990s as a coaxial machine gun on the AVGP Cougar—will always remind me of the now-defunct Indoor Miniature Range on Highbury Avenue in London, Ontario, where we practiced Cougar gunnery using lasers and a table covered with model tanks, and where Brad Glenn and I stripped the C5 down as far as we could, beyond the normal limits of the detailed strip and assemble, and learned the functions of its myriad parts, its Rube Goldberg construction. The tricky piece on the C5 was the breech-lock cam, a small metal block which, if installed backwards or upside-down—an easy error to make, the difference being a tiny chamfer on one side of the sneaky little bastard—would disingenuously allow you to assemble the entire machine gun, only to lock its workings into immobility when you first cranked back the cocking handle. You were not supposed to mess with it. Naturally, we did.

Brad and I, both master corporals at the time, departed that winter for Canadian Forces Base Gagetown, where we were to become qualified as gunnery instructors. The regiment also sent two officers; the adjutant warned them in a stage whisper that if they didn't finish the course ahead of Brad and me, they would be on extra duties, so the game was on. We were young, we were cocky, and a few weeks later Brad had graduated second on the course. In some dusty corner of Gagetown's Armour School there's a trophy awarded to the top candidate on that course, a polished 76mm casing with a wooden shell, and on its base one of the nameplates reads MCpl Somerset A.J. The officers got their extras. And I can still tell you, twenty-two years after the fact, that the ten factors affecting elevation in armoured gunnery are range, angle of sight, jump, droop, drift, propellant temperature, trunnion tilt, parallax, barrel wear, and … I can only ever get nine. I'd like to say "wind, especially at the target end," but this is a factor affecting line.[128] I sing the song of obsolescence, the crew commander's action drill: muzzle ends clear, driver's hatch closed, no obstructions; my side free to traverse, two hundred pounds, SRB removed and stowed, bore clear, coax half-loaded. None of these things ever leaves you, and reciting them now produces a disturbance of the spirit, an unsettled chest, perhaps *saudade*. Two hundred pounds, and what do you get? Another day older and deeper in debt. The final truth is that we're only young once and what you pissed off a bridge is lost in the sea.

The Cougar is long gone, the few remaining examples converted to gate guardians at various military bases, their crew commander's hatches now welded shut, the guts of their guns removed. I no longer handle these guns, not the 76mm Gun L23A1, or the C5, or the C6 that replaced it; not the FN I carried on my recruit course, or the SMG, or the slick and efficient C7, the little C8 with its collapsing stock, its continual stoppages. Nowadays I carry only a shotgun: my Browning pump, a 20-gauge side-by-side, or a 12-gauge over-under. But one thing leads to the next. If I had never shot that sweet, tight group with the FNC1, would my dog now mope beside my desk, dreaming of grouse breaking cover in winter cedars, woodcock busting out of red osiers?

In ten years, she will be dead. In twenty, I will break open my little side-by-side and smell burnt powder, and I will remember. None of these things ever leaves you. In the top left drawer of my desk this autumn I discovered a small piece of steel with a flattened tail, the recocking lever from a C5 bolt. The beaver dives into the pond, we

128 The answer is air density. Just as shotgun patterns and shot strings are matters best left to shotgun geeks, I will not explain what is meant by jump, droop, and drift.

advised gunnery students, demonstrating how to fit the recocking lever into its slot in the breech block. I intend to grind a slot in the beaver's head, and thus fashion my machine gun recocking lever into a beer bottle opener. Other nations dream of beating their machine guns into ploughshares, but I am Canadian. And south of the border, thousands upon thousands of men like me sit back in easy chairs and remember: none of these things ever leaves you. Can it be that the Wellspring of Crazy lies here? Can it be that the roots of American gun culture lie in American militarism, that the nation has for far too long dreamed of beating its ploughshares into guns?

I AM A ROAD WARRIOR. I lug my heavy laptop bag through departure lounges, speakers squawking we are boarding this flight by zone, this is a gate change announcement, please do not leave your luggage unattended. Please watch your step while exiting the moving sidewalk. In Detroit a disembodied voice invites soldiers to relax in the Freedom Center Military Lounge, which we are told provides a home-like atmosphere created to thank them for their service. On United Airlines, priority boarding for soldiers in uniform. South of the border any mention of the few years I spent readying to fight the Russians produces a reflexive thanks-for-your-service, repeated like a prayer, a Nicene Creed for the American nation. The calendar marks Veterans' Day, Memorial Day, Armed Forces Day. "Armistice Day was sacred," wrote Kurt Vonnegut, who observed a cultural shift, "Veterans' Day is not." When the guns stopped, Vonnegut wrote, the sudden silence was like the voice of God. There is no sudden silence here, where this is a pre-boarding announcement for Delta flight 1847 with service to Seattle and Anchorage. We cannot hear the voice of God.

Militarism places its faith in military might and holds military service as its highest ideal. In 2013, the United States budgeted $613.9 billion towards that ideal, of which $88.5 billion was for "Overseas Contingency Operations," which is to say remaining at war. And the United States has been at war, hot or cold, more or less continually since the Japanese bombed Pearl Harbour. After World War II, there was the Korean War, the Vietnam War, the invasions of Grenada and Panama, the Gulf War, and the War on Terror (including both Afghanistan and Iraq), to say nothing of many dozens of limited operations that saw

US forces bombing whatever unfortunate state had made that week's Presidential Shit List. Personnel costs alone for 2013 were $130 billion, more than the entire military budget of the next biggest spender at the House of Mars: China. That's a lot of soldiers trained, brought up through the ranks, sent overseas to do what they were trained to do, and then released back to civilian life. Thousands upon thousands of Americans boys shuffle into one end of that big, camouflage-painted machine and march out the other proud, trained, and comfortable with firearms. And Americans, of course, shoot each other more than twice as often as the people of any other Western nation. Can it be a coincidence that the United States spends more money than any other country in training its boys as killers?

It's a trenchant question. The US military puts special emphasis on transforming ordinary people into killing machines, because it believes that ordinary people simply can't bring themselves to kill. At the end of World War II, after interviewing members of more than four hundred infantry companies in the Pacific and in Europe, the US Army combat historian S.L.A. Marshall wrote, "we found that on average not more than 15 percent of the men had actually fired at the enemy positions or personnel ... The best showing that could be made by the most spirited and aggressive companies was that one man in four had made at least some use of his fire power." This was the "ratio of fire": more than three-quarters of combat infantrymen, Marshall said, never fired their weapons because they could not bring themselves to do it.

Like the father of a freshly minted MD who's just received the news that she intends to forgo medicine and open a dog-grooming business, the US Army was dismayed to discover that, after it had given its men weapons, ammunition, uniforms and rations, and invested countless valuable hours in their training, they had simply sat and gazed stupidly at the enemy. Small-unit commanders could not be expected to run from foxhole to foxhole, encouraging their men to fight. The modern infantryman had to be trained to fight on his own initiative. He had to overcome his reluctance to kill his fellow man. The ratio of fire had to be increased.

And so training for the Vietnam War saw a new emphasis on killing. The Figure 11 target, my good friend Ivan, replaced the traditional bullseye so that the soldier would become accustomed to firing at a suitably dehumanized human figure. Lectures stressed killing the enemy with machine gun, rifle, bayonet, grenade, and whatever other weapon came to hand. And when recruits marched in mass formation, they recited inane chants about killing, supposedly to lower their inhibitions against pulling the trigger. The army was determined to turn boys into killers.

But does this training carry back to civilian life? In *On Killing*, now required reading for US Army officers, Lieutenant Colonel Dave Grossman sets out to examine how boys become killers and how killing affects them, proposing a new field of study that he obnoxiously dubs "killology." Grossman takes as his premise Marshall's ratio of fire, and the underlying assumption that humans are naturally reluctant to kill. Everywhere he looks, in the long history of men at war, he finds soldiers unable to kill each other. When men fired in combat, Grossman suggests, it was often only to make noise; the gun, loud and impressive, was mostly a posturing device. It's a wonder that anyone managed to die at all. But modern training has changed all that by reprogramming the human brain.

To Grossman, modern military training is essentially operant conditioning, little different from dog training.[129] Conditioning soldiers is necessary, he explains, because intense fear paralyzes the forebrain processes that would normally govern the soldier. In combat, the midbrain takes over—but the midbrain is inhibited by a powerful, innate resistance to killing, so the soldier does not open fire.[130] Operant conditioning in training turns off that midbrain inhibition. The result is a dangerous condition that Grossman calls "acquired violence immunity deficiency," and he warns that "Severe psychological trauma becomes a distinct possibility when psychological safeguards of such magnitude are overridden." Once the crisis of combat is past, the soldier may have difficulty living with what he has done. He may become what we now call a "psychiatric casualty." He has become a victim of his own government, of "psychological warfare conducted not upon the enemy, but upon one's own troops."

It's an attractive explanation for American gun violence. You take young men, introduce them to guns, train them and encourage them to kill people, and then release them into society. Should anyone be

---

129 I propose that Grossman knows jack about training dogs. But this is neither here nor there.
130 This idea is bizarre, as the forebrain is usually credited with inhibiting our behaviour and limiting our violent impulses.

surprised by the resulting body count? But if former soldiers were responsible for all those murders, surely someone would have noticed. Grossman suggests that military discipline keeps soldiers from killing people without orders, and points instead to video games, which he says have all the effects of military training without the discipline. It's a pretty shaky explanation. But there is a broader problem with Grossman's theory: the whole thing turns out to be bullshit.

The bullshit starts with S.L.A. Marshall. Roger Spiller, of the US Army Command and General Staff College, pointed out that Marshall could not possibly have carried out group interviews with four hundred infantry companies in the time he had available; to do so would have had him interviewing well past the end of the war, rather than immediately after each action, as he claimed. His methods, too, were questionable. On Marshall's death, no statistical analysis, not even notebooks containing his raw data, came to light. A man who had worked with Marshall in Korea subsequently described the informality of his approach, suggesting that in many cases Marshall did not even raise the question of whether men had fired their weapons. A Canadian military historian, Robert Engen, has pointed out that Canadian records don't support Marshall's claims either—and the Canadian Army drew its recruits from a culture almost identical to that of the United States. Why would Canadians be so different? Could it be all those hockey fights?

It transpires that Marshall had a history of fibs. He padded his World War I resumé, boasting of leading men in combat as the youngest American commissioned officer in France; in fact, he was not commissioned until after the war was over. He wrote that he spent Armistice Day in a front-line foxhole; in fact, he was behind the lines, taking a course in an non-commissioned officers' school. He claimed, on different occasions, to have served in combat in three different units; in fact, he spent World War I in an engineer unit, doing construction work behind the lines.

In reality, people don't need to be trained to kill. Killing each other is a natural human behaviour, if not a particularly laudable one. Throughout the long history of our species, there has never been any evidence of a reluctance to kill.[131] But Marshall's ratio of fire, implausible

---

131 Steven Pinker's *The Better Angels of Our Nature* (2011) provides a convincing overview of that history, complete with body counts.

as it is, attracts adherents because it just seems to fit. "Everything in war is very simple," Clausewitz cautions, "but the simplest thing is difficult." For military leaders, the experience of command becomes a nightmare in which, no matter how hard you run, you never quite get anywhere. Men stop. Platoons don't get to where they're supposed to go. Attacks are repulsed. Yet casualties, when one considers the amount of metal flying around at high speed, are often surprisingly low. Then along comes S.L.A. Marshall, with a simple explanation … well, we all love a simple explanation. And so the US Army and its allies changed its basic infantry training in response to his ideas. The eminent military historian John Keegan incorporated Marshall's ratio of fire into his seminal 1976 study of men in battle, *The Face of Battle*. Grossman wrapped an entire book around Marshall's ratio of fire, currently on the US Marine Corps commandant's reading list. *On Killing* remains required reading for US Army officers, despite the fact that it's utter nonsense.

Although it may well be true that America's exceptional homicide rate is somehow related to American militarism, it's not because the military reprograms boys into killer robots. These are not the droids we're looking for. We'll have to look elsewhere. Perhaps, if the problem doesn't come from all those trained killers, it springs from the culture that celebrates them.

THE BUCKSKIN-CLAD FRONTIERSMAN recalls the mounted knight, his squire now Chingachgook, the man who knows Indians. Hawkeye begets Shane, the professional killer dressed in frontier buckskin who, however reluctantly, fights for justice. But the modern battlefield allows no space for knightly heroism. "Que pleust à Dieu que ce malheureux instrument n'eust jamais esté inventé," lamented Blais de Monluc, a sixteenth-century French general, in his *Commentaires*, after seeing knights cut down by foot soldiers armed with arquebuses: "Would to God that this unfortunate instrument had never been invented." He would not be the last to make that wish. Shakespeare parodied the sentiment, as did Cervantes in *Don Quixote*:

> Blessed be those happy ages that were strangers to the dreadful fury of these devilish instruments of artillery, whose inventor I am satisfied is now in Hell, receiving the reward of his cursed invention, which is the

cause that very often a cowardly base hand takes away the life of the
bravest gentleman …[132]

Duckboard paths through the cratered mire, star shells hanging in the
ghastly air, and the chatter of machine guns chewing the bodies of men
caught up in the wire. Rats will finish the job. On the Somme, British
engineers dug a tunnel under the Hawthorn Ridge Redoubt and packed
it with forty thousand pounds of high explosive, which they blew ten
minutes before zero hour. One minute you're picking lice and the next
you're one part flesh and nine parts atomized countryside. What pass-
ing-bells for these, who die as cattle?

But there, up there, is Snoopy in his Sopwith Camel, high above all
of that, hunting the Red Baron. The hero climbs out of the trenches and
joins the knights of the air: a return to chivalry, to individual combat,
the horse now a roaring sputtering clattering machine twisted by the
torque of the mad, spinning cylinders of its wild rotary engine, spraying castor oil from snorting valves. But by the dawn of the jet age the
knight of the air has lost his romance. Now he flies at twice the speed
of sound, strapped to a howling jet engine, following vectors provided
by the disembodied voice of a radar operator who sees only blips on a
screen; death is delivered by guided missiles that fly themselves into his
enemy. His cockpit filled with flashing lights and alarms, with buttons
and switches, the pilot is a technician who operates a machine with all
the cachet of a data-entry clerk.

The hero returns in the form of the Special Forces Operator, his face
painted, his movement silent, the American Rifleman reborn to visit
death on his enemy in single combat. Like the knight riding before a
yeoman army he is an elite soldier, at his best when he works alone or
with a small group of his fellows. He stands ready to serve, his identity
secret, an anonymous hero who asks for no laurels, only the respect of
his peers and the satisfaction of having served with that elite brotherhood. He keeps his visor lowered.

Sir Gareth of Orkney, that Sir Kay called Beaumains, lives a year as
a kitchen knave in Arthur's court, concealing his noble birth, and then
rides forth with the damsel Lyonet to rescue her sister, whose castle
is under siege by the Red Knight of the Red Lands. Gareth slays and

---

132   From *Don Quixote*. The Shakespearean iteration is in *Henry IV*.

overthrows knight after knight, each more powerful than the last, and after each victory Lyonet derides him as a kychyn knave who stynkyst all of the kychyn, his clothis bawdy of the grece and talow. In *Under Siege* (1992), Casey Ryback (Steven Seagal) is a former Navy SEAL working as a cook on the battleship *USS Missouri* when a rogue CIA agent takes over the ship with plans to steal its nuclear warheads. Ryback teams up with Jordan Tate (Erika Eleniak), a stripper hired to pop out of a cake at the captain's birthday party, which is rudely interrupted when the band turns out to be terrorists. It's hard to find a good event planner these days.

> JORDAN: So who are you? Are you, you, like, some Special Forces guy or something?
> RYBACK: Nah, I'm just a cook.
> JORDAN: A cook?
> RYBACK: Just a lowly, lowly cook.
> JORDAN: Oh my God, we're gonna die.

Only later, on witnessing Ryback's feats of arms, will Jordan realize the truth: "You're not a cook," or as Lyonet has it, "I mervayle what thou art and of what kyn thou arte com; for boldely thou spekyst and boldely thou hast done." The knight's skill at arms is proof positive of his honour and high birth. And just as the Hollywood hero never runs out of ammunition until the script demands it, so Sir Gareth breaks an endless supply of lances.

This is what it means to be a warrior.

THE MILITARY IS A NATION within a nation, a culture unto itself. It prizes its history and its traditions; it has its own deep customs. Soldiers speak their own language, an English in which the same words convey a different understanding. Their language even has words of its very own. "Numpty" is Scots slang for "idiot," not used in Canada outside the Maritimes, but spread coast to coast by master corporals describing the failures of their charges. "Buckshee," describing an item that has fallen through the cracks of the supply system, derives from the Persian "baksheesh": money given as charity, a tip, or a bribe.[133] It probably came

133 Many people will define it to mean "free of charge," but this does not capture the nuance. It normally refers to military-issue items that are no longer on the books and therefore can be given

into the Canadian Army via the British, in World War II, and never seems to fall from the lips of civilians. Meanwhile, Troopie's bogged two hundred plus of the defile. Every military develops its own language. These are nations apart.

When Noah Richler decried the decline of Canada's peacekeeping mythology in *What We Talk About When We Talk About War*, he neglected the fact that, for some Canadians, the "nation of peacekeepers" myth has always been just that. Whatever the public believed its army was for, their soldiers had their own ideas. I didn't train to keep the peace in Cyprus; I trained to fight Russians. The Figure 11 was named Ivan, and the AFV recognition posters on the walls, with "Know Your Enemy" in bold letters at the top, showed Russian tanks.[134] Everyone knew that no sooner did you key your pretzel switch than the Russian artillery had your number.[135] We were a war-fighting force and peacekeeping was just something we did from time to time, a secondary role. And the public, with its obtuse notion that we were a nation of peacekeepers, just didn't get it. Ask any of us: those dumb fucks didn't even know what peacekeeping *was*. Witness Bosnia.

In wartime, the soldier is a hero; in peacetime, he is an outsider, or believes himself so. One popular analogy sees the army as the big dog you keep chained up outside: nobody likes that dog until someone comes along and tries to break into your house. And the soldier loves this analogy. He loves to see himself as a noble outcast. He is Sir Gareth of Orkney, enduring Lyonet's insults up until the moment she realizes he has saved her; then, happily ever after and fade to black. He is Casey Ryback, Hawkeye, Shane, Dirty Harry, and Will Kane.

In his follow-up to *On Killing*, *On Combat*, Dave Grossman introduces his sheepdog fable, now a staple of self-defence nuts. Grossman

---

away or traded. If I find a rifle-cleaning kit in the field and can't find its owner, I could turn it in to the regimental quarter master, but I probably won't; it is buckshee, and I will trade it to someone who needs it, either for some other buckshee item or for future considerations. If I did turn it in, the RQMS would himself squirrel it away as buckshee and use it to cover future losses. Now, if I *do* give the RQMS a buckshee cleaning kit, he'll owe me one and this will help me out when I lose some item next month: future considerations. It helps if we're on beer-drinking terms. "Free" does not quite describe this. "Baksheesh," with its illicit connotations, does.

134   AFV recognition: Armoured Fighting Vehicle recognition, the skill of distinguishing friend from foe on the mechanized battlefield.

135   "Pretzel switch": the press-to-transmit switch of a radio. Corruption of "pressel switch" (a push-button switch), used to describe any press-to-transmit switch even if it is not in fact a pressel switch.

attributes the fable to "one Vietnam veteran, an old retired Colonel," and proceeds to mix his own ideas into the story.[136] The result is a heady mix of junk science and obvious bullshit.

The sheepdog fable divides the world into three groups. The most numerous are the sheep, "kind, gentle, productive creatures who can only hurt one another by accident." Then we have the wolves, who as one might expect, "feed on the sheep without mercy." Wolves obviously lack any inhibitions that prevent them from killing; killing is what they do. They prey on the poor little sheep. Standing against them are the sheepdogs, who "live to protect the flock and confront the wolf." Sheepdogs, like wolves, lack the midbrain inhibitions that prevent us from killing each other, but fortunately they are constrained by some other moral sense, which Grossman does not clearly define. "What if you have a capacity for violence, and a deep love for your fellow citizens?" asks Grossman. "Then you are a sheepdog, a warrior, someone who is walking the hero's path. Someone who can walk into the heart of darkness, into the universal human phobia, and walk out unscathed."

Sheep make up 98 percent of the population. Grossman decides that they just happen to be the 98 percent who, as the US Army's World War II research showed, will inevitably break down under the stress of combat and become psychiatric casualties. Isn't it neat when all the numbers match? They also happen to be the same people who can't bring themselves to shoot the enemy in combat.[137] Sheep are incapable of hurting each other because they share the natural midbrain inhibition that prevents humans from killing each other. This means, of course, that if you *can* bring yourself to shoot, you must either be a wolf or a sheepdog. And since sheep are by definition harmless, anyone who harms anyone else becomes a wolf: a predator, a morally degenerate, psychologically abnormal, bad person. It's all very convenient.

Grossman's appeal to his chosen audience is obvious: he blows sunshine up the sheepdog's ass. They are Sir Gareth of Orkney and Dirty Harry: soldiers and police officers, neatly conflated into a single, noble profession of arms, natural warriors all. They have voluntarily chosen

---

136 Both of Grossman's books frequently use anecdotes from experienced soldiers who are almost always left anonymous. One suspects they are horse pucky, with some justification: among his few cited sources in *On Killing* are articles from *Soldier of Fortune* magazine.

137 Oops—the numbers no longer match. Never mind!

"the hero's path," and volunteered; this, in itself, is enough to prove that they are among the exceptional 2 percent. But fluffy as sheepdogs may be, they also have big, shiny, wolf-like, sheep-frightening teeth, and so the foolish sheep reject them. You poor, honourable sheepdogs, outcasts in the society that you nobly dedicate yourselves to protect! You art become Will Kane: the man who gets the job done, who protects a nation of shopkeepers that has long since abandoned the torch passed by its frontier forebears, protectors of a society barely worth protecting.

In William Luther Pierce's *The Turner Diaries*, the ideal of fascist masculinity is a brave, selfless man who preserves civilization by taking up his weapon and his shield and going out daily to confront predators, by accepting his lonely duty to protect the stupid, complacent sheeple who fear and distrust him, by sacrificing and if necessary dying for a cause that the broader public is too stupid to understand. The duty to protect civilization falls to the elite few willing to take up that gauntlet:

> How fragile a thing is man's civilization! How superficial it is to his basic nature! And upon how few of the teeming multitudes to whose lives it gives a pattern does it depend for its sustenance!
>
> Without the presence of perhaps one or two per cent of the most capable individuals—the most aggressive, intelligent, and hardworking of our fellow citizens—I am convinced that neither this civilization nor any civilization could long sustain itself.

In a bizarre echo of *The Turner Diaries*, Grossman argues that without soldiers our civilization would perish, and then proceeds to elevate his sheepdogs—his noble two percent—above all other vocations:

> One US military leader (whom I have promised to keep anonymous) wrote these words as he watched his soldiers engage in great acts of valor:
>
>> Dear God, where do we get such men? What loving God has provided, that each generation, afresh, there should arise new giants in the land. Were we to go but a single generation without such men, we should surely be both damned and doomed.
>
> Think about it. If we went but a single generation without men (and women) who are willing to go out every day and confront evil,

then within the span of that generation we should surely be both damned and doomed.

We could go for a generation without the doctors, and it would get ugly if you were injured or sick, but civilization would continue. We could go for a generation without engineers and mechanics, and things would break down, but civilization would survive. We could even go for a generation without teachers. The next generation would have to play "catch-up ball," and it would be hard, but civilization as we know it would survive.

It's the same old story: civilization is created and sustained not by the decadent intellectual's pen, but by the pure, hard sword. Dave Grossman is surely not a neo-Nazi, and has probably never read a piece of trash like *The Turner Diaries*, but this same old rhetoric has floated on down through the air and alighted on his pen, as sure a sign of cultural transmission as any. This idea that weapons are essential to civilization is a central tenet of the gun culture. It also appeared in Buffalo Bill Cody's Wild West program, in an essay entitled "The Rifle as an Aid to Civilization":

> [While it is] a trite saying that "the pen is mightier than the sword," it is equally true that the bullet is the pioneer of civilization, for it has gone hand-in-hand with the axe that cleared the forest and with the family Bible and school book. Deadly as has been its mission in one sense, it has been merciful in another; for without the rifle ball we of America would not be to-day in possession of a free and united country, and mighty in our strength.[138]

Buffalo Bill, or whoever wrote that essay, was not alone in thinking it trite to say the pen is mightier than the sword. Don Quixote agreed: "Let none presume to tell me that the pen is preferable to the sword; for be they who they will, I shall tell them they know not what they say." The Knight of the Woeful Countenance instructs us that peace is preserved not by lawyers, but by armed men; not by legal mumbo-jumbo, but by those who speak plain Renaissance Spanish. He even foreshadows Grossman's argument: while we could get along just fine without scholars, and things would get rough for a little while, if we had no soldiers to pursue the goal

---

138 Slotkin, Richard. *Gunfighter Nation: The Myth of the Frontier in Twentieth-Century America.* (New York: Atheneum, 1992), 77.

of peace our civilization would be overcome by war—presumably within a single generation. Arms is the nobler path.

Nothing could pander more purely to the warrior culture. And Grossman is eager to link his sheepdogs, his militarized police and his professional soldiers, to that same chivalric tradition:

> Have you ever wondered why police officers wear a shield on their left side? This is a direct, intentional, overt reference to the knights of old. There really were knights. They woke up every day and donned armor. They hung a weapon on their hip and a shield on their left side. And they went forth and did good deeds and administered justice in the land.
>
> Gunpowder defeated armor, and the knights went away.
>
> Today, for the first time in centuries, in both the military and law enforcement communities, we have warriors who don armor every day, take up their shields, strap on their weapons, and go forth to do good deeds.
>
> If that is not a knight, if that is not a paladin, a new order of chivalry, then you tell me what is.

"The method and language Don Quixote used in delivering himself were such that none of his hearers at that time looked upon him as a madman," Cervantes tells us. But Don Quixote *is* a madman, of course; he has spent too much time reading romances, and has lost the ability to distinguish reality from the myths of the age of chivalry. The guy's got a shaving basin on his head, people: he's flat-out loopy.

There seems to be a lot of that going around.

THE SHEEPDOG IS HUMBLE. He endures the proud man's contumely, and a woman's scorn. He does not seek a fight, but stands ready when one is offered. His identity is secret, except to men like himself, men of honour. And so the knight of medieval romance went anonymous, his visor lowered, his name secret, revealing his identity only to those men who could best him in single combat. The captain knows who Casey Ryback is, and shares a glass of whiskey with him; to the junior officer who supervises him, Ryback is merely a cook, and an insubordinate, disrespectful one at that. The farm boy Westley, disguised as the Dread Pirate Roberts, endures Princess Buttercup's insults in the 1987 film *The Princess Bride* until she recognizes him by the words "as you wish." In the 1975 thriller *Breakheart Pass*, Deakin (Charles Bronson) is derided as a common criminal, a prisoner in transit, until he reveals himself as a federal agent sent to stop a plot to run Winchester rifles to the Indians. And today, Special Forces soldiers are photographed with their eyes blacked out by censors. The censorship serves practical purposes but nonetheless feeds off and in turn reinforces the same symbolism.

This warrior culture is not the stuff of fringe wingnuts. It's the mainstream. And to see that, we need only turn to what American men read in bestseller-making numbers. Tom Clancy exalts the sheepdog archetype in *Clear and Present Danger* (1989) before the story even begins, in the acknowledgments, where he thanks "Ed, commander of warriors," and laments, "would that America served you as faithfully as you serve her." In the novel, the United States begins a clandestine war against Colombian drug lords after they assassinate the FBI Director. Clancy's complex plot soon puts the whole gun-culture mythos in play: the rifleman myth, the sheepdog archetype, and most of all, the conflict between the law and violent, retributive justice, between lawyers and people who speak "plain American."

Sheepdogs recognize each other and form a brotherhood. *Clear and Present Danger*'s Dan Murray, a senior FBI agent, describes himself and his friend Jack Ryan as "warriors," although one is a police officer and the other a spy.[139] Similarly, the CIA operative John Clark immediately recognizes Chavez, a sniper selected to go into Colombia, as exceptional. Chavez is the American Rifleman, the fate of nations resting on his capable shoulders. And as such, he must move out of the army's anonymous ranks, and join America's secret warriors, its clandestine order of sheepdogs. Not for them the faceless, plodding career of robot infantry; they must find scope for their American individualism.

The code of the sheepdog also governs the novels of W.E.B. Griffin, another American writer who has succeeded in becoming a brand name, a masculine parallel to Danielle Steele. Like Clancy, Griffin writes series that follow the careers of small brotherhoods of true warriors as they rise through the ranks, although the careers of Griffin's characters are marginally less improbable than Clancy's. Clancy's Jack Ryan rises from Marine Corps second lieutenant to university

139 In the world of the sheepdog, the police are fully militarized, an extension of the profession of arms into the civil sphere.

professor to Deputy Director of the CIA to President of the United States—this last against his will: no sheepdog would willingly enter the compromised world of politics. Kenneth J. "Killer" McCoy, the protagonist of Griffin's *The Corps* (a series of ten novels), is commissioned from the ranks, but only attains the rank of major, a career arc that is possible, if improbable.[140] The means by which these heroes rise, however, and the forces that oppose them, are the same: true warriors, sheepdogs, are promoted on merit, in spite of the opposition of false warriors, mere bureaucrats.

We first encounter McCoy as a Marine Corps PFC stationed in China. He has just taken the examination for promotion to corporal, a promotion he is likely to win, for he is exceptional. He can type seventy-five words a minute, a skill that he has concealed from the Corps out of fears that they will make him a clerk. He is quick at math and an expert shot. Unlike most China Marines, McCoy took advantage of the Chinese girl he hired as a housekeeper, not in the usual way, but by convincing her to teach him Cantonese. He also speaks French, Latin, and Italian. He is a man who knows Indians, and his unique skills will see him pulled out of his machine gun company and given a job in military intelligence, the natural territory of the sheepdog.

In the early pages of *Semper Fi*, the first book of the series, McCoy becomes "killer McCoy—a nickname he detests—when he is waylaid by a group of Italian marines and fights back with the Baby Fairbairn knife he keeps strapped to his wrist, killing two of his assailants.[141] He is unperturbed by the moral ramifications of his act, quoting "he who lives by the sword shall die by the sword." Like Jack Ryan, he does what he has to do free from the burden of morality. This marks him as a true sheepdog, one of Grossman's 2 percent; none of the weeping and wailing and moral quandaries of the pisswilly sheep for him.

These characters are frontiersmen set loose outside the nation's borders; they are each of them the American Rifleman, whose marksmanship decides the outcome of battles. Combat—the last frontier, the

---

140   For example, Angus Duffy joined the Canadian Army as a private, became regimental sergeant major of the Hastings and Prince Edward Regiment, and then commissioned from the ranks, rose to the rank of lieutenant colonel, and became the unit's commanding officer.

141   The Baby Fairbairn knife Griffin gives his protagonist is presumably a smaller version of the Fairbairn-Sykes fighting knife developed by William Fairbairn and Eric Sykes for use by British commandos in World War II, although that knife had not been invented at the time McCoy was in China. A full-size Fairbairn-Sykes would be too large to conceal strapped to your wrist.

"universal human phobia" into which Grossman's sheepdogs fearlessly walk, and emerge from unscathed—is the Darwinian crucible within which men are tested and bureaucrats found wanting. The dumb die first. It is skill, rather than luck, that keeps you alive. Combat is not the inhuman realm of artillery and aerial bombs and buried mines and machine gun bullets delivered from a thousand yards; combat is personal. "Infantry combat is the business of death, at the personal level, where you could usually see what you were doing and to whom you were doing it," writes Clancy. Infantry combat is about the rifle. Neither Chavez nor McCoy suffers from fear. Fear is for sheep.

Fiction must deal either with sheepdogs or with wolves, for reasons that are immediately apparent in the Looney Tunes cartoons featuring Sam Sheepdog and Ralph E. Wolf: sheep are just plain dull.[142] Ralph and Sam arrive at work each morning, punch in at the time clock, and then proceed to their business, Ralph to catching sheep, and Sam to snoozing in the sun and thumping the snot out of Ralph as required. The sheep, for their part, confine themselves to munching grass.

If the lives of Ralph and Sam seem humdrum and routine, imagine making a cartoon about the sheep. No heroic novel of America at war could concern the men of an undistinguished infantry company of an undistinguished battalion, shivering in their filthy foxholes as artillery shells fall around them, dying at random. We create myths to escape the truth, to overcome our anxieties. The mythology called on by *Clear and Present Danger* and *Semper Fi* asserts that, whatever the evidence of our everyday lives, we are not mere flotsam caught in currents beyond our control. We can step outside the herd and control our destinies—and all we have to do to become sheepdogs, as Grossman tells us, is to pick up a gun and step into the role:

> If you are in a war, you are a warrior. Is there a war on drugs? Is there a
> war on crime? Is there a war against terrorism? Are you confronting and
> containing aggression as a peace officer at home, a peacekeeper in some
> distant land, or a warrior combating terrorism around the world? Or
> perhaps you have chosen to be a martial arts practitioner or an armed
> citizen, seeking to defend yourself or your loved ones in their hour of

---

142   Ralph E. Wolf closely resembles Wiley Coyote, and shares the latter's faith in the products of the Acme Corporation in spite of the demonstrated unreliability of Acme explosives. This has often led the public to confuse Ralph with his more famous cousin.

need? Are there people who wake up every morning determined to send you back to your family in a box?

Then you are in a war and you are a warrior.

Arm yourself against an imagined threat, and you become a warrior; your commute to the office is a journey across a battlefield. You are the Knight of the Woeful Countenance and your Dodge Caravan is Rocinante.

Most of the population of the United States now lives in cities and drives back and forth to work in air-conditioned vehicles. Americans work in cubicle farms, before glowing computer screens; they eat fast food and shop in glowing shopping malls. There is no place here for Hawkeye in his buckskins. Marshal Will Kane does not stalk those shiny floors alone, his eyes darting from the Taco Bell to the Wal-Mart entrance, looking for the Miller boys.

But America is also a nation of Quixotes, forever reaching into the past and reviving the heroes of myth, shrugging off cognitive dissonance much as Quixote did: All this is enchantment! All America becomes a fantasy theme park, a fictional world in which we can play out our sheepdog fantasies. Death lurks even in the Tastee-Freez. The sheepdog must seek the wolf, as Hawkeye must seek the frontier. The old frontier was a physical place, a territory lying out beyond the boundaries of civilization, where violence became inevitable. The new frontier is violence itself, and America is determined to seek it.

Kingdom of Fear

The Collapse of the Social Contract and the Culture of Armed Self-Defence

Las Vegas is a society of armed masturbators.

—Hunter S. Thompson

WE SURVIVE, DAY TO DAY, in brutal times. Ask anyone. You just can't trust people anymore, not with these gangs and these drugs and the kids today with no respect. Just yesterday two of them broke into this guy's house, this older guy, and they robbed him and beat the shit out of him with a baseball bat. Guy's in hospital. The cops got the guys and they say just an isolated incident, no danger to the public, which of course is bullshit. They just want you to go back to sleep. This kind of stuff never happened when we were growing up, we never did that kind of stuff. You had break-ins, sure, but that was just break-ins and never when people were home. But now, now they just don't care. There's no respect anymore. You get in the way, they just kill you. All for a few bucks, just enough to pay for their next fix.

Not like it was. Time was, you never even locked your doors. And that was when we lived with honest God-fearing people. You went to church on Sunday and you wore your Sunday best and that meant something, you know? You wore a suit. Not like now, the kids show up in jeans if they show up at all. Maybe they go to the mosque instead, I don't know. Wear towels on their heads. But that's okay, I don't mind those people. Good neighbours, and you know why? They know what family is. They look out for each other. They got values.

People used to stick together. You looked out for your neighbours. But anymore, people just don't care. You could be drowning and nobody throws you a line. You forget to lock your car one time and the next morning they cleaned the change out of your ashtray. Society is falling apart.

I wait for him to finish, let him say his piece, the same old story. The usual old man's get-off-my-lawn litany of social ills. Guy's about eighty, house and yard neat as a pin, lawn always mowed like a golf green. I'd smile and nod and walk on down the street but something he said caught my ear: *people used to stick together.* Maybe this crazy old coot was there when it all went down. Maybe he knows something.

"Where'd you grow up?"

"Place called Paradise Valley."

"That's out west someplace, right? I'm looking for someone came from there." I give him the victim's name.

"Oh, him," he says. "He's been dead for years."

"I met his granddaughter," I say, lying through my teeth. "She was wondering what happened to him."

"I didn't think he had any kids."

"Don't ask me. Maybe not the same guy."

Guess not, he says. But then he starts to talk, this guy. And he's older than you'd think, way old. I'd pegged him at about eighty but he's more like eight hundred and he's still sharp, he remembers it all. He remembers medieval England where the murder rate was like a Mexican drug war, then the Renaissance, as safe as the Sudan. By the time we sailed off to fight the Boers, the crime rate was more like Switzerland. And here I thought he said things were better back when.[143]

People learned, he says. We figured out we're all in this together. I need a car, I could go kill you and take yours but then I'm looking over my shoulder all the time. Makes more sense to make a deal and shake on it. And when I shake it better mean something, you better know you can trust me, right? My word better be my bond.

"And what if I say it isn't?"

"Pistols at dawn." He spits on his perfect lawn. "Nowadays, you sue. Anyways, next thing you have is a sheriff. You got a problem, you go to

---

143   Steven Pinker's *The Better Angels of Our Nature* provides a convincing overview of the evidence that crime and violence have in fact fallen over time, but, unlike my source, his reports are second-hand. It definitely helps to know someone really, really old.

him. You don't go stabbing people or whacking them with shillelaghs. You let the sheriff take care of it."

"'The king and his courts shall be the *vindices injurarium*,'" I say.

"The what?"

"Nothing. I guess it's the good old Leviathan."

"The what?"

"The Leviathan. Hobbes, you know."

"You smokin' dope or something?" Shaking his head. I know what he's thinking: these kids today. Me with my tinnitus, I'm still a kid to him.

"Anyway, you take it to the sheriff," I say. And that'll teach me to keep my mouth shut.

Yeah, he says, so you take it to the sheriff. Because we need each other, right? You want to live in Paradise Valley, you want to prosper, you got to live together. An eye for an eye makes the whole world blind, you know who said that? (I shook my head; I'd sworn off quotations and allusions by then.) Smart guy that Gandhi. Most of the time, anyway. Telling the Jews to turn the other cheek to Hitler, that was kind of dumb. So anyways, we learned to live together and things got a lot quieter. Things in Paradise Valley were good.[144]

"When did you leave?"

"Back in the sixties. You remember the sixties."

I admit I don't. I wasn't even born until the end.

"Peace and love, my ass. The Summer of Love? Bullshit. That was when the murder rate took off again. Six years down the road and the violent crime rate about doubled. And it just kept on getting worse and worse."

"So what happened?"

He looks at me as if I've started quoting Blackstone again. "Whattaya mean, what happened?"

"I mean who killed him?" I need to know. I need to find out when we all decided that we're not in this together anymore, and why.

"I don't know," he says. "That was about the same time I moved away. I wasn't there."

So I leave him there to rake his leaves and go back to the office and stare at the wall. I'm no closer and the clock is winding down. That's

---

144 The accepted explanation, that the spread of gentle commerce and a growing state monopoly on violence taught us increased self-control is covered by Norbert Elias's 1978 book, *The Civilizing Process*. He wasn't there, either.

what you get for taking on a cold case. But I'm getting ahead of myself. Let's start at the start.

THIS IS A MURDER MYSTERY.

It's a long way from the dusty streets of Will Kane's showdown to a quiet suburb in London, Ontario, on a cool spring evening, but there I was, walking alone. I don't remember what time it was, but it must have been late because it was already dark, and there must have been a chill in the air, because I was wearing my grey fleece jacket with the black trim, the warm one. As any witness to a crime will tell you, it's funny what you remember.

I also remember the car: a black Lexus RX that slid to a stop by the curb beside me, idling, its tinted passenger window sliding down to reveal some skinny teenaged kid with close-cropped blond hair, hunched forward in his seat.

"Excuse me ... we're kind of lost."

"Well, where are you going?"

"Look, can you show me ..." The kid fumbling with a map, turning it in his hands, trying to find which way was up. And something about him. He seemed nervous. Somewhere deep in the back of my mind an alarm bell was ringing, the ground radar warning of something on the move, out beyond the wire. But we're in the quiet suburbs, and this is just some kid in Daddy's Lexus, so I stepped forward as he held out the map, pointing at some street or another, and I turned my head to look down at his map, trying to place myself, barely aware of the rear passenger window now sliding down.

Something hit me, square in my left ear. Something wet and cold. And I am your sucker, have a good laugh, as I straightened and turned to face the rear passenger window and half-saw the figure crouched there before something coming at me, coming fast, and it hit my left eye, and I reeled back, blind.

The Lexus peels away with peals of laughter, the little shits. Blinking to clear my eyes, blind and unable to read their plate, swearing, my legs now pumping at a flat-out sprint to catch those little fuckers at the stop sign, drag that little shit out the window and drive his head into the pavement, hammer the curb with his face until he starts to convulse and twitch with yellowish cerebrospinal fluid dribbling from his ear. And I am through the stop sign now, legs still pumping uphill, the Lexus now out of sight. At the top of the hill I stopped, drawing air into my heaving lungs, the smell of vinegar in my nostrils. What the hell did they throw at me? My mouth filled with the taste of it, unable to name it, the tears streaming from my burning left eye, still half blind.

You little shits. You little cowards. It takes a lot of spine to drive away. You've got me outnumbered at least three to one and you still don't have the balls to stand and fight. Spineless little turds. The best part of you ran down your mother's leg. I could have been your father but the dog beat me up the stairs. I have a fine line in barrack-room insults, all of them futile.

So I walked on home, back down the hill in the dark with whatever-it-was running down my neck and over my grey fleece jacket with the black trim. Past the scene of the crime, a cup there that they had thrown at me, dark fluid splashed on the ground. Cars catching me in the glare of their headlights, drivers slowing to stare and then tromping the gas to speed away. My wife coming out from the living room, fear flooding her face.

"There's gonna be a fuckin' killing," I said.

But she thought there already had been a killing, because that vinegary smell, that taste I couldn't quite place, was ketchup: red ketchup covering the left side of my head, running from my hair, dripping down my jacket, and of course at first she thought it was blood because the worst is always possible, and who expects to see her husband walk through the front door covered in ketchup? And this, too, is why every car that passed me slowed and then accelerated suddenly away.

And so the police were called, and I went upstairs and showered the ketchup out of my hair and washed the ketchup out of my ear canal, and I threw my shirt and jacket and jeans in the wash and sat at the kitchen table while some cop scribbled in his notebook. The cop told me their cup was gone, that evidently they'd come back to pick it up, and I made a mental note that next time, next time you wait in the shadows and ambush the poor bastard when he returns to the scene of the crime, rush him fast so he never knows what hit him. As if there's going to be a next time. And then, on the cop's advice, the vision in my left eye still cloudy, it was down to the emergency room where an eye chart confirmed that I still could not see properly out of my left eye, which led me to two more appointments and finally to a specialist who suggested that my fuzzy vision was due to scratches to the cornea, which eventually would heal—although, as it turned out, my vision never did improve.

There are lessons here. Among most important is that when the ground radar picks up movement outside the wire, you ought to pay attention. Pull up and ask me directions today, and you are standing into danger. Do not stop me in the street to ask me for a light. If you ask me the time, I'll say I don't wear a watch, my eyes on you all the while. The vision in my left eye never did recover, and I am not fucking around.

Another is that ketchup is bad for you. My son, considering a plate of french fries, asked me to pass the stuff on over.

"The what?"

"The ketchup."

I gazed on him in wonder, trying to decipher his alien language, and my wife stood up and reached across and seized the ketchup for him.

"Oh," I said. "You mean the bottled evil."

I no longer use ketchup as a condiment, or for any other purpose, not because of some kind of post-traumatic stress but simply because when you've had that stuff in your ear and in your hair and in your eye and up your nose, it loses whatever appeal it ever held. The only appropriate substrate for ketchup is a grilled-cheese sandwich, which is a mistake in the first place because a grilled-cheese sandwich is essentially a pan-toasted heart attack. And I delight in impersonating Clint Eastwood as Dirty Harry in *Sudden Impact*, squinting: "Nobody, but *nobody*, puts ketchup on a hot dog."

But the greatest lesson of all is that if you find yourself walking home down some suburban street after dark, with your head and upper body dripping with what appears to be blood, nobody will stop to help you. You become a suburban Will Kane. The stalwart homesteaders of our ersatz Paradise Valley will slow down and goggle and then tromp the gas pedal and speed away before they risk getting embroiled in whatever is going on out there in the dark. So, although the killing I longed for never did happen—fortunately for everyone involved—something did die out there. Or something has gone missing, since we never did find the body, and we can't be entirely certain the killing ever actually occurred. Something waylaid our sense that we're all in this together. And me, with my tinnitus and my damaged vision and my guns stacked quietly in the safe: I am your Marlowe. I aim to find the killer. I know these streets, and I will take your fool's errand for the usual fee, plus expenses. Love is a hard-luck dame in cheap sunglasses, and I always was a sucker.

Oh, and one final lesson: it doesn't matter how mad you are. You can't outrun a Lexus.

LET US MAKE A LIST of the known suspects. Some point to rising divorce rates, the decline of the family, falling church attendance, and that despicable rock n' roll; things pretty much went to hell when that Elvis Presley began gyrating his hips. Others suggest that the mass migration from the peaceful countryside to the urban jungle done did it. Lieutenant Colonel Dave Grossman points to all of the above, and to Hollywood: once Hollywood dropped the Production Code, he complains, our entertainment became violent and depraved, and society followed suit. Lurking beneath many of these explanations is the usual racism couched in coded language: the problem is kids growing up without fathers (black people), the problem is hip-hop culture (black people), the problem is inner city gangs.

The criminologist James Q. Wilson, best known as a proponent of the broken-windows theory of policing, provides one of the more plausible explanations for the crime wave of the 1960s and 1970s: the problem was these kids today. Specifically, too damn many of them. Violence has always been a young man's game. Each generation of youth is a cohort of barbarians, and it falls to their elders and betters to civilize them. But with the arrival of the baby boom, Wilson argued, youthful barbarians overwhelmed society by weight of numbers, and the result was steadily rising violent crime that peaked, leveled off, and then declined again as the baby boomers matured into something resembling adulthood. And now, as the boomers approach their dotage, crime is falling back to pre-boom levels, and we're all pretty much getting back to normal except that the 1910 Fruitgum Company remains an indelible blight on the national consciousness. Some crimes, no jail sentence can ever erase.

Yet the arrival of the next big cohort of barbarians, the millennial generation, failed to produce a similar crime wave, unless we count crimes against common sense, in the form of an endless series of stupid articles on how special they are, written by supposed marketing experts.

Something else must have been at work, and by strange coincidence, the 1910 Fruitgum Company provides a clue. The cover of the band's 1968 album *1, 2, 3, Red Light* features a crime in progress: a cartoon young couple smooching innocently on a park bench while a moustachioed British bobby blows his whistle and raises an enormous white-gloved hand in the universal signal to cease and desist.[145]

Neither the 1910 Fruitgum Company nor their fans possessed any special social insight, but the artist who designed that album cover did understand something about the spirit of the age: the thing about the Man is, he doesn't want you to have fun. Public smooching is out. So are loud music, boisterous laughter, motorcycles, fast cars, tight and colourful clothing, suggestive dancing, drinking, and recreational drugs. All of these things offend the old, the fat, and the slow, and of course, the old, the fat, and the slow are in charge around here. Stop that, stop that, commands the bobby in his best Monty Python English: Move along, now, move along.

The problem was not these kids today so much as a society that had collectively lost faith in its institutions, in the government that makes its laws, the courts that interpret them, and the police that enforce them. When enough people lose faith in the bobby with his whistle and his white-gloved hand, the bobby loses his authority. Sir Robert Peel, who set up Britain's first professional police force in 1829, recognized that police ought to prevent crime, not arrest criminals after the fact. And they could only do that if the public trusted them. The police are the public and the public are the police, Peel's principles insist, "the police being only members of the public who are paid to give full-time attention to duties which are incumbent on every citizen in the interests of community welfare." The police could only hold onto trust by choosing persuasion over force and by impartial service to a law that, presumably, was fair and just. "The power of the police to fulfil their functions and duties is dependent on public approval of their existence, actions and behaviour," as Peel's principles have it. That the public must also approve of the laws the police uphold goes unsaid.

It is not police or the army or the king's strong arm that holds a stable democracy together, but consensus, our sense that we live in a shared

---

145   The author hastens to add that he does not own and has never seen a copy of this album, has never listened to it, has never heard the title track, and discovered the cover art only by accident while investigating the crime against humanity known as 1960s bubble-gum pop.

community, our faith in the institutions of democracy, our consent to be governed. The problem is that not everyone buys in—because, perhaps, they toil in dirty coal mines for a dollar a day, their life expectancy limited sharply by explosion, fire, cave-in and black lung, or perhaps because our shared community has decided that, because of their skin colour, they will be relegated to the back of the bus, to a separate drinking fountain, to the shabby neighbourhoods down where the freeway cuts through the old swamp.

But not everyone has to buy in. We just need enough people, a critical mass. Someone has to take the scab work, to join Don Chafin's makeshift army, to fill the ranks of the white police force that raids the wrong Detroit bar late one July night. And usually, there is no shortage of recruits. In *Harlan County, USA*, the strikebreakers stand convinced that the unions are full of communists and that the American economy is a zero-sum game: if we give those miners more money, we'll end up paying more for everything and we'll all be that much poorer for it. All across America, the white middle class had long been united by a fear of black men, as expressed in *The Birth of a Nation*. If you let those folks get above their station, everything falls apart. So things were not good, before the 1960s. Not for everyone. But things were stable.

In 1955, Rosa Parks declined to give up her seat on the bus, and young white people were ready to take her side. Women were disinclined to remain in their post-war kitchens. The Vietnam War further strained the social contract: the nation asked young men to die for it, and young men were not entirely sure that was a good deal. The old, the fat, and the slow didn't want you smooching in public, and they sure didn't want you smoking all that groovy grass, no matter that you never hurt nobody. And now the government was the enemy and the cops were the pigs, and you sure as hell weren't going to call the pigs on anyone. The counterculture made heroes of the Black Panthers, regardless of their criminal excesses, their murders of police officers, their rapes. They were on the right side, if only because they stood against the Man. The Man was the enemy.

FOR HUNTER S. THOMPSON, the turning point was the 1968 Democratic Convention in Chicago. For a follow-up to his first book, *Hell's Angels*, Thompson offered Random House a book on the death of the American dream—not so much the death of that vision of a house in the suburbs with two-and-a-half children and a car in the carport, but the death of do-your-own-thing, of an America within which you might carve out a space within which to live on your own terms. It was a half-formed idea. He had no idea how to deliver the book he had promised, no idea what shape or form it might take. He needed material. Thompson headed to Chicago, flying blind.

Thompson's experience there so shook him that at first he would not even speak of it. Limited details came out later, in his letters. Crossing a police line, he had shown his press pass; after a short, one-sided discussion of its validity, a cop speared him in the gut with his billy club. "That scene in Chicago made all the Berkeley protests look like pastoral gambols from another era," he wrote. "On Monday night I saw 3,000 lined up behind a barricade of park benches and garbage cans, beating on the cans with clubs and shouting: 'Pigs eat shit!' ... at a mass of 400 cops, about 100 yards away, chanting 'Kill, Kill, Kill ...'" Thompson knew which side he was on: "... in terms of the book I think I've come out of a fog."[146]

But Thompson was never able to turn that experience into the book he had promised. He struggled with it for three years, unable to find his way out of the "mire of information"; he had no shortage of material, but no handle with which to pull it together. Everything he wrote ballooned out of control, like his assignment on the NRA for *Esquire*, which grew to 140 pages. "Maybe the only way to get at the vitals of the American Dream is to come at it crab-wise," he wrote, which is exactly how he found it, when a *Sports Illustrated* assignment for a short piece on the Mint 400 motorcycle race turned into *Fear and Loathing in Las Vegas*.

Fear and Loathing in Las Vegas was Thompson's high-water mark as a writer. America itself is distilled in Las Vegas, a town filled with savage lizards, a "nest of armed loonies." It is the main nerve of the American dream: a greed-driven, anarchic culture awash in money fleeced from the rubes. Thompson's alter ego, Raoul Duke, and his attorney Dr. Gonzo, exist entirely outside the American consensus, travelling to cover a district attorneys' conference on narcotics and dangerous drugs with a suitcase full of drugs and a car called the White Whale, as if Moby Dick had surfaced alongside the *Pequod* to have a peek at Ahab. The 1960s are over, and the mood is paranoid. Gonzo, armed with a

---

146   Letter to Jim Silberman at Random House, September 3, 1968. Hunter S. Thompson, *Fear and Loathing in America: The Brutal Odyssey of an Outlaw Journalist, 1968–1976 (New York: Simon & Schuster, 2000), 119.*

.357 Magnum and a hunting knife he ordered from room service "to cut the limes," brims with violence. In a diner where Duke hoped to find safe haven from all the madness, Gonzo provokes the waitress and then threatens her with the knife. In Terry Gilliam's film adaptation, the scene is a turning point; Gonzo's gratuitous aggression tells us the joke has gone well past far enough. America in the 1960s was fun; in "this foul year of Our Lord, 1971," the joke is over.

"We are all wired into a survival trip now," Duke muses, as he reflects on the failure of the "essential old-mystic fallacy of the Acid Culture: the desperate assumption that somebody—or at least some force—is tending that Light at the end of the tunnel." And when survival is on the line, America goes armed. In a 1969 letter to Selma Shapiro, a publicist at Random House, Thompson wrote that he was "amazed … to find out how many people are seriously preparing for a street-war—and most of them want it." His acquaintances in the counterculture were "on a violence trip." There was no America anymore, no sense of a nation. There was instead a flag, a flag that stood for whatever your own thing happened to be. In place of "We the people," Thompson's new Declaration of Independence read, "Good luck—you're on your own."

We are all alone in our modern-day cities, each of us an isolate. On the shuttered streets of suburbia at dusk on a spring evening you might as well be Will Kane in his worthless little town, abandoned to face his fate, as I discovered with a face full of ketchup as blank-windscreened SUVs scurried past me in the darkness. And if I am your Marlowe then perhaps it's fitting that I should be suckered into a wild goose chase, trying to solve a murder that never happened. For there was no murder here. Nobody killed off Paradise Valley. It just died on the long road into Center City, like Granma Joad, just another victim of the Great Migration given a pauper's burial in some forgotten grave. Natural causes: old age, exhaustion, and a bad heart. And so here I am again, out in the dark; walking past rows of suburban windows illuminated by the soft light of televisions around which a nation of isolates huddles like cavemen around their campfires, fearing whatever lurks just beyond that circle of flickering light.

A CENTRIFUGAL MADNESS GRIPS THE NATION. City splits from country, left from right, youth from middle age. The family collapses, and its lonely fragments scatter. Gas prices spike and huge cars lie stranded and gasping in the desert like beached whales. Third-rate dictators burn the flag in contempt as the crumpled, melted wrecks of a helicopter and a C-130 Hercules lie in deadly embrace on an Iranian plateau. Decent folks have fled to the suburbs, and brutal times are upon us. Happiness is a warm gun.

If it bleeds, it leads—unless of course there is no video, in which case nobody cares. In the news business, video is gold. Any crappy old home video or security camera footage of a crime will do. Home invasion robberies captured on security cameras outlive their newsworthiness, but are preserved on YouTube for repeated viewing by people who like to frighten themselves. One such video of a home invasion in Tucson, on October 28th, 2012, aired on *Good Morning America*. In it, three men arrive at the home's front gate, apparently offering to do yard work; when the homeowner approaches, they overpower him, pull guns, and rob him and his family. One man was identified from the security camera footage and quickly arrested, but the other two remained at large, the television host gravely intoning that "they are already planning more robberies"—although this, of course, is something he could not possibly have known. The dramatic footage aired all over the United States, although the thieves got nothing more than wallets and cell phones.

Television, too, offers self-defence advice on shows such as the Outdoor Channel's *The Best Defense* and the Sportsman Network's *Personal Defense*. Hosted by a group of gun writers and former police officers, *The Best Defense* claims its hosts continually examine trends in crime so they can create "a model of violent crime" to better predict what you may face next on the mean streets of the suburbs. Crime scenarios are staged, and the reaction of the armed citizen critiqued for our education. The scenario repeats until he or she gets it right, rather like a video game.

The scenarios played out on *The Best Defense* push the fear meter's trembling needle into the red zone. On one episode a wife and daughter are followed home from the mall by criminals who park behind them in the driveway, walk boldly up to the door, and push their way into the house. The feckless husband, sitting on the couch watching television, is shot out of hand. Then the thugs drag the women upstairs: game over.

Michael Bane, who hosted *The Best Defense*, also hosts *The Shooting Gallery*, which features similar home-defence scenarios. "We're going to step you through a home invasion," a wide-eyed Bane warns in the intro to one episode. "Is it going to be scary? You bet!"

Bane and his guest, "top civilian and law enforcement trainer" Mike Dalton, go through what you need to do to prepare for the home invasion that surely threatens your family. You need a lock on your bedroom door. You need a cell phone, because your land line can be cut. Dalton goes on to advise us to arrange our bedrooms so that the bed is farthest from, and facing, the door. The bed itself should have a heavy, wooden headboard and footboard, so that it can stop or slow bullets. Your bedroom should be set up so as to provide a concealed, protected firing position where you can wait, gun at the ready, after calling 911.

And of course you need a loaded gun.

"In general, a gun for self-defence needs to be loaded," Dalton warns, before clarifying that if you have kids in the house, then, well, your gun still needs to be kept loaded. For safety, however, you could keep a loaded magazine in the gun without loading a round into the chamber, or perhaps keep your loaded gun on a shelf where the kids can't reach it.[147] But don't stick your gun in the nightstand drawer, because this is the first place the bad guy will look. Instead, you should sleep with a gun on the floor beside your bed, concealed under a newspaper or magazine. Or you can keep it in your closet, so when the bad guy bursts in and shoves you into the closet—something Dalton seems strangely confident he will do—you'll have it handy.

Another option, which Bane and Dalton neglect to mention, is The-Backup, a gun rack designed to attach to the side of your bed so you can keep your loaded shotgun within arm's reach as you sleep. When the home invader breaks through your locked bedroom door, you simply reach down, grab your gun, and greet him with a hail of deadly buckshot. "A shotgun sprays its ammunitions [sic] so you don't need a great shot to get the job done," promises the manufacturer's website, while neglecting to mention that the spread of a shotgun pattern in the distance between bed and bedroom door might be only three inches.

---

147   A gun with a loaded magazine inserted into the receiver should be considered loaded whether there is a round in the chamber or not. And putting a loaded gun on a shelf where the kids can't reach it is about as effective as putting the cookies on the top shelf of the cupboard. Neither of these suggestions is in the least safe.

On *Personal Defense*, meanwhile, our solemn host warns that "home invasions are scary ... they're things horror movies are made of." In the segment that follows, he demonstrates two incorrect ways to respond to the sound of a man breaking into your home, followed by the correct response. In the first run through, he stays put and calls the police; while he's on the phone, the bad guy comes into the room and shoots him. Next, he tries running down the hall and hiding while he calls the police, but again the bad guy comes into the room and shoots him. The key to survival, we soon learn, is to forget calling the police. Anyone who breaks into your house intends to kill you, and he will shoot you on sight; your only recourse is to take cover and shoot him first.

America is a nation of snake-oil salesmen, and fear is a hot commodity. "With residential invasions and break-ins consistently on the rise, leaving your home safety to chance is an extremely large risk," advises the website for The-Backup, neatly ignoring the fact that the rate of "residential invasions" is not actually measured, and that burglary rates are actually falling. Those facts make not a dent in our fear of the home invader.

"With more home invasions and break-ins, it's really important not only to secure your firearms but also to have them readily available," YouTube warns us, and then advertises ways to hide your gun in plain sight using "Tactical Walls"—mirrors, whiteboards, shelves and so on that open to reveal secret hiding places for guns. Tactical Walls helpfully sells a whole series of accessories so that you can customize your ready gun storage to hold extra ammo, flashlights, knives and other tactical paraphernalia. Another company makes the Flashbang and the Marilyn, holsters that attach securely to a woman's bra, allowing her to carry a concealed handgun without showing an obvious, unsightly bulge on her waistline. They also make the Betty and the Ava, for those days when you want to wear your gun on your belt—and you need all of these, of course, so that you always have a holster appropriate to your outfit. In a consumerist world, a gun is not just a weapon; it's a lifestyle and fashion accessory.

Fear motivates us and gives our boring lives meaning, and if no one is willing to scare us, we delight in scaring ourselves. The Internet has democratized the business of fearmongering, and a simple search reveals many takes on how to repel the dreaded home invasion. The dynamics of Internet discussion lead towards extreme preparation. Anything less than complete preparedness is "asking for it," the error of the naïve. It's not enough to keep a loaded gun around someplace, not with all these home invasions and robberies. "I am an advocate of carrying on the body at all times, even at home," declares a woman in her YouTube review of the Marilyn holster. "You never know what's gonna happen. You never know if someone's gonna bust through your front door and, um ... and ... wants to harm you and your family." Another YouTube expert, wide-eyed still, speaks of surviving a home invasion; yet as the story emerges, this "home invasion" turns out to have been nothing more than a late-night knock on the door. Another man heard a bump in the night, outside his suburban home. It could have been anything: a drug addict looking for money, a rapist looking for victims, a home invader looking to kill him just because, or even a raccoon getting into the garbage can. He reached for his gun and shouted out that he was armed. "My wife is pretty shaken up," he tells us. "I am pretty shaken up."

It's just another moonlit night in the Kingdom of Fear.

IT'S ENOUGH TO MAKE ME GLAD, once again, that I live in Canada, that safe land of socialized medicine, staunch Mounties, and multicultural harmony. Nobody here is going on TV to preach that I need to keep a gun hidden under the newspaper in my bedroom, the better to roll out of bed in a combat stance to ice some fucker who wants my iPad or my life. Nobody here is advertising bedside gun racks, Kevlar bedsheets, concealment holsters that clip to a bra, bedroom mirrors that slide up to reveal your handgun hidden in a recess in the wall. Here, you can't even buy a handgun for "home defence"; your stated purpose has to be something innocuous, like target shooting, and you have to keep that handgun locked away in a safe and disabled, its ammunition stashed away elsewhere.

But if Canada lies outside the Kingdom of Fear, it is at least a colony. In small-town Ontario you'll find men afraid to visit Toronto because they're convinced that, as *Globe & Mail* columnist Margaret Wente once told us, to witness a shooting in Toronto is a simple matter of setting up your Muskoka chair at Jane and Finch and brooding there until something goes down. Home invasions are on the rise, they insist. The Canadian Shooting Sports Association tells us that the good cower in their homes while the bad try the locks, while up in Ottawa the ugly have disarmed us and made it illegal to fight back. You can't even keep a gun handy; you have to keep it locked up in a safe where it will do you no good at all. And you can bet the criminals aren't keeping their guns locked up. As the home invader beats the life out of you with a length of pipe, you can take comfort in knowing that your gun is safely locked away where he can't get to it unless he really, really wants it.

Canada's gun nut sees his American big brother having all the fun, and he longs to join in. To own a gun is to seek justification, and if target shooting isn't enough then frightening yourself over crime will do. If only we could keep our guns handy, just in case; if only our government would just trust us, and treat us like adults. If only we could carry concealed handguns, we could go fearless into the dark night of Toronto, protected by our talismans. We could regain the security, autonomy, and power that Pierre Trudeau's Liberals took from us. We could regain our pride and become men again! And always, in the wings, there is some American listening in, who tells us in a stage whisper how glad he is that he doesn't live in Canada, where we have no rights, where we are, for all intents and purposes, the slaves of an overweening socialist government, where we wait like sheep for the slaughter.

To people who actually live in Toronto and who walk its not-so-mean streets daily, this is like listening to space aliens who, having abandoned sexual reproduction millennia ago, now puzzle and argue over the function of a vibrator recovered from a sex shop in Los Angeles by a deep-space reconnaissance team. It's probably for mixing some kind of cake batter. For loosening drywall screws. For opening champagne bottles by slowly agitating the contents: see, as you apply vibration, pressure slowly builds until suddenly—pow!—and the pressure is released and the champagne flows, just like that. Little green men of indeterminate gender nod their oversized crania in agreement: a plausible hypothesis at last!

Who are these goddamned Martians? Have they ever been to Toronto? Probably not, truth be told. And strangely, their small towns are statistically more dangerous than Toronto, which, unless you happen to involve yourself in the drug trade, is one of the safest cities in

Canada.[148] In the annual Statistics Canada homicide-rate sweepstakes, Toronto, a perennial also-ran well back in the pack, never figures. The smart money bets on smaller places, on Thunder Bay or Prince George or Abbotsford. And if you want to take a long shot and bet on a major city, you would bet on a Western city, on Winnipeg or Regina. The common thread, although StatsCan carefully avoids being specific, is that Canada's most dangerous places are troubled First Nations communities, places where alcoholism and drug use are distressingly common and young men—the people most likely to do violence in any community—see little hope for the future. This is, of course, not a problem with First Nations communities themselves, because these same communities are also places where people get out of bed each morning and go off to work and raise their families. It's a problem with Canada. It is the same problem we see in the so-called urban jungle, where crime rates are highest among young black males, and where murder rates are highest of all among those young black males who choose careers in crime. For these communities, the social contract has nothing to offer. For these, Canada is a failed state.

But these communities have nothing to do with our conservative, small-town male, who's convinced that his front door could crash in under the weight of two armed and determined home invaders at any time. His world is quiet and safe, no matter how he frightens himself. Of course, he can always tell you otherwise. All he needs to do to scare himself is to turn on his TV and watch the news.

ON APRIL 8, 2009, eight-year-old Tori Stafford left school in Woodstock, Ontario, a sleepy little town of about 38,000 people known best for having been hit by two F4 tornadoes way back in 1979. Security cameras recorded Stafford leaving in the company of a young woman with dark, ponytailed hair, wearing a white jacket. That young woman was eighteen-year-old Terri-Lynne McClintic. Pathetic and needy, McClintic had fallen for Michael Rafferty, a sociopathic creep who pimped out women he picked up through online dating services and fantasized about breaking into homes to rape single mothers. Rafferty had picked up McClintic at a pizza joint by the simple expedient of referring to her as a "hot little number"; she returned the

---

148   Joycelyn Francisco and Christian Chenier, "A Comparison of Large Urban, Small Urban, and Rural Crime Rates," Canadian Centre for Justice Statistics (2007).

compliment by hopping in his car and fucking him in a parking lot while her mother's pizza got cold. To Terri-Lynne McClintic, Michael Rafferty was all that: he had his own car, and his own Blackberry, and he actually *liked her*.

McClintic did exactly as she was told. She took Tori Stafford to Rafferty's car, as he had instructed, and they drove off. At the Home Depot, McClintic went in to buy garbage bags and a hammer while Rafferty waited in the car with Stafford. Then Rafferty drove to a secluded spot where he raped the girl and then beat her to death with the hammer as McClintic stood by. Rafferty left Stafford's body in a garbage bag wearing only a Hannah Montana T-shirt and a pair of earrings she had borrowed from her mother.

Reason howls its demand for a rationale, and finds none. God shrugs: the girl died just because. And as Rafferty goes to trial, with McClintic now the Crown's star witness, a reporter from the local newspaper treks dutifully to some park and finds parents clinging tightly to their kids. One parent remarks that you just can't be too careful anymore, you just can't let your kids out of your sight. Suburban parents insist on driving their kids to school in the morning, a distance of two whole blocks. And, it being an ordinary day in Canada, six people will be killed and 474 injured in car accidents.[149] Some of them, no doubt, will be on their way to school.

Fear sells. Neil Postman, in his 1985 book *Amusing Ourselves to Death*, suggested that, as an inevitable consequence of the medium, TV news has reinvented itself as entertainment. Television keeps viewers riveted by feeding them a continual stream of stories more stimulating than informative, more entertaining than accurate. And as sociologist Barry Glassner pointed out in *The Culture of Fear* (1999), the journalist's ideal crime story has a predictable structure that lends itself to dramatization. The victim is likeable and innocent, the perpetrator is clearly a villain, the details are simple and unambiguous, and finally, the story suggests a frightening trend, the better to thrill the viewer. You could be next!

Reporters find evidence of a trend because they are looking for it. Events that might otherwise go unremarked receive heavy coverage just so long as some imaginary connection creates a news hook.

---

149   Based on 2009 data from Transport Canada: 2,209 killed, 172,883 injured.

Days after Justin Bourque shot five police officers in Moncton, New Brunswick, in 2014, Canadian media breathlessly reported that parts of Dartmouth, Nova Scotia, were under lockdown as police sought a man who had been seen on a rooftop with a rifle. That man was never found. On the same day, police in London, Ontario, arrested a man who was seen in a busy city park with what turned out to be a pellet gun. But although the local paper dutifully alluded to the Moncton shootings, the story received no coverage outside London. There was no City On Lockdown, and no fear of a Gunman At Large. Efficient arrests of armed men who actually exist are less frightening than scares inspired by imaginary gunmen on rooftops. One makes national news; the other is a footnote.

Spend enough time in front of the tube and you'll come down with the mean world syndrome, the conviction that the world is a nasty, dangerous place filled with cruel predators who live just to do you harm. Television news, which relies on drama but provides little background or context for the events it reports, is the vector for the mean-world parasite. The more sensationalist the stories, the stronger the effect. People who like sensationalist stories are predisposed to distrust humanity, and the stories they watch feed that predisposition, like Jimi Hendrix's guitar squealing directly into its own amplifier. Keep your eyes on the tube, and you'll soon be scared silly.

Still, no one admits to his fear, least of all the armed citizen. True Men are not afraid. Dirty Harry continues chewing his hot dog even as he guns down bank robbers. Fear is an emotional state, and men pride themselves on being rational creatures, devoid of emotion, whatever the evidence to the contrary. It's unmanly to admit you're afraid to walk to the corner store after dark, past that apartment parking lot where some guy was stabbed two—or was it three?—years ago. To suggest that fear of crime motivates handgun sales, that the gun is the great American security blanket, is to attack traditional masculine values using the language of traditional masculinity. The sheepdog's reaction is predictably furious.

But to borrow from Forrest Gump, fearful is as fearful does. Neutralize the negative connotations; call it apprehension, worry, concern, or awareness. The entire culture of armed self-defence, which insists that a man's role is to protect his family and that women need to be armed to protect themselves from rapists, is propelled by fear. Talk to the self-defence advocate about break-ins, and he will tell you about home invasions.[150] To a man who owns guns for self-defence, criminals are not losers who commit crimes because it's all they can do, and who are mostly after money; criminals are predators who intend harm for harm's sake, who are motivated by a sociopathic desire to hurt others.

The General Social Survey has asked Americans if there is "anywhere near where you live—that is, within a mile—where you would be afraid to walk alone at night" since the 1960s, and since the early 1970s, almost half of Americans have consistently answered Yes. Criminologist and sociology professor Mark Warr has noted, "Americans react to [the fear of crime] through a variety of precautionary behaviours so pervasive and normative that they form a significant and defining element of American culture."[151] In simpler terms, the fear of crime is so widespread that we don't even notice the myriad precautions we take to try to keep ourselves and our families safe. We may say we're not afraid, but our actions say otherwise. Fearful is as fearful does. When the going gets scary, the scared go armed.

"ANYBODY IN POSSESSION OF A WEAPON and the ability and will to use it immediately gains some security, autonomy and power, even if he is alone—as most people are in American cities," writes William Vollmann.[152] Fixated on the potential victimhood of every woman he knows, and on his own, he will illegally conceal a .45-calibre pistol in his pocket to accompany his fiancé as she walks her dog through the foggy Sacramento night. The Sacramento newspapers are filled with

---

150   A burglary is a property crime in which the perpetrator typically tries to avoid any contact with his victim; a home invasion is a crime of violence, in which the perpetrator seeks out the victim for the purpose of robbery. Home invasions are repeatedly used as evidence that safe-storage regulations endanger lives, although home invasions are in fact quite rare. Fear sells. I have been told that "hundreds" of home invasions occur each year in rural Ontario, always by people with no idea how many really do happen but who long to keep loaded guns handy, and who want to believe they're common. In fact, no statistics are kept on the Canada's home-invasion rate, but in most break-ins the homeowner is not even at home; and in most break-ins where the homeowner confronts the burglar, the burglar flees.

151   Mark Warr, "Fear of Crime in the United States: Avenues for Research and Policy," in *Criminal Justice 2000, Volume 4: Measurement and Analysis of Crime and Justice* (Washington: US Department of Justice Office of Justice Programs, 2000), 452.

152   William T. Vollmann, *Rising Up and Rising Down: Some Thoughts on Violence, Freedom, and Urgent Means* (New York: Harper Perennial, 2005), 61.

mayhem and Vollmann's fear is palpable on the page. No one, perhaps, has so eloquently expressed the appeal of going armed. Security, autonomy, and power: Vollmann's .45 is no childish security blanket, but a powerful talisman, heavy in his coat pocket, against the rising sense of helplessness that cripples us when violence lurks in dark corners. "Mr. Nine Millimetre here," says Jules (Samuel L. Jackson) in *Pulp Fiction*, while pointing said 9mm at Pumpkin's head, "he's the shepherd protecting my righteous ass in the valley of darkness."

Fear makes us impotent; weaponry restores our power, because weapons are above all sources of power. "The power that weaponry confers has been conventionally treated as exclusively violence-enhancing," writes the criminologist Gary Kleck.[153] "This is an unduly restrictive conceptualization of the significance of weaponry. A broader perspective starts with a recognition of weapons as sources of power, used instrumentally to achieve goals by inducing compliance with the user's demands." Or, guns restore freedom of action to those who might otherwise be induced to comply with the demands of others—or they restore security, autonomy, and power to those whom fear might otherwise control. The gun is about power.

The security and power afforded by the loaded .45 carried illegally in your coat pocket are illusory, given that a potential assailant is probably likewise armed, but its cold metallic immanence restores your faith that a greater power watches over us. That power enables Vollmann to walk as chivalric escort into a foggy Sacramento night, protected even from those who likely meant him no harm to begin with. "That night when I went out with the Asian woman to walk her dog (a lonely, foggy night when anything could happen), I did not feel afraid when two men sauntered towards us. I nodded at them, my hand on the loaded .45 most feloniously concealed in my coat pocket. They sneered back. They were ugly, intimidating men. But I didn't feel intimidated. They walked on, and the fog ate them."

The gun is my shepherd; I shall not want. He restoreth my courage: he leadeth me in the True Man's path of righteousness. Yea, though I walk through the valley of the shadow of death, I will fear no evil: for thou art with me; thy rod and thy staff they comfort me. Thou preparest a table before me in the presence of mine enemies: thou anointest my

---

153   Gary Kleck, *Targeting Guns: Firearms and their Control* (Hawthorne, NY: Aldine de Gruyter, 1997), 218.

head with oil; my cup runneth over and I fret not that I flash a nice watch in a bad neighbourhood. I am bad-ass.

THE DOG DEMANDS HER WALK.

She is not precisely subtle about this, my Sadie: she sits down in front of me as I watch television or read, and she stares.

This dog could stare down the Sphinx. I can keep right on reading, but I can see here there from the corner of my eye, sitting absolutely still. I've tried staring back, but she doesn't blink. Must be some canine inner-eyelid thing. If I try to startle her, she barks. Hold out too long, and she puts a paw on my knee: Look, buddy, a dog's gotta do what a dog's gotta do, if you catch my drift, and it ain't my carpet is all I'm saying. So I find my shoes and jacket and the leash. I still have the grey-fleece jacket with the black trim, and it must have been five or six years back. The ketchup didn't stain. I can still point out the driveway where it all happened.

I'm not twitchy about it. Understand this: I rarely even think of it. The kids who did this thing have probably all graduated university by now—I think if you're cruising the streets in Daddy's Lexus, you're bound for university whether you like it or not—and they might even be settling into their first real jobs, and probably never think of it at all. Or they're off to law school. Likely they don't even know that they did any permanent damage, thought the whole thing was just a joke. My left eye is blurry at any distance but my right is better than 20/20 so it more or less makes up for things; if I have to read fine print I can always cover the bad eye. But I would make a lousy pirate. I am left-eye dominant and shoot left-handed, my bad eye guiding the muzzle to the bird. The brain picks out what it needs and with both eyes open it seems the right fills in the details. Otherwise, I wouldn't be able to hit a thing.

All of which is beside the point. Yes, you caught me: I spent that last paragraph avoiding the real question. No, I am not afraid to walk those same streets at night. If I were, I would not take the dog. You can hit me in the eye with your bottled evil but the dog is another matter. And I could go armed, too, in spite of the law, but feel no need. My mother will tell me to be careful, and this is the first lesson: when the ground radar picks up movement out beyond the wire, pay attention. It's a simple rule, really.

But I wonder, at a time like this, when I am touring the Kingdom of Fear: what if I did go armed? What if I lived in Florida, and could stand my ground? Would I go armed, if I lived there? Or would I even walk the streets at night? Would some dipshit kid be dumb enough to try a joke like that if he knew the guy he pulled it on might be carrying a concealed 9mm pistol, a nasty little job with a black composite slide that'll make three quick holes for your life to leak through, all over Daddy's leather Lexus seats? It's easy to think you're not that guy on the news but then, you've never been there.

What if I lived in Detroit? There's a place where you could make a good case for going armed: all those empty city blocks and a murder rate like El Salvador. Alternatively, New Orleans. It's all well and good to read the research, as I have, and to know that even in these places your risk depends in large part on who you are and who you know; the wolves prey on the wolves more than they prey on those poor old sheep. But you'll forget those studies when you're out at night against the best advice and that black Lexus sidles up to the curb. I'll guarantee that.

I see that eyebrow, the one you're raising at me, Miss Fancy Therapist. Yes, I know you caught that. You want to know just how I react when that black Lexus slides up beside me, even now. You want to know what goes through my head.

Not fear. Not exactly.

Because real men are not afraid? Come on, now. I read that last bit you wrote, too.

What's fear, then?

Let's see: "Call it apprehension, worry, concern, or awareness." You wrote that. Or have you forgotten?

Apprehension, maybe. Worry, no. Concern or awareness, yes. Once bitten, twice shy and all that. That black SUV slides up as its window slides down and I make damn sure to take a good look at who's in that passenger seat. Usually she's about seventy and her husband is driving and they really are lost. But I'm not taking one step off that sidewalk until I'm sure just what's going on. And yes, some back corner of my brain is running down a list of options. Such as? Such as, what's your escape route.

And if I went about armed? Yes, then that would make the list of options. Concealed nine, inside-waistband holster. I'm right-handed but left-eye dominant, tilt my head to the right and shoot a handgun with my left eye. Not that I've actually shot a handgun in about twenty-five years.

And when that black SUV rolls up? What then?

Molon Labe

The New Constitutionalism and the Paranoid Style in American Politics

Once you take away the guns, you can do anything to the people.

—Timothy McVeigh

JESSE JAMES LIES DEAD, DEFEATED, slain by the coward Robert Ford. The Leviathan smiles, baring long yellow teeth, and flexes its claw, its cold metallic grip tightening that net of steel, like a constrictor encircling its prey. The great snake is patient. It does not squeeze, but simply waits for you to breathe out and then draws up the slack, ratcheting its grip ever tighter until you cannot inhale. The realm of possibility shrinks: rails vibrating with the power of the hissing beast morph into wires thrumming with strange electricity, their messages zinging from point to point at the speed of thought: names, faces, credit card numbers, personal histories. You can't check into a hotel or rent a car without a credit card, and as soon as it slides into the machine's greedy slot they have your number, bub, they know where you buy your groceries and what you eat and how much ammo you have in the basement and, yes, they know all about your thing for cheerleaders. You exhale again and the beast tightens its grip, the air itself now humming with its power, the whispering of the wireless world. They know where you live and they know where you are, your cell phone silently ratting you out by GPS. You cannot fight the power of the Great Snake, your shrinking autonomy. On the Internet you read that the Department of Homeland

Security is stockpiling ammunition and they know you have read that because the NSA is watching, they know that you know and now you are marked, the snake watching you with its baleful red eyes. They know you know about the weather control, the chem trails, the bird kills from their weapons tests, but the snake is ever patient, calm, waiting for you to exhale one more time so it can tighten its grip and crush the last of your autonomy, security, and power. In the darkness, the thwop of helicopter blades: a small constellation of blinking nav lights skims the treeline. They are out there.

The same great migration that uprooted people from the land and sent them looking for work in the cities brought us the welfare state. And as the state grew and began to do obnoxious things like taxing the rich to feed the poor, an inevitable backlash arose. Objection to the New Deal fed post-war anti-communism and created a movement that soon departed from common sense and went spinning off, out of control, according to its own mad logic—logic that led eventually to the conclusion that only guns can keep us free, and that any attempt to take our guns away must be the ploy of tyrants determined first to disarm and then to enslave us. And thus was born perhaps the nuttiest wing of the American gun culture: the patriot movement. Less a cohesive political movement than a loose collection of paranoid, ultranationalist ideas flying in close formation, the patriot movement wraps itself in the flag and adopts the symbolism of the Revolutionary War, preaching that traitors in Washington have moved the nation far from its roots and betrayed the constitution. That the Second Amendment is the single most important sentence in the Bill of Rights is taken on faith. But to understand why the patriot movement reveres the Second Amendment, we must start at the start.

Robert Welch, a retired candy maker and the inventor of Junior Mints, started out on the loopy, far-right fringe of post-war anti-communism. By the late 1960s, Welch had developed into a flat-out paranoid crackpot, having convinced himself that a shadowy conspiracy of international bankers—some shadowy They—controlled world events. The organization he founded, the John Birch Society, lies so far to the right that it denounced Nixon and Reagan as liberals and declared that Eisenhower was a communist agent. "Almost every day I run into some whole new area, where the Communists have been penetrating and working quietly for years, until now they are in virtual control of everything that is done in that slice or corner of our national life," Welch declared at the founding meeting of the John Birch Society, in 1958. "You have only a few more years before the country in which you live will become four separate provinces in a world-wide Communist dominion ruled by police-state methods from the Kremlin."[154]

Later, Welch changed his tune from nutty to crazy: the masterminds of the global conspiracy were not, in fact, the communists in the Kremlin, which conveniently explained the Kremlin's failure to impose world-wide communist dominion or even to keep the Soviet Union under its thumb. Instead, Welch's shadowy They morphed into the Illuminati, or later, "the Insiders": international bankers and captains of industry who controlled world affairs to their own ends. The Insiders controlled both the United States and the Soviet Union and were manipulating global affairs towards a socialist "New World Order," the culmination of their two-hundred-year conspiracy. The Insiders had already succeeded in perverting the very idea of the United States in the minds of its own people: the United States was never intended to be a democracy ruled by the whims of the populist mob, as the Insiders had led its people to believe. It was a constitutional republic in which the only legitimate power was the enlightened will of the founders, embodied in the constitution, which would provide for the good of all. And the enlightened will of the founders naturally aligned with Welch's rightwing libertarianism: Americans were to be free of any encumbering regulation that might interfere with the ideal commonwealth of every-American-for-himself. To Welch, government existed for the express purpose of stomping on the personal autonomy of citizens, which, until the New Deal came along and wrecked everything, had properly been the role of free enterprise.

Even in its heyday in the early 1960s, when it boasted one hundred thousand members, the John Birch Society lay on the outer fringe of the American right. But by wrapping themselves in the flag at the height of the Cold War, the Birchers placed themselves above criticism.[155] And

154 The founding principles of the John Birch Society are laid out in *The Blue Book*, the complete text of Welch's remarks at the organization's founding meeting, which has gone through many revisions as times have changed. Anyone who needs a good dose of crazy can track down a copy online.

155 Anti-communism was sufficiently powerful in the 1960s that Bob Dylan was barred from performing "Talkin' John Birch Paranoid Blues," which mocked the Birchers, on the Ed Sullivan

their ideas carried like the smell of an outhouse on a hot day: even one hundred yards downwind you can still pick up a faint whiff. Today's patriot movement reeks of the Birchers.

Anti-communism morphs easily into a general paranoid conspiracy theory, drawing ultimately on the Protocols of the Elders of Zion, and leading to the conviction that government exists for the very purpose of enslaving American citizens. To the paranoid right, this is the only reason men seek power. But before they can enslave you, they'll have to take away your guns. Gun control, therefore, must flow from the desire to enslave you. Any step to restrict guns must be the precursor to a campaign of genocide. Why else disarm the public? Even apparently reasonable attempts at gun control are a short skid down the slippery slope, a ploy of the "gun grabbers," who seek to chip away at gun rights until nothing is left.

Fortunately, the founding fathers had the foresight to include the Second Amendment in the Constitution of the United States. You owe it to them, and to the flag, not to give one inch. To protect your guns is your solemn duty as a Patriot.

IN 480 BCE, WHEN THE PERSIAN army threatened to encircle the Greeks at Thermopylae, it fell to a force of three hundred Spartans to fight a delaying action to cover the Greek retreat. Xerxes of Persia issued the hopelessly outnumbered Spartans an ultimatum: Surrender your arms. King Leonidas of Sparta responded with *"Molon labe,"* which essentially translates to "come and take them." Being uttered in ancient Greek lends gravitas to this schoolyard taunt, and so it has been passed down through the ages and adopted by American gun-rights patriots, who have given the events that followed their own unique spin: the courageous Spartans, who were slaughtered, bought time for the Greeks to arm themselves, prepare, and ultimately defeat the Persians, thus saving Greek democracy and guaranteeing that the founding fathers could look to it as they sat down, with God guiding their quills, to create the Constitution of the United States. Little did he know it at the time, but at Thermopylae, Leonidas fought for the Second Amendment itself: he was a true American hero, two millennia before the fact.

show. Mainstream America would let you say anything you wanted, as long as you were anti-communist. But a grubby folk singer, making fun of anti-communists? Far too controversial.

Molon labe entered the discourse of the great American Gun Kerfuffle in the late 1990s and has since become ubiquitous among gun rights hardliners. Those two Greek words now appear on T-shirts, hats, pens, buttons, embroidered patches, bracelets, dog tags, belt buckles, bumper stickers, coffee cups, water bottles, mouse pads, knife blades, trigger guards, AR-15 ejection port covers, and anywhere else one might care to stick an ancient Greek slogan. They appear on the stylized Greek helmets selected by gun activists as their online avatars. Inspired by fears of the UN Arms Trade Treaty, one image circulating online depicts a UN blue helmet with a bullet hole through it, and the slogan "*Molon labe.*" *Molon labe* is also the title of a novel by one Boston T. Party, an insurrectionist fantasy imagining Wyoming's brave stand against the federal government.[156] Often written in ancient Greek lettering, an alphabet most of its proponents cannot even decipher, *Molon labe* has become the new watchword of the gun.

This insurrectionist, come-and-take-them mindset is not limited to scattered militia fantasists who boast online of their willingness to take on the government from suburban basements. The paranoid constitutional ideology that began with the Birchers is so widespread today that even American soldiers now speak of fighting the US Army, and American police officers of resisting American police. Oath Keepers, an organization of American soldiers and law-enforcement officers who promise not to obey orders that violate the US Constitution, asks its members to take its *Molon Labe* Pledge:

> We will never disarm. We will never surrender our military pattern, semi-automatic rifles and the full capacity magazines, parts, and ammunition that go with them. The fundamental purpose of the Second Amendment is to preserve the military power of We the People so we will have effective means to resist tyranny. Regardless of what unholy, unconstitutional filth issues from the mouths of oath breakers in "Mordor on the Potomac" our answer is MOLON LABE.

---

156   Mr. Party's novel reminds me of the Seinfeld episode in which Jerry complains that his comic nemesis, Tim the Dentist, has only converted to Judaism for the jokes. Does this offend Jerry as a Jew? "No, it offends me as a comedian." *Molon Labe* is a rare foray into fiction for Mr. Party, who is better known for numerous books loosely defined as non-fiction, including *Surviving Doomsday: A Practical Guide* and the helpful (if unnecessary) *Boston on Surviving Y2K*. Boston T. Party is the psuedonym of Kenneth Royce.

If "Mordor on the Potomac" insufficiently explains Oath Keepers' attitude towards the federal government, reading a bit more of the pledge may help clarify it:

> We will not register ourselves or our arms. Registration is the prerequisite to confiscation, which is the prerequisite to dictatorship and extermination. We will NOT be photographed, finger-printed, tracked, and subjected to psych-evaluations like convicted sex-offenders just for owning semi-automatic rifles. Doing so is itself an act of surrender and submission, taking the mark of the slave (it is akin to taking the mark of the Beast).

The *Molon labe* pledge, which declares that any law banning firearms would be "an act of war against the American people, and thus an act of treason," is that Oath Keepers will not enforce gun-control laws, and specifically will not enforce any laws creating a gun registry, banning so-called assault weapons, or banning high-capacity magazines. But it doesn't stop there. Oath Keepers promise to actively resist the enforcement of such laws: "We will interpose ourselves between the people and the oath breakers and traitors who try to disarm them." Any law-enforcement officers who attempt to enforce a gun-control law will be acting outside the constitution and are "no better than violent street criminals"—and you know how the sheepdog responds to the wolf. For Oath Keepers, the Second Amendment has become the entire constitution.

Though there are only a few thousand Oath Keepers, many outside its official ranks are believers. Following the Sandy Hook massacre, as Congress debated a renewed assault-weapons ban, twenty-eight of twenty-nine Utah sheriffs aped Oath Keepers pledges and promised that they would not enforce laws that violated the constitution. Later, when Colorado introduced new gun-control laws, Colorado sheriffs vowed not to enforce them, and fifty-four county sheriffs subsequently sued to have those laws struck down.

They lost.[157] And here is the problem with letting the sheriff, or any other citizen, decide which laws are constitutional and which laws are

---

157 On July 26, 2014, US District Chief Judge Marcia Krieger ruled that the laws were constitutional. She had also ruled that the fifty-four county sheriffs had no standing to sue the state in their capacity as sheriffs, requiring them to sue as private citizens.

not: none of us can say, and if we think we can, we are likely wrong. This is what the courts are for. Given that the Supreme Court of the United States has never ruled that an assault-weapons ban would be unconstitutional—the language of *DC v. Heller* suggests it might be, but carefully allows room for the alternative—Oath Keepers has overstepped its bounds, unless some of its members moonlight as Supreme Court justices when they aren't arresting shoplifters. And given the well-documented record of police forces treating civil rights as an inconvenience to their investigations, their sudden zeal for the constitution seems misplaced.

But in the new constitutionalism, interpreting the meaning of the Bill of Rights is not the job of lawyers or the courts, and their reinterpretations of its meaning are inherently suspect. No; the meaning of the constitution's text is plain, and easily accessible to anyone who can read. Constitutional fundamentalists borrow from their religious counterparts by adapting the Protestant *sola scriptura* to the Bill of Rights: the only authority on the Bill of Rights is the Bill of Rights itself, and all of its important meanings are plain. As the *Westminster Confession of Faith* put it in 1646, "those things which are necessary to be known, believed, and observed, for salvation, are so clearly propounded and opened in some place of Scripture or other, that not only the learned, but the unlearned, in a due use of the ordinary means, may attain unto a sufficient understanding of them." In short, not everything about the Word of God—be it the Bible or the Constitution of the United States—is plainly obvious, but all the important things are. And so, in spite of the wide latitude for gun control left by *DC vs. Heller*, the Second Amendment's plain meaning is unambiguous to the true believer: Shall Not Be Infringed.

It is no coincidence that constitutional fundamentalism and religious fundamentalism fly in close formation. Both reassure a worldview that has little tolerance for ambiguity, nuance, or contradiction. In place of those messy, contradictory, slippery facts, scripture offers laws, a Holy Trump Card to conquer all. Moses had two stone tablets, carven by a divine chisel; the United States has better calligraphy.

NOTHING IS SO DANGEROUS AS A bad idea with a loaded gun. Bad ideas have always found their agents in disaffected young men, men with lousy jobs and money problems, men with a history of bad luck with women. Men whose problems are not of their own making, but are instead the product of dark forces and conspiracies. Not conspiracies against them personally—that would be paranoid!—but against *their people*. Violence, that used-car salesman, lays down its catalogue of wrongs and asks which we would like to avenge. America's paranoid right chooses Ruby Ridge and Waco.

During the 1980s and 1990s, the patriot movement became increasingly entangled with a resurgent white supremacist movement. The two had always been close neighbours; many basic patriot tenets, such as the shadowy conspiracy of international bankers it opposes, have obvious anti-Semitic roots. And so, on the fringes of the right, America's love affair with autonomy via the gun found expression in fantasies of a last stand against the New World Order's Zionist Occupation Government, or ZOG. Bush the Elder and Mikhail Gorbachev stoked the fire with their remarks that the end of the Cold War had ushered in a "new world order"—the choice of those specific words by both the Soviet and American leaders indicating, to the paranoid right, that the conspiracy the Birchers had long warned against was now approaching fruition.

In the early 1980s, Randy Weaver bought a twenty-acre property near Ruby Ridge, Idaho, just forty miles from the Canadian border and more or less in the middle of nowhere, to wait out the apocalypse that his devoutly Christian wife, Vicki, had convinced herself was imminent. Weaver was a white separatist and a former Green Beret who had joined the US Army during the Vietnam War, hoping to see action. He was disappointed to find himself posted instead to Fort Bragg in North Carolina while the army in its wisdom sent unwilling conscripts to fight the communists, so he quit the army and moved back home to Idaho. In 1986, at a meeting of the Aryan Nations, Weaver met an informant for the Bureau of Alcohol, Tobacco, Firearms and Explosives (ATF) who tried to talk him into selling two sawed-off shotguns. The ATF hoped to use the threat of National Firearms Act charges to get at what they really wanted: another informant.

Weaver refused to play along. He had sold two shotguns, but insisted that the ATF's informant had sawed them off after the fact. He insisted also that he was not a member of the Aryan Nations, and could not give the ATF any information anyway. So the ATF made good on its threat, and moved on the shotgun charges. Weaver was given notice, through his lawyer to appear in court on February 20, 1991. But a probation officer also sent Weaver a letter with the court date erroneously cited as March 20. Perhaps because of that confusion, Weaver never appeared in court, and on August 21, 1992, a group of US marshals moved in to reconnoiter the Weaver cabin, preparing to arrest a man the federal authorities considered armed and dangerous.

But the marshals alerted Weaver's yellow lab, Striker, who ran off uphill to investigate, with Weaver, his fourteen-year-old son Sammy, and Kevin Harris, a family friend, following close behind. "I realized immediately that we had run smack into a ZOG/NEW WORLD ORDER ambush," Weaver later wrote. Sammy Weaver, Deputy US Marshal Bill Degan, and Striker were shot and killed. Kevin Harris claimed that the US marshals shot the dog first, that Sammy then shot back, and that he then killed Bill Degan in self-defence; the marshals' version of events has Degan challenging Harris, Harris shooting Degan, and then a general firefight during which Striker and Sammy were killed. Kevin Harris would ultimately be acquitted of killing Degan, on grounds of self-defence. But before Kevin Harris would come to trial, he would have to be taken into custody. And with a US marshal dead, the feds weren't messing around.

Given Weaver's history, the authorities saw him as a dangerous wingnut. Vicki Weaver was herself loopier than a bag of cold spaghetti, and had sent the ATF threatening letters that did little to improve her husband's image. She promised that "the tyrant's blood shall flow" and that "whether we live or die we will not obey you … war is upon our land." Mindful of a threat profile that painted Weaver a dangerous extremist, the FBI came up with permissive rules of engagement, which allowed their snipers to shoot any armed adult without warning—rules of engagement that never received official approval, but which FBI snipers believed were in force.[158] When Weaver left the cabin, armed, to sit with the body of his dead son in an outbuilding, FBI sniper Lon Horiuchi opened fire, hitting Weaver in the arm. Weaver ran back to the cabin, and Horiuchi fired again. His bullet passed through Vicki Weaver's head, killing her, and seriously wounded Kevin Harris. It was the first day of a twelve-day siege.

---

158 Under normal rules, snipers would only fire at someone who represented an immediate threat.

On the second morning, FBI negotiator Fred Lanceley, unaware that Vicki Weaver was dead, called down on a loudspeaker: "Good morning, Mrs. Weaver. We had pancakes this morning. And what did you have for breakfast? Why don't you send your children out for some pancakes, Mrs. Weaver?" Meanwhile, Mrs. Weaver's body was lying on the cabin floor, covered with a sheet, while her children sat by. There was no hope that FBI negotiators could build any kind of rapport with Randy Weaver now.

The siege at Ruby Ridge ended only after the FBI brought in Colonel Bo Gritz, a former Green Beret and a hero to the patriot movement. Gritz, Weaver could trust: in 1988, Gritz had briefly been the infamous white supremacist David Duke's running mate on the Populist Party ticket, and he was known for his opposition to the New World Order. With Kevin Harris in grave condition with wounds to his chest and arm, the Ruby Ridge survivors surrendered. Weaver would face only one charge: failing to appear in court. Among patriots, the Weavers were martyrs, the victims of a tyrannical government bent on stamping out any opposition to its rule.

Months later, the New World Order would make new martyrs to liberty, at Waco, Texas, after a siege better remembered for its fiery conclusion than for the events that led authorities to move in. The Branch Davidians, a breakaway sect of a breakaway sect of the Seventh-day Adventist Church, had experienced a schism of their own following the deaths of their leader, Benjamin Roden, in 1978, and his wife, Lois in 1986. Roden's son, George, considered himself heir, but Lois favoured a young man named Vernon Howell, who tried to seal the deal by becoming her lover. In 1984, the Davidians split into two factions, one each led by Howell and George Roden. Three years later, George Roden dug up a dead follower and challenged Howell to prove his divinity with a good old-fashioned resurrection; Howell responded by complaining to the police that Roden was abusing corpses, and proceeded to the Davidians' compound at Mount Carmel to get photographic evidence. Roden, being a good Christian, took up the Uzi. The resulting gunfight lasted twenty minutes, and although Howell and his group faced charges, none was convicted.

Good things come to those who wait. Two years later, one of George Roden's followers confessed to having had a vision of himself as the chosen Messiah of God. Roden guided his wayward disciple back to the true path by applying an axe to his head. With his rival now confined to the loony bin, Howell took over Mount Carmel, gave himself a new name—David Koresh—and announced to his followers that God had chosen him to make many babies. He was entitled, he said, to 140 wives, and proceeded to marry girls as young as thirteen years old. But what got Koresh in trouble with the law was not his underage wives. What got him into trouble was his guns.

Medieval monks sustained their monasteries by such initiatives as making honey and brewing beer for the greater glory of God; the Branch Davidians had a gun business. Women sewed ammo vests, which the sect sold through gun shows. But Koresh or his followers had also illegally converted AR-15 rifles to fully-automatic fire. On February 28, 1993, although they were aware that the Davidians had been tipped off and might be prepared for their arrival, the ATF attempted a raid on the Mount Carmel Center. In the firefight that followed, four ATF agents and five Branch Davidian members were killed; a further sixteen ATF agents were wounded.

The siege lasted fifty-one days. Early on the morning of April 19, 1993, the FBI smashed holes in the walls and poured CS gas into the building. Their plan was to gas the Davidians for two days, or at least until they gave up, whichever came first. But by noon, the Davidians had set fire to their own compound in a mass murder-suicide. Of the seventy-eight dead, twenty had been shot, including Koresh. One three-year-old child had been stabbed to death. Only nine survived.

Conspiracy theories persist, holding that the fire was set by the FBI or started by CS gas grenades, and that the subsequent investigation was a cover-up. To the patriot movement, Waco was a cold-blooded massacre of innocents by the FBI and the ATF, agents of a government that kills anyone who stands up to resist slavery. Following Ruby Ridge by less than a year, it was a call to arms.

Violence found its agents in Timothy McVeigh and Terry Nichols, who bombed the Alfred P. Murrah building in Oklahoma City in 1995 in explicit retaliation for the federal government's perceived violations of the constitution: Ruby Ridge, Waco, and the Brady Handgun Violence Prevention Act. McVeigh, a Gulf War veteran, had left the army after his Special Forces application was denied and then drifted from one job to another. Nichols had worked a series of odd jobs before joining the army in 1988, at the age of thirty-three, where he and McVeigh formed a friendship based on their mutual racism. But Nichols' military career was short. He received a hardship discharge following a divorce in 1989, and married a seventeen-year-old mail-order bride from the Philippines who was already pregnant with another man's child. That child died by suffocating in a plastic bag at the age of two while under Nichols' care; divorce followed. By the time he met up with McVeigh again, Nichols was selling army surplus gear and copies of *The Turner Diaries* on the gun-show circuit. Both Nichols and McVeigh were losers, unable to manage their money or to keep a job. They had fucked up everything they touched. Clearly, the government was to blame.

On April 19, 1995, the anniversary of both the FBI assault at Waco and the battles of Lexington and Concord, McVeigh and Nichols detonated five thousand pounds of ammonium nitrate fertilizer primed with nitromethane racing fuel packed into a Ryder truck rented under a fake ID, in front of the glass-plated façade of the Arthur P. Murrah building. The blast demolished half the building, killing 168 and wounding 680. Nineteen of the dead were children in the building's daycare centre.

Police stopped McVeigh only ninety minutes after the bombing, for driving a car with no licence plates, and then arrested him for illegally carrying a concealed weapon. He was wearing a T-shirt printed with *Sic semper tyrannis* (thus always to tyrants)—the slogan that John Wilkes Booth had shouted when he assassinated Lincoln—Jefferson's "The tree of liberty must be refreshed from time to time with the blood of patriots & tyrants," and carrying pages torn from *The Turner Diaries* describing a truck-bomb attack on the FBI headquarters in Washington.[159] This was a man who had quit the NRA because it was too soft. To the cop who stopped him, Timothy McVeigh must have seemed a perfect loon.

From his jail cell, McVeigh claimed victory, believing that the FBI negotiated a peaceful resolution to the 1996 Montana Freemen standoff because they feared further bombings. "Once you bloody the bully's nose," he said, "he's not coming back around." Even as the author of the deadliest act of terrorism on American soil at that time, the mass-murder of 168 people, he played the victim to the end. Poor little

---

159   When Terry Nichols was arrested, police found a copy of William Luther Pierce's other novel, *Hunter*, in his home. *Hunter* is the story of a man who decides to strike a blow for all that is good and holy by patrolling the streets at night and gunning down interracial couples.

Timothy McVeigh had been turned against the government by his terrible experience of inhumanity during the Gulf War, or so he said, forgetting that he had actually applied for Special Forces, and been refused, on his return.

Whatever McVeigh's claims—and there were many—no one should be fooled.[160] Nothing the federal government did provoked the Oklahoma City bombing. The 168 victims of McVeigh's bomb were simply scapegoats for his failure to get into the Special Forces and his inability to keep a job, to manage his gambling debts, or to find a girlfriend. He found in the patriot movement's fear of federal power something to pin his failures on and to hate, and he glommed onto it like a limpet to a boulder. McVeigh's hatred of the federal government went before Waco, and gave his life meaning by allowing him to step onto the stage and be a hero to himself.

This was a Patriot.

IT'S GETTING HARDER AND HARDER to be a wackjob these days. A figure like McVeigh presents something of a problem. He's embarrassing—not because of his views but because of, you know, those dead kids. And this is to say nothing of the small problem presented by the FBI and ATF: it turns out that when you bloody the bully's nose, he develops a serious interest in identifying all your fellow travellers and cutting them off at the knees before they can throw the next punch. Add the Patriot Act, which gave federal agencies sweeping anti-terrorist powers, and everyone lining up behind the President after the 9/11 attacks, and it gets downright difficult to be a true, flag-waving, barrel-sucking, constitution-worshipping, government-hating patriot.

Opposition to the Iraq War attracted new recruits from the progressive, anti-war left, people who were predisposed to think that the whole thing was some kind of set-up. If the World Trade Center had been destroyed by the government of the United States to provide a pretext for a war to secure an oil supply, then maybe there was some truth to all this stuff. We all know the banks and the big corporations are too powerful. And the Bilderberg Group, that annual conference of political and business leaders: we all know they're secretly setting the global agenda for their own nefarious ends, stacking the deck, rigging

---

160   Even Gore Vidal should not have been fooled, although he allowed himself to be.

the game. We all work for them, you know. We're willing dupes drifting through life with our eyes closed to the truth, suckers used to fulfil the secret ends of an international elite. The gulf between the outer fringe of the left and the radical right turns out to be much smaller than it appears.

Alex Jones, a self-described libertarian and ardent constitutionalist who seems never to have met a conspiracy theory he didn't like, is the bridge across that narrow chasm. Jones produced *Loose Change*, one of the most influential films of the truther movement, a loose movement of conspiracy theorists who believe the official account of 9/11 is false and that the attacks were in fact the work of the US government. He believes also that federal agents were behind the 1993 World Trade Center bombing, and that the Oklahoma City bombing was an inside job in which the federal government killed 168 Americans as a pretext for a crackdown on right-wing militias. Russia's short 2008 war on Georgia was engineered by NATO. The moon landings were faked. FEMA is building concentration camps across the United States to imprison Americans. Jared Loughner's shooting of Congresswoman Gabrielle Giffords and eighteen others was the result of government mind-control techniques, to which mentally unstable persons such as Loughner are particularly vulnerable, whose goal was to take our guns away. And the Sandy Hook massacre was a "false flag operation," a faked event staged for the media using actors.

Jones is a child of Waco: as he watched the congressional hearings into the incident on C-SPAN, he became convinced that the original ATF raid was a publicity stunt by an agency afraid of losing its funding, and that the investigation into the subsequent massacre was a cover-up. This was his first conspiracy theory, which he no doubt remembers with the same fondness with which other men recall the first time they got their hands up a girlfriend's shirt. We all remember the first time.

Jones is best known to the general public for his bizarre, angry appearance on CNN's *Piers Morgan Tonight* following the Sandy Hook massacre, during which he ranted, raved, shouted, and ultimately challenged Piers Morgan to a fist fight. This was, no doubt, just what Morgan had hoped for: the only thing better than demonizing gun nuts is provoking them to demonize themselves. But to Jones' followers, his bizarre appearance on CNN was a simple case of some British media-elite smart-ass trying to make a fool of a good American patriot's passionate love for his country.

Morgan had invited Jones to appear after Jones had promoted a petition for Morgan's deportation. Morgan's crime? Undermining the Constitution of the United States. Jones is a patriot, and Morgan had suggested that in a modern representative democracy such as the United States, the Second Amendment is actually rather silly. As far as Jones was concerned, this amounted to sedition.

The central tenets of Jones' world view are the "eugenics agenda," which seeks to bring about a scientific dictatorship within which the practice of eugenics can proceed, the steady militarization of police forces with the goal of imposing a police state, and a UN agenda to control the world under a New World Order, one-world government—the fundamental idea, it seems, behind all great American conspiracy theories.[161] As kooky as Jones's ideas may be, they are steadily creeping into the mainstream, as evidenced by CNN's decision to invite him on *Piers Morgan Tonight* as a guest: even if he had only been invited there to make a fool of himself (and, by association, of gun owners in general), he was still invited. And he has a growing audience. Jones lost his first radio job when he refused to moderate his views, but his current radio show now airs on about seventy AM and FM radio stations across the United States, and his estimated audience, over the air and online, has grown to two million listeners—far greater than the John Birch Society ever had.

And unlike the Birchers, Jones's audience is not limited to older men with money to spare. The movement of right-wing conspiracy theories towards the mainstream manifests also in the popularity of former congressman Ron Paul, who, like Jones, is particularly popular among young people. The kook constituency grows younger, even as we watch middle-aged Tea Partiers rant on our televisions. In *The Paranoid Style in American Politics* (1964), Richard Hofstadter noted that the paranoid style—the reliance, that is, on external conspiracies and traitors among us to manufacture an atmosphere of crisis—had originally belonged to those in power who feared secret societies and Jesuits. But the radical right, which in Hofstadter's time meant the

---

161   Like others before him, Jones has adopted anti-Semitic ideas while discarding their expressly anti-Semitic content. We can still rant on about "international bankers," having grown out of the idea that all bankers are Jews. It's almost as if we're thinking like adults!

John Birch Society, had turned it into a complaint of the dispossessed, in which the traitors in our midst now controlled our own government. Still, the Birchers' view was privileged; they were men who owned businesses and had money that they feared losing. It seems that in the age of the Internet, the paranoid style has moved further still from the corridors of power and now belongs to people with no money in the bank, to wage slaves under employment-at-will[162] with too much debt and too little security.

Following 9/11, with a Republican in the White House, an external threat in Al-Qaeda, and a war to cheerlead in Iraq, the patriot movement went quiet. But the election of Barack Obama brought it roaring back to life. Once again, the evening news featured Americans wrapping themselves in the constitution, urging the impeachment of the president and making veiled threats to resort to "Second Amendment solutions" should the government do anything dastardly, such as forcing health insurance on them. Conspiracy theorists convinced themselves Obama was a foreign-born Muslim mole. For the racist right, the election of a black president was particularly galling. Obama's election to a second term was preceded by overt threats of rebellion, which failed to materialize into anything more violent than sotto voce grumbling. With the push for gun control following the Sandy Hook massacre, that grumbling again swelled into open threats that any new attempt at gun control would lead to civil war or a revolution. Each year, indeed, calls arise on the Internet for a "Second American Revolution" to begin on July 4; each year, the uprising fails to occur as planned.

That the election of a Democrat to the White House inevitably brings armed resistance to the government, whether at Bundy Ranch or Jordan, Montana, is one of the less salutary indications of American democracy—but then, those responsible insist that the United States is not a democracy at all, but a republic. The old Bircher argument, that the United States was never meant to be a democracy, resonates with people who find themselves on the losing end of the popular vote. They suck their thumbs and appeal to the absolute principles embodied in a constitution created by wise, prescient men. That "democracy" and

---

162   Employment-at-will is the name given the prevalent arrangement in the United States, under which an employer may fire an employee at any time without notice or severance pay, and without proving any cause.

"republic" are not mutually exclusive categories makes little impression; that being a grown-up means accepting that you won't always get your way makes no impression at all.

To be Canadian is to be susceptible to a smug sense of national superiority when it comes to the wackier extremes of the American gun culture. Those people are crazy, what with their assault rifles and their handguns hidden in the wall and their insistence that only an armed populace can save us from the tyranny that is otherwise inevitable. We do not have an armed populace, nor any real or imagined right of insurrection, nor any right to bear arms, as Bruce Montague discovered to his cost, but look! Our government has yet to pack us all away into labour camps and work us as slaves towards the enrichment of some secret cabal of international bankers. We enjoy freedom of speech, freedom of association, and if we lack the right to keep and bear arms we're still able to shoot and eat bears. Not bad for a gang of unarmed slaves.

But the notion that Canada has no gun culture died shortly after seven o'clock on the evening of June 5, 2014, when a twenty-four-year-old man dressed in army-surplus camouflage and carrying a Norinco M305 rifle and a Mossberg 500 tactical shotgun went for a walk in Moncton, New Brunswick, with no plan of ever returning home. He walked down his street of shabby trailers and then turned south, through the woods, into an affluent suburb. Neighbours spotted him, and immediately called 911 to report an armed man, exactly as he hoped they would. His name was Justin Bourque, and his plan was to attract the police, and then kill them.

Constable Fabrice Gevaudan was searching for Bourque near a house at 15 Bromfield Court when Bourque fired his first shots. Those two shots missed Gevaudan, who shouted into his radio, "He's shooting at me! He's shooting at me!" and ran to the fence behind the house next door. Bourque fired three more shots and killed him. "I don't know what he was thinking," Bourque later said. "Obviously not a very combat-savvy guy." The shots had come from behind, and Gevaudan was unsure where his assailant was hiding.

Bourque moved on. Constable David Ross, a police dog handler, spotted him walking south on Mailhot Avenue towards Hildegard Drive, and drove towards him. Bourque raised his rifle and opened fire. Ross fired back through his truck windscreen, but missed. Bourque didn't. Ross's truck was still in gear, but rolled to a stop, its fuel line cut by a bullet. "I don't know where they get these guys," said Bourque. "I just, what was it? Like, two or three shots anyways, just to the window. Obviously it would go through, because it was the .308 ... I'm pretty sure I tagged him the first [shot]. I just kind of double-tapped." Ross had left a family barbecue, and rushed to respond to the emergency call.

Tim Daley, whose house overlooked the street where Constable Ross lay slumped in his truck, dying, asked Bourque if he should go inside. "Probably," said Bourque. He walked another block down Mailhot, where he told Mildred Stewart not to worry. "I'm not out to kill civilians," he said. "I'm only after government officials."

Bourque cut through somebody's backyard, pausing to shout a challenge to the cops to come and get him, and then moved down Hildegard where Constable Darlene Goguen blocked his progress. Another officer, Constable Martine Benoit, had stopped her car at the intersection, cutting off Bourque's retreat. "I was about to get cut off down Hildegard, so I went down with suppressive fire," said Bourque. Unable to see where the shots were coming from, Benoit tried to back out of the intersection, but the shooting had disabled her car. Another officer, Eric Dubois, drove up next to Benoit's car to provide cover, and the two officers huddled behind the vehicles for three minutes before Bourque opened fire again, wounding Dubois and Goguen. Bourque then turned and walked off, crossing Hildegard and walking south as a man took his photo, a photo that would soon spread coast to coast via Twitter.

Bourque again cut through backyards, back towards Mailhot, where Constable Doug Larche had just parked his unmarked car. Larche was in plain clothes but was wearing body armour and was armed with his service pistol and a shotgun. "I don't know, he had his gun half ready, but not ready enough, so," said Bourque. "He saw me and I think, like, fired two shots and then after that I tagged him, but I think I hit him in the neck ... anyways I went around and flanked to see if he was still alive and he wasn't."

Bourque looked down at Larche's body, and walked off, yelling "Bring me more cops!"

A little over an hour after the shooting started, the police had a name, thanks to one of Bourque's neighbours, who identified him and warned police that he had an extensive gun collection. But by this time Bourque had slipped away into a wooded area, and a full-scale man-hunt was underway, with the neighbourhood under lockdown and the Emergency Response Team sweeping the area as an airplane equipped with a thermal camera flew overhead. Shortly before midnight, the camera spotted Bourque's heat signature, and ERT members wearing night vision goggles moved in. The thermal camera footage shows Bourque standing, raising his hands over his head and walking forward to give himself up. His words to the police were widely reported: "I'm done."

The times being what they are, thousands of curious eyes had already tracked Bourque down on Facebook, where they found his repeated posts attacking the government and the police. One photo featured a uniformed R. Lee Ermey, in uniform in his role as *Full Metal Jacket*'s drill sergeant, jabbing his finger at the camera, the caption declaring that people who don't think ordinary citizens should be armed are the reason ordinary citizens should be armed. Another post questioned the militarization of the police, with photos of police in full riot gear. Captain Jack Sparrow explained elsewhere, "We need your guns, they said. So I shot them." A photo shared from "Anonymous ART of Revolution" warned that a man named Jacob Rothschild, who was worth $500 trillion, owned nearly every central bank in the world, our news media, our oil, and our government, and that his family had financed both sides of every war for the past two centuries. Further down the page, Minutemen faced down the Redcoats: "Free men do not ask permission to bear arms," while a blue ribbon campaign urged us to have liberals spayed and neutered.

It transpired that Justin Bourque was a full-fledged gun nut.

In custody, Bourque's inability to keep his mouth shut soon confirmed that he was all that he seemed. Tossed into a holding cell with an undercover officer, he soon boasted that "as long as this stays between you and me, I killed three cops." He went on to describe his rifle and the full metal jacket ammo he had used, the same ammo used by the military. Under interrogation, he soon abandoned the advice of his legal aid lawyer and spilled the whole story, apparently compelled to brag about his tactical prowess and the "combat skills" he had learned from playing the video game Metal Gear Solid. Then, having fallen for the under-cover cellmate trick, having allowed his interrogator to manipulate him into admitting everything, and having been tricked into confessing in writing in the form of a letter to the families of his victims, Justin Bourque confided that "I just don't trust the police, well, obviously." Like most fools, he considered himself the smartest guy in the room.

"Having a free mind is never an advantage in a socialist world, my friend," Bourque confided to his interrogator. Borque was homeschooled, which he seemed at once to celebrate and regret. Homeschooling taught him to be an independent thinker, to avoid the socialist indoctrination of the public school system, but also made him an outcast, unable to relate to his peers, whom he saw as products of that socialist indoctrina-tion. "I dated a lot of public school girls and it didn't work like 99.9% of the time," he admits. "And you know, that had to do with the fact that I didn't act like, you know, act like other guys."

During his police interview, Bourque continually regurgitated gun-culture clichés. "It's your responsibility, shouldn't it be, to pro-tect your own?" he asked, recycling the popular complaint that wait-ing for the police is a deadly mistake. "Not wait three minutes for a policeman to come. It should be your own, shouldn't it?" We keep fire extinguishers because the fire department can't always be there, first aid kits because we can't wait for the paramedics, but we're not allowed to prepare to defend ourselves and, true to standard-issue self-defence rhetoric, "that's sad for women especially." Similarly, he soon reminded his interrogators that Samuel Colt made equalizers. "Back in the wild west every man was equal, right? because if this man was five-feet tall and this eight-foot guy says, 'Hey, you know what, you're small, you have no rights,' well, guess what, you're wrong, buddy." As his interro-gators probed him, he rambled on about socialism, social engineering, the rule of tyrants, freedom of speech, senseless drug laws, libertari-anism, big oil, the Russians and the Chinese, William Wallace, work camps, and something called "the black curtain," an apparent reference to a Megadeth song. Justin Bourque, free thinker, had not one original thought in his head.

Asked why he did it, Bourque went to "Hook in Mouth," another Megadeth song, the lyrics to which he had posted on Facebook on the day of the shootings. "You're just a fish along for the ride whether you like it or not, you know you got a hook stuck in your mouth wherever you're going," he explained. He believed he was out of options. "You either get work at a call center, go to college and put yourself in further debt or … you fight for your freedom with couple of kicks and screams." Any of the options he had rejected seems preferable to murdering three people and spending your life in jail. But Bourque had the notion that his jaunt through Moncton would demonstrate what one determined man could do with a rifle. He hoped to prompt a wider uprising, although his notable lack of allies among his public-school educated peers ought to have given him pause on that score.

Bourque was a soldier with a cause, at least in his own mind. "Somehow I just got the mentality to be a soldier," he lamented, "but I just never found my war." So he made his own. He had planned to strike against Big Oil by setting gas stations on fire and then sniping at the police when they showed up, but he had some kind of problem with his bicycle and decided instead to set out on foot and wing it.[163] That pathetic detail, perhaps more than any other, defines Justin Bourque. He had set out to start his private war carrying baby powder, explaining later that it was good for preventing trench foot, but neglected to bring water. Still, he sure knew the lingo, or what he imagined the lingo to be, speaking of "suppressive fire," "cover and concealment," and "tagging" his victims. His incompetence was utterly unequal to his combat fantasies, yet he was too incompetent to realize it.

In a word, Justin Bourque was a loser, a dope-addled sad-sack nobody who bounced through a series of lousy jobs, complaining all the while that his considerable talents were wasted; he could, he said, do just about any voice on the Cartoon Network, which ought to have been good for something, yet there he was working crappy warehouse jobs. His love life was no more successful: "Being homeschooled, you gotta imagine it was just difficult as hell keeping a girlfriend, especially in this day and age." But he hadn't done himself any favours. One co-worker from an old job at Wal-Mart recalled Bourque tagging along with the gang on a camping trip. He had spent most of the night drinking while fondling the gun he had inexplicably brought along. He wasn't invited back.

---

163 Bourque had no car, having lost it some months earlier when a friend was caught driving it with an expired plate. He could not get the plate renewed because the car had failed a safety inspection.

His notions of freedom, the freedom he felt he was denied in socialist Moncton, were equally out of touch with reality. Pressed on this point, he began to ramble. "Well, just like I said, just the way you meet people, you know, it's just, I like heavy metal, everybody else likes rap and hip hop, and it's just, they're so one-minded, and I don't like a lot of the new movies that come out because I find that, you know, they release the same movie over and over again." He had no freedom, he said, because he'd been fired from a warehouse job for speaking his mind. That his friend Eric had hung himself was not a private tragedy, but a great social injustice. That Bourque's own life was a hopeless mess, it seems, was not his fault, but the doing of Big Oil and International Bankers who wanted his precious guns. "Socialism is socialism whether it's Naziism or Communism," he explained, demonstrating his firm grip of wingnut political science. "The capitalism has created socialism just to control, you know what I mean."

He could have expressed himself through heavy metal, but couldn't get a band together: Mike played bass and he played guitar, and that wasn't much of a band. So it was guns that restored his sense of security, autonomy, and power. Guns were the only thing that made Justin Bourque feel he could be powerful or important. He bought his guns and created out of patriot-movement rhetoric a fantasy of himself as a freedom fighter on an international stage, just as Timothy McVeigh had elevated himself from a sorry loser selling junk on the gun show circuit to an American freedom fighter by acting out the part in which he had cast himself.

Canada's National Firearms Association had responded to Bourque's shooting spree as only people lacking professional public relations advice can, by issuing a press release before Bourque had even surrendered.[164]

The NFA deplores the terrible actions by a clearly deranged individual that led to these deaths and injuries. Incidents like these demonstrate the validity of the mounting evidence that none of Canada's firearms control efforts over the past 50 years have had any effect on preventing violence, or otherwise stopping bad people from carrying out their evil deeds.

---

164   It is also painfully evident that no one at the NFA can write a coherent English sentence, much less an elegant one. "Demonstrate the validity of the mounting evidence?" "Support a health care system which could be better enabled," etc.? It's as if they took a special course on how to write bullshit.

It is clear that Canada's excessive firearms control system has failed again. The excessive rules in place do not in any way increase public safety, but merely contribute to an expensive and unnecessary regime which harms only those of lawful intent. Resources wasted on this fundamentally flawed firearms control regime could be better placed to support a health care system which could be better enabled to diagnose and treat conditions that put people's lives at risk.

Incidents like these demonstrate no such thing, and the NFA made a wild assumption in announcing that a better mental health system would have caught Justin Bourque before he did any harm. A court-ordered psychiatric assessment would in fact later conclude that he was entirely sane. There was also the question of timing: as Tony Bernardo, head of the rival Canadian Shooting Sports Association, had it, "I thought it was pretty premature." The Coalition for Gun Control, for the first time in recorded history, agreed with the CSSA: "It's too early to have this discussion. We will not participate at this point." Surely, if an award were available for the most tasteless press release of the year, the NFA would win it. But these are mere quibbles. The NFA's press release was not simply dumb as a wet, dead stump; it was also utterly oblivious to Justin Bourque's self-evident motives. Bourque was no crazed madman acting out some agenda only he could comprehend. He was a creature of the gun culture with a head stuffed full of *Molon labe*.

And the NFA might well have kept quiet, for the NFA itself is one of the chief importers of the *Molon labe* mindset to Canada, to the tune of about three thousand tons of bullshit annually. The organization had spent most of the previous year bashing the RCMP and the Army over their seizures of firearms in High River, Alberta, after the town had been evacuated during the 2013 Alberta floods. It even suggested that the police had worked from a secret list of guns, using long-gun registry data which, by law, was supposed to have been destroyed.[165] Only one day before Bourque stepped out of his trailer with his rifle in his hand, the NFA had published a promotional video on YouTube in which,

---

165   The report of the Commission for Public Complaints Against the RCMP tells us that there was no such list, that there was no plan to charge gun owners with unsafe storage, and that there was no agenda to take advantage of the crisis to confiscate guns. There was simply miscommunication, unclear orders, overzealous execution and the usual catalogue of minor errors that a suspicious mind inflates into conspiracy.

to strains of inspirational music, various talking heads explain why they support the NFA. One man declares, "I became involved in the NFA shortly after the G20 in Toronto that happened, where Premier McGuinty and the police chief of Toronto secretly brought in martial law in downtown Toronto, and I was aghast at what they had done." The same NFA that, on June 5, decried Bourque's shooting spree as "the terrible actions by a clearly deranged individual" had, on June 4, promoted gun ownership as a counter to police and government power.

It's getting harder and harder to be smug.

SOMETIME IN JUNE 2011, I found myself standing at the window of a Calgary hotel room, staring out over a landscape of low, blocky industrial buildings. I had to drive to Fernie, British Columbia, to give what turned out to be a surprisingly well-attended reading at the Fernie library, and I was thinking about what I ought to say. And then it occurred to me that I was staring out the hotel window at an ugly industrial landscape, and that I spent a lot of time staring out of hotel windows at ugly, limited landscapes and that this had certainly informed a novel whose protagonist spent a lot of time staring out of windows at various landscapes whose already limited possibilities were drearily restricted by intervening panes of glass. The whole world is out there, and there is no place to go.

I spend a lot of time in hotel rooms and airport departure lounges and confined to hurtling titanium tubes at thirty-eight thousand feet. That month I flew to Halifax and then to Calgary, drove to Edmonton, drove back to Calgary and thence to Fernie, and I can't recall on what day I read at the Fernie library or stood at that hotel window. But that doesn't bother me, because I'm sure Canada's Communications Security Establishment can fill in the gaps.

Beyond that transparent pane the dead industrial air of Calgary thrums with wireless whispers, the patient hiss of the Great Beast tightening its grip. My cell phone tracks me by GPS all the way down to Fernie, down through the hardscrabble foothills and up through the Crowsnest pass where the scale of the mountains crushes you. The watchers are watching. And all of this would seem simply paranoid if we did not now suspect, thanks to Edward Snowden, that the Great Snake tracked Canadians as they logged into free WiFi in airport departure lounges and hotel rooms and followed them for weeks thereafter, regardless of the Charter of Rights of Freedoms and heedless of the law and in spite of the insistence of CSE chief John Forster that "CSEC does not direct its activities at Canadians and is prohibited by law from doing so."

Who can you trust? The RCMP murdered Robert Dziekanski in Vancouver Airport and if there had been no video, no one would ever have been held to account. The Ontario government invoked a draconian and arguably unconstitutional 1938 law, the Public Works Protection Act, during the G20 summit in Toronto; Toronto's chief of police, Bill Blair, lied outright about the powers it granted him.[166] As stupid and obnoxious as the black-clad protesters were, proclaiming their non-violence while smashing windows and making threats, one cannot excuse the excesses of the police. We all wish to inhabit a society of laws but our police prove as willing to discard those laws as anyone; they also possess the unique power to exonerate themselves. So we killed a guy in the airport: he was violent and we did what we had to do. Wait, there's a video? Oh, well. Too bad, so sad.

In a room in the fabulous Mint Hotel in downtown Las Vegas, Raoul Duke stares out the window at a giant machine in the sky, "some kind of electric snake." The question at hand is whether to shoot it, or study its habits. My guns are in the safe. And for now, there is no need to shoot that giant electric snake. I study its habits. I still have faith that the law will be our *vindices injurarium* and that the democratic institutions we have created can hold the snake to account.

In short, I get it. The gun hanging on the wall leaves you the option of remaining master of your fate regardless of the police, regardless of the constrictor tightening his grip, regardless of the faceless computer at the NSA that knows what you had for dinner last night. Yet the ridiculousness of those words is evident as soon as you say them. The only option that gun offers is to become a crazy on the evening news, an armed loony blockaded within his house waiting for a bullet from the tactical team's sniper. Your options exist only in fantasy, a fantasy created to justify the gun. In the real world, you are John Steinbeck's Okie sharecropper, staring down Joe Davis's boy with his old rifle: there

---

166 No, I do not moonlight as a constitutional lawyer; thus, "arguably." And as it happens, the Public Works Protection Act has since been repealed and replaced by more balanced provisions. The snake has been held to account.

is nobody to shoot. Your gun is just the touchstone of a cranky old man, Clint Eastwood in *Gran Torino* leveling his rifle at the transgressor who has smashed his garden gnome, hissing, "Get off my lawn." If only you could, the world could be yours. If only. If only.

TEOTWAWKI

Survival Fantasies, Disaster Myths, the Zombie Apocalypse,
and the End of the World as We Know It

"Life is real again, and the useless and cumbersome and mischievous have to die."
—The Artilleryman in *The War of the Worlds* (H.G. Wells)

MY SON CAST A DUBIOUS GLANCE in my direction, and then turned to
the television: "You call this research?"

Why such skepticism? The gun culture is found in the culture, my
boy, and the culture is found on our television screens. Pay no attention
to these empty beer cans, these few remaining potato chips, this coagulating chip dip, the scattered survivors of some junk-food apocalypse.
I am a Professional Writer, and I am hard at work watching *Jericho*,
a short-lived television series that aired for a single season on CBS in
2006, capitalizing on fears of terrorist attack and cynicism over the war
in Iraq.[167] In it, the residents of the small town of Jericho, Kansas, find
themselves isolated after nuclear attacks knock out the major cities of
the United States and cripple its government. With no idea who has
attacked their country, or why, the people of Jericho must survive as
the power grid goes down and food distribution ceases. Some of them
naturally find the time to fall in love. As my son looked on, a small boy

---

167   After CBS cancelled *Jericho*, protests by its die-hard fans led the network to bring it back
in 2008 for a short run of seven episodes, which tied up any loose ends as rapidly as possible. By
"protests by its die-hard fans," I refer to the shipping of some forty thousand pounds of nuts to
the network's offices, a reference to Brigadier General Anthony McAuliffe's response to a German
ultimatum to surrender during the Battle of the Bulge, which the final episode had quoted.

standing on the roof of his parents' home watched a distant mushroom cloud climb into the atmosphere over Denver.

"What, another apocalypse?" he said. "What is it with you and apocalypses?"

I do like a good apocalypse, or more precisely, a post-apocalypse. The thing about apocalypses is the scope they create for fantasy. The landscape is emptied and your only task is to get through one more day; there is no future beyond tomorrow. You can't even find a green banana. Instead, you're back to basics: survival rations, water, shelter, fire if you can risk it—you don't know who is out there, just beyond the circle of light, sizing you up for your last can of beans, your boots, your thread-bare blanket. You'll need your wits about you. Also, a strong knife, a rucksack, something to start fires. And guns. Lots of guns. Looters and marauders stalk that depopulated landscape, and they are armed. In a world where two is one and one is none, you are going to need lots and lots of guns and ammo.

That empty landscape is a landscape of possibility, a new frontier. And it is a frontier made for our times. The open road is rife with speed traps, our money is in plastic and our names have become numbers. Even our idle chatter is sifted by dark computers in secret basements. Where is the landscape of possibility now? How is the hero to find his frontier? That's easy: you blow it all up and start again. You take away the electricity that powers the computers, tear down the society that pays the police to man the speed traps, smash the social contract that binds us to our common interest. And then you hit the road where the killing gets done. All the old rules are gone. There are no tables set for tea. As the artilleryman of H.G. Wells's *The War of the Worlds* put it, "Life is real again, and the useless and cumbersome and mischievous have to die."

H.G. Wells didn't care about the post-apocalyptic landscape for its own sake. He didn't care about the frontier. *The War of the Worlds* is concerned with Darwinism and brings about an apocalypse to make its point. But Wells nevertheless created the template that post-apocalyptic fiction would follow. Disaster overtakes us. Government control collapses, the army and police forces dissolve, panicked people fill the streets, and soon everyone is running and hiding. We fall back on our base instincts and soon fall to fighting over whatever resources remain.

And our hero staggers through a kind of post-apocalyptic picaresque, colliding with one archetype after another: the curate, driven off his rocker, the artilleryman with his grand and impractical plans for a new society, and, in later iterations, the looter, the brigand, the warlord.

True post-apocalyptic fiction waited on the Cold War, which brought us the real possibility of an apocalypse. When *The Day of the Triffids*, John Wyndham's science-fiction masterpiece, appeared in 1951, satellites and genetic engineering were visible just beyond the horizon. Wyndham set his novel in the mid-1970s, when he imagined these things would exist. Trigger one satellite weapon and blind almost everyone, let governments collapse, let the bodies start to pile up and disease to sweep through the cities, and we are back to square one, struggling for survival. We don't really need walking, man-eating plants to make this one work, but we've got 'em anyway, just to liven things up.

Unlike Wells, Wyndham *did* care about the post-apocalyptic landscape for its own sake. In the wake of a destructive war driven by competing political ideologies, *The Day of the Triffids* is interested above all in how we might build a new society and what form that society might take. And so our hero, Bill Masen, meets up with a series of would-be leaders: academics with visions of an ideal society, the essentially socialist Coker, a group of religious nuts, and ultimately the neo-feudal warlord, Torrance. But *The Day of the Triffids* is also English, and something is missing: even Torrance puts persuasion before violence. Wyndham's cosy catastrophe lacks guns and paranoia.

But guns and paranoia are two commodities of which the United States has an abundant supply. When American writers play in the post-apocalyptic sandbox, building imaginary worlds in which government has disappeared, in which the rule of law is but a memory and our hero must survive by his wits, they inevitably graft on their guns and paranoia. The American vision of post-apocalyptic survival rarely resembles *The Day of the Triffids*; it is usually closer to *Mad Max* or *The Walking Dead*. And when Americans prepare for some expected disaster, they cast themselves in leading roles in those fictional worlds, worlds that justify arming themselves appropriately. All the world's a stage, and we imagine no small actors.

Jerry Ahern was an American pulp fictioneer who spent his entire career in the post-apocalyptic sandbox, imagining the worst as he stepped from non-fiction to fiction and back again. Ahern freelanced for *Guns & Ammo*, *Knife Digest*, and *Petersen's Handguns*; he also wrote several non-fiction books on such helpful topics as "how to carry concealed weapons and know when others are."[168] He was president of the handgun manufacturer Detonics USA from 2004 to 2007, when the company was bought by Bruce Siddle and Steve Stahle, who in turn sold a stake to none other than Lieutenant Colonel Dave Grossman. Shortly before his death in 2012, Ahern published a survival manual, *Survive! The Disaster, Crisis and Emergency Handbook*, which offers "real-world advice that can save your life and the lives of the ones you love" in the event of hurricanes, blizzards, tornadoes, flu pandemics, and power blackouts. He was, in short, a gun writer with one foot firmly in the mainstream and the other on the fringe.

Ahern is perhaps best known, however, for a series of trashy pulp novels called *The Survivalist*, born out of the climate of anxiety created by Reagan's acceleration of the arms race in the early 1980s. The survivalist of *The Survivalist* is one John Rourke, who graduated medical school but opted for the CIA over medicine, got shot up in a Central American jungle, crawled back to the United States, and eventually built himself a state-of-the-art survival retreat in the Smoky Mountains. "There are enough loonies loose in the world today to screw up the planet so bad that survivalism training is going to be the only thing that'll keep people alive—maybe," he advises in the opening pages of *Total War*, the first of the series, just before he spots the Russians invading Pakistan. With that, World War III is on, and, well, it turns out that "survivalism training" is the only thing that'll keep people alive. Maybe.

Ahern's novels are the wildest of fictional fantasies, drawing on science fiction as much as Ahern's non-fiction work as a gun writer. Although Ahern based the first novels of the series firmly in the world of 1981, he gives Russia particle-beam weapons, the better to defeat the United States and give Rourke an enemy to fight. He also uses sci-fi staples such as cryogenics, a handy way to get around the problem of nuclear radiation. But as goofy as it is, the *Survivalist* series nonetheless has something to tell us about the mindset of the real-world survivalist.

---

168   Jerry Ahern, *CCW: Carrying Concealed Weapons* (Blacksmith Press, 1996).

Ahern combines the gun writer's love of guns with the sci-fi writer's penchant for excruciating, unnecessary detail, giving the reader such clunkers as "Small H-K MP5SD3 integral silencer, collapsible stock 9-mm submachine guns in their white-knuckled fists, they stormed the two dozen turban-clad opium smugglers on the highway, clinging to the four stake trucks." A combat scene typically sees Rourke work his way through his entire personal arsenal: a Colt CAR-15 carbine; twin Detonics Combat Master .45s carried in shoulder holsters; a Colt Python .357 Magnum revolver with a Mag-na-Ported barrel, Metalifed frame, and Pachmayr grips; and an A.G. Russell Sting 1A boot knife.[169] He wears a Rolex Submariner and rides a Harley Davidson Low Rider. The emphasis on brand names, on special, custom-modified guns, combines the gun-magazine gadgeteer's fantasy with the role-playing gamer's equipment list. At least part of our fascination with guns is a fascination with gadgets, and at least part of the attraction of "survivalism" is simply that it provides an excuse to collect them.

The books celebrate the assumptions of American gun culture. Partisans armed with "American sporting arms" hamper the invading Soviets; America is at once a formidable nation of armed citizens and a wasteland overrun by looters and brigands. A KGB officer reflects that it was a pity his leaders had nuked New York, because the "weaponless, fear-ridden" people of the Northeast would have been so much easier to control than the "heavily armed and fiercely independent" people of the West and South. Rourke's wife, Sarah, on the other hand, is certain that the brigands overrunning the South are not locals. She knows her Southern neighbours to be good and gentle folk; the brigands are, no doubt, residents of the "weaponless, fear-ridden" cities of the Northeast who have somehow found themselves weapons. The good guys are good and the bad guys are bad. Looters loot; Rourke, picking through the ruins for things he can use, is "foraging."

---

169   For those who care, the Colt CAR-15 is a short, carbine version of the AR-15 rifle. The Detonics Combat Master was the first handgun made by Detonics, a compact redesign of the 1911 pistol made before Ahern got involved with the company. A Mag-na-Ported barrel has ports cut in the upper side of the barrel to vent propellant gases and control muzzle lift when the gun recoils; Metalife is a protective coating for firearms. Pachmayr is a manufacturer of various accessories, most notably grips and recoil pads. The Sting 1A was an all-metal, double edged knife about which Ahern once wrote a piece for *Knife Digest*. All of these names are the trademarks of various manufacturers.

Rourke is a practical man who does manly things in a man's world; he knows the score. Sarah, who has separated from him because of his violent job, illustrates children's books for a living. A lifelong inhabitant of a fantasy world, she soon learns the error of her ways. Looters and brigands begin raping and pillaging within hours of the catastrophe. Human violence waits only for some event to crack the fragile seal of civilization that contains it. And with that, we are back to basics, red in tooth and nail, scrabbling and fighting to survive. The prepared survive and the unprepared receive an education, nasty, brutish, and short. Thermonuclear war is a bad thing, but at least it has restored what the good gun nut longs for, as expressed in a thousand Westerns: a world in which we survive by our wits and our guns, where men are men, women are women, and people speak plain American. Life is real again, and the useless, the cumbersome, and the liberal have to die.

For the survivalist, this is paradise.

PERHAPS YOU SLEPT IN. Hung-over, maybe. There is precedent: this is how Bill Masen's companion Jo escaped blindness in *The Day of the Triffids*. Or perhaps you work nights, or had to cram for an exam. It happens. Any of a thousand scenarios could keep you out of it, unaware. You miss the start of the thing and wake up some sunny day, sleep in your eyes, halfway rested, and have plenty of time to brew your coffee before it hits you. Something is off. It's quiet. Too quiet. And as you shake off that movie cliché, you realize just *how* it's too quiet. You hear birds, the neighbour's flag cracking in the gusting wind, its halyard snaps ringing off the pole, the coffee maker's persistent, lazy drip, but nothing else. No traffic noise from the main road, no horns, no lazy Cessna Skylane puttering through a procedure turn as it heads back to join the pattern, another student at the controls. Not one human sound.

Out the back window, a smudge of smoke mars the horizon. Which would be of little concern were it not for this eerie not-quite-silence, so upstairs you go, coffee in hand, still in your slippers. A higher vantage point avails you little: it's still just a smoke column of indeterminate cause, a house fire somewhere, perhaps, although you hear no distant sirens. There ought to be sirens. Oughtn't there? Did you miss them? And then you see it, a movement out of the corner of your eye, much

closer, down in the neighbour's yard. It's Mike, and he's bent over someone, someone hurt. You push the window open and yell down and he
looks up, blood all over his face, blood drooling from his slack-jawed
mouth, empty eyes and Holy crap on a crap-cracker he's *eating* her.

It's at times like this you thank the sweet Lord you had the foresight
to stock the gun cabinet and lay in a few thousand rounds of ammo,
because by Christ you're gonna need it now. The boots, the knives, the
machete, the baseball bat, even that Japanese katana you shouldn't have
wasted good money on. Things are gonna get ugly, but the good news
is that, if you live in Canada, getting through the apocalypse really just
means making it through the rest of the summer. You just wait for winter to freeze the bastards solid, and then dispatch them with snowballs
to the deliquescent brain-pan.

It's a good thing you watched all those zombie movies.

All those zombie movies. *Night of the Living Dead* originated the
zombie genre in 1968. Its sequel, *Dawn of the Dead*, didn't appear until
1978. In more recent years, we've seen *Hell of the Living Dead*, *The Evil
Dead*, *Day of the Dead*, *Return of the Living Dead*, *Evil Dead II*, *Night of
the Living Dead*, *Dawn of the Dead*, *Land of the Dead*, *Diary of the Dead*,
Flight of the Living Dead, and *Survival of the Dead*, which last has some
comment to make about the genre, given the dead's stubborn refusal to
go ahead and die. In 2010, zombies made the jump to television in *The
Walking Dead*, which offers me the opportunity to point out to the kids
just how well prepared I am for the zombie apocalypse, and just how
well trained to survive it, although they are skeptical of my claim that
The Walking Dead is a documentary.

Anyway, that's a lot of zombies, particularly since 2002. But it's
not just the zombie *movies* that have grown more numerous; it's the
zombies themselves. In the original *Night of the Living Dead*, a small
group of people rides out a limited zombie outbreak in a cellar until
help arrives (and shoots one of the survivors). But in later iterations the
zombies multiplied until they were everywhere. Nowadays, as soon as
you get a zombie outbreak, civilization is overwhelmed and no help is
to be found. The authorities, which responded effectively to the zombie threat in *Night of the Living Dead*, have become powerless against
the zombie apocalypse. Neither can we rely on our fellow survivors. If
zombie movies teach us anything, it's that in times of crisis we're on our

own. And the living dead have evolved. No longer the slow-moving, shambling creature seen in the *Night of the Living Dead*, your modern zombie can run just as fast as a living human, although of course his (its?) skull is so soft that you can kill him with a pocketknife.

Bill Masen could dream of driving the triffids from the land and starting afresh; John Rourke could dream of holing up with his family and getting by, to pass on the job of rebuilding to future generations. But the characters in zombie movies have only a shared dream of terror, flight, and eventual death. Survival is now a futile struggle, but one in which we persist simply because we must. And the swelling popularity of zombie apocalypses following the 9/11 terrorist attacks must have something to tell us about ourselves. Zombies give expression to fears of savage enemies who are not open to negotiation, but perhaps also to the ongoing American fascination with crime. We live day-to-day among the faceless hordes. The zombie apocalypse is end times for the Kingdom of Fear.

In the shorthand of online discourse, survivalists and armed citizens use the word "zombies" to stand for both the marauders of a post-apocalyptic landscape and the feared home invaders of contemporary America, even as they buy up zombie targets. *Guns & Ammo* magazine has published stories with titles like "Avoid the Bite: Tips for Unarmed Self-Defense from Zombies," "How to Create a Secure, Zombie-Proof Home," and "How to Pick the Best Zombie Pistol." These stories are presented tongue-in-cheek, but they also have a serious purpose, allowing the writers to cover the evergreen topics of self-defence and survival from a fresh angle. Securing your home against zombies involves the same steps as securing it against post-apocalyptic marauders, and the best zombie pistol is surely also a dandy pistol for self-defence. The zombie lurching wildly towards us represents that point at which fantasy blends with reality, it is at once an expression of deeply-held fears and a harmless gag.

The ammunition manufacturer Hornady, which has taken advantage of the zombie fad by marketing Zombie Max ammunition made just for killing the undead, felt the need to publish a disclaimer:

> Hornady® Zombie Max™ ammunition is NOT a toy (IT IS LIVE AMMUNITION), but is intended only to be used on ... ZOMBIES, also known as the living dead, undead, etc. No human being, plant,

animal, vegetable or mineral should ever be shot with Hornady®
Zombie Max™ ammunition. Again, we repeat, Hornady® Zombie
Max™ ammunition is for use on ZOMBIES ONLY, and that's not a
nickname, phrase or cute way of referring to anybody, place or thing.
When we say Zombies, we mean … ZOMBIES!

Hornady wishes to make it clear that their Zombie Max ammo is made
for target shooting as part of an ongoing gun-industry gag that has produced zombie targets, "zombie-stopper" sights, zombie ammo cans, and
a three-position safety catch for AR-15-style rifles marked Live, Dead,
and Undead. Chiappa Firearms manufactures a "Zombie Blaster" shotgun, and Mossberg has produced zombie-themed variants of its popular
Mossberg 500 pump-action shotgun. There are even "zombie shoots":
zombie-themed target shooting competitions in which competitors
armed with shotgun, rifle, and pistol compete over a course of fire to
survive the undead and win a trophy.

All this is in good fun, of course. Same as it ever was: eight-year-olds
dressed in cowboy gear fought out backyard gunfights that translated
Cold War anxieties into harmless play. Conflict and violence inspire fear
but are also the fundamental stuff of entertainment. But zombie shooting games have provoked stern disapproval from people who don't think
anyone should ever have fun with a gun. Some finger-wagging nitwits
even suppose the zombie shooting fad demonstrates that gun nuts are
so entirely paranoid they are unable to separate movie plots from real
life. But zombie shooting is a tongue-in-cheek game, a send-up of the
tactical firearms market that demonstrates a shocking truth, hitherto
undiscovered: the gun culture has a healthy sense of humour, too.

Zombieland has become the fantasy theme park of American gun culture. And all those people blasting away at zombie targets with Zombie
Max ammo ought not to concern us, because those people at least have a
firm grasp of the boundary between fantasy and reality. We ought to be
much more concerned by those who labour to make their fantasies plausible, who seek ways to find parts they can play out for real.

On my bookshelves are *The SAS Survival Handbook*, Petersen's *A Field
Guide to Edible Wild Plants: Eastern and Central North America*, and *The
Official Wilderness First Aid Guide*, published by St. John's Ambulance.

My kids amuse themselves by watching Les Stroud in old episodes of *Survivorman*, and ranting at disaster movies: "Build a fire, you idiot! Don't you know how to build a fire?" I own two survival kits containing such items as NATO boat matches—which burn even when dropped in a puddle—signal mirrors, button compasses, firesteels, and water purification tablets. I have water filters, compact stoves, backpacks, and survival blankets. I own more knives than I can easily count. Each of them is sharp enough to shave with, should I ever feel the urge.

I will not plead insanity here. All of these things I own with good reason. My kids learned to light fires and put up shelters as prerequisites to canoe-tripping. Thus, also, the survival kits, the water purification tablets, the stainless-steel water bottles suitable for boiling, the water filter. Anyone who hunts and fishes owns knives, perhaps more knives than he or she really needs. Sometimes, you look at this stuff and shake your head. Will I ever use a survival blanket? But last season I went grouse hunting in unfamiliar territory, and got turned around. Snow fell in big, wet flakes, and the dog and I were soaked. I'd left the topo map in the van. No way to navigate by watch and sun under that overcast. But I had a button compass in the survival kit I'd tossed in my vest in idle consideration of a snapped ankle in bad weather. I consider myself vindicated.

But to be completely honest, some of these things I own simply because, to borrow from Hunter S. Thompson, once you get locked into a serious gadget collection, the tendency is to push it as far as you can. Well-made folding knives are like potato chips in that it is impossible to own just one. Gadgets of all kinds exert a magnetic pull. The question ceases to be "what do I need?" and instead becomes "hey, how could I use that?" The game of what-if, so central to preparedness, soon moves from such practical considerations as "what if I twist an ankle out there in the rain and have to wait hours for help" to rather more remote possibilities like "what if the canoes are lost to a waterfall and then the food pack is torn to pieces by a bear, and a freak lightning strike sets our remaining gear on fire, leaving us with nothing but canoe paddles, belt knives, and our wits?" A need to justify your collection of gadgets creates fantasy scenarios that make those gadgets necessary. Soon, worst-case scenarios take over entirely. You become a kook.

The Internet, that tool of technological civilization that offers untold boons to all humanity, has been especially kind to kooks. Here, the otherwise-isolated nutbar can seek out his fellow travellers. Survivalists, now rebranded as "preppers," flock to emergency preparedness websites like February squirrels to a bird feeder, there to chatter loudly and engage in amusing squirrel spats over various nuttery. On a discussion board devoted to wilderness survival, you might expect to find tips on what to do when you dunk your canoe on the Winisk River, sixty zillion miles from the nearest road, and how best to get yourself found and rescued before you starve. You would expect wrong. Instead, a stranger in a strange land, you will stumble into discussions about how to *avoid* being found or rescued, and warnings that you better unload your weapon before coming into *my* camp. On YouTube, a self-proclaimed survival expert lays out his plan to buy a Hagglunds BV206, a tracked, amphibious utility vehicle, against the inevitable day when the shit hits the fan; in a moment of rich and alarming self-parody, he laments that he lacks a .50-calibre machine gun so will have to settle for .30-calibre.[170] Kooks, extremists, and fringe wingnuts abound, spreading a rich layer of horseshit with which to fertilize the next generation of kooks, extremists, and fringe wingnuts.

It is probably wise to stay off the Internet.

Inevitably, online prepper communities have adopted their own unique shorthand. All preppers prepare for SHTF (when the Shit Hits the Fan) when we can expect to find ourselves WROL (Without Rule of Law). If it hits the fan hard enough, we'll be facing TEOTWAWKI (The End of The World as We Know It). In SHTF, you'll need your BOB (Bug-Out Bag), in which you'll have packed all the basic supplies you'll need to survive for a few days.[171] You should already be carrying your EDC (Every-Day Carry), which probably includes a knife or a multi-tool and a powerful LED flashlight as well as your sidearm. Throw your BOB in your GOOD vehicle (Get Out of Dodge) and you're good to go.

Survivalism is Hobbesian: disaster banjaxes the fragile machinery of civilization and throws us back into our natural state of savagery. Gone are frocks, drawing rooms, and strawberry socials, to be replaced by

---

170   The video was still on YouTube when this book went to press, but had been made private; perhaps the author was concerned about the security implications of sharing his plans with the rest of the world.

171   The Bug-Out Bag originates from the military and has passed into general usage. In the security office of a nickel plant in northern Alberta, a place where poison gas leaks could force emergency evacuation at any time, I saw a row of bags stacked along the wall under a placard: "Bug-Out Bags." I had to shave off my beard, for the first time since leaving the Army, in case I had to don a gas mask. Here, at least, one could bug out with good cause.

ravening hordes armed with improvised weapons, lusting after blood and gasoline. When the shit hits the fan, predators will take over the streets. Accountants and real estate agents and business consultants for large software companies based in Atlanta, who ordinarily seem to perform no useful function at all, must turn to violence or perish. The unprepared, lacking food, water, and survival gear, will take what they need by force. And those happy few who had the foresight to prepare, to get themselves a Hagglunds BV206 and stick a .30-calibre machine gun on top, will soon have to fight just to keep what little they've got.

Every movement needs its thought leaders, and James Wesley Rawles is among the most prominent of TEOTAWKI preppers.[172] Rawles operates a website, SurvivalBlog.com, and has written several non-fiction books in addition to a series of novels beginning with *Patriots: A Novel of Survival in the Coming Collapse*. According to his official biography, Rawles was a US Army intelligence officer from 1984 to 1993, but resigned his commission as soon as Bill Clinton was elected president. After leaving the military, he worked as a technical writer, and now works as a freelance writer and self-proclaimed survival expert from his survival retreat on a ranch somewhere in the Rocky Mountain West, regarding the precise location of which he is coy: "I'm not at liberty to discuss where I live." It is, of course, equally possible that he is writing from a suburban basement in New Jersey.

Like any good self-proclaimed guru, Rawles presents himself as the progenitor of an entire school of thought, which he calls "Rawlesian survivalism," and as the originator of a political movement, the "American Redoubt" movement, which promotes the relocation of conservatives, Christians, and Jews to Idaho, Montana, and Wyoming, to ride out the coming collapse. Rawles, who proclaims his opposition to racism, explains that he wants Christians and Jews for neighbours because only the religious have the firm moral grounding that will make them trustworthy when society collapses (atheists and Muslims, apparently, are in the same amoral, godless boat). Rawles would not feel safe, he says, with a Marilyn Manson fan for a neighbour. There are moral absolutes, he warns, and we must choose our friends and neighbours wisely. Kids with black hair and purple lipstick should not be among them.

---

172   Rawles insists on spelling his name with an extraneous comma: "James Wesley, Rawles." This supposedly separates his given names from the name belonging to his family. I will not gratify the faux-aristocratic affectation.

In his 2009 book, *How to Survive the End of the World as We Know It*, Rawles lays out his twenty-two tenets. Rawlesian survivalism essentially takes standard-issue survivalism, with its emphasis on a well-armed survival retreat where one can go back to the land, and grafts on a moral dimension derived from evangelical Christianity. It rejects the racism of anti-Semitic, white-supremacist survivalist movements of the 1980s in favour of contemporary anti-Muslim religious intolerance, a dubious improvement. Most of all, though, Rawles is about guns. Fully one-third of Rawlesian principles revolve around self-defence. In the Rawlesian worldview, armed violence is not just a possibility lurking beyond the weak, flickering light of your campfire; it is inevitable. One must show restraint, he advises, but always have recourse to lethal force. Buy life assurance—guns, that is, and ammunition—not life insurance. Rawles even suggests you buy a masonry home, solely because masonry stops bullets. And since the collapse is imminent, the time to fortify is now.

In the self-proclaimed guru business, it's never enough to have a quasi-original doctrine; you must also proclaim the vital importance of your doctrine. And to a survivalist, this means warning that the collapse is both inevitable and imminent—essentially, to tote a sandwich board announcing that the end is nigh. Rawles presents nightmare scenarios that seem all too plausible, if only we willingly suspend disbelief as we might in a movie theatre. What if there was an outbreak of a highly virulent, rapidly transmitted influenza strain, one that kills 50 percent of infected patients? As the disease spreads, fear driven by hysterical media reports paralyzes North America. People stay home rather than risk infection by going to work. Trucks cease carrying food into supermarkets that are no longer open. Police officers refuse to go in to work, leaving the streets to criminals and predators. The power grid goes down. Hungry, desperate people emerge from their homes and fall on each other in an orgy of looting and violence. As looters empty supermarket shelves, the starving masses leave the cities and roam the countryside, looking for food. Anyone who had the foresight to prepare for the catastrophe by stockpiling food becomes a target.

What are you smirkin' at, Pollyanna? You don't think a flu pandemic is likely? There's always an economic meltdown, an attack with nuclear, chemical, or biological weapons, World War III, an oil embargo, an invasion by some foreign power, climate change, peak oil, a major earthquake, an eruption of the Yellowstone super volcano, or an asteroid strike. "What do you need," John Rourke asked in the first of Ahern's *Survivalist* novels, shortly before World War III broke out and demonstrated his foresight, "A runaway laboratory virus, a global economic collapse, a world crop failure?" Take your pick. There are so many possible disasters that one is certain to hit sooner or later. More likely sooner. The time to prepare is *now*.

Preparing for the collapse means, above all else, preparing for violence. To Rawles, violence follows TEOTWAWKI as surely as spring follows winter, and violence follows a script derived from the pulp novels of Jerry Ahern and from Hollywood movies. Regardless of the disaster that gives Rawles' movie its premise, the plot plays out the same way: power failure leads to the failure of water pumping stations, the disruption of the food supply, the collapse of law and order, riot, fires, and looting, and finally a massive, desperate migration out of the burning cities and into the countryside, where the prepared must fight just to keep themselves alive. It's inevitable. History proves this, although it has never actually happened.

The drive to prepare goes before the need. The man who fears tornadoes makes sure that he has a strong cellar, and keeps his television tuned to the 24-hour weather channel, where continual, breathless warnings of impending weather disasters reinforce his fears and justify his preparations. The man who fears violence buys guns, and imagines increasingly violent scenarios—muggings, break-ins, organized home invasions—that justify his preparations. But the survivalist is also a fantasist, a collector of survival gadgets who, in imagining storylines that vindicate his preparations, casts himself in the starring role of his own imaginary movie. He is John Rourke come to life.

And so the prepper's plans begin to read like descriptions of a fantasy tree fort. You will live in a masonry house with steel doors and a fireproof roof, hidden away behind dense hedges backed by a chainlink fence and a strong gate on a large lot that provides a clear field of fire. Under your windows, you will plant thorn bushes. You'll have a big, quiet, yet menacing dog—or better yet, two. You'll have a large vegetable garden, hidden away behind rows of flowers and shrubs so nobody can tell it's there, and a large, secure outbuilding just to hold all your supplies. In SHTF, you'll break out the concertina wire—just one of the goodies you keep stashed in that outbuilding—and ring your property with steel. And when things start to get ugly, you'll block your driveway by parking a Caterpillar tractor across it and disabling the ignition—a suggestion Rawles arrives at as if everyone has one stashed away in the shed.

So you'll need to buy a Caterpillar tractor, it seems, one that you can afford to abandon as a roadblock. But that's not all. You also need night-vision equipment, IR floodlights and starlight scopes. And you don't want to set up your perfect tree fort just anywhere. Ideally, you'll find a place with its own natural gas well or surface coal seam, or at least one with a good stand of timber (sustainability matters). But you should also be sure to locate it within a libertarian paradise featuring low taxes, small government, and a low population. People are a threat, community is a pain, and the only numbers that count are those within your own castle. You'll want three families—meaning six adults—so that you can have a two-man (or one-man, one-woman) security detail patrol the grounds in shifts. Clearly, you're going to need to find some crazy friends. And if you can find some crazy friends with a Caterpillar tractor, you can save yourself a few bucks.

The time to move is now: after TEOTWAWKI, real estate values in the Rocky Mountain West are going to shoot up. Even a small place will end up costing you an arm and a leg, or at least a gunshot wound or two. So you need to quit your job, sell your house, and move out to the American Redoubt, far from the decadent cities of the Northeast. If you can't afford to quit your job, you might have to build your survival retreat while keeping your place in the city, but then you'll have to make the perilous trip to the survival retreat in SHTF, WROL, fighting your way through marauding bands of looters. Good luck with that.

If you're foolish enough to stay behind in the city, you'll need to take special precautions. In SHTF, the city will soon become so dangerous that your only hope of survival will be to remain hidden. The streets will go dark, and your lights will be a beacon to predators. You'll need to completely black out your windows using black plastic and heavy blankets, and then use sensitive night-vision equipment to make sure there are no light leaks. Since municipal water supplies will fail, you'll need to use buckets in place of your toilet, and treat the contents with lime to cut the smell. Simply disposing of your waste by dumping it could give you away and get you killed; likewise digging a latrine in the backyard.

Above all, wherever you are, you'll need guns. Lots of guns. "It is not realistic to think that you can survive with just one gun, or even just one rifle, one pistol, and one shotgun," Rawles warns. If you're on a budget, you might "get by" with a big-game rifle, a shotgun with two barrels—one for hunting, and a short "riot gun" barrel for everything else—a .22 rifle for small game, and a .45 pistol. (Who could get by without a handgun?) But to handle all the routine work that crops up around the homestead, you should really double that arsenal, and include a complete set of web gear tailored to each long gun you carry. Ammunition? Two thousand rounds for each "battle rifle," five hundred for each hunting rifle, eight hundred for each handgun, two thousand for each .22 rifle, and five hundred for each "riot gun." Those are minimums. You really ought to have three times that. Remember, "ammo is best bought by the 3/4-ton pickup load."

So that's the plan. Somewhere in the heart of the Rocky Mountain West is a deep well of crazy that continually replenishes the American consciousness, and John Wesley, Rawles, has found its main spring.

THERE EXISTS A SPECIES OF DISORIENTATION peculiar to the hour of zero dark stupid, when you have been in the field however long and have been asleep for what seems only minutes before you are again prodded awake, in complete darkness, your body slick with sweat, your uniform greasy with it, the rough lump of your buttpack under your head. Your eyes open but your brain refuses to awaken. In that moment you do not know your name, or where you are, or why you are there; you are not even entirely sure that you are alive. Someone is shoving you and saying, *Sergeant.* The brain wheezes into action like a rusted gear. We call it zero dark stupid because that is what you are.

"Bravo's not back yet. What do we do with the sentries?"

Duty calls: I must rejig the sentry roster because my twelve-man troop is down a quarter of its strength. Our Bravo callsign broke down, again, en route to the harbour—this sweaty, mosquito-ridden patch of woods—and they stayed with the boat. And so I am down three men. I need two on sentry and one on radio watch at all times. Crew commanders take radio watch, and the drivers and gunners pull shifts on sentry, two-hour shifts, staggered. So it ought to be a simple matter except that I am the first up in the morning and the last to go down at night and I have a two-hour shift of my own and also they wake me up for every little fucking thing, and I can't remember how the system works, and I can't remember who is in what crew or who is on sentry when or how the shifts are staggered because it is zero dark fucking stupid and this has been going on for days and Jesus fuck I can't even add two and two much less figure out who's on first.

"Sergeant?"

"Kennedy."

"He's at SHQ."

Of course the dumbass squadron headquarters has pulled away one of my soldiers to act as a runner, as if you need both a runner and a radio watch. So this means I am down to five. The mind will not function: all of the gears are spinning free, something is stripped, something has come off its goddamn trunnions. In the dim red glow of a filtered flashlight, I am staring stupidly at a sheet from a field message pad where the sentry rotation is written. I feel like a prehistoric tortoise staring at a technical manual from the space shuttle.

And that was my lowest moment, not because I cared about the sentry roster or the SHQ or whether Bravo was back, nor even because I wanted dearly to go back to sleep, but because my mind could not manage the simplest of tasks, could not figure out a sentry rotation that was deliberately made simple for just this reason: Bravo could have gone over a mine or been killed by a Sagger or suffered any of a dozen fates worse than mechanical breakdown. That is why you train. And this is what sleep deprivation does: it transforms you into a drooling idiot and chips away at your will to go on.

My task was to keep a small patch of woods secure, night in and night out, with nine adults—twelve, on the rare occasion that Bravo's antediluvian machine held together and all the boats made it into harbour. And so I can say with some confidence that when John Wesley Rawles suggests that rotating two-man security patrols can adequately protect a property of at least twenty acres—and probably a great deal larger, given the need to have a stand of timber large enough to provide a long-term fuel source—against heavily armed and organized "home invasion gangs" and large bands of looters, then John Wesley Rawles is full of shit. Give any serious consideration to the requirements of securing the homestead, of farming, foraging, hunting, and keeping the machines running, and you soon arrive at an inescapable conclusion: you need more manpower. This is why the aristocracy in feudal societies developed into a warrior class that lived parasitically off an enslaved peasantry. If Rawles is right, if the end really is nigh, you're going to need more than a couple of crazy friends with a Caterpillar tractor. You're going to need about two-dozen serfs. But these realities do not penetrate the survivalist mindset, because the survivalist inhabits fantasyland.

Among the hints that we're in fantasyland—as if the lists of gear, the surface coal seam, and the Caterpillar tractor don't make it obvious—is the number of truckloads of ammunition that the survivalist plans to stockpile. In the movies, the bad guys fire countless rounds at our hero, kicking up dust, perforating car doors, and shattering windows, yet the good guy escapes without a scratch. At worst, he's wounded in a mentionable place. But reality is that by the time you've fired two thousand rounds from your "battle rifle" (much less the six thousand rounds that's preferred), someone else will assuredly have fired back using his own battle rifle, and ruined your entire day, or at least the days of several of the five other adults (and however many children) with whom you share your fortified compound.

We face a choice: we can prepare to survive real-world disasters, or we can prepare to inhabit a movie set. Again and again, survivalists choose the movie set. Real-life scenarios, such as the 1998 Quebec ice storm, are boring; fantasies are fun. The survivalist insists that he has learned from the lessons of history, but in truth, his fantasies derive from fiction. The outbreaks of looting, pillaging, and gratuitous violence that survivalism predicts simply don't happen in real-life disasters. Yet we believe they do, and that belief creates a new reality. We expect the movies, and because we expect the movies, we play out our movie roles.

Media accounts of Hurricane Katrina in New Orleans told of a city gripped by looting and violence. New Orleans Police Superintendent Edwin Compass warned that tourists were being raped and robbed in the streets. Looters were everywhere. Desperate people looking for food and water emptied store shelves, while organized gangs of thieves stole electronics and guns. News reports repeatedly described the city as a "war zone." According to the *Washington Post*, New Orleans was as bad as "Baghdad on a bad day." Gangs worked their way through the Superdome and the convention centre, which had been set up as relief centres, robbing, raping, and murdering the people sheltering there; the hopelessly outnumbered police were powerless to intervene. It was an object lesson in why you don't want to find yourself in a relief shelter, disarmed and helpless: safety lies in armed autonomy.

But as the floodwaters receded, it transpired that there had been few rapes and murders at the Superdome, or anywhere else. Edwin Compass, who eventually resigned his post, conceded that there were "no official reports to document any murder. Not one official report of rape or sexual assault." Police investigated each and every report of rape at the Superdome, where about twenty-five thousand people took shelter, and found that only two sexual assaults had occurred. Reports of looting, too, turned out to be exaggerated. While looters had indeed stolen consumer goods from businesses, most of the looting was not violent and was confined to poor neighbourhoods. No gangs of ravening looters rampaged through the city. And even at the height of the crisis, police had distinguished between looters stealing consumer goods and people scrounging for food, which the news media had not.[173]

At the beginning of the atomic age, governments had a vital interest in how people might react to a nuclear attack, and so they invested in research. Researchers soon identified three prevalent "disaster myths": that large-scale disaster will cause widespread panic, that fear will drive people into a state of emotional and mental paralysis in which they cannot care for themselves, and that violence, crime, and looting will become widespread as people revert to an essentially feral state. But in reality, communities tend to unite in the face of disaster. Large-scale looting generally does not occur, and organized gangs of marauders do not ravage the countryside. Indeed, victims themselves take the initiative and often make important contributions to disaster relief through self-help. Following the 9/11 attacks, for example, boat owners took it upon themselves to help evacuate people from lower Manhattan. In times of crisis, we pull together.

---

173 In at least one well-known instance, a photograph of a black man with food he had scrounged was accompanied by a caption that called him a looter, while the caption of a similar photograph of a white couple said they were "finding food." These two captions were written by different photojournalists working for different agencies, but nonetheless stand as examples of a double standard in news reporting.

People who had lived through bombing already knew this. Britain's war experience shows up in *The Day of the Triffids*, where, despite the fact that most of the population is blinded and predatory plants are on the loose, most people calmly cooperate. But America has never experienced aerial bombing, and its disaster myths keep their deep hold on the national subconscious. We may not see panic and bedlam in real disasters, but we see them in Jerry Ahern's novels and in John Wesley Rawles' survival manual and in countless Hollywood movies, and we believe the fiction.

If you wanted to see what America might look like after the apocalypse—after a major pandemic or a complete economic collapse—you might go to Detroit. Real-world Detroit slid into bankruptcy following an economic meltdown arising both from the collapse of its industrial base and the flight of much of its tax base. The city's population fell from 1.8 million to just over 700,000, hollowing out the city more effectively than even the Black Death might have, had Detroit existed in 1375. Buildings, roads, street lights, bridges, sewers: all have fallen into disrepair. Police response times for a crime in progress may be up to an hour; buildings sometimes burn down before the hard-pressed fire department even arrives. So completely has the city's economy collapsed that in some areas even groceries are hard to come by. And the city is violent, the most dangerous city in the United States, with a murder rate ten times the national average. Rates of robbery, rape, assault, and arson are all correspondingly high. Detroit is the perfect image of the failure of our civilization, because there, the city as an institution has failed.

This is one of the nightmare scenarios that Rawles and his fellow travellers imagine. Rawles of course is riding out the collapse of Detroit from the safety of his ranch somewhere in the Rocky Mountain West, which might seem to prove his point. But for those left behind, Detroit is not a jumble of frightening ruins within which one must stay hidden from sight armed with a battle rifle and six thousand rounds of ammunition to ensure one's very survival. Despite an economic collapse and the disappearance of more than half the population, people in Detroit still find jobs. They still get up in the morning and go to work and come home at night and cook meals and wash dishes and raise children and do all the other things that normal people do throughout the world, in spite of crime, in spite of a dearth of opportunity, in spite even of privileged hipsters who see their city as a kind of theme park for creative bullshit. Detroiters do these things because this is what people do. When there is no work, people find work, or they make work. People get by. We hang together, because humans are social animals and, at the deepest level, we know that we depend on each other. And so, although most of the concealed handgun permits issued by the state of Michigan are held by Detroiters, Detroit is not a city of fortified compounds, of masonry houses with fireproof roofs and front lawns set up as kill zones. It is, instead, a city where, because the police are too stretched to respond to calls, neighbours band together and patrol their own neighbourhoods for their mutual safety. In Detroit, you will find not a post-apocalyptic wasteland, but the Homesteaders of Center City.

But Detroit is less fun than fantasyland, so we take our cues from imagination's sandbox: fiction. Both Jerry Ahern and John Wesley Rawles have written not only post-TEOTWAWKI survival manuals that purport to tell us how things *will* be, but also novels that lay out their imaginings of how things *may* be—visions that happen to coincide. As we watch movies and read novels, we assess their realism not against experience, but against their own internal logic and against their precedents. "That seems realistic," we nod, as the mayor of New Bern, Kansas sends armed men to seize farms outside Jericho, even though it is not realistic at all. It seems realistic because the logic of the story argues that it must happen, like it has in stories right back to H.G. Wells and *The War of the Worlds*.

Survivalism is fantasy. Jerry Ahern's novels do not set out to understand how otherwise peace-loving people might get by in the aftermath of a nuclear exchange, in a kind of *Little House on the Post-apocalyptic Prairie*. Instead, Ahern's novels use a nuclear exchange to bring about the collapse of society as the premise for their author's violent fantasies. Disaster is only the enabling event. All survivalism needs—or wants—is a means of getting rid of the government and breaking down social norms: a satellite weapon, a nuclear device, a zombie epidemic. A runaway laboratory virus, a global economic collapse, a world crop failure? Any disaster will do. The apocalypse is the end, and the end justifies the means.

Fantasy is, of course, all about escape, and survivalism offers escape from a world that is increasingly connected, civilized, and controlled. The scope for individual direct action is increasingly constrained.

Everything we do leaves technological fingerprints. Our buying habits can be tracked through bank and credit card records, our reading habits by our electronic trail through the Internet. Our movements can be tracked through our cellular phones. Facial recognition technology allows security cameras to identify us on sight. In the computer age, almost everything we do can be tracked and monitored. And we cannot fight back, because there's nobody to shoot.

But TEOTWAWKI promises to do away with all that. TEOTWAWKI promises a world in which the only currency is barter or gold. Computers are as useless as the megaliths of Stonehenge, and our governments, assuming they have survived, have no reach or power. To gain this freedom, we must first trade away all the conveniences of modern life, and the security provided by police. You have to give something up to live in the world you want: a world free of government interference in which you make, and protect, your own fortune. TEOTWAWKI is a consummation devoutly to be wished. The survivalist's greatest fear is not that our society will collapse into violence. His greatest fear, his greatest disappointment, is that it will not.

PART III

ALL ARE PUNISH'D
The Consequences of Never Growing Up

Something About Our Republic
Consumerism, Identity, and the Culture of Negligence

> *Place your clothes and weapons where you can find them in the dark.*
>
> —Lazarus Long in *The Notebooks of Lazarus Long*
> (Robert A. Heinlein)

WHAT IS IT ABOUT THE REPUBLIC that makes its people go armed?

We have stalked the highways of the Kingdom of Fear and seen its frightened people, yet most Americans do not pass their days in fear—least of all those Americans who are most likely to carry guns, the inhabitants of small cities and towns where crime rates are low and there is little to fear—from one day to the next. We have completed our taxonomy. We have come as close as we dare to the Wellspring of Crazy, which lies in the shadow of the great migration off the land, yet none of the madness there really explains why so many apparently ordinary people go about armed. It is time to ask how we came to this pass.

Perhaps the simplest explanation is the best. Perhaps the something that makes its people go armed is simply the republic's otherwise most salient feature, its rampant consumerism. Americans buy things because they want them, and because they can. And having bought things, Americans seek to justify themselves, to push back buyer's remorse. And so perhaps Americans become people of the gun simply because they have money to burn. For as long as you have money to burn in the United States, someone will be happy to sell you a match. And in selling you a match, he or she will be only too happy to tell you why you ought to own matches, why you as an American have a God-given right to buy matches, and why you should carry your matches with you wherever you go, just in case something needs burning. And so you carry your matches, so you can reassure yourself that you're the kind of person who's smart and prudent enough to make sure he has a match handy, even though you quit smoking twenty years ago.

I fear that to track down the missing piece of our puzzle, we shall have to travel deep into the heart of darkness. Get in the minivan, kids. We're going to the mall.

Out here in the suburbs, little gives us meaning. We watch the game on our flat-screen TVs, mow our lawns, wash our minivans, and walk our dogs. The annual rite of lawn fertilization that confirms membership in the conformist tribe of the suburban male rewards us with a lush sward that denotes our worth and worthiness. But this is no landscape of possibility. Our network of roads and rails has long since squeezed possibility out of existence, compressed the earth and cut it into tiny squares and left us with this, our very own lawn. Granddad's rifle is long gone from its place over the back door and the frontier is nowhere to be found. But to be an armed citizen—to join the tribe of the sheepdog—is to step outside the dreary prospects of everyday life and become a new man.

Today is Saturday, and today I will go grocery shopping. I will drive to the supermarket in my minivan and buy red peppers, onions, a loaf of bread, a package of chicken breasts, and certain other sundries, and then I will drive home again. But I will make that trip as an armed citizen. I will wear "tactical" pants, originally designed for police departments and now sold to my sheepdog tribe, which feature myriad pockets to hide my gadgets. I will wear a long shirt, untucked, to hide the grip of the 9mm handgun I carry in an inside-waistband holster. In my pockets I will carry an LED penlight, a small multitool, and a razor-sharp folding knife—an Emerson CQC-7 with a nub on the blade's spine designed to catch the corner of my pocket and pull the blade open as I draw the knife. I will also carry a notebook and a pen, a "tactical" pen with a knurled body of machined titanium, designed as a striking weapon. I will wear designer sunglasses and a Swiss watch; I can see myself taking martinis shaken, not stirred. Before I leave the house, I will load my pistol.

I know from *The Best Defense* that the supermarket parking lot is a potentially dangerous environment. I am alert. The other shoppers here today are sheep, living their lives in Condition White: unaware and unprepared. I am the sheepdog. I step from my minivan on Condition Yellow: relaxed alert. Today may be the day I have to defend myself.[174] I walk erect, taking note of my surroundings, a habit of mind I have developed through practice, and by reading *Personal & Home Defense* magazine. I take nothing for granted. I take note of eleven other shoppers in the parking lot. Inside the supermarket, I help an elderly woman get a can of diced tomatoes from a high shelf. I do not carry my grocery bags back across the parking lot, because having my hands full would make me vulnerable. Instead, I push the cart (a potential improvised weapon in itself) back to my minivan, checking that no one is loitering there as I approach.

Or at least, I like to think I do these things. Alertness takes effort, and nothing much ever happens around here. And so my gun and my knife and my little flashlight become a sort of sheepdog uniform that creates my identity, like one of the hats that settles onto Elmer Fudd's head in the old Looney Tunes cartoon. I wear sheepdog clothes, carry sheepdog accessories, and view the world through a sheepdog lens. Not for me the boring, comfortable lives of the suburban sheep. I am alert, armed, and ready. My life will not be reduced to a bit part. Instead I play the part of Jack Ryan in a novel that Tom Clancy never got around to writing. I perform the sheepdog.

THIS STORY IS WELL KNOWN. Five days after Christmas, Veronica Rutledge packed her two-year-old son and her three nieces into her car and drove to the Wal-Mart in Hayden, Idaho, to redeem Christmas gift cards. Over her shoulder, she wore a purse she'd received from her husband as a Christmas gift, and in which she carried her 9mm Smith & Wesson pistol. In the electronics section of Wal-Mart, she left her purse unattended for moment, a long enough moment that her son had time to unzip its rear compartment, pull her loaded handgun from its holster, and accidentally fire it. The bullet struck Rutledge in the head, and she died on the floor.

---

174 Condition White and Condition Yellow are the first two of four states of the combat mindset described by Jeff Cooper, who loved such systems. The others are Condition Orange (specific alert) and Condition Red (fight).

Veronica Rutledge made news because she was a white woman shot by her toddler with her own gun, in a public place, right after Christmas. Reporters stressed that she had been her high school's valedictorian (although they generally failed to mention that her rural school had only a few dozen graduates each year), and that she had graduated from the University of Idaho with a degree in chemistry and gone on to work at the Idaho National Laboratory, where she had written papers on nuclear waste processing. Some reports called her a "nuclear research scientist," which may have been stretching the case, but the point was that although she loved hunting and reportedly carried her gun daily, she was certainly not the redneck of popular stereotype.

When a story like this one hits the news, the questions that arise are predictable. Among the first was why Veronica Rutledge would have carried a gun to Wal-Mart, given that she (a) was a woman, (b) had an education and all her teeth, and (c) lived in a place where there was essentially no crime. The first two are, of course, matters of stereotype, but the third approaches a serious question. Rutledge lived not in Hayden, but in Blackfoot, Idaho, population 11,000; Hayden itself has a population of only 13,000, and is hardly the concrete jungle. This is not really the kind of place where you need to carry a gun. But as a friend told the *Washington Post*, Rutledge "wasn't carrying a gun because she felt unsafe. She was carrying a gun because she was raised around guns."

Veronica Rutledge was carrying a gun because guns were a part of who she was. Her Facebook likes included the NRA, Guns.com, and a local trapshooting club, which the media dutifully reported. They also included various recipe-sharing communities, her church, and a couple of romance writers, which the media dutifully ignored in their rush to portray her as an obsessed gun nut. She was a fan of *The Princess Bride*. She liked Western movies, country music, and Victoria's Secret. In other words, she was an ordinary young woman who happened to like guns. She was carrying a gun because for the Rutledge family, guns were not scary instruments of killing, but ordinary, everyday tools. And she was carrying a gun because carrying a gun was not an unusual thing to do in her family and community, and because she could—she held a concealed-carry permit, and had every legal right to do so. Quite possibly, she thought she should carry a gun because of her duty to protect her son. How far the Kingdom of Fear intruded on her consciousness, we can never know. It's not important. We know the important reason: as her father-in-law, Terry Rutledge, said, "We're gun people."

WHAT DOES IT MEAN to be gun people?

It means, first of all, that you are The Other. Even if you live in Blackfoot, Idaho, among the People of the Gun, you look to the media and feel the weight of elite opinion press against your way of life. And when you know you are The Other, when you know you are a different breed, the tendency is to pledge allegiance to Sheepdog Nation. You accept its core values and its principles, as set down by its thought leaders, gun writers like Colonel Jeff Cooper and self-defence experts like Massad Ayoob. And you perform your membership in the nation, as a Christian goes to church, by enacting its rituals. You slide your loaded handgun into its concealment holster as a Catholic prays the Mysteries of the Rosary. And you buy things: guns, holsters, handgrips, knives, perhaps even tactical pens, because with every purchase you confirm your membership in the tribe, just as granite countertops are the membership dues of the Nice Kitchen tribe, or as driving a BMW announces your success.

I've already admitted that I own more pocketknives than I actually need, a common problem among people who like knives. You keep on buying them because, like Goldilocks, you're looking for the one that's just right, or so you tell yourself. You keep right on buying them, also, because you have a little money to burn and there are so many good knives and also, perhaps, because every time you buy a knife you reiterate that you're a member of the Be-Prepared tribe of former Boy Scouts. And once you have a half-dozen or more pocket knives lying in a drawer, they begin whispering to you. Nothing sinister, I hasten to add. They say things like, "Why did you buy me, if you're just going to carry that other knife all the time? Wasn't I a good knife to you? Was it something I cut?" And then the guilt sets in, and you start rotating them, a different knife each week, because they demand to be used. Head to a site like BladeForums.com, where knife nuts gather to talk about blade steel and sharpening and which knife to buy next, and you will find people who solve this problem as only knife nuts can: they carry four knives at once, reassuring themselves all the while that each serves some unique and necessary purpose.

Once you have a gun, what are you to do with it? Imagine a world in which you were not allowed to carry those pocketknives, and so they all lay in their drawer bickering with each other and begging to be carried. I won't ever buy a 1911 pistol or a Browning Hi-Power, although should the zombie apocalypse arrive I would surely want one, simply because in Canada they are useless instruments. You can use them in only one place, on an approved range, and there is no need for them anywhere else.[175] I am not sufficiently interested in handgun target shooting to spend the money, and if I were, the gun would be a .22-calibre target pistol, which is much cheaper on ammo. That Browning Hi-Power would become a safe queen: an expensive piece of hardware that never sees use, unless you count the occasional cleaning. Like all those pocketknives, the handgun begs to be used, or at least to feel useful. So naturally, people who have spent money on handguns want to carry them. That's what handguns are for. You don't have to be afraid of anything, and you don't have to want to shoot anyone.

This is the single most important reason that Americans carry guns: because they can.

IT ISN'T COLD UNTIL YOUR NOSTRIL hairs freeze as you inhale. We all draw our lines someplace, and that's where I draw mine. And that morning, it was cold: nostril hairs frozen, snow crunching underfoot, cheeks stiffening. Just how cold, I wasn't sure, because I was in Walled Lake, Michigan, in the outer orbit of Detroit, and people there speak a foreign language called Fahrenheit. But that wasn't important, partly because the only thermometer I really needed was freezing together each time I inhaled, and partly because I had other, more pressing concerns. It was still pitch dark, with not a hint of light in the eastern sky, and I was late for work. And I was lost.

Walled Lake is far enough out of Detroit's orbit that getting lost is not especially worrisome from the standpoint of personal safety. The previous year, I'd missed my exit from the interstate in the heart of Detroit and taken the next exit to turn around, a short adventure that gave new meaning to "lost": buildings burned out and boarded up and

---

175 In Canada, there is arguably good reason to carry a handgun if you are a trapper or a prospector or otherwise make your living in a wilderness setting, where that handgun might actually be useful. Trappers, in particular, find them handy for dispatching animals in traps. But I'm not a trapper.

not a soul in sight save a lone man, sitting on a bench, staring at the ground. It seemed important not to disturb him. It seemed important also to get right back on the interstate, not because I feared he would jump up and do me harm but because this seemed like a bad neighbourhood to wander in, to make wrong turn after wrong turn, with no real notion of how to get back to the highway, in a minivan with I'm-not-from-around-here licence plates. My instincts were right: the intersection of Livernois and West Chicago, it turns out, is one of the most dangerous parts of the city.

Walled Lake is not. And so my concern was not to avoid being shot, but to find a place where I could turn around and retrace my steps. I turned down a small side street lined with what looked like small summer places, and turned into a driveway. It then occurred to me that here in the outer orbit of Detroit I could actually get shot for turning into a driveway in the middle of the night, simply because Detroit is a scary idea and sometimes the people living close to that scary idea allow it to govern their actions. Not that I broke into a cold sweat, or felt a sudden quickening of the heart, or suffered some other sweeping melodrama. It simply popped into my head unbidden, as one might wonder, did I remember to lock the garage door?

The sudden glare of your headlights brightens the dark living room where a man lies on the couch of his summer place, sleeping off the Jack Daniels he'd knocked back after his wife kicked him out. He peeks out from behind the curtains to see your van idling in his driveway, motionless. He's had break-ins here, more than once, and he's not about to stand by while it happens again. And there you sit, staring at Google Maps and trying to figure out where you went wrong, only to look up and find yourself on the wrong end of a 12-gauge shotgun.

That's a remote possibility, of course, about as likely as being struck by lightning. But if you make a habit of golfing in the rain, death by lightning strike is not unthinkable. Everyone out here in Walled Lake has guns. At the warehouse shipping dock, the shipper has slapped a bumper sticker up on the bulletin board, courtesy of the local Safari Club chapter: "Hunt with your kids, not for them." In the warehouse office is a bulletin board whose every square inch is covered with hunters' snapshots: last year's buck, a limit of geese, wild turkeys. Everyone wears camo: camo ball caps, camo hoodies, camo coats. I note the shipper's boots: Wingshooters, by Irish Setter. I have a battered pair of my own.

Nobody here is worried about guns. In fact, nobody even talks about them. It's just who they are: they're gun people, just as people in northern Ontario or rural Montana or the Miramichi or northern Idaho are gun people. Nobody ever thinks about this stuff. In gun country, you get up in the morning like everyone else, and you go off to work and then come home and take care of the kids, and life is much the same as it is anyplace else. The culture of everyday gun ownership is entirely distinct from the activist gun culture, yet we insist on conflating the two, on believing that anyone who goes shooting once a week must be gun obsessed, violence-obsessed, dangerous. But they're just people who like to shoot, because—here's the secret truth—guns are fun.

And if my own orbit decays, if I slow and fall towards Detroit, and find myself moving along its empty streets, among its blackened and boarded houses, what then? It's one thing to say that there is no need to carry a gun from the safety of London, Ontario, where the worst threat I face is a shot of bottled evil from some bored suburban teenager out for kicks. It's another thing entirely to say you have no need of one in Detroit, the most violent city in the United States, where the murder rate stands at ten times the national average and where, if you call for help, the police may take over an hour to respond. And although Detroit has the highest number of concealed-carry permits of any place in Michigan, its violence does not come from the number of guns kicking around. Its violence comes from the failure of the city as an institution, from an economic and civil collapse that has driven half the population elsewhere, and left almost half of those who remain living below the poverty line. Taking away guns will not make Detroit a peaceful and happy place. The only solution for Detroit is to rebuild Detroit.[176] And in the meantime, you have to live there. Carrying a gun in Hayden, Idaho, might be a matter of sheepdog performance, or of giving in to the Kingdom of Fear. But

---

176 American criminology has sought since the 1960s to establish relationships between gun ownership and violence, with inconclusive results. Rates of violence rise and fall independently of gun ownership and gun control. Guns make ordinary violence more deadly, but they don't cause the violence itself. Neither does carrying guns actually reduce crime, as John Lott has argued. A good overview of research on this question is Jens Ludwig and Philip J. Cook, *Evaluating Gun Policy: Effects on Crime and Violence* (Washington: Brookings Institution Press, 2003).

carrying a gun in Detroit starts to look like a rational choice. I can't say what I would do if I lived in Detroit.

I worked in Jamaica for several weeks in 2005, when that country had the highest murder rate in the world. What's more, I worked in Kingston, where most of the murders take place, a city the US State Department warns its employees is "a Critical crime threat post." A high wall, topped with razor wire, protected the warehouse, and at the gate you passed a uniformed guard toting a shotgun. Delivery trucks occasionally met with hijackers. On the way in from the airport, my driver took Mountain View Avenue, which the embassy advises us not to do. At every intersection along that street, lanky, bored police in flak jackets and helmets slouched beside their cars, toting shotguns and M16s. "We've had some trouble in Mountain View," my host cryptically explained. The trouble in question was the aftermath of a by-election; the parish seat had changed hands, and now there was a settling of accounts among gangs tied to political parties that had seen nightly gun battles and shootings.

It is a troubled island, wrecked by Cold War interference, rampant corruption, and the War on Drugs. Nobody carries a gun, at least not legally, because private ownership of guns is banned in Jamaica. Those who can afford to live in gated neighbourhoods protected by armed private security guards, who respond quicker than the police and who know exactly who signs their paycheques. Houses lie behind high stone walls topped with iron spikes. And in the midst of it all, bright-scrubbed children in smart, clean uniforms skip down the shabby streets to school. Life is normal when it's the only normal you know. "It's the same as anywhere," said my host, although quite obviously it is not. "There are just some places you shouldn't go." Mountain View Avenue is one of those places.

Nobody goes about armed, although going armed in Kingston might well be a rational choice. But there is a difference between going armed because you must, and going armed because you can, which takes us from Kingston, Jamaica right back to Hayden, Idaho.

WHEN YOU CARRY A GUN, you carry a weighty package of consequences, a point that the media and the police carefully talked around following the death of Victoria Rutledge. This was an accident, they insisted, which no one could have predicted, an Act of God. Nothing more should be said. "It's a terrible, terrible incident," said Terry Rutledge, choosing the most neutral word available: it was a thing that had happened that was bad. From nearby Spokane, Washington, KREM-TV reporters called it "a very, very tragic accident" and "a terrible, terrible accident," noting that Rutledge was "as responsible as they come," but also reporting the view of the local police, who hoped this terrible, terrible accident would "serve as a reminder to always, always protect your gun."

This was the gentlest possible approach to the point that nobody wanted to make in the politically loaded climate of the Great American Gun Kerfuffle: Veronica Rutledge was dead because she had left a loaded gun unattended, however briefly, with a child. Terry Rutledge was quick to lash out at anyone who did raise that point. "They are painting Veronica as irresponsible, and that is not the case," he insisted, pointing to her experience with guns, her handgun training, and her concealed-carry permit. Also, in apparent response to the image of a reckless young woman with a gun loose in her purse, "this wasn't just some purse she had thrown her gun into." It wasn't; it was a Gun Tote'n Mamas 0014 Concealed Carry Shoulder Bag, which distinguishes itself from a regular purse in its rear zippered compartment, which holds a holster to fit a pistol. But that's neither here nor there, for a concealed-carry shoulder bag's zippered compartment is no more secure than the zippered compartment of an ordinary purse if you leave it unattended with a two-year-old.

Nobody possessing any degree of sensitivity wants to call Victoria Rutledge irresponsible. She is dead at twenty-nine, and her son will face a difficult and uncharted road when he is old enough to understand what happened. There is no call to pile on with social condemnation, or moral opprobrium, or conclusions drawn about her character. But we can understand how she came to be killed, for the sake of future prevention: she had a loaded gun, with a round in the chamber, and she left that gun unattended for long enough that a child was able to unzip the compartment it was stored in and remove it from the holster that covered its trigger.

There is no violent crime to speak of in Hayden, Idaho, neither did Rutledge fear it. So why was the gun loaded, with a round up the spout? The finger of blame here points not at Victoria Rutledge, mother, but at the armed-camp vision of America, the culture of complete preparedness that insists you must go armed, that you must at all times have a loaded weapon within reach, with a round in the chamber, ready to fire. Just in case. No matter that crime is falling, no matter that you live in a small town where nothing much ever happens. It *could* happen, just as you could win the lottery or be struck by lightning or, conceivably, be swallowed by a sinkhole and washed out to sea and eaten by sharks. Sheepdog Nation's thought leaders tell us this is so, and so we must enact the ritual.

Veronica Rutledge's death was not the tragedy of a young mother's negligence with a loaded handgun. It was the tragedy of a culture of negligence. The game of "what if" has normalized keeping loaded guns to the point that American gun owners increasingly forget to treat them as if they are—which is, of course, the first rule of firearms safety. And there is no shortage of accidents. In North Carolina, a man unloads his gun but forgets he left a round in the chamber and is shot and wounded by his three-year-old grandson. In Florida, a two-year-old finds a gun in the glovebox and shoots himself in the chest. In Missouri, a five-year-old boy finds his grandfather's loaded handgun and accidentally shoots his nine-month-old brother. The sheriff, in this last case, calls it "a tragic, cautionary tale," but, as usual, we seem to be long on tragedy and short on caution. No charges are laid, in any case.

The triumph of the culture of negligence surely took place on January 19, 2013. On this, the inaugural Gun Appreciation Day, created in response to federal gun-control efforts, five people were shot in three separate incidents at gun shows across the United States. At a gunshow in Raleigh, North Carolina, a loaded 12-gauge shotgun was accidentally fired while it was being removed from its case at the entrance to the show, wounding three people. Its owner had brought it there to sell it, and had apparently forgotten that it was loaded. In Indianapolis, a man leaving a gun show accidentally shot himself in the hand with his .45 while he was loading it. And at a gun show in Medina, Ohio, a dealer who had just bought a gun was showing it to a friend when he accidentally fired it. The magazine had been removed, but a round was left in the chamber.

In none of these cases was a charge laid.

In September 2011, two men brought a Mauser rifle into Ellwood Epps Sporting Goods near Orillia, Ontario. There was something wrong with the gun, and they had partly disassembled it before bringing it in. As the older of the two put the gun down on the counter, it discharged, critically wounding the younger man and also injuring an Epps employee. The gun was still in its case. The man, Peter Arnold, was charged with three criminal offences: careless use of a firearm, handling a loaded firearm causing bodily harm, and transporting a loaded firearm.[177]

Canadians once saw accidental shootings as nothing more than terrible, terrible incidents. When someone pointed a revolver at a friend, not knowing it was loaded, that was not a matter of criminal irresponsibility, but a tragic, tragic accident that should remind us to always, always take care. But earnest repetition is no solution. Anyone handling a gun has a duty to take care. Carelessness is not tragic, tragic, nor terrible, terrible. It's criminal negligence.[178] In the Canadian military, any accidental discharge will lead to charges, regardless of whether anyone is hurt—even when using blank ammunition.[179] For civilians, any shooting accident looks like Careless Use of a Firearm, as close a thing to absolute liability as you will ever find in the Criminal Code: if you weren't careless, how did this happen? The result is a culture of accountability.

And shooting ought to have a culture of accountability. Guns do not "go off." Barring mechanical failure, or someone dropping the gun, they fire only when somebody pulls the trigger. This is why we observe basic rules of firearms safety: control what the muzzle is pointing at, keep your finger off the trigger, and assume the gun is loaded until you've proven otherwise—not simply by removing the magazine, but by opening the action and checking that the chamber is empty. To these we can add one more rule: a loaded firearm remains under your control at all times. Not in the glovebox, not in a drawer, not in your tactical purse, but in your hands or on your body. These are not advanced concepts, and they are not controversial ideas. These are basics.

Basic firearms safety ought to dictate that you don't leave loaded guns lying around, nor do you load a gun when there is no clear reason

---

177 At time of writing, this case was still before the courts.

178 Actually, it's covered both by Criminal Negligence (Section 219) and Careless Use of a Firearm (section 86) under the Criminal Code of Canada. Criminal Negligence Causing Death carries a four-year mandatory minimum sentence when a firearm is involved.

179 The same holds true in the US military, where accidental discharges are referred to as "negligent discharges."

to do so. There is no reason to have your concealed handgun loaded in the Wal-Mart, if you don't expect to face a bad guy there. But you cannot make this suggestion without provoking howls of derision. How will you protect yourself if your gun isn't loaded? Do you only wear your seatbelt when you're about to crash?[180] Are you comfortable with becoming a statistical outlier? The Great American Gun Kerfuffle has come down to culture war. The armed-camp vision of America, which perhaps exists solely to justify gun ownership, insists you must be locked and loaded at all times. And to suggest that anyone unload his gun, put it in the safe, or even be criminally liable for safe handling is dismissed as just so much squawking from the antis. The culture of negligence has become entrenched. Fatal accidents are just the price of freedom.

THAT THIRTY-THOUSAND-ODD AMERICANS are killed each year with guns is an American tragedy, and it has become a commonplace of the gun-control movement that behind this great tragedy lies a great evil. That great evil needs a face, and so gun-control activists have come to blame gun manufacturers. The firearms industry pours money into the NRA, which helps to fund its various campaigns and also to pay the salaries of its staff and its full-time lobbyists. And so anti-gun activists now point to gun manufacturers as Big Gun, a firearms analogue to Big Tobacco, profiting from death even as they deny the common-sense fact that their products are dangerous and prevent any meaningful progress on gun control through their puppet, the NRA. It ought to be clear to anyone that, while a gun doesn't up and kill someone all by its lonesome, it surely is a great aid to the killer's work. And by woeful misinterpretations of the public health research, which demonstrates that the presence of firearms is a risk factor for both homicide and suicide, we arrive at the conclusion that guns themselves are simply not safe, that no one can be trusted to own a gun because the statistics prove that people with guns are more likely to shoot people than people without guns, and you just never can know.[181] "Firearms safety" is just a fiction

---

180 No, but I only wear my seatbelt when I am driving. I do not wear one when I'm sitting on the couch, for example, although an earthquake could at any moment throw me to the floor and injure me.

181 That this is a serious misinterpretation of the research ought to be obvious. Although the various researchers (Dr. Arthur Kellerman being one of the leaders) have shown that guns are "independently" correlated with homicide and suicide, they are of course only independent of the other variables in the models. A careful look finds strong hints that the homicide risk, for

Big Gun concocted to fool America into thinking their products aren't actually dangerous, that people can own guns without putting their lives and the lives of their families at risk.

But firearms safety is not a fiction, as the grim facts of accidental shooting on accidental shooting testify: in each of these cases, the problem is simply that people have failed to take basic, common-sense safety precautions. If Big Gun preaches firearms safety through the National Shooting Sports Foundation—an organization that truly is its puppet, being organized and funded entirely by gun manufacturers—then the reasons are likely much less cynical than its opponents suggest. Not even the executives of Sturm, Ruger & Co. actually *want* to see people killed when kids get their hands on loaded guns, and not only because it's bad for business. It was William Ruger himself who suggested that the practical legislative solution to the problem of semi-automatic firearms was to limit magazine capacity, a suggestion that now prompts torrents of angry bile from gun activists convinced that only 30-round magazines can keep the goblins at bay.[182] And the NRA is hardly Big Gun's puppet. When Big Gun shows signs of cooperating with gun control, the NRA has encouraged its members to boycott those gun makers, as Smith & Wesson discovered to its cost.

Big Gun is a fiction. There is no conspiracy. There are no puppet masters pulling the strings. No great evil lies behind the great American tragedy. As usual, what appears to be an organized, coordinated program is nothing more than the isolated acts of a large number of people whose interests happen to coincide. Guns are big business, but they're a big business made of many small businesses, of range operators and shooting instructors and gun writers and gun-shop owners

---

example, is related to domestic violence: the odds ratio for women killed by domestic partners in Kellerman's original study is striking. And of course, firearms do not cause suicidality; they simply offer a means that appears to be more certain and less painful than others. More recent research has suggested a worrisome connection between carrying a gun, anger, and impulsive behaviour. Pro-control activists might make more progress if they were to abandon the argument that people in general simply can't be trusted with guns, and instead focused their efforts on identifying the kinds of people who ought not to be trusted with guns, and making sure that they aren't. We might, for example, look at people's driving records as one indication of whether they are responsible and trustworthy, but we do not. And incredibly, many American states don't see the nexus of domestic violence and gun ownership as a pressing problem that demands attention. But that's a question of gun-control policy, which is beyond the scope of this book.

182   Canada adopted William Ruger's suggestion, limiting centre-fire semi-automatic ammo capacity to five rounds for long guns and ten rounds for pistol magazines. The history of mass shootings in the US and Canada suggests this was a fairly effective measure.

and self-defence gurus and survival "experts" and magazine publishers and pawnbrokers and accessory makers and whoever else makes a dollar from America's love affair with the gun. Many of these businesses, like Slide Fire Solutions with its Chicago billboards, are fully involved in pumping sludge through the Wellspring of Crazy. For some, bottling Crazy and selling it is the entire business plan. The problem is not Big Gun; it's the culture, a culture that continually reiterates stupid and dangerous ideas, for a profit. If I buy into those ideas, then that culture becomes a part of my identity. And your attempt to regulate my guns becomes an attack on their business, and an attack on me. The whole mass pushes back, with increasing vehemence. Nobody controls this beast anymore, not even the NRA.

The NRA's gun safety program for kids, in which Eddie the Eagle encourages youngsters to leave the area and get an adult when they find an unattended gun, would be laughable if its failures were not so tragic.[183] But this is not Big Gun selling us a lie. It's a half-assed excuse for firearms safety promoted by people who simply can't admit to themselves that keeping a loaded gun handy is not only unnecessary, but foolish. Quixotes keep their guns loaded, in case of windmills. Fearful men carry them feloniously in the Sacramento night, as talismans to ward off evil. Actors cast themselves in larger parts, and slip guns into their holsters as props. Disenfranchised wingnuts grip their guns and mutter about the constitution. The reasons are numberless, and of course the overarching reason is that somebody is making a buck off it, just as someone makes a buck off every diet fad, every fashion craze, every tabloid. Jesus himself is a commodity.

There is no great evil behind America's great tragedy. There are only small men. For America's tragedy is tragic in the classical sense. The nation is not laid low by dark forces and conspiracies beyond its control. It lays itself low, again and again, through its hubris and its greed.

---

183   As has been repeatedly demonstrated, kids so instructed do not Stop!, Leave the Area!, and Tell An Adult! Instead, they pick up the gun and mess with it. See, for example, Baxley and Miller; Farah, Simon, and Kellerman; Hardy; Himle, Miltenberger, Gatheridge and Flessner; and Jackman, Farah, Kellerman, and Simon. From the other side, see Lott and Whitley, who (surprise!) warn us that safe storage laws actually lead to perverse results; in *More Guns, Less Crime*, Lott informs us that safe storage laws actually increase violent crime. But John Lott has yet to find a gun-control law that doesn't.

You'd Have to Be Crazy
Home-Grown Terrorists, Lone Wolves, and Mass Shootings

The only lesson that can be learned from this is don't home-school your kids.

—Justin Bourque

On October 20, 2014, Patrice Vincent, a fifty-three-year-old warrant officer working at the Canadian Armed Forces base in Saint-Jean-sur-Richelieu, Quebec, was deliberately run over in a parking lot and killed. Vincent's attacker, Martin Couture-Rouleau, was already on an RCMP terrorist watch list, and his passport had been revoked. He had been waiting in that parking lot for hours, looking for a suitable victim, and after running down Patrice Vincent and a second soldier, he called police to explain that he had acted in the name of Allah. But Allah does not appear to have cared much for Couture-Rouleau, who died in hospital after losing control of his car, running at police with a hunting knife, and being shot several times. I received this news from my clock radio, which awakens me with the latest in bad news each morning. I recall thinking two things: first, that it was a hell of a thing to be run over in a parking lot on your lunch hour simply because of the uniform you were wearing, and second, that a car makes a handy weapon if you live in Canada and can't easily get your hands on a gun and don't know how to build a bomb. I wrote it off, like most people did, as a senseless killing.

The following morning, Michael Zehaf-Bibeau took a Winchester Model 94—a lever-action rifle with a design dating back to the nineteenth-century revolution in firepower—and shot Corporal Nathan Cirillo twice in the back as Cirillo stood ceremonial guard at the National War Memorial in Ottawa. As Cirillo bled to death on the concrete steps of the memorial, Zehaf-Bibeau drove to the Parliament buildings and ran into the Centre Block. His attack had media traction because it was a shooting, because it was an attack on Parliament itself, and most of all, perhaps, because it came so soon after the attack that killed Patrice Vincent. A photograph of Zehaf-Bibeau with his rifle, his face covered by a keffiyeh, circulated on Twitter. Rumours of a second gunman and a third shooting, at the Rideau Centre mall, kept Ottawa on lockdown. And, of course, fear spread and multiplied, and rumours flew, because when we know little about a frightening event, we try to fill in the gaps with speculation. This is how rumours work: one person's speculation becomes another's possible truth and then a third's reality, and the next thing you know there is a gunman at the Rideau Centre mall and cops have been shot and ISIS is on the move in Canada. The nation was under attack—except that it was not, as the RCMP soon clarified. There was no second gunman, and the attacks were unrelated. They were just the work of a pair of troubled and angry young men who had glommed onto the same cause.

It seems odd to begin a discussion of mass shootings with two isolated, politically motivated attacks in which only two people were killed, particularly since one of those incidents did not even involve a gun. But the difference between a mass shooting and a single casualty can be a bullet that stops the shooter in time. The difference between a terror attack and a crime is only the label we put on the shooter's cause. Why worry about how many are killed and with what? The same questions demand answers regardless. What motivates the killer? How could we have stopped him from acting? Are these isolated incidents, or part of some trend?

Comment is a team sport these days, and most of us make sure to work from the playbook, running the same plays on offence and defence as the situation demands. To the right, Michael Zehaf-Bibeau was a terrorist acting according to a larger agenda; to the left, he was a mentally troubled young man who had resorted to violence. To the left, Marc Lépine was an anti-feminist terrorist; to gun activists in Canada, a mentally troubled young man who had resorted to violence. Mental health is our secular equivalent to "the Lord works in mysterious ways": if you can't figure out what to do, or you don't like the obvious solution, you talk about mental health spending as if putting money in a bucket will somehow take care of everything.

Was Zehaf-Bibeau a mentally troubled lone wolf, or a terrorist? The truth, which ought to be obvious, is that he was both.

WHAT CAN POSSIBLY MOTIVATE SOMEONE to take up a gun and walk into an elementary school or a movie theatre or some other public place where people go innocently about their business, and deliberately gun down complete strangers? The mind reels. One cannot fathom it. And so we decide that something must be broken inside that shooter, that his mind can't have been operating according to the usual rules, that some mental virus must have infested his operating system. In short, he'd have to be crazy.

It's a cop-out, of course. The mind needs a way to explain away the inexplicable and reduce the enormity of events to manageable dimensions. In the media glare of the aftermath, there is never any shortage of acquaintances and grief-stricken relatives and "experts" stepping forward to tell us of the shooter's irrational behaviour and strange obsessions, all to reassure us that he was nuts. What is incomprehensible and frightening becomes merely frightening, and we move on to other things.

But "you'd have to be crazy and therefore he was" is clearly circular reasoning, and you can't diagnose someone as mentally ill after he's dead, which the shooter usually is by the end of his rampage. Mental illness isn't like having strep throat or measles. It's not a question of whether you're sick or not, whether some pathogen is in your mental wiring. Many mental illnesses lie at the extreme end of a continuum, where the ordinary reactions of the human mind become so imbalanced that one ceases to cope.[184] Our shooter may have had an inflated sense of his own worth, and a need to feel admired, but who doesn't? This is not the same thing as narcissistic personality disorder. Before we could say he suffered

---

184   The recent fuss over DSM-5 (the fifth edition of the Diagnostic and Statistical Manual of Mental Disorders) illustrates the point. DSM-5 created new illnesses and loosened the definitions of others. *Maclean's* magazine (among many others) fretted that DSM-5 had pathologized grieving and turned normal worry into "generalized anxiety disorder." At issue was at what point normal behaviour became illness.

from narcissistic personality disorder, we would have to establish that our shooter's delusions of grandeur and need to feel admired significantly impaired his day-to-day life, that he was unable to form normal relationships because he looked on others primarily as mirrors reflecting himself, and that these problems persisted day to day, regardless of the situation.[185] And this is difficult to establish, unless you've been able to lay him on a couch and interview him at length. We cannot simply declare people crazy because it's convenient to see them that way, and then assume that by putting more money in the mental health bucket we might somehow prevent future shootings—although more money for mental health would certainly benefit people who really do have mental health problems, people who in spite of our prejudices are no more likely to go shooting rooms full of people than anyone else.

Yet we declare the shooter crazy, again and again. Michael Zehaf-Bibeau was widely assumed to be a mental-health case on the word of his mother, who said that he was not entirely well although she had barely spoken to him in recent years.[186] Marc Lépine is posthumously assumed to have suffered from acute narcissistic personality disorder.[187] Martin Couture-Rouleau's next-door neighbour insisted Couture-Rouleau was not a terrorist, just a young man who needed psychiatric help. The NFA suggested, in a press release, that Justin Bourque's shooting spree might have been prevented by "a health care system which could be better enabled to diagnose and treat conditions that put people's lives at risk," before Bourque had even been captured. That psychologists found Bourque mentally competent seems not to have penetrated the NFA's ironclad confidence. Nor is Bourque unique. Rarely is the shooter actually insane, at least not clinically so.

But if mass shootings are not a mental-health problem, what are they? Are they, in truth, all about guns? This seems self-evident: they are shootings. And they seem to be growing more common as guns grow more common, as more and more black rifles circulate.

---

185   Based on DSM-5 criteria. "Significant impairment" that is "relatively stable across time and consistent across situations" are key criteria that must be met for a personality disorder to exist.

186   Susan Bibeau clarified that she did not think her son was crazy, merely that he was not well.

187   Thanks to the remarks of a police psychiatrist, the assumption that Lépine suffered from narcissistic personality disorder is widespread. The psychiatrist's own warning, that we cannot posthumously diagnose Lépine, seems to have been ignored. See, for example, Lee Mellor's book, *Rampage: Canadian Mass Murder and Spree Killing*, which claims that Lépine's life was "shaped by a major personality disorder."

Gun-control advocates seem keen to prove that mass shootings are simply a problem of too many guns, and publish statistics proving that we are seeing more mass shootings than ever before.[188] Gun-rights advocates reply by picking apart their definitions. What differentiates a mass shooting from an ordinary, everyday shooting? Should "school shootings" include all shootings that take place at schools, regardless of the number of casualties and of motivations, or should it include only the Columbines and Écoles Polytechniques, incidents in which the shooter's aim is to cause the greatest possible number of casualties without regard to whom he kills?

So let us begin by defining the problem, lest we mistake talking for thinking. Our definition ought to begin not with the setting, or with the number of casualties. Michael Zehaf-Bibeau killed only one man before he was shot down. Marc Lépine killed fourteen women. But does anything really set these two men apart? Does it matter if the shooting is actually a mass shooting? Timothy McVeigh killed 168 people with a bomb. Is he any different? Need our killing be a shooting at all?

Maybe we can start by looking under another rock entirely.

RATHER THAN CHASING DOWN DEFINITIONS and arguing how many mass shooters can dance on the head of a pin, let's creep up on the mass shooter crabwise. Let's consider a possible prototype: Gavrilo Princip.

Princip only shot one person, but his act carried greater consequence than Michael Zehaf-Bibeau or Justin Bourque could dream of. His assassination in Sarajevo of Archduke Franz Ferdinand of Austria ignited World War I, which led directly to the Russian Revolution; the unresolved conclusion of the Great War propelled into power a little maniac named Adolf Hitler and led directly to World War II and its holocausts; this war, in turn, gave us the atom bomb and led us into the Cold War, which gave to us Korea, Vietnam, and however many brush fire proxy wars no less vicious; that same Cold War and its noxious ideological conflict destabilized the politics of countless small nations, plunging nascent democracies into a cycle of political thuggery; and

---

188   See, for example, *Mother Jones* magazine, which made a major project of collecting data on mass shootings and published its results in May 2014. Using this data, researchers at the Harvard School of Public Health found that the rate of mass shootings was increasing, a claim also made by *Mother Jones*. *Mother Jones* carefully defined "mass shooting" for their purposes, which naturally leads to quibbling over the definition.

when the whole thing finally fell over, we found ourselves back in Sarajevo, fighting again over the nationalist aspirations of an insignificant nation. Sarajevo bookends the bloody twentieth century, and it all leads back to one man standing outside a café with a pistol in his pocket. Not bad for a morning's work.

Princip may not seem much like Bourque, Zehaf-Bibeau, McVeigh, Lépine, and the rest. But he has all the same traits found in the likes of Bourque and McVeigh. He is young, slight, and weedy. His health has always been poor. He had attempted to join Serbian guerillas fighting the Turks, but was rejected because of his health and small stature. And so, desperate to belong to a cause and to become a hero, he is recruited into an assassination plot, one that requires him to commit suicide by swallowing cyanide. We cannot say for sure that Princip shares the same pathology as our mass shooters and homegrown terrorists, but he certainly looks the part.

How are we to stop him? Can we keep the gun from his hands? The gun is a Belgian-made FN Model 1910 pistol, supplied by Serbian military intelligence. Like my bottom-ejecting pump shotgun, a Browning BPS, like the Colt 1911 pistol, like the Browning Hi Power pistol, like the M2 .50-calibre machine gun and its little brother the M1919 machine gun, like the Browning Automatic Rifle, it is a John Browning design. John Browning is responsible for the telescoping bolt, which is the design innovation behind modern semi-automatic pistols. He invented the gas-operated machine gun, a concept that leads directly to the machine guns and assault rifles of today. He designed the Winchester Model 1887 lever-action rifle. John Browning's shadow falls everywhere. Even the Makarov pistol used by the Soviet Red Army was a knockoff of the same gun that killed the Archduke: a John Browning design.

Might the world be a better place had John Browning never been born?

I would be out a shotgun. Though that is a small concern when weighed against all the consequences of John Browning's work. But what of those consequences? Can we believe that, deprived of John Browning's amoral genius, human ingenuity would not have found equally effective designs, or even arrived at the same solutions? Are we to believe that, deprived of their machine guns, Allied forces could not have found some alternative, and still defeated Hitler's armies? Necessity is the mother of invention, and something in humanity's murderous nature its father.

So many culprits. Let us absolve the gun and its designer, and instead call to the stand young Jelena Milisic, Princip's girlfriend. Milisic spent the evening of June 27 with Princip in a city park, where she defended her virtue against Princip's repeated importunities.

"A man can suffer terrible complications if he doesn't release the pressure," said he.

"That is nonsense," said Jelena. "And were it not, I am confident you could take the matter in hand."

"But I may die a hero's death in the morning."

A rolling of eyes: this is what you get for consorting with revolutionaries. Jelena realizes now that she should have listened to her mother. Come morning, according to a friend, Princip was frustrated enough "that he would have shot God himself." And, for want of a hand job, three empires were lost.

Perhaps.[189]

Seeking something, or someone, to blame, we finally have only Gavrilo Princip himself. After all, guns don't kill people; people kill people. Or so the NRA advises us, neatly ignoring the role weapons play in facilitating the procedure. But let's accept the NRA's line for a moment. Given that it is people who kill people, would the world be a better place had Gavrilo Princip never been born?

Let us, armed with knowledge of the flux capacitor, build a time machine and return to 1914 Sarajevo to assassinate the assassins. We know their names. We know all the details, and they should not be difficult to find. But for every would-be assassin we cut down, another would surely spring up. Europe seethes with nationalists, with anarchists, with socialists and communists. Assassination is in the air, and the deadly machinery of alliances is oiled and awaits only a push to spin its first lethal gear. And so our deadly game of whack-a-mole is doomed to fail.

It was not Gavrilo Princip who assassinated Franz Ferdinand; it was Serbian nationalism. Princip was a naïve teenager, nineteen years old, 145 pounds and sickly: only a pawn in their game. Bob Dylan, little

189 I may have fabricated the dialogue. The rest of this story, which may be apocryphal, is from David DeVoss, "Searching for Gavrilo Princip," *Smithsonian* magazine, August 2000.

older than Princip when he wrote the song of that very name, was just as wrong, for there is no "they," no dark and powerful conspiracy of shadowy power brokers, no chess master pushing his pawns forward. There is only the complex of bad ideas that proclaims the right to take up a pistol and shoot the Archduke in the interest of forming a greater Yugoslavia.

And so Princip becomes a national hero to Yugoslavia. In 1953, Marshal Tito opened a Princip Museum in Sarajevo, to preserve his memory. In 1964, the peasant shack in which he was born was declared a national landmark. A pair of footprints, embedded in the concrete sidewalk, marked the spot from which he fired the fatal bullets. But nationalism has its own dire quantum mechanics. The quantum that is Princip's bullet tears the cloth of Archduke Ferdinand's uniform, severs his jugular vein, and lodges against his spine, exciting the atom that is Europe. The energy of this quantum binds together a greater Yugoslavia, but this energy must inevitably decay; Yugoslavia spins apart, emitting heat, light, and blood, and the atom returns to its ground state. In Sarajevo, the embossed footprints that commemorate the hero's act are removed. Croatian troops destroy the peasant shack, and Bosnians shut down the Princip museum.

Princip is neither hero nor villain. He is a mere foot soldier, a member of that class that most often does violence in the service of bad ideas: young men. It is not the bullet that ignites the powder, nor the gun that pulls the trigger, nor the teenaged killer who manufactures destiny. Guns don't kill people; ideas kill people. And the power of ideas comes not from some lentil-munching, herbal-tea-sipping, Ghandi-quoting moral superiority, but from the simple fact that swords cannot extinguish them. They persist until either they get their way, or they go out of fashion. For good ideas, such as human rights, democracy, and the rule of law, permanence is a wonderful thing. But bad ideas persist also, so long as people can be convinced to believe them. And nothing is more dangerous than a bad idea carrying a loaded gun.

A bad idea needs an agent to carry its gun, and that agent is always the same: an angry young man. Here, we find a clear and consistent pathology. The coroner's report on the École Polytechnique massacre tells us all we need to know: that mass killers have fantasies of power and success and a burning need for recognition. Their high expectations are continually disappointed, of course, by the everyday reality of their lives, and they scapegoat groups they imagine are responsible for their failings and retreat into violent and grandiose fantasies of revenge that compensate for their own essential impotence. It does not matter if they kill one, or twenty, or if their motive is political or personal, or, indeed, if the weapon is a gun or a bomb. These men are all the same.

Consider our cast of characters: Marc Lépine, a self-absorbed loser who blamed women for his failures; Timothy McVeigh, a self-absorbed loser who blamed the government; Justin Bourque, who could do every Cartoon Network voice and felt that oughta be worth something, like a minor character from *The Trailer Park Boys* come to life. Michael Zehaf-Bibeau, Dylan Klebold, Jared Loughner: the common thread is a kind of deadly incompetence, as if the killer's genetic marker is the Loser Gene. The anti-terror expert Brian Michael Jenkins has suggested we should call our homegrown terrorists not lone wolves, but stray dogs. They glom onto their causes because causes are what they most desperately need, causes to elevate their lives above the banality of the everyday, to the significance they feel they deserve.

Bad ideas need their agents, and stray dogs need their causes. Serbian nationalism assassinated the Archduke, just as anti-feminist backlash killed fourteen women at the École Polytechnique and the gun culture killed three Mounties in Moncton. Princip, Lépine, and Bourque—troubled young men all—pulled the triggers. Nothing separates Lépine from McVeigh, except the means of murder; nothing separates Anders Breivik from young men fighting for ISIS.[190] It's time to stop asking if public atrocities are the work of terrorists or mentally troubled lone wolves. It's time to admit that they're really just the same thing. And above all, it's time to discard the assumption that mass shootings are a unique problem, and to see them for what they are: nothing more than the point in three-dimensional space at which a stray dog intersects with a cause and a loaded gun.

One of these things we can do something about, because Princip differs from our other shooters in one important respect: he cannot be stopped, because he is history's agent. But not everyone gets his gun from Serbian spies and acts in the interest of a movement that will

---

190 On July 22, 2011, Anders Breivik killed 77 in Norway, 8 by bombing and the remainder in a shooting massacre at a teenagers' summer camp. His ideology, expressed in a long, detailed manifesto, was based on Islamophobia.

arguably provoke a world war regardless. If we stop the next Justin Bourque, no co-conspirator will take his place. And we do have a way to stop him, even if we don't know who "he" is.

We can do something about the gun.

ONE OF THE MOST STRIKING POINTS in the coroner's report on the École Polytechnique shootings is made seemingly in passing: "They thought it was an end of session joke, and that the attacker was firing blanks."

Nobody thinks it can happen to them, of course, right up until the moment it does. But in 1989, school shootings were not yet regular fodder for twenty-four-hour news channels. Canada had not seen a school shooting in more than twenty years. And so, as Marc Lépine burst into a classroom with a rifle, fired into the ceiling and ordered the women there to line up against the wall, it was still possible to imagine that he was just kidding, that this was all some sort of elaborate joke whose punchline would soon become clear.

It is inconceivable today that anyone would think the man with the rifle was just kidding, and this is really all the evidence any sensible person needs to establish that mass shootings have indeed become more common. Only a fool would dispute it—although, the times being what they are, there is no shortage of fools stepping forward to do just that. If you were to admit that mass shootings had grown more common, then you would come perilously close to admitting that America had some kind of gun problem, which would be an act of treason against Mom, apple pie, the constitution, and Jesus. And so the games begin, with rhetoric spiralling into debates over what a mass shooting actually is, how many victims are required, how the victims can relate to the shooter, and for what reasons the shooter is permitted to open fire. If you can rig the definitions, you can skew the numbers to prove anything you please.

If gun activists do confront the idea that mass shootings have become more common, they will lay the blame on some new pathology: on video games (a favourite of Lieutenant Colonel Dave Grossman) or on anti-depressants or on a general collapse of society's moral standards. But the pathology of the killer is not new at all. He is the same old angry young man he always has been.

The truth is inescapable: mass shootings have grown more common not because society has grown sicker or more violent (in fact, the opposite is true), but because the gun has become the angry young man's weapon of choice, and because ordinary people have replaced soldiers and politicians and Austrian archdukes as his preferred targets. Perhaps it is a consequence of the much-ballyhooed End of History: with no great cause to join, we fall to killing people at random, citing whatever justification we can dream up.[191]

Angry young men have turned to shooting, and this is, in part, a simple consequence of the world gun culture has wrought. Guns have become America's *vindices injurarium*, for injuries real and imagined. The AR-15 has usurped the place once held by the anarchist's bomb and the airline hijacker's pistol as the nation itself has become fascinated with things "tactical," with military and paramilitary equipment, weapons, and tactics. Simply put, black rifles are cool. Going out to shoot a bunch of people with an old hunting rifle is the act of a loser, a pathetic weenie who couldn't find a real weapon. Going out to shoot a bunch of people with a black rifle and a tactical shotgun while wearing a black tactical pants and combat boots and a load-bearing vest stuffed with ammo is still, of course, the act of a loser, but at least the loser can look at himself in the mirror and imagine he's something more than that, just as Justin Bourque imagined that he might start a revolution as he stepped out of his trailer wearing camouflage. On a whiteboard in his trailer, Bourque had listed the members of his army. First Lieutenant Justin Bourque's skills are support, gunner, marksman, medic, and knife combat; his primary weapon is the M14S, his secondary the Mossberg 500 12-gauge, his CQC weapon the Glock tactical knife. In his fantasies, the shooter is a soldier, and a soldier needs a soldier's weapons.

It can hardly be coincidence that mass shootings have increasingly seized our imagination over the past decade, and that the Clinton-era assault-weapons ban, which made paramilitary rifles harder to get, expired in 2004. Angry young men turn to the black rifle because the black rifle is easy to get. When your entire life is stamped with marks of incompetence, and you're angry enough to kill, going postal is as easy as finding a gun shop.

THIS WAS NOT SUPPOSED TO BE a book on gun control. Gun control is too transient, too of the moment. You make the case for universal

---

191 The rise of homegrown terrorism reminds us that history is not, in fact, dead, and gives angry young men a new Great Cause in which to fight.

background checks, and what you've written becomes obsolete the next year when the law changes. But we cannot address mass shootings, it seems, without asking for solutions, and so we have to ask the question: How do we stop a shooter?

We cannot keep the gun from Gavrilo Princip's hands, because Serbian military intelligence is aiding him. But we can, perhaps, keep the guns away from Justin Bourque and Marc Lépine and Jared Lee Loughner, none of whom has spies for friends. Loughner bought the 9mm Glock pistol he used to shoot US congresswoman Gabrielle Giffords only a few months before the shooting, when, according to acquaintances, his everyday behaviour had already become noticeably erratic. Background checks could not stop him from buying it, because he had as yet done nothing, but a licensing system such as Canada's might have. That licensing system, which did not yet exist at the time, might also have stopped Marc Lépine. A fragile, narcissistic loner or a paranoid schizophrenic may find some difficulty providing the necessary character references. But no licensing system is perfect. People slip through. Justin Bourque had passed a firearms safety course, and held a firearms licence. So had Kimveer Gill, who carried out the 2006 Dawson College shooting in Montreal—in fact, Gill had a restricted licence, which requires more extensive background checks. But at least some shooters will be stopped if access to guns is restricted.

Anyone who is sufficiently determined may find a gun anyway, of course. Eric Harris and Dylan Klebold, the Columbine shooters, were both underage and unable to buy guns legally, so Klebold got his prom date to make a straw buy for them.[192] And nobody knows how Michael Zehaf-Bibeau got his gun. But Zehaf-Bibeau's gun is notable: a Model 94 Winchester is quick-firing but slow and inconvenient to load compared to modern semi-automatic rifles. It is not a gun you would choose to attack Parliament, unless of course you couldn't get your hands on an AR-15 or something of that ilk. And Zehaf-Bibeau couldn't, without turning to the black market: he had a lengthy criminal record, and a prohibition order barring him from ever owning guns. He was limited, weapons-wise, to whatever he could easily find. So was Martin Couture-Rouleau, who was on a terror watch list. He used his car, presumably because it was the most dangerous weapon he could get.

---

192   A straw buy is a firearms purchase by a legal buyer on behalf of someone who isn't.

The fact is that, whatever the gun lobby's protests to the contrary, gun control works—provided, of course, that we think of gun control in terms of specifics rather than in obtuse generalities. Following the 1996 Port Arthur massacre in Tasmania, in which thirty-five were killed, Australia effectively banned semi-automatic and pump-action guns.[193] The UK banned semi-automatic centre-fire rifles after the 1987 Hungerford massacre, and did the same with handguns following the 1996 Dunblane massacre. Gun-control activists will hasten to point out that, since that time, Australia has had no mass shootings, and Great Britain hardly any—but this, of course, argues *post hoc ergo propter hoc*, and founders on the fact that neither the UK nor Australia had many shootings to begin with. A more important point may be that the low rate of mass shootings in both countries reflects the low availability of guns. By contrast, the country with the worst mass shooting problem, the United States, also happens to be the place where just about anyone can buy a gun, no questions asked: all you have to do is go to a gun show.

Mass shootings occur where a stray dog and a bad idea meet a loaded gun, and the easiest of these three to control remains the loaded gun. And so nothing scares the gun lobby as much as mass shootings. This is why Canada's NFA rushed out a press release in a mistaken attempt to "control the narrative" even as Justin Bourque ran from police. And this is why conspiracy theories—that the Sandy Hook and Port Arthur massacres, for example, were false-flag operations by governments determined to usher in gun controls—prove so popular, despite being obvious bullshit. The gun lobby fears mass shootings because mass shootings give momentum to gun control. Mass shootings dominate our imagination when we think of guns.

But they ought not to.

The mass shooting belongs to the Kingdom of Fear: events frighten us most when we face dreadful consequences for reasons we cannot understand—when, for example, twenty elementary school kids are gunned down with an AR-15 because … because why? You'd have to be crazy to do that. And so the mass shooting dominates the media and

---

193 Semi-automatic and pump-action guns are not entirely illegal in Australia, contrary to popular belief, but are tightly restricted. These restrictions may fall under the "obtuse generality" category; the Port Arthur shooter, Martin Bryant, was somehow able to get guns despite being unlicensed and despite the challenge of a significantly subnormal IQ. This suggests some less restrictive measures, such as registration, might have achieved the same goals.

becomes, for most people, the leading reason for gun control, when in fact the number of people killed in mass shootings in the United States is but a tiny proportion of the thirty thousand Americans who die each year by shooting, two-thirds of whom are suicides.[194] The mass shooting is a trick of a slick shell-game operator, who has us continually looking under the wrong cup. The real threats are much more mundane.

And even when we do face the shooter, we fail to see him for what he is. The typical mass shooter profile is no mystery. There it is, in the coroner's report on the École Polytechnique. The US Secret Service, tasked with protecting the president from lone wolves and stray dogs, knows it well. In a free society, we can never spot them all, but it certainly doesn't help that we don't think it's up to us. When the weird guy they invited along on their camping trip showed up with a gun then sat and fondled it all night long, Justin Bourque's Wal-Mart co-workers apparently never thought to call the cops and say, Hey, that was kind of weird. Instead, they just decided not to ask him to come along next time.

Might someone have reacted differently if, instead of "You'd have to be crazy" and the assorted bullshit of talking heads pushing their pet theories, the media asked the right questions? What if media coverage of mass shootings led not to generalized fear, but to some kind of understanding of what makes a shooter tick? Would someone have reacted differently if, following any given mass shooting, we could actually talk about the problem like adults, and learn to recognize the stray dog?

Maybe. But nobody ever thinks it will happen to them, so this is a forlorn hope.

I HAD HOPED TO AVOID DISCUSSING mass shootings in this book, as I had hoped to avoid discussing gun control, albeit for different reasons. This is a book about gun culture, about the mainstreaming of increasingly loopy ideas, and about my rejection of those loopy extremes. And mass shootings have little to do with this.

The mass shooting, unlike the Western or post-war American militarism, has nothing to tell us about why we find it so hard to give up the gun. We find no ideas in the mass shooter that can explain this. On the

---

194   Since 1999, approximately thirty thousand Americans have been killed each year with firearms, from a low of 28,663 in 2000 to a high of 33,636 in 2013 (more recent data are not available). Slightly less than two-thirds of these deaths are suicides: 58 percent in 2000, for example, and 63 percent in 2013. CDC data collected at gunpolicy.org.

rare occasions we do find those ideas—in the case of Justin Bourque, for example—they are simply inherited from somewhere else. And there is no inherent connection between the mass shooter and the patriot movement, or survivalists, or any other division in our taxonomy. He is connected to the surging popularity of black rifles, but the causal arrow points not from him, but at him. The mass shooter lies in the realm of consequences.

Some will object to my dragging in Gavrilo Princip and Michael Zehaf-Bibeau, who are not mass shooters, or Martin Couture-Rouleau and Timothy McVeigh, who were not shooters at all. But all these men share the same pathology. We are talking not about shootings, but about manifestations of violence. And that this particular species of violence manifests itself so often in shooting lies also in the realm of consequences, which is why discussing the mass shooter simply can't be avoided.

We have mass shooters because we have guns, obviously. But mass shootings are not simply a consequence of allowing people in our societies to own guns. They are, instead, a consequence of the gun culture itself. The stray dog chooses the gun because it is so easy for him to get a gun, because resistance to gun control is so entrenched. And he chooses the gun because the gun he can easily get is a black rifle with a high-capacity magazine, a weapon suitable for fighting his own little war, because the gun he can get fits his fantasy of himself as a soldier for a cause. We have mass shooters because of the armed-camp vision of America. We have mass shooters because we have sheepdogs, living in the fantasy worlds of the forever-prepared. All that separates the stray dog from the sheepdog is his attitude to sheep.

The stray dog will always be with us. We can't heal him, or prevent him turning to bad ideas, or even hope to find him before he does. But this doesn't mean we are helpless. We can address the culture that leads him to the gun.

Kulturkampf

Guns, the Culture War, and the Triumph of the Radical

Of course there is no dialogue. Given a choice between the NRA and animal rights I'll choose a rowboat anytime.

—Jim Harrison

ON APRIL FOOL'S DAY, 2013, Nelson, Georgia (population 1,300), enacted its Family Protection Ordinance, which made gun ownership mandatory for all heads of household, except convicted felons and anyone who conscientiously objected to owning a gun. You might have thought that, by allowing conscientious objectors to opt out, the law was empty enough as it stood. But not everyone agreed, and on May 16, the Brady Center to Prevent Gun Violence sued the town and its council for violating residents' Second Amendment right *not* to own a gun. The city settled out of court, and quickly amended their Family Protection Ordinance by adding a clause saying that all the foregoing was unenforceable and would never be enforced, and that there was, in any case, no penalty for anything therein even should someone try to enforce the unenforceable. And so, in spite of Nelson's Family Protection Ordinance, which remains unenforceably in force, a resident of Nelson, Georgia, can want to own a gun but choose to flout the law by not owning one, and no one can do a damn thing about it. You can go around not owning a gun in broad daylight, on the steps of city hall, and all the police can do is cluck and wag their fingers in stern disapproval, because the Second Amendment guarantees your right not to own a gun in defiance of the law.

The Second Amendment is getting weird.

"Some people have security systems, some people don't, but they put those signs up," explained Councillor Duane Cronic, who had originally tabled the ordinance. "I really felt like this ordinance was a security sign for our city. Basically it was a deterrent ordinance to tell potential criminals they might want to go on down the road a little bit." Nelson's council even voted to put up a sign in the town advising potential criminals that Nelsonians were armed, by law (except, of course, for those who weren't). But criminals, those nasty predators lurking in the shadows of the American mind, had been ignoring Nelson as it stood. The local chief of police, Heath Mitchell, who commanded a large and sophisticated modern police force consisting entirely of himself, admitted that crime in Nelson was restricted mostly to petty property crime. The town hadn't seen a homicide in five years.

When we ask why this Family Protection Ordinance exists, and why it remains on the books even after being amended so as to be completely without force, Duane Cronic cannot help us by musing about lawn signs and security systems. The Great American Gun Kerfuffle is really just a battleground in a wider conflict. If the law is the essay in which we describe our values, then the question when we sit down to write it is who gets to hold the pen.

Nelson's Family Protection Ordinance is very much like a sign you put up on your front lawn. But this is not a sign saying, "Criminals, stay away." Instead, it says, "Liberals, go home." It expresses in law the values of Sheepdog Nation by declaring that in Nelson, Georgia, gun ownership is a force for good that protects families and that gun owners are good, dutiful, civic-minded citizens who protect and defend their neighbours. Sheepdogs are welcome, and the sheep ought either to stop complaining about their teeth or to find other, unprotected pastures. The Family Protection Ordinance may not actually do anything, but that hardly means it is entirely empty of meaning. It is a drooling, neutered sheepdog, ecstatically humping a couch cushion just to prove it can.

This is the culture war, the reality that has turned the discourse on guns into a verbal Passchendaele. Mired in this slime, no breakthrough is possible. All we can do is bring up more artillery. It does not help us to find the Wellspring of Crazy or to analyze the sludge that oozes forth, sludge carrying such a heavy lunatic charge that even brief contact can make the Family Protection Ordinance seem sensible. We will find no solution. What doesn't kill you makes you dumber, slows the mind and, by some alchemical magic, anneals it into hammer-hardening steel whose obtuse edge toughens with every blow. Nothing can be achieved. Nobody is going to compromise.

I LIKE GUNS.

Is that declaration in itself disturbing? Does it suggest some personal flaw, a deficiency of character, a minor derailment on the way to full adulthood? Have I, perhaps, come too close to the Wellspring of Crazy?

Astronauts land on Mars, descend from their shining space capsule, and greet the Martians, their message carefully devised by scientists and encoded in a universal language based on that constant of the universe, the atomic weight of hydrogen: "We come in peace for all mankind." But to the Martians, cowering and peeking from behind their Martian mud huts, this sounds a lot like "All your chocolate chip are belong to us." Savage interplanetary war ensues. Which is to say, every message is decoded through the recipient's frame of reference, whatever its originator may have intended. I say, "I like guns"; you hear your own assumptions.

Like our ill-fated entreaty to the Martians, the simple declaration, "I like guns," stands to be mistranslated as, "I like violence, war, and murder." Or a gun, thanks to a superficial understanding of human psychology gained through undergraduate exposure to Freud, is purely phallic; "I like guns" becomes "I am compensating for my sexual insecurity or inadequacy." Or guns are all about power, and "I like guns" becomes "I am compensating for a sense of weakness." In any case, it means nothing good. Perhaps I should keep my mouth shut.

But look, I also like typewriters: old, mechanical typewriters, the kind that were already obsolete long before computers came on the scene. Not the huge, heavy ones that once adorned the desks of secretaries and newspaper reporters, but the portable typewriters used by writers on the move. I own a nice Remington Quiet-Riter, a Royal Quiet Deluxe that I plan to refurbish someday, and a sweet little ultra-compact West German Adler Tippa. I bought a late-1970s Smith-Corona Galaxie 12 from a bemused neighbour's garage sale a few short years ago. But the pride of my small collection is a near-mint Olympia SF. SF stands for "Schreibmaschine Flach," or flat typewriter, and it is: it's just as small as the Tippa, all metal and German-made. You can pick one up, fully refurbished, for around five hundred dollars, or you can cruise garage sales until you find someone who thinks he's ripping you off at ten bucks, as I did. It is smooth and loud, with a clear, crisp typeface, one of the best portable typewriters ever made, enough to make you sorry the personal computer was ever invented. Enough to make you want to sling your Leica M3 over one shoulder, pack up your Olympia SF, and head west along some temporal latitude, in search of a time when there was still such a thing as Kodak Tri-X Pan. But you know you're just going to hit the ocean, long before you reach that promised land.

No one criticizes or complains about my typewriter collecting, except perhaps my wife, who feels that these useless artifacts clutter up the house. Nobody suggests that my affection for the tactile thwack of keys striking paper reveals my concealed propensity for battery, or illustrates some sexual perversion, or suggests some problem with my masculinity. I just plain like manual typewriters. I like them for their elegant mechanical complexity, their historical association with writing, and simply for that thwack of keys on paper, which is the sound of progress, word by word, the sound of work getting done. Most of all, I like them because they're fun to use. Typewriters are neat.

Why can't guns offer similar attractions? Their mechanical elegance is interesting in itself, whether it is found in the Rube Goldberg workings of a Browning M1919 machine gun or the far simpler workings of a boxlock shotgun. I own a 20-gauge side-by-side with an Anson and Deeley boxlock action. It's a design that caught on right away, way back in 1875, because in place of external hammers that you have to cock with your thumb, it has internal hammers that recock automatically when you reload. These guns are still being made simply because the design leaves little to improve. It has just three moving parts: a hammer, a main spring to power the hammer, and a cocking dog, which recocks the hammer. You push the top lever to the right to release the Greener cross bolt, an 1865 innovation that locks the barrels closed, and as you swing the barrels down to reload, the fore-end pushes against the cocking dogs and re-cocks the hammers.

Mine is the simplest of side-by-sides. It has a manual safety and double triggers, the front trigger for the right barrel and the rear trigger for the left, each trigger with its own hammer, sear, and cocking dog. Many people prefer the more complex single selective trigger, a recent invention that lets you choose which barrel to fire by moving the safety catch. (It matters because your two barrels have different chokes, which gives them different effective ranges.) A gun with two triggers looks odd to the rifle shooter, and people expect that a single-trigger gun would be a quicker-handling gun in that sudden rush when a bird breaks from cover. But your hands soon commit the double triggers to muscle memory. The dog is working out to the side and puts up a bird flying hard and away, and you shoulder the gun and think to yourself, this calls for the tighter choke, and your finger simply finds the rear trigger on its own. A double-trigger side-by-side shotgun is light and quick, the perfect upland bird gun, elegant as much as utilitarian, ingenious in its design, perfected a century before I was born. How can you not admire it?

This gun is not simply a mechanical device, however. Every device has its purpose. Mechanical typewriters do not kill people, except when used as blunt instruments. Guns do. And although expressions like "hunting rifle" or "trap gun" testify otherwise, it is axiomatic to the anti-gun side that the sole purpose of guns is to kill people. Guns are not merely capable of violence; they are inherently violent. Chekhov's Gun, the dramatic principle that cautions playwrights that a rifle hanging on the wall in Act I must be fired by the end of Act III, somehow seems to apply to real life: every gun must eventually express its true purpose, violence. And so blogger Tom Harvey, writing on suicide at the Huffington Post, argues that "a gun is too powerful a symbol to be ignored," that the gun worms its way into its owner's thoughts and encourages him to kill himself, whether he is suicidal or not. Harvey even suggests that guns encourage people to kill themselves by noose, sleeping pill, and razor blade, thanks to their "powerful suggestive nature."

This makes no sense at all. But when it comes to guns, our conclusions go before our reasoning. Our positions are firmly entrenched and impervious to evidence. We embrace what supports our prejudices, and reject what threatens them. We cannot even agree what the word "gun" means. It means exactly what we choose it to mean. And consequently, our discourse is no more fruitful than a treetop war between troops of monkeys: we howl; we screech; we throw monkey shit at each other. This, we call politics.

WHEN A GANG MEMBER'S BULLET KILLED Jane Creba, a fifteen-year-old white girl, on Yonge Street, Toronto's city council reacted by bringing in "City Based Measures to Address Gun Violence," which included banning guns from city property. That ban had no effect on gang members, of course, because the guns they carried were illegal to begin with. One more by-law would hardly matter. But it did inconvenience target shooters, whose range at Union Station was shut down, and the annual Toronto Sportsmen's Show, which lost the use of the Canadian National Exhibition grounds.[195] Kicking the Sportsmen's Show out of the CNE grounds did absolutely nothing "to Address Gun Violence," of course, but that was never really the point. City council intended to write into law its disapproval of guns and the people who own them. It was a move against the gun culture.

Councillor Gord Perks was frank about his reasoning: "We took a position as a city council that the promotion of guns, the sale of guns, and the display of guns in our city reinforces and builds the culture of guns in our city." Alas, nobody thought to ask what he meant by "the culture of guns," which would surely have been revealing. It certainly appeared that council had mistaken talking for thinking. City council evidently saw no difference between the hunters who attend the Sportsmen's Show each year to see the latest in hunting gadgetry and the gang-bangers who shoot each other in apartment stairwells at Jane and Finch. Everyone shared the same culture of guns. "Keep them out of my city," said Councillor Adam Vaughan, his choice of words inadvertently betraying the true bone of contention: this was not a struggle over guns, but over whose city Toronto would be.

In 2010, Councillor Josh Colle sought to create an exemption that would allow the Sportsmen's Show to come home. "Yes, we have a problem with guns, and it's a huge one," said Colle, "but it's not going to be solved by us debating whether [the Sportsmen's Show] is at the CNE or the convention centre." Toronto's problem was illegal handguns smuggled over the border, that ended up in the hands of drug dealers who

195 People asked why on earth there was a *shooting range* at Union Station. The range had originally been built to train railway police, and had since been leased by a recreational shooting club.

showed little concern for who might be caught in the crossfire. Colle was frank about the views of his constituents in gang-ridden neighbour-hoods: "They see this as a debate that makes downtown—I hate to say it—white people feel better that they've done something, when they're suffering from this gun violence day after day."

Councillor Perks' reply took oratory to new heights: "Fuck off."

But Colle was right, which explains in part why Perks found himself without an intelligent rejoinder. Toronto's ban on firearms on city prop-erty was never anything more than a symbolic act. And as it became clear their position was lost, the anti-gun wing of council again struck symbolic blows, demanding that the Sportsmen's Show devote free floor space to domestic violence organizations and to the hunter's sworn enemy: animal rights groups. These were not serious anti-violence pro-posals so much as schoolyard taunts in the culture war. If the hunters were to have their way, they would be made to eat a few bites of crow.

Two years later, a twenty-three-year-old gang member named Christopher Husbands opened fire on two gang rivals in the food court of Toronto's Eaton Centre, killing two and wounding four more, including a thirteen-year-old boy from Belleville who was visiting the city with his family. Councillor Vaughan went after the root of the problem, and proposed a by-law to make illegal handguns even ille-galer. "I'm tired of the violence and I'm tired of dealing with a bunch of privileged people that complain their hobby is being impacted," he proclaimed. He hoped to ban guns in Toronto, period. When it turned out that this was beyond the city's powers, he proposed instead to ban sales of ammunition. "There's no rational reason to own a gun in the city," he said. "I appreciate that people like them as a sporting hobby. I appreciate that people like their guns and their activities, but those are emotional arguments."

There are reasons to own a gun in the city, of course; one is that you engage in shooting "as a sporting hobby." What Vaughan wrote off as an emotional argument could fairly be summarized as "I want to live a lifestyle that I enjoy." And that may be an emotional argument, but the rational argument tied to it is that living the lifestyles we enjoy is a matter of freedom of expression.

This is not a constitutional trump card. Freedom of expression is not absolute, and it can't be used to justify doing things that put others in danger, such as carrying a loaded handgun just because you can. I am not free to express myself by frightening people, or by harassing people, or by driving through residential neighbourhoods at outrageous speeds. If Vaughan can make such arguments regarding gun ownership in general, let him; the problem was that he didn't think he had to, that vague references to privilege and emotion were sufficient.

Freedom of expression is not simply an "emotional argument," to be dismissed with a wave of the hand. It is one of the bedrock values that define us. Or, perhaps more accurately, it's one of the bedrock values that we pretend define us, because while we jealously protect our own freedoms, we are only too happy to dismiss the rights of others. We are far less keen on Live and Let Live than we pretend to be. Instead, we long to declare that the city is ours to live in according to our lights—and that if you don't like it, you can go live someplace else. And when, inevitably, we don't get our way, we stamp our feet and suck our thumbs like petulant children, outraged at the very idea of compromise.

WHOOPS—SILLY ME. Here I am, using words like "compromise." I was actually about to suggest that it might be helpful to attempt some kind of reasoned and respectful discussion, which is a goddamn laugh riot, because *guns*, and because *Internet*. It's as if I'd wandered into the Holy See and clapped my hands together and shouted, "Okay. Let's watch a porno!" The pained silence stretches just thin enough that some muscle strain is evident in my frozen grin. And then the Holy Father replies: "Dude. That's not what we do here."

What was I thinking?

Writing at the Huffington Post, Josh Horwitz, executive director of the Coalition to Stop Gun Violence, picked up on a post made by an NRA member on the Facebook page of the Committee to Stop Gun Violence.[196] The anonymous commenter said that Veronica Rutledge "deserved to die she was so abysmally stupid, the gene pool is better for it and the rest of us are safer for it." Beneath all his layers of poisonous rhetoric and gratuitous insult, the guy actually had one valid point: Rutledge died because she left her gun unattended with a round in the chamber. But Horwitz seemed to be in full agreement that this had not

---

196 Why members of the NRA would want to engage in slanging matches on the CSGV Facebook page is a mystery; and that anyone would take the time to read their posts is utterly baffling. But many people seem to enjoy this pastime.

been a preventable accident; it was a terrible terrible tragic tragic tragedy made inevitable by the fact that Rutledge owned a gun. Anyone who suggested it was a preventable accident had "thrown [Rutledge] under the bus" and derided her "as singularly 'stupid,' 'careless' and 'irresponsible,'" all to avoid addressing the truth: that guns are inherently dangerous. "The point of such rhetoric, obviously, is to squash introspection about American gun culture in the wake of horrors," Horwitz wrote. He complained also that the gun culture had "inculcated a mentality in many gun owners that is reckless."

The levels of contradiction soon become difficult to navigate. Gun activists complain about anti-gunners' grandstanding; anti-gunners complain about gun activists' grandstanding. The gun culture had made people reckless with guns, yet addressing that recklessness head-on was an attempt to squash introspection about the gun culture. Gun activists say this was a tragic, tragic accident; anti-gunners shake their heads and say this was a terrible, terrible event. It was either completely unpredictable, or sadly inevitable, but the one thing we are not permitted to suggest, the one great heresy, is that it was *preventable*—because this would lead us to practical questions, and addressing practical questions is a lot less fun than being right at the other guy's expense.

The introspection Horwitz demanded was not a conversation about gun safety—that would suggest Rutledge had been negligent, which would be throwing her under the bus. No, the discussion was to be about how the NRA had duped Rutledge into believing that owning a gun is not itself risky. Citing the usual research, Horwitz insisted that gun ownership is a risk factor for both homicide and suicide, and that our careful introspection should be directed not at safely handling the guns we own, but at renouncing the gun entirely.[197] Introspection regarding the general evils of the gun culture is always welcome.

Horwitz's moral outrage would be more convincing if it weren't directed solely at gun activists who had called Rutledge negligent (or worse). There was no shortage of anti-gun bloggers willing to discard good taste in favour of page views. And so, at news and opinion site

---

197 Owning a gun has indeed been shown to be a risk factor for both homicide and suicide (see, for example, Kellerman *et al.*), but these findings are abused by activists who suggest the risk is inherent to the gun itself (see Tom Harvey, also writing at the Huffington Post, above). Guns do not *cause* suicides or homicides; they make it more likely that homicides and suicides will be successful. People who are not at risk of shooting themselves or others don't suddenly become likely suicides or murderers by dint of owning guns.

The Daily Banter, Editor-in-Chief Ben Cohen wrote that Rutledge was an idiot who had terminated her life via extreme stupidity.[198] "While a huge amount of sympathy should go out to the family," wrote Cohen, displaying no amount of sympathy, nor any facsimile thereof, "it is difficult to feel too sorry for someone so reckless and stupid." He made sure also to suggest that she clearly needed "a very thorough psychiatric evaluation" simply because she owned a gun and carried it.

This is just one example. Another blog, Wonkette, reacted to a series of gun accidents with generous helpings of snark and the kind of sensitive touch that only a sociopath can muster. In response to the Florida two-year-old who shot himself with a gun he found in the glovebox of his parent's car, Matt Carpenter wrote that it was tragic that "he shot himself instead of one of his idiot parents." In regards to a man (yet another man) who had shot himself with his own pistol at a gun show, Jeff Wattrick channeled the NRA to ask who can stop a moron with a gun? "The answer is a moron will stop himself. With his own gun!" Everyone is a moron, an idiot, a lunatic, a crazy-ass gun nut who deserves whatever happens to him because he is a Bad Person and, more importantly, because he belongs to the wrong monkey tribe.

The most infantile of these contributions comes from another blogger, Tom McKay, who wins an extra prize for dishonesty for his remark regarding the man who had been shot by his wife through the bedroom door while bringing her "actual breakfast in bed, which apparently doesn't happen in this household very much." McKay was too busy taking cheap shots at the victim's marriage to report what had actually happened: the man had left for work, but then returned home to surprise his wife and managed to set off his own burglar alarm. With her husband gone and the alarm hooting, the woman had every reason to think there was an intruder in her home, and she made a grave error: she shot through a closed door without knowing who was on the other side. But what's the fun in telling the whole truth? We snort smug giggles into our hands at the crazy gun nuts and their marital problems.

---

198   Cohen boasts of his site's "highly quality journalism [sic], unfiltered commentary and snark." He also suggests that Rutledge was "completely obsessed with guns," a second-hand opinion recycled from the *Washington Post*, based on the fact that her Facebook likes included the NRA and Guns.com. But recipe exchange groups outnumbered gun sites on her Facebook page by about four to one. If she were completely obsessed with guns, how are we to describe her attitude to cookies? If Cohen had checked for himself, he might have reached a different conclusion—but *highly quality journalism* doesn't bother with that these days, I guess.

It's easy to see why Canada's NFA might lose whatever tenuous grip on common sense it possessed and start spewing ill-advised press releases. The Coalition for Gun Control may have been silent as Justin Bourque rampaged through suburban Moncton, but on the Internet, there's always someone yapping away somewhere. To the NFA, their opponents are "grave dancers," who cynically use every tragedy as an opportunity to advance their political agenda. This, they feel, is in bad taste. And so the NFA responded to Justin Bourque's rampage with its infamous press release; to the Charlie Hebdo shootings and Michael Zehaf-Bibeau's failed attack on the House of Commons in October 2014 with calls to allow Canadians to carry concealed handguns just in case; and to Christmas with a poster of Santa Claus giving an excited boy his first AR-15, and admonishing him not to shoot his eye out. "We are controlling the narrative," they boasted on Facebook, with Justin Bourque still on the run and every news outlet in the country deriding them. "The NFA is changing the culture in this Country and in order to win we need to confront these people."

One thing is clear: the NFA, which for some time had been essentially moribund, has been revitalized. To go along with its new attitude it has a new logo, a stylized maple leaf combined with the silhouette of an AR-15, with the slogan, "No Compromise." To the true believer, this says, "we will never stop fighting." But to everyone else, it looks a lot like "we can't play nice in the sandbox and will throw tantrums until we get our way."

Almost forty years ago, CASAL won its fight against Pierre Trudeau's majority by a persistent campaign of grassroots pressure applied through letters and local riding associations. The leaders of Canada's gun lobby exhorted gun owners to join the party of their choice and work at the riding level. With the NFA floundering after the death of its president, David Tomlinson, in 2007, the CSSA led the push to have the long-gun registry abolished, and stayed largely out of the public eye. But the new, No Compromise NFA seems determined to make a public spectacle of itself and grab all the headlines it can with brash, ill-advised stunts like its Santa poster, which drew criticism even from gun owners. Perhaps the Canadian gun lobby has been emboldened by its success with the long-gun registry, and delights in poking its opponents just because it can.[199]

---

199 It ought not to. Although the gun lobby won a victory against the long-gun registry, it soon found that the Harper government was unwilling to roll back other gun controls. The topic was too contentious. Only as the 2015 federal election looms has the government made new promises to shore up its base.

But the same increasingly confrontational style has also appeared south of the border.

Take, for example, Open Carry Texas, a group that has taken pro-gun activism to new depths. It is no longer enough to join the NRA and write earnest letters to the editor and to elected representatives and to get out to vote. Nor is it enough to participate in the occasional public rally. Trolling the Committee to Stop Gun Violence on Twitter and Facebook seems to have palled, although plenty of people still find time to do it. Similarly, you can post only so many altered photos of Shannon Watts of Moms Demand Action before that game gets boring. The time comes when you have to take your act to the streets.

Open Carry Texas is, strangely enough, the love child of Eldridge Cleaver and the 12-gauge shotgun, a gang of white Texans who feel the best way to stand up for their rights as an oppressed minority is to take to the streets with rifles strapped to their backs. And in Texas, as in many places, this is entirely legal, as it was in California when the Black Panthers marched into the legislature. The Panthers were defending their right to keep and bear arms as a counter to the power of a major-ity-white police force in black neighbourhoods. Open Carry Texas has now taken up the fight, defending the right to keep and bear arms in the local grocery store as a counter to something or other, but mostly to poke gun-control activists in the eye.

Open Carry Texas and Moms Demand Action have been at war for well over a year, and while the war has featured any number of misogynist assaults on Moms Demand, and armed counter-protests at Moms Demand events, the primary campaigns have been waged in the semi-public spaces of retail chains and restaurants. Open Carry Texas chooses its battlefields: Chipotle, Home Depot, Kroger super-markets, Target. Their activists seize the territory, move in with rifles and shotguns slung over their backs to shop for renovation supplies or groceries or whatever. And then Moms Demand responds with letter-writing campaigns, Twitter campaigns, and media advertising targeting that unfortunate business with demands that they ban guns in their stores.

Strangely, I sympathize with the corporations. There you are, an innocent greedhead just trying to make money the good old American way, only to find yourself caught in the No Man's Land between the wacky fringe of a powerful gun lobby and a determined gun-control group bankrolled by Bloomberg. One side can call on the full power of the NRA and its boycotting hordes, while the other represents the even larger number of Americans who think the sight of some fat oaf eating at Chipotle with an AR-15 across his back is, well, kind of disturbing. Either way, your business is now going to be the victim of protest and counter-protest. The poor CEO is caught between a rock and a crazy place, and there is no easy solution.

Moms Demand has won most of the battles—as well they should, because their opponents are obvious wackjobs. Ronald Reagan's remark about the Black Panthers, that it is simply not acceptable to carry weapons with the aim of influencing your fellow Americans, clearly applies—although Open Carry Texas repeatedly stresses that they aren't out to intimidate anyone. No, they just want you to get used to the sight of wackadoodle dingbats with AR-15s and AKs, because then wackadoodle dingbattery will be normalized, and America will come to accept going about armed with rifles and shotguns as part of everyday life.

The most surprising casualty of Open Carry Texas has not been gun control, but the NRA's control over the pro-gun message. In April 2014, as Open Carry Texas fought a losing battle against Moms Demand for control of the Chipotle restaurant chain, the NRA came under increasing pressure from Texas lawmakers to rein in the pro-gun protests. Like the Black Panthers, Open Carry Texas was making people nervous, and the NRA was worried that, like the Black Panthers, the group stood to provoke a backlash that would roll back many of the NRA's successes. NRA leaders pressured C.J. Grisham, the man behind Open Carry Texas, to back off. But Grisham would not budge. Like Canada's NFA, he crowed that he was in control of the narrative, that he was proving to Texans, day after day, that wackadoodle dingbattery was nothing to be alarmed about. Even as his group was kicked out of Starbucks, Wendy's, Chipotle, Chili's, Applebee's, and Jack-in-the-Box, Grisham insisted that he was winning the war.[200]

---

200 Restaurants have proven to be a poor battleground for the Open Carry army. This was particularly true of licensed establishments, which could pass the buck to liquor laws and kick out armed patrons. The war soon moved to the retail floor, where Open Carry troops were better able to use the terrain to their advantage. And although General Grisham lost the battle of Target, he would score his first major victory at the Battle of Home Depot, before marching on Kroger supermarkets.

Following well-publicized and embarrassing Open Carry demos at Chili's and Sonic in San Antonio, the NRA issued a press release distancing itself from the group. Enough was enough.

> Recently, demonstrators have been showing up in various public places, including coffee shops and fast food restaurants, openly toting a variety of tactical long guns. Unlicensed open carry of handguns is legal in about half the U.S. states, and it is relatively common and uncontroversial in some places.
>
> Yet while unlicensed open carry of long guns is also typically legal in most places, it is a rare sight to see someone sidle up next to you in line for lunch with a 7.62 rifle slung across his chest, much less a whole gaggle of folks descending on the same public venue with similar arms.
>
> Let's not mince words, not only is it rare, it's downright weird and certainly not a practical way to go normally about your business while being prepared to defend yourself. To those who are not acquainted with the dubious practice of using public displays of firearms as a means to draw attention to oneself or one's cause, it can be downright scary. It makes folks who might normally be perfectly open-minded about firearms feel uncomfortable and question the motives of pro-gun advocates.

These open carry protests, the NRA said, defied common sense and showed "a lack of consideration and manners." This was not, the organization insisted, the Texas way: "And that's certainly not the NRA way."

Unlike Grisham's group, whose unearned confidence seemed utterly impenetrable, the NRA actually understood how ordinary people might feel about the sight of a bunch of guys with paramilitary weapons slung over their backs showing up at some restaurant: nervous. The NRA was ready to admit that this kind of behaviour was "downright weird," not to mention impractical, scary, and just plain impolite. It was like a flashback to 1934: it was, again, almost as if the NRA were *reasonable.* I could imagine having a *beer* with these people, if only they knew anything about hockey.

But it didn't last. To NRA supporters, it seemed like a fumble. The press picked up the ball and ran with it, hard and fast, and gun activists watched in alarm as they neared the goal line. The NRA press release had made Open Carry Texas look bad, which they richly deserved, but that meant that Moms Demand was winning. And if Moms Demand was winning then gun owners had to be losing, because politics is a zero-sum game. Open Carry Texas called the NRA release "disgusting and disrespectful," and threatened a boycott. And so Chris Cox, the NRA's chief lobbyist, announced that the original release had been the work of some junior staffer, who had since been put to the rack, and who had recanted after his fingernails were pulled out with pliers. His body had been thrown out of a helicopter somewhere over the Atlantic, and he would no longer be a problem. "Unequivocally, we support open carry," said Cox. "We've been the leader of open carry efforts across this country."

America likes to believe that the NRA controls gun politics in the United States, thanks to the funding of the gun manufacturers who pull its marionette strings. But the truth is that nobody is in control anymore. After the Revolt at Cincinnati, a newly radicalized NRA did indeed take control, and gun manufacturers were only too happy to give it money. The NRA used the power of groupthink to whip even gun manufacturers into line, organizing boycotts to punish Smith & Wesson and Ruger for failing to push back hard enough against gun control. It built a monster out of spare parts, out of fear of government and fear of foreign conspirators and fear of crime and fear of black men, out of pride in American history and pride in American arms, and it jolted that monster to life and set it lurching out to do its work. But now it has lost control of its creation, and finds itself backing up the stairs as the monster lurches forward, demanding love.

The villagers are going to have to put the torch to this thing.

As PRESIDENT OF THE NRA, Charlton Heston frankly declared a "cultural war" against "blue-blooded elitists." He extolled "the America ... Where you can pray without feeling naïve, love without being kinky, sing without profanity, be white without feeling guilty, [and] own guns without shame." It's a bulk set of ideals, bought whole-sale, appealing to God, apple pie, and the good old days—the same old longing for Paradise Valley. And only one of these ideals has anything to do with guns. The rest exist to remind the faithful that this is not really about gun control at all. The gun grabbers want your guns because, like the terrorists, *they hate your way of life.* "In sum," writes lawyer and pro-gun activist Don Kates, "indispensable to gun lobby success is an anti-gun discourse that suggests 'gun control' is not a legitimate social imperative aimed at criminals but a matter of cultural or moral hatred directed at gun owners."

And it is not the anti-gun side, but the gun lobby itself, that most encourages gun owners to believe they and their guns are hated. Pro-gun groups happily distribute anti-gun cartoons and articles to their membership, and gun activists gleefully share them online. The effects of zero-tolerance programs in schools are a perennial theme, with endless examples of kids being suspended after pointing pieces of gun-shaped toast at one another. Look at how crazy these anti-gunners are! And look at how they indoctrinate your own children to believe that guns are evil! In Canada, the NFA continually tells gun owners that they are a hated minority, that they are blamed for the Montreal massacre. "The stigma of firearms ownership was hurled upon us after the Poly-Tech," says an NFA Facebook post explaining its Justin Bourque press release, "and we have become accustomed in [sic] wearing that shame in silence for every mass killing thereafter."

Culture war favours the blowhard, and by framing gun control as culture war, the NRA distracts us from serious policy questions while silencing internal dissent. Everyone thinks it's a good idea to keep guns out of the hands of criminals and the insane, including the NRA. But as soon as anyone proposes a reasonable, practical measure such as universal background checks, all the NRA leadership needs to do is drop the appropriate keywords—elitist, gun-grabber, registration—and background checks become an attack on Mom, apple pie, democracy, and Jesus himself. There will be no talk of gun control as a pragmatic question of policy. As the treetop squawking and screeching begins, the loudest monkeys take over, and the moderates find better ways to spend their time—partly because, as moderates, they don't worry too much from day to day about apple pie, democracy and the AR-15. The ranting of anti-gun blowhards, too, serves only to strengthen pro-gun radicals. Redneck, slack-jawed yokel, barrel-sucking gun nut: all this accomplishes is to warn the gun-owning moderate that he has no friends here. And so the podium is left to the radical, who's the only one who really wants to stand at the mike and rant. The thing about living in a septic tank is the nasty stuff floats.

Moderates disappear, also, because nobody *wants* to see them. Nothing sucks the wind out of a windbag so quickly as complexity and nuance. We like our stories simple. And the media are only too happy to keep selling us simple stories. And so, on July 12, 2013, *US News* reported that gun owners were "still overwhelmingly white males." In the accompanying photo of a gun-rights rally in Albany, New York, not one non-white face is to be found, there are also precious few women. The demonstrators carry signs, two of them with AR-15s and the slogan "Come and take it"; another declares, "Live Free or Die. I'm ready." And then there's the obligatory flag bearing a coiled rattlesnake: Don't tread on me. "White men represent just a third of the US population," the article declares, in clumsy newspaper prose, "but about 60 percent of adults with guns in America today are white men."

Let's apply our minds to these numbers, shall we? If six of every ten gun owners are white men, then *four* in every ten gun owners are *not* white men, which is almost, what, 40 percent or something, isn't it? Isn't that close to, you know, *half*? So the dominance of white men is hardly as overwhelming as the headline or the photo suggest. And in fact, the *rate* of gun ownership—that is, the number of guns compared to the number of people—is highest among black males. America is a gun culture, but that gun culture contains multitudes. Not every gun owner is a forty-five-year-old white male carrying a protest sign declaring his willingness to fight the gummint.

It hardly helps that the hosts of shows like *The Best Defence* and *Personal Defence*, the gun writers who fill the pages of *Guns & Ammo*, and the leadership of the NRA are predominantly conservative white men. It is white males who most ardently resist change—or, more accurately, a subset of white males who happen to be particularly vocal and whose resistance is so effective that it has been dubbed "the white male effect."[201] John Lott, Dave Grossman, John Wesley Rawles, Michael Bane, Jerry Ahern, and Jeff Cooper are (or were) all white men. The people whose ideas fill this book are mostly white men. This is not the reality of gun ownership, but it is the face of what we call the gun

---

201   Dan Kahan and Donald Braman, law professors at Yale and the George Washington School of Law, have published a series of papers exploring resistance to gun control (among other issues) using the cultural theory of risk. They suggest that the white male effect owes not to white males in general, but to those with a hierarchical, individualist mindset. See Dan Kahan and Donald Braman, "Culture and Identity-Protective Cognition: Expanding the 'White Male Effect' in Risk Perception," *Journal of Empirical Legal Studies* 4(3), 2007.

culture. And since we so often forget to think about what we mean by "the gun culture" before starting to talk about it, the extreme begins to represent the whole.

When we talk about gun owners, we think of gun nuts. But Open Carry Texas is tiny. Even the NRA has only about four million members, while at least fifty million Americans own guns. And repeated surveys of American gun owners find them at odds with the NRA over issues such as universal background checks, with nine out of ten in support. One survey, now more than twenty years old, even found that most NRA members disagreed with NRA policies.[202]

We love and will not relinquish our stereotypes, because they provide convenient handles. But they make us stupid. Beside the desk where I write these words stands a safe, and in that safe are my guns. I am as tired as anyone of infantile bloggers invoking Freud and telling me I'm a sexually insecure moron for owning a gun. Yet I will not let the NRA stand for me, and the wordy email updates I get from Canada's CSSA, filled with malapropisms and fallacies, amuse and irritate me in equal proportion. Dave Grossman, John Lott, and John Wesley Rawles do not think for me. I have been called a Fudd, an elitist, and a faggot, and although I have never been accused of loving a man-purse or drinking soy lattes, the day is yet young. There is no shortage of gun owners who don't give a damn about the NRA or its politics, although they rarely stand up and say, "You don't speak for me." If the villagers want to put the torch to the monster, they are going to need these people.

But consensus is hard, and snark is easy. When Adam Vaughan announced his plan to ban ammunition sales in Toronto, his fellow travellers took up the fight. Enzo DiMatteo, associate news editor at Toronto's weekly *NOW* magazine, wrote, "gun and ammo retailers are required by the feds to log a buyer's name and licence number," but the federal government had "signalled its intention to do away with the recording of ammo transactions." The first claim was an error. The federal government imposes no such requirement; it comes instead from Ontario's Ammunition Regulation Act.[203] The second was an outright

---

202 I refer to Weil and Hemenway, "I Am the NRA: An Analysis of a Random Sample of Gun Owners," which found that most NRA members supported waiting periods and handgun registration, which the NRA opposed.

203 DiMatteo ought to have been aware of this fact, having cited the supposedly lax requirements of that very law two paragraphs later. In this, too, he erred, writing that the law only requires the buyer to be over eighteen and to show photo ID. In fact, the Ontario law requires the retailer

fabrication, as was his bizarre assertion that "Ontario may decide not to abide by the new rules, but other provinces like Alberta will, opening the door to the possibility of interprovincial movement of ammo." The federal government had not, in fact, signalled its intention to do away with rules it had never made, and there was no reason to believe that Alberta would happily go along and sell ammunition under imaginary new rules that would replace old rules that did not exist—although apparently DiMatteo found reason to imagine it. If Canadian journalism offered a prize for the greatest number of errors and fabrications in a single news story, *NOW* and Enzo DiMatteo would have trumped even now-defunct Sun News.

But DiMatteo's piece produced what was surely the desired effect: a flurry of enraged correspondence from Canadian gun owners who had read it online. One Drew Lynch called DiMatteo a "big-government-loving, hysterical pussy boy" and a "soy-latte-drinking, yoga-loving, man-purse-wearing faggot," whom Lynch counted among the "freedom-hating, nanny goofs." Another letter suggested that the solution to violence in Toronto was to ban all Jamaicans from Canada because, "Murder is part of their culture." Naturally, *NOW* diligently printed this correspondence. After all, the only thing more fun than demonizing gun owners is provoking them to demonize themselves.

WELL, WHO BETTER TO DEMONIZE than gun owners? Everyone else is blameless. But we can demonize the guns, too, as if guns played some active role in matters. And we repeatedly do just that, if only subconsciously. The dead, for example, become victims of "gun violence," as if shootings somehow differed from other forms of violence. Shooting someone is a good deal more lethal than punching him in the face, or even stabbing him with the nearest steak knife, but this hardly places gun violence in a special category. Nevertheless, while other violence is just plain old violence, gun violence is gun violence, a genetically distinct subspecies endemic to the United States.

Of course, gun violence *is* a special category in the United States, which, among developed nations, is a statistical outlier when it comes to both rates of gun ownership and rates of armed mayhem. But the

to record the buyer's home address, and the Ontario Chief Firearms Officer had issued a policy requiring retailers to record the number of the buyer's firearms licence in lieu of his home address. It was therefore not possible to buy ammunition in Ontario without a licence, as DiMatteo asserted.

idea of gun violence carries also the tacit suggestion that the two words are linked, that the first leads to the second. We love facile explanations, and the facile explanation for gun violence is that guns cause violence. And as facile as it is, that explanation has attracted more than its share of research funding. In 1967, the psychologists Leonard Berkowitz and Anthony LePage published a seminal paper proposing that the mere presence of a gun encouraged violent behaviour—something they called the "weapons effect."[204] And although later research has substantially debunked their proposal, the idea has stuck.[205]

Paradoxically, the weapons effect is often espoused by people who insist at the same time that there is no link between video games and violence, just as it is denied by followers of the NRA, who insist that violent video games are much more important as causes of school shootings than the fact that you can walk into just about any sporting-goods store and buy yourself an AR-15. It has not occurred to either group that both ideas rest on the same theoretical premise. But logic and evidence are not in play: you believe what you want to believe, based on whether you like video games, and whether you like guns. Our conclusions go before the evidence. If you like playing games, then video games can't possibly cause violence, and no number of impressive, jargon-choked papers whose multiple authors come bedecked with entire alphabets of credentials can ever convince you otherwise. Likewise if you like guns. And if you don't like guns, well, they're obviously the problem.

As soon as we convince ourselves that the guns themselves are the problem, or at least that the guns themselves are a large part of the problem, a simple solution leaps forth: get rid of the guns. Or at least, a simple-*seeming* solution: with three hundred million guns in circulation, many owned by people devoted to hanging onto them in spite of the law, the prospect of degunning America is even more daunting than demining Afghanistan. It would be a project not of years, but of decades, or generations. And it is a project that would, in my view, leave

204   Leonard Berkowitz and Anthony LePage, "Weapons as Aggression-Eliciting Stimuli." *Journal of Personality and Social Psychology.* 7 (1967).

205   Some researchers have replicated the original result, but others have failed. One interesting experiment compared subjects who were unfamiliar with firearms with subjects who were, and found the weapons effect was absent among the people who actually owned guns—which somewhat undermines the original suggestion that owning a gun makes you violent. (B.D. Bartholow, C.A. Anderson, N.L. Carnagey, and A.R. Benjamin, "Interactive Effects of Life Experience and Situational Cues on Aggression: The Weapons Priming Effect in Hunters and Nonhunters," *Journal of Experimental Social Psychology* 41(1) (2005))

America poorer, for it takes as its premise that millions of American gun owners whose guns will never kill anyone are somehow irrelevant, that their views can be ignored, that their voices need not be heard. They're just gun nuts anyway.

And so I don't like to read the words "gun violence," or to hear that however many women or children are "victims of guns," or to be told owning a gun is irresponsible because it puts my family at risk because I might murder them.[206] It puts my back up because these people are telling me that *my* guns are part of the problem, that *my* guns ought to be taken away. Never mind that my guns in fact threaten no one; nevermind my right to live according to my own lights. As the Canadian Advisory Council on the Status of Women argued, I don't even deserve a voice in the matter; or, as Adam Vaughan suggests, I am a privileged guy whining about his hobby, and ought to be ignored. Political dialogue is a freight train. You can stand on the tracks and make all the arguments you like but you're just going to get smeared like a bug.

I get it. I know why Bruce Montague hid guns in his vault, why he buried the Luger his grandfather brought back from the trenches of France. Nobody is listening and nobody is prepared to compromise and real values are at stake and you do what you feel you must. I do not fear my side-by-side shotgun will be outlawed—these are the least restricted of guns, even in Britain or Australia—but I know what it feels like to face that train, nonetheless. You can lie down, stand up, or dance a hornpipe and that train won't give a damn. You thought you were a citizen, with rights and a voice, but as every election reminds us, voting is little more than a formalized way of pissing into a hurricane.

And so I insist, again, that the guns themselves are not the problem. The gun does not pull the trigger. It does not sit in its safe, encouraging murder and suicide in sly and subliminal whispers. A machine has no intent. It takes a person to pull the trigger. Violence is a human problem.

It's at about this point I realize that I'm starting to sound like the NRA: guns don't kill people, people kill people. Okay, then. You got me. In the end, perhaps I'm just another gun nut. Maybe I'm a bad person: a redneck, a racist, a homophobe, a general-purpose bigot-by-association. Because if we have to join teams, I guess it's pretty clear

---

206   This is the unfortunate subtext of the popular interpretation of Arthur Kellerman's papers: that, on the basis of a statistical correlation, all gun owners are incipient murderers.

where I'm going to land. Should have been, anyway, as soon as I started whining about freedom of expression and living the life I want to live. I'm with the gun people. I didn't want to be on this team, but nobody in this fight gets to be on the side of the angels. Being on the side of the mouth-breathers and nutjobs will just have to be good enough. It's that or the *NOW* magazine crowd, who won't have me anyway.

But no, I'm not joining the NRA. It is true, of course, that people kill people, but it is also true that they often use guns to do it. And the problem is that, in the United States, guns are all too available to people who kill people, a problem about which the NRA proposes to do nothing at all. Indeed, the NRA devotes itself to resisting any attempt to make guns less available to people who kill people, for the simple, unacknowledged reason that any group of people who are likely to kill people forms its own constituency among the NRA's membership. When the NRA resists attempts to restrict gun sales to men convicted of misdemeanour domestic assault, we should hardly be surprised. This has nothing to do with principle. Any organization devoted to protecting the rights of gun owners will inevitably attract those gun owners who feel their rights are most threatened, which includes those who ought not to enjoy those rights at all. And others will line up with them simply because they fear the antis will win unless someone stops them, and they believe the NRA can. You don't look for a nice guy when you need a litigator. You hire an asshole, because that's what the job requires.

Violence—gun violence, if you will—remains a human problem, not because it is humans and not weapons who do the violence, although that is indisputably true, but because the solutions lie in politics, and politics is a human problem. This is why I have sought the Wellspring of Crazy: not because gun owners are crazy, or because gun owners all believe only their guns can save them from the black helicopters in SHTF, or because gun owners fear a race war or imagine themselves loyal sheepdogs, because most gun owners do not believe these things. I set out on this quest because these ideas are swimming loose in the foul and stinking bilge of our politics, stinking up the water, and their pull is just strong enough to make a difference. These ideas provide the ideology that resists even the most tentative of gun-control measures. This is what powers American gun violence: not guns, not gun owners, nor even the gun lobby, but the deeply rooted ideas that call us to resist change.

The culture is the problem, and so the problem is intractable. Cultures are nigh immovable. You can't simply dive into the bilge, fish these things out, and kill them. Perhaps in time, we could starve them to death. But before that could happen, we would have to stop flinging monkey shit at each other, to come down from the treetops, and conduct ourselves like adults, or at least like children who had mastered the basic rules of sandbox citizenry.

I'm not holding out much hope.

Burds

An Epilogue

You may break your heart, but men will go on as before.
——Marcus Aurelius

WRITING THIS BOOK has been like diving for pearls in a vast, polluted river, down, down in the murk and sludge kicking and grasping and then up for a moment gasping for air in a bright and foreign world, each muscle sick with strain, and no idea where in hell the ceaseless current has carried me.

One grows tired. The days grow shorter and the mornings cold, and nobody wants to be swimming—which is to say, anything one might write regarding the endless gun kerfuffle seems increasingly pointless. The quickening days of autumn remind us that life is short. No one is listening. No one is ready to hear even that he is not prepared to listen. In the land of ranting deaf men, the man with tinnitus grows slowly hoarse.

What's a boy to do? I took Sadie hunting.

ON THE WALL CALENDAR by the front door, the opening day of bird-hunting season and every Saturday and Monday thereafter is marked with a scribble that looks like "BURDS." My wife, who uses this calendar to plan the kids' school days and other family events, raises a skeptical eyebrow. I shrug, and point to the dog. You know me; my spelling is better than that. I is a writer! The dog wags her tail, a willing fall girl for my graffiti. We two, we have everyone fooled.

My dog Sadie bounds and bounces like a puppy, runs down field edges picking up burrs, stops to lick up the dew that bends the grass. She feels obliged to help with my bootlaces although she is hampered by her woeful lack of opposable thumbs, also knot know-how. She checks my right boot to make sure nothing is hiding in it while I lace up the left, mouths the tongue to make sure it is out of my way, paws at the toe, tail working all the while. She is, in other words, a pain in the ass. She's a goof, a joker, a stand-up comic among gun dogs, but all is forgiven in those electric moments when she is on a bird, fur soaked with dew, steam rising backlit in the early morning sunlight. When she picks up the scent of woodcock she is all business, quicksilver in brambles, low under tangles of wild rose and hawthorn, a natural-born killer with a goofy, ceaseless-wagging tail.

Some hunters buy dogs so they can hunt; others hunt so they can work their dogs. And from the time the snow melts in March she is working. It takes years to fully train a flushing spaniel, and when the discipline of training gives way to hunting there is always a certain amount of backsliding. I am not much of a trainer, but I am lucky to have good teachers. We progress through quartering drills, shaping the dog's instinct to cover ground and work the wind. Then steadying: we expect the dog to charge in on a bird and put it to flight and then, as every instinct screams to give chase, we demand that the dog calmly sit, mark the fall, and wait for the signal to retrieve. And throughout, endless retrieving. First, simple marks, where the dog marks the fall and retrieves the bird.[207] Then water retrieves, retrieves over obstacles, and doubles. In a memory retrieve, the dog marks the fall but is then heeled to another position and sent on a line—pointed in the direction of the bird, and released to go out and find it. This builds the dog's confidence for blind retrieves, in which the dog is simply told "Dead bird," given the line, and sent to retrieve a bird it has never seen. A fully trained spaniel is a wonder to behold. I confess I hunt in part just to work with dogs.

---

207 Gun dog training is perhaps the only field in which the word "mark" is still used in the old sense, to observe or pay attention: a marked retrieve is one in which the dog observes the fall of the bird. Except in the idiomatic "mark my words," this usage has faded from the language. Interestingly, some gun dog trainers still send their dogs on with the command, "Hie on," which is probably the only remaining use of "hie."

When the season opens we take our game into thick edge cover—hawthorn and raspberry and wild rose—where birds take shelter. When the leaves start to fall we get perhaps one month on woodcock before they fly south, and then it is grouse, not the dopey northern grouse that you can pot on the ground with a .22, but cagey, wild-flushing birds that have seen dogs and know what they're about. You hear the sudden burst of wingbeats back in the cedars and the bird is already gone, unseen. Sadie works on, head down. We trek through stark and empty woods. I know some good territory for grouse, and we cover it, putting up maybe six birds in a morning. This yields one shot. My phone's GPS informs me I've hiked some eighteen kilometres. Sadie has covered several times that distance and, after three days in a row, she looks it.

Aches and pains on Sunday mornings. Her first season, she was out at the end of November with a knee injury, took it easy through the following spring. The second season, a thorn deep in a pad sidelined her with ten days of antibiotics, and then another pad cut on the ice in December. The dog comes up lame at mid-morning and you find an inch-long hawthorn sticking out of her paw. Pick it out and she's off and running: another day afield. Frost on goldenrod and my breath hanging in the air. Vest, hat, gloves, whistle, the brass bases of shotgun shells cold in my hands. Sadie bursts out of her travelling crate and runs, nose to the ground.

We are alive in the work of killing. Sadie moves with purpose. She put up a pheasant rooster from a tangled hedge along an old fence line, the bird bursting out of the hedge with a distinctive cackle, a high flyer that seemed to shoot up vertically and then hang in the air, and I hit it square with the first shot, a burst of loose feathers from the impact of the pellets. The bird was heavy and warm in my hand, limp, its head flopping. Blood in its nostrils, blood on my deerskin gloves.

We kill to live, whether we buy our meat at the supermarket or do the job ourselves. A clean shot is satisfying. Now and again you'll cripple a bird and have to dispatch it by hand, and wringing the bird's neck takes the satisfaction out of things right quick. For this purpose I made what British fly fishermen call a "priest" by drilling the end out of a piece of deer antler, filling it with lead, and capping it with epoxy. I administer the last rites with a quick, downward blow.

Last fall I took a not-very-good shot at a woodcock and downed it, and when Sadie retrieved it, the bird was still alive and alert. Its deep brown eyes seemed enormous, limpid, and filled with numinous intelligence. I put a finger over its beak, bent its head down, and broke its neck with a sharp blow of the priest, and its eyes went dull and black, from quick to dead. I shot a rising woodcock over a thicket of wild rose, a snap shot at close quarters before the bird levelled off, and one pellet struck the back of its head and caved in the fragile skull. But this is not how death usually visits. When the bird falls directly at the shot the cause is usually a broken wing, a pellet breaking the bone at the shoulder. And not every shot is a clean shot. The woodcock I killed with my priest had taken a single pellet that cut into the abdomen; when I plucked it, one flank was swollen with blood beneath the skin.

One learns how death arrives. The shotgun spews seven hundred tiny lead pellets and they stream invisibly to their target. It only takes a few. Perhaps one. A pellet intercepts the flying bird, cuts through breast feathers and punches through the loose skin beneath, trailing feather barbules as it carves its path through muscle, splinters bone, and comes to rest. On the kitchen table the pheasant autopsy proceeds: cut the skin at the neck and peel it back to reveal the breasts, the crop swollen with soy beans, the dark meat of the thighs. Note the blood spotting the left breast, the dark swelling of the abdomen behind its thin membrane, the bruising of the flopping left thigh. One pellet has penetrated the thigh and shattered the femur into tiny, sharp splinters that sliced the contracting muscle, the pellet passing through into the abdomen where it has punctured the liver and filled the belly with thick, dark blood. Another has penetrated the breast, its path marked by feather barbules trapped in the wound channel. A third has punctured a lung, spilling blood into the chest cavity. Two of these wounds are fatal.

This is how death arrives: internal organs bleed. Blood pressure plummets. The body goes into shock, shutting down the extremities to compensate for blood loss. If a pellet has punctured the chest cavity then the diaphragm labours to draw air into the lungs, each breath instead sucking air into the chest cavity itself, putting pressure on the lungs, collapsing them. Or blood floods a punctured lung, blood at the beak its tell-tale.

Such a candid inventory of trauma will no doubt offend some. But unless you're a vegan, you are at some level complicit. I would rather make a clean kill than a slow one but there is no sense pretending that guns visit instant death. And there is no escaping the understanding that how guns kill birds is how guns kill people, that this catalogue of trauma underlies the story on the morning news, the body in the Regent Park apartment stairwell, the bystander felled by a bullet to the chest, the school shooting. When we talk about putting armed guards in schools, when we talk about carrying concealed handguns, when we talk about what shotgun to choose for home defence, we skip glibly past the pages of this catalogue, imagining the double tap that stops the bad guy in his tracks. We do not imagine the bleeding. But if you have killed anything with a gun, then you know how guns kill. You know it is all about blood.

I CAUGHT UP TO HIM IN some cheap little diner on the north side of Center City. I was way out west, out where fictional characters go when the story is over. No readers, no viewers, no civilians allowed. Only ideas of people, who can never die. I wrote my way in, as a cheap-jack Marlowe in a roadside diner with chipped Formica tables and pie in a glass case and a flickering neon sign out front. The kind of place where the waitress calls you Honey. She had a run-down look, the flip side of a dream gone south. A familiar face but I couldn't quite place her. I took a stool at the counter and asked for a cup of Joe. It was the kind of place where you could still say that without raising an eyebrow.

She set the cup down harder than she had to, black coffee slopping over the edge. Nobody was calling me Honey today.

"You see that bastard Gonzo, you tell him he's still not welcome here."

So that was her. I told her I didn't know him.

"I thought you writers all knew each other."

"Only in awards season," I said. "Anyway, I'm pretty sure he's dead."

"Well," she said, and crossed her arms over her chest. "Good riddance."

"I'm looking for someone." I reached into an inside pocket and took out the picture and laid it on the counter. "Name of Roy."

"You some kind of cop now?"

"Private dick."

"Today's your lucky day." She nodded to a table in the corner where a man in a shabby brown suit sat with his back to the room. It didn't look like him. The clothes were all wrong. But I picked up my coffee and walked over and slid onto the bench opposite.

It was him: older, careworn, that broad trademark smile now long gone, no sign of the embroidered shirt, the chaps, the gun. His suit had a stain on the lapel and his shirt collar was frayed.

"Jig's up, Leonard," I said.

He looked up at me for a moment and then looked down at his coffee. It was cold, and the cream had formed a scum on top. He'd been sitting here a long time.

"Nobody's called me that in years."

"Times change."

"Don't I know it."

"You're out of uniform."

"No one wears that cowboy getup anymore."

"You're breaking the rules," I said.

He laughed. "And you?"

"I'm in mufti."

"And I'm a special case. I'm Roy Rogers *and* Roy Rogers." He picked up his spoon off the Formica and folded the scum layer back into his coffee. "They all still come in here, you know. Wyatt and Harry Callaghan and everybody. We all live in Center City now. There's no place else to go."

And this, of course, was how I knew I'd find him here, sooner or later. Even Shane still comes in from time to time. He'd tried to kill himself a while back but of course it didn't work. Nobody here can die. So he still drops in wearing his buckskins, sits at the counter and eats a BLT with fries and chats with Chingachgook and the Pathfinder, who are about the only people he can still stand. All of them have long since run out of west.

"I don't have your answers," he said.

"I didn't ask."

"You're overthinking it. I was just an actor playing an actor playing a cowboy."

"I hate to break it to you, but you're really just a symbol."

He laughed, without humour. "Well, you about rode me right into the ground."

"How's Trigger?"

"That's a low blow, Mister." He lifted his coffee cup and sniffed at it, put it down again. Stone cold. "Thought you were gonna get all the answers, did ya?"

"I just wanted to find better questions." You ask a stupid question, you get a stupid answer. We have all the stupid answers and it's about time we came to better questions. About time we dispensed with stupid generalities for good.

"Find any?"

"Which way to Paradise Valley?"

"Not my movie."

"But you've heard of it."

"What do you hope to find there, anyway?"

"Refuge," I said. Just another sunken-eyed man on a road clogged with streams of refugees walking like ghosts to anyplace the war is not. "I'm about ready to make a separate peace."

"They paved it over and turned it into a shopping mall." And now, for the first time, that Roy Rogers smile. "Or a megachurch, I can't remember which."

The sun had slipped below the window lintel and I reached back and twisted the handle of the shade. Slats of light tightened on the table, shadows falling across Roy's face like bars.

"It wasn't supposed to be this way," he said. "Nobody was supposed to get hurt."

"Nobody blames you."

"It was just the movies. Nobody was supposed to take it seriously."

"They invented you because they took it seriously."

"You gonna take me in?"

"Nobody can take you in, Roy. You're the Good Guy." And besides, he didn't do it anyway. It was just that we all moved out to Center City. And we never could let go, never could accept that the West is not forever wild. We invented Roy and we can never take him in, and we can never let him go. I put a five on the table and told him to get himself a slice of pie.

"So long, Leonard."

"Happy trails to you," he said, and gave me the finger.

> *The totalitarian states can do great things, but there is one thing they cannot do: they cannot give the factory-worker a rifle and tell him to take it home and keep it in his bedroom. That rifle hanging on the wall of the working-class flat or labourer's cottage, is the symbol of democracy. It is our job to see that it stays there.*
>
> —George Orwell

I SET OUT HERE TO UNDERSTAND the gun culture. I fear this was a mistake. America is a gun culture, as Richard Hofstadter argued, but "the bad thing about people with guns"—*the* gun culture—is a figment of our imaginations. We err, as Toronto's anti-gun councillors did, when we presume that there is a single "culture of guns," that all things in heaven and earth fit neatly onto our limited canvas. The picture is difficult to paint. Perspective eludes us. We expect that all lines will converge at the horizon, but of course they do not. Some of them do not converge at all.

The Internet tells us that the world is full of gun nuts. The Internet tells us also that everyone who owns a gun is a gun nut. We know this because websites tell us so. We know, also, because we can go and find those gun nuts. We can track down their blogs and their discussion forums and read their discussions and satisfy ourselves that we have found the gun culture. Brave anthropologists, we can observe the habits of the NRA member on Twitter and describe his strange rituals, and then we can publish our papers on the gun culture, which are sure to be almost as accurate as nineteenth-century accounts of travels among African tribes. After all, the Internet also tells us also that 86 percent of our waking hours are spent in acrobatic sex.

Not everyone wraps his identity around his gun. Not everyone who owns a gun needs to take the frontier myth seriously, or become a full-fledged Patriot, or take his family off to the woods and build a survival retreat. But the archetypes of American gun culture—the rifleman, the frontiersman, the sheepdog, the True Man—do rattle around in some corner of our minds, regardless. We cannot escape them. They are not of the fringes, but belong to mainstream thought. They are in the pages of our novels and on our television screens. They are part of us all.

When George Orwell wrote that it is our job to see that the rifle remains hanging on the wall of the labourer's cottage, he was right. And of course, gun activists are fond of that quotation. There's George Orwell, a socialist, telling the truth! The rifle must remain! But Orwell never said that the rifle was the guarantor of democracy, as America's gun culture now insists; he said it was a symbol. I am not free because of the guns resting in the safe beside my writing desk; guns can rest in the safe beside my writing desk only because I am free. And it is our job not to preserve those guns, but to preserve a society within which we can be privileged to own them.

Our job, because it falls to each of us. "The Home Guard could only exist in a country where men feel themselves free," Orwell also wrote, which was perhaps untrue. But it *is* true that the Home Guard could only have existed where people felt they shared a common stake. Orwell wrote those words in the *Evening Standard*, in January 1941. France had fallen. The United States stood on the sidelines, debating whether Hitler was really on the side of the anti-communist angels; the Soviets were still enjoying the peace of the Molotov-Ribbentrop Pact. U-Boat wolf packs were winning the Battle of the Atlantic, savaging Britain's tenuous lifeline. Everyone on Orwell's isolated, bomb-battered island knew they were in it together.

We no longer face any unifying threat. Instead we huddle in the circle of flickering light cast by our screens, and stamp our accelerator pedals to speed away from the stranger in the street spattered with bottled evil. We band together in the treetops to hoot and fling monkey shit at each other. There is no sense that democracy is a shared commitment, the product of a shared act of will and of our faith in the institutions we have created to preserve it, at the heart of which is a parliament, a place where we come together to speak. Instead we confront the noxious idea that democracy is preserved only by armed men, prepared to kill enemies both foreign and domestic—that latter category meaning, in essence, their political opponents.

This is the greatest threat to the rifle hanging on the wall of that labourer's cottage: that the society within which he can be privileged to own it will sink so far into violence and distrust that the privilege will be removed. And the people who most promote that violence and distrust are not Moms Demand Action or the Committee to Stop Gun Violence or the Coalition for Gun Control. They are the NRA, the Gun Owners of America, the Oath Keepers, Canada's National Firearms Association. The greatest threat to the guns resting in my safe is not your fear that they will do harm, but the people who fight to keep them available to nuts, loons, batterers, and angry, impulsive men. I have met the enemy, and he is us.

Perhaps, as the 1960s generation passes on, the picture will change. Perhaps some of the corners I have set out to illuminate will darken, get covered over by grime. Times change, movements pass. The vehemence of the culture war may be the last rearguard fight of ideas that are losing their sway. But Alex Jones, the conspiracy theorist who tells us that FEMA is building concentration camps and stockpiling coffins, that the Department of Homeland Security is preparing to confiscate everyone's guns, and that the US federal government is spawning tornadoes and steering them into American cities just because it can, finds an attentive audience among the young. Perhaps, then, we are fucked.

Paradise Valley has become a ghost town, a jumble of ruins and rotted boards. You will not find it on your fancy GPS. You'll need an old map to drive out to that happy place where we still had some sense of our greater community. And in all my searching, I never did find that map, just as I never did find the spot they buried Granma Joad, on the road into Center City. I have been your man who knows Indians, sought out your bloody frontier, moved from civilized drawing rooms to Doc Holliday's poker table. And I have found no community. I am left a man without a country, in a land without a frontier. All that remains is my republic of one. The rest is up to you.

So I will return to the business of writing stories, and take the dog hunting.

THREE SHORT ROADS TO NOWHERE are laid out in a triangle, and at its southern apex is a cane-filled depression out of which Sadie puts up a pheasant rooster which takes me by surprise and wheels away to the south heedless of the shot that passes behind. I endure a glare of disgust from the dog: she critiques my shooting, and I the choices she makes in working cover. But she puts up more birds than I hit. I am losing this debate on the numbers.

If you were plunked down here you might well question who laid out this triangular field, planted with soy beans, and bounded it with raised roadways, each eight-hundred-odd paces long. You might ask why a paved surface persists in places, considering that none of these roads leads anywhere. But I do not, because among my enthusiasms—mechanical typewriters, black-and-white photography, wooden boats, all things that sing the song of obsolescence—are antique aircraft. We are standing on a runway.

This was the No. 4 Bombing and Gunnery School of the Royal Canadian Air Force. In the 1950s all of the buildings were torn down and most of the runway pavement broken up. The Air Force, in its wisdom, felt that air gunners might learn to lead German fighters if they first learned to lead clay targets on the skeet range, and after the war the machines from those skeet houses ended up at the St. Thomas Gun Club, where I go shooting today. The base itself became a wildlife management area run by the Ontario Department of Lands and Forests as a demonstration of wildlife-friendly farming. Farmers rent the fields and raise corn and soybeans and winter wheat.

More than six thousand men graduated from No. 4 Bombing and Gunnery School. A plaque at the gate lists the names of eighteen who were killed flying from these runways: Leon Hood, Ernest Bourne, Johnny McNally, Norman Lavoie, Robert Prentice, Richard Gray, Ralph Hilchie, Kenneth Nicholson, Lionel Renaud, Earl De Planche, Keith Joyce, Ivan Rees, Edwin Hawkins, Robert Sharp, Sidney Turner, James Allan, Lawrence Watt, William Neville. A nineteenth man, Donald McLay, appears in casualty records but does not appear on the plaque.

All these intolerably nameless names. The runways are overgrown, bordered by strips of bush. All that remains of the hangars is their concrete pads. The Earth keeps wildly spinning through space and we crawl around on its surface feeling tremendously important, shouting on about guns and abortion and gay marriage and who gets to be the mayor of Toronto. When the Cougar's main gun fired the whole boat rocked and the turret filled with smoke. The tracer on the shell was orange and it seemed improbably slow at ranges over a kilometre, hanging in the air as it arced down onto its target. We called the gun a pumpkin launcher. In the summers I taught courses at the Meaford tank range, now built up into a proper training base. Back then it was a tent city and as instructors we slept in one of a few hard shacks, smoked at a picnic table we had dragged behind a screen of poplars, "the Emerald

Forest," the inside joke being that those poplars rendered us invisible. We were young and everything we said was funny.

All this is gone. The Cougar is gone and the Emerald Forest is paved over. Nothing remains but memory and that dies with us. McNally was engaged, on only his second or third flight; his plane crashed into Lake Erie. Allan was married. Leading Aircraftsman McLay is not on the plaque. Twenty children died at Newtown. All are punished. And I am tired of swimming. The days are getting shorter, the planet leaning away from the sun.

Along the east runway Sadie puts up another pheasant out of thick grass bordering an entanglement of wild rose, its tail streaming, and it seems to hang in the air for one long moment until the shot cuts feathers, hits it square, and it folds and falls, wings broken. Death arrives. Breast feathers float down through the air. I take the bird from the dog, blood at its nostrils, the body slack and heavy, feathers shifting under my grip. Another rooster, its feathers a riot of colours, beautiful. The head rolls at the end of its limp neck, dead.

A Note on Sources

THIS IS NOT AN ACADEMIC TREATISE, and so I have chosen not to clutter the text with a dense mass of citations, which for most readers would accomplish little more than to slow the reading experience and evoke unpleasant memories of slogging through required reading for some disappointing course taught by a tiresome drone. However, a word on sources seems appropriate.

I would be remiss not to acknowledge a few books and essays that took on central importance to this one. Richard Hofstadter's essay "America as a Gun Culture" and, less obviously, his book *The Paranoid Style in American Politics* cannot go unmentioned. Steven Pinker's *The Better Angels of Our Nature: Why Violence Has Declined* tells us far more about the gun culture than perhaps Pinker himself intended; his allusion to Hobbes' Leviathan is apt, and the Leviathan took on teeth and claws and scales in my retelling. Richard Slotkin's *Gunfighter Nation* gave me the archetypes of the frontier myth, and makes a convincing case regarding the crisis that arose from the closing of the American frontier. Blake Brown's *Arming and Disarming: A History of Gun Control in Canada* also proved invaluable.

It was Rod Paschall's *The Defeat of Imperial Germany, 1917-1918* that first introduced me to the myth of the American rifleman, perhaps twenty years ago. The revolution in firepower comes from several sources, but one of the most valuable was Robert L. O'Connor's *Of Arms and Men: a History of War, Weapons, and Aggression*. For the history of American labour conflict, I am particularly indebted to Lon Savage's *Thunder in the Mountains: The West Virginia Mine War, 1920–21* and to Thomas G. Andrews' *Killing for Coal: America's Deadliest Labor War*, not to mention of course Barbara Kopple's film *Harlan County, USA*.

Papers by Garrett Epps, Jeannie Suk, and others guided me through the history of American self-defence law, the English common law, and the duty to retreat; without these signposts, I would still be wandering the wilds of Blackstone's *Commentaries*, faint from hunger and dehydration. Adam Winkler's *Gun Fight: The Battle Over the Right to Bear Arms in America* provides a useful overview of the history of American gun control, and also a detailed look at *DC v. Heller*. I am not a lawyer and these people are, so I hasten to add that any errors are my own, etc.

I have cited crime statistics in several places. For American crime statistics, the primary source is the FBI's Uniform Crime Report. In Canada, Statistics Canada helpfully publishes annual summaries of homicide, police-reported crime, and violent crime.

Hunter S. Thompson's autobiography contributed its title, *Kingdom of Fear*, as the title of a chapter here, and as a description of America today, or at least a corner of the American mind.

Bits and pieces of many things—Wilfred Owen, Hunter S. Thompson, Bugs Bunny—have found their way into the text here and there, and may convince some pedant to accuse me of plagiarism, owing to a lack of quotation marks. It seems to be all the rage these days. But the entire process of language is love and theft, so there you go.

Finally, it seems appropriate also to apologize for, or at least to explain, my continual use of masculine pronouns where the reader has come to expect gender-neutral language. The reason here is simple: gun violence and the gun culture are predominantly masculine phenomena. It is true, for example, that the US military trains both boys and girls, but until very recently it was exclusively the boys it trained for the killing roles and in American society as a whole, it is the boys who do most of the killing. It is the boys, also, who promote the ideas of the gun culture, which (as I point out in the text) relies on traditional masculine archetypes. I have chosen, therefore, to use masculine pronouns in most cases.

Sources
Books, Academic Papers, And Periodicals

Introduction

Brown, R. Blake. *Arming and Disarming: A History of Gun Control in Canada*. Toronto: University of Toronto Press, 2012.

Butcher, Steve. "'Knife culture' slammed after box cutter attack in Blackburn pizza restaurant." *The Age*, November 22, 2013.

Hofstadter, Richard. "America as a gun culture." *American Heritage*, October, 1970.

Hope, Christopher, and James Kirkup. "'We're out of touch on knife crime,' says top judge." *The Telegraph*, July 9, 2008.

Lott, John. *More Guns, Less Crime*. Chicago: University of Chicago Press, 2010.

Rodriguez, Meredith. "'Pure American' rifle billboard assaulted." *Chicago Tribune*, February 1, 2014.

A Nation of Riflemen

Brown, R. Blake. *Arming and Disarming: A History of Gun Control in Canada*. Toronto: University of Toronto Press, 2012.

McGrath, Roger D. "The American Rifleman in the Revolutionary War." *The New American*. September 13, 2010.

O'Connell, Robert L. *Of Arms and Men: A History of War, Weapons, and Aggression*. Oxford: Oxford University Press, 1989.

Paschall, Rod. *The Defeat of Imperial Germany 1917-1918*. Boston: Da Capo Press, 1994.

"Police riflemen." *The New York Times*, June 8, 1873.

"Rifle Practice." *The New York Times*, April 7, 1872.

"Rifle practice. Necessity for a school of marksmanship—what the State Militia should do about target practice." *The New York Times*, May 3, 1873.

Slotkin, Richard. *Gunfighter Nation: The Myth of the Frontier in Twentieth-Century America*. New York: Atheneum, 1992.

"The Canadian rifle match: Capt. Fullerton makes twenty-eight points." *The New York Times*, August 17, 1874.

"The Canadian rifle matches." *The New York Times*, August 19, 1874.

"The Rifle Association: The National Range at Creedmoor. A review of the first season of the New York Rifle Society." *The New York Times*, December 13, 1873.

The Tendency of the American Mind

Blackstone, William. *Commentaries on the laws of England*. Philadelphia: J.B. Lippincott Company, 1893.

"Brian Knight says he didn't mean to shoot ATV thief." *Red Deer Advocate*, January 14, 2011.

Brown, Richard Maxwell. *No Duty to Retreat: Violence and Values in American History and Society*. Norman, Oklahoma: University of Oklahoma Press, 1994.

Cheng, Cheng, and Mark Hoekstra. "Does Strengthening Self-Defense Law Deter Crime or Escalate Violence? Evidence from Expansions to Castle Doctrine." *Journal of Human Resources*, 48(3), 2013.

Christensen, Dan. "NRA Uses New Florida Gun Law as National Model." *Daily Business Review*, May 17, 2005.

Epps, Garrett. "Any Which Way but Loose: Interpretive Strategies and Attitudes Toward Violence in the Evolution of the Anglo-American 'Retreat Rule.'" *Law and Contemporary Problems* 55(1), 1992.

Keaton, Angela F.. "Backyard Desperadoes: American Attitudes Concerning Toy Guns in the Early Cold War Era." *Journal of American Culture* 33(3), 2010.

Lerner, Renee Lettow. "The Worldwide Popular Revolt Against Proportionality in Self-Defense Law." *Journal of Law, Economics & Policy* 2 (2006).

Montgomery, Ben. "Florida's 'Stand Your Ground' law was born of 2004 case, but story has been distorted." *Tampa Bay Times*, April 14, 2012.

Robinson, Paul H., and Robert Kurzban. "Concordance and conflict in intuitions of justice." *Minnesota Law Review* 91, 2007.

Suk, Jeannie. "The true woman: scenes from the law of self-defense." *Harvard Journal of Law and Gender* 31, 2008.

Vollmann, William T. *Rising Up and Rising Down: Some Thoughts on Violence, Freedom, and Urgent Means*. New York: Harper-Perennial, 2005.

Weinstein, Adam. "How the NRA and its allies helped spread a radical gun law nation-wide." *Mother Jones*, June 7, 2012.

The West is Still Wild

Barra, Allen. "Who was Wyatt Earp?" *American Heritage*, December, 1998.

Slotkin, Richard. *Gunfighter Nation: The Myth of the Frontier in Twentieth-Century America*. New York: Atheneum, 1992.

"The OK Corral Inquest. 1992. 'Statement of Wyatt S. Earp in the Preliminary Hearing in the Earp-Holliday Case, heard before Judge Wells Spicer, November 16, 1881.'" Accessed July 18, 2015, http://law2.umkc.edu/faculty/projects/ftrials/earp/wearp-testimony.html

"Westerns: The Six-Gun Galahad." *Time*, March 30, 1959.

Winkler, Adam. *Gun Fight: The Battle Over the Right to Bear Arms in America*. New York: W.W. Norton, 2011.

The Secret History of the Second Amendment, Part 1

Andrews, Thomas G. *Killing for Coal: America's Deadliest Labor War*. Cambridge, Massachusetts: Harvard University Press, 2008.

Benson, Jackson W. *The True Adventures of John Steinbeck*, Writer. New York: Penguin, 1984.

Boren, Lyle H., Congressional Record, 76th Cong., 3rd Sess., pt. 13, LXXXVI (1940), 139-40.

"Mingo marchers fight with police; five miners fall." *The New York Times*, August 29, 1921.

"President's proclamation ordering dispersal of insurrectionary marauders in West Virginia." *The New York Times*, August 31, 1921.

Savage, Lon. *Thunder in the Mountains: The West Virginia Mine War*, 1920-21. Pittsburgh: University of Pittsburgh Press, 1990.

"Sid Hatfield slain before courthouse." *The New York Times*, August 2, 1921.

"Sid Hatfield was victim of plot." *The New York Times*, August 3, 1921.

Slotkin, Richard. *Gunfighter Nation: The Myth of the Frontier in Twentieth-Century America*. New York: Atheneum, 1992.

Steinbeck, John. *A Life in Letters*. New York: Penguin,1976.

Steinbeck, John. T*he Grapes of Wrath*. New York: Viking, 1939.

"West Virginia mob orders troopers away." *The New York Times*, August 14, 1921.

The Secret History of the Second Amendment, Part 2

Bogus, Carl T. "The Hidden History of the Second Amendment." *UC Davis Law Review* 31(2), 1998.

The Kerner Commission. *Report of the National Advisory Commission on Civil Disorders. Washington: National Criminal Justice Reference Service*, 1968.

Kleck, Gary. *Targeting guns: Firearms and Their Control*. Hawthorne, NY: Aldine de Gruyter, 1997.

Papachristos, Andrew V., and Christopher Wildeman, "Network Exposure and Homicide Victimization in an African American Community," *American Journal of Public Health* 104(1), 2014.

Pierce, William Luther (as Andrew Macdonald). *The Turner Diaries*. Hillsboro, WV: National Vanguard Books, 1978.

Ruane, Michael E. "Artifacts show a Rosa Parks steeped in freedom struggle from childhood." *The Washington Post*, Feb 3, 2015.

Seale, Bobby. *Seize the Time: The Story of the Black Panther Party and Huey P. Newton*. Baltimore: Black Classic Press, 1991.

Sherrill, Robert. *The Saturday Night Special*. New York: Penguin, 1975.

Smith, Aaron. "2 gun stores near Ferguson say sales are soaring." CNNMoney, 14 August, 2014. http://money.cnn.com/2014/08/14/smallbusiness/gun-sales-ferguson/

Smith, Aaron. "Ferguson-area gun sales surge ahead of jury decision." CNNMoney, 20 November, 2014. http://money.cnn.com/2014/11/20/smallbusiness/ferguson-gun-sales-riots/

Tonso, William R. "Gun Control: White Man's Law." *Reason*, December, 1985.

Winkler, Adam. "The Secret History of Guns." *The Atlantic*, September, 2011.

Winkler, Adam. *Gun Fight: The Battle Over the Right to Bear Arms in America*. New York: W.W. Norton, 2011.

An Uncertain History

Achenbach, Joel, Scott Higham, and Sari Horwitz. "How NRA's true believers converted a marksmanship group into a mighty gun lobby." *The Washington Post*, January 12, 2013.

Ascione, Alfred M. "The Federal Firearms Act." *St. John's Law Review* 13, 1939.

Atwood, Margaret. *Survival: A Thematic Guide to Canadian Literature*. Toronto: House of Anansi Press, 1972.

Brown, R. Blake. *Arming and Disarming: A History of Gun Control in Canada*. Toronto: University of Toronto Press, 2012.

Davidson, Osha Gray. *Under Fire: The NRA and the Battle for Gun Control*. New York: Henry Holt, 1993.

Frederick, Karl T. "Pistol Regulation: Its Principles and History, Part I." *The American Journal of Police Science* 2(5), 1931.

Frederick, Karl T. "Pistol Regulation: Its Principles and History, Part II." *The American Journal of Police Science* 3(1), 1932.

Frederick, Karl T. "Pistol Regulation: Its Principles and History, Part III." *American Journal of Criminal Law and Criminology* 23(2), 1932.

Frye, Brian L. "The Peculiar Story of United States v. Miller." *NYU Journal of Law & Liberty* 3, 2008.

Halbrook, Stephen. *That Every Man be Armed: The Evolution of a Constitutional Right*. Albuquerque, NM: University of New Mexico Press, 1984.

Henigan, Dennis A. "The Heller Paradox." *UCLA Law Review* 56, 2009.

Levinson, Sanford. "The Embarrassing Second Amendment." *Yale Law Journal* 99, 1989.

Levinson, Sanford, "Some Preliminary Reflections on Heller." June 26, 2008, accessed 19 July 2015, http://balkin.blogspot.ca/2008/06/some-preliminary-reflections-on-heller.html

Malcolm, Joyce Lee. "The Right of the People to Keep and Bear Arms: The Common Law Tradition." *Hastings Constitutional Law Quarterly* 10, 1983.

Malcolm, Joyce Lee. *To Keep and Bear Arms: The Origins of an Anglo-American Right*. Cambridge, Massachussets: Harvard University Press, 1994.

Malcolm, Joyce Lee. *Guns and Violence: The English Experience*. Cambridge, Massachusetts: Harvard University Press, 2002.

Malcolm, Joyce Lee. "The Supreme Court and the Uses of History: District of Columbia v. Heller." *UCLA Law Review* 26, 2009.

May, Elizabeth. "10 Reasons Why Harper Isn't Really Canadian." The Huffington Post, 6 June 2013, accessed July 19, 2015, http://www.huffingtonpost.ca/elizabeth-may/harper-not-canadian-elizabeth-may_b_3395713.html

Merkel, William G. "The District of Columbia v. Heller and Antonin Scalia's Perverse Sense of Originalism." *Lewis & Clark Law Review* 13(2), 2009.

Posner, Richard A. "The Incoherence of Antonin Scalia." *The New Republic*. September 13, 2012.

Richler, Noah. *What We Talk About When We Talk About War*. Fredericton, NB: Goose Lane Editions, 2012.

Thompson, Hunter S. *Fear and Loathing in America: The Brutal Odyssey of an Outlaw Journalist, 1968-1976*. New York: Simon & Schuster, 2000.

Thompson, Hunter S. *The Proud Highway: Saga of a Desperate Southern Gentleman, 1955-1967*. New York: Ballantine, 1997.

Webber, Alan C. "Where the NRA stands on gun legislation." The American Rifleman, March, 1968.

Winkler, Adam. *Gun Fight: The Battle Over the Right to Bear Arms in America*. New York: W.W. Norton, 2011.

Wright, James D. and Peter H. Rossi. *Armed and Considered Dangerous: A Survey of Felons and their Firearms*. Hawthorne, New York: Aldine de Gruyter, 1994.

Zimring, Franklin E. "Firearms and Federal Law: The Gun Control Act of 1968," *J. Legal Stud*. 4 (1975).

Judged by Twelve

Bloomfield, Warner. "Montagues face civil forfeiture of their property." *The Dryden Observer*, September 28, 2005.

Crossley, Lance. "Gun law rides into Haliburton." *The Haliburton Echo*, March 22, 2005.

Gauthier, Dan. "Man facing weapons charges argues Firearms Act is unconstitutional." *Kenora Daily Miner and News*, March 20, 2007.

Gibson, Janet. "Dryden gunsmith charged with firearms, explosives offences." *The Kenora Enterprise*, September 25, 2004.

Grozelle, Jerry. "C-68 challenger hosted by outdoors association." *The Highlands Courier*, April, 2005.

"King of the hill in Eton-Rugby Township." *The Dryden Observer*. March 31, 1998.

"Law body won't punish Christie but flays ties to 'lunatic fringe.'" *Canadian Press*. February 24th, 1993

Mauser, Gary A. "Armed Self Defense: The Canadian Case." *Journal of Criminal Justice* 24(5), 1996.

Mazza, Brian. "Legal challenge to gun registration underway." *Rocky Mountain House Mountaineer*, February 15, 2005.

McKay, Cindy. "Still standing against C-68." *Interlakes Spectator*, August 19, 2005.

"Montagues change legal counsel." *The Dryden Observer*. December 15, 2004.

Nemeth, Mary. "Fighting back: farmers, hunters and firearms enthusiasts are turning the gun-control debate into trench warfare." *Maclean's*, June 5, 1995.

"NW Ontario man fires lawyer, stalling constitutional challenge of Firearms Act." *The Thunder Bay Chronicle-Herald*, March 23, 2007.

"Ontario man vows to take constitutional challenge of Firearms Act to top court." *Canadian Press*. November 7th, 2007.

Papineau, Laurie. "Charges laid against CUFOA member, wife." *The Dryden Observer*, September 15, 2004.

Paterson, Jody. "An uneasy peace: at 56, controversial lawyer Douglas Christie now worries for his children." *The Victoria Times-Colonist*, March 3, 2002.

Williams, Garett. "Montague found guilty on 26 firearms-related charges." *Kenora Daily Miner and News*, December 7, 2007.

Wilson-Smith, Anthony. "Rock fights for gun control." *Maclean's*, June 5, 1995.

A Woman's Right

Bailey, J.E., A.L. Kellerman, G.W. Somes, J.G. Banton, F.P. Rivara and N.P. Rushforth. "Risk factors for violent death of women in the home." *Archives of Internal Medicine* 157(7), 1997.

Bordua, David J., and Alan J. Lizotte. "Patterns of legal firearms ownership: a cultural and situational analysis of Illinois counties." *Law & Policy* 1(2), 1979.

Brown, R. Blake. *Arming and Disarming: A History of Gun Control in Canada*. Toronto: University of Toronto Press, 2012.

Bugg, David, and Philip Q. Yang. "Trends in women's gun ownership, 1973 – 2002" (paper presented at the 99th Meeting of the American Sociological Association, Aug 14-17, 2004).

Carpenter, Catherine L. "Of the enemy within, the castle doctrine, and self-defense." *Marquette Law Review* 86(4), 2003.

Dressler, Joshua. "Feminist (or 'feminist') reform of self-defense law: some critical reflections." *Marquette Law Review* 93(4), 2010.

"Eighth Annual Report of Domestic Violence Death Review Committee." Office of the Chief Coroner, Province of Ontario, 2010.

Kellerman, Arthur L., Frederick P. Rivara, Norman B. Rushforth, Joyce G. Banton, Donald T. Reay, Jerry T. Francisco, Ana B. Locci, Janice Prodzinski, Bela B. Hackman and Grant Somes. "Gun ownership as a risk factor for homicide in the home." *New England Journal of Medicine* 329(15), 1993.

Lott, John. *More Guns, Less Crime*. Chicago: University of Chicago Press, 2010.

Sheley, J.F., C.J. Brody, J.D. Wright, and M.A. Williams. "Women and handguns: evidence from national surveys, 1973 – 1991." *Social Science Research* 23(3), 1994.

Sinha, Maire. "Family violence in Canada: a statistical profile, 2010." Statistics Canada, May, 2012.

Smith, Tom W. "Armed and dangerous statistics: media coverage of trends in gun ownership by women." *The Public Perspective*, May/June 1990.

Smith, T.W., and R.J. Smith. "Changes in firearms ownership among women, 1980 – 1994." *Journal of Criminal Law and Criminology* 86(1), 1995.

Terry, Allison. "Why gun ownership among US women is climbing." *Christian Science Monitor*, 15 February, 2013.

Thompson, C.Y., R.L. Young, and W.L. Creasey. "Women's emancipation and the ownership of firearms." *Women and Criminal Justice* 7(2), 1996.

Fudds

Carpenter, David. *A Hunter's Confession*. Vancouver: Greystone, 2010.

Pinker, Steven. *The Better Angels of Our Nature: Why Violence Has Declined*. New York: Viking, 2011.

Richards, David Adams. *Facing the Hunter: Reflections on a Misunderstood Way of Life*. Toronto: Doubleday, 2011.

Collateral Damage

Bouffard, L.A. "Examining the relationship between military service and criminal behavior during the Vietnam era: a research note." *Criminology* 41(2), 2003.

Chambers, John Whiteclay II. "S.L.A. Marshall's Men Against Fire: new evidence regarding fire ratios." *Parameters*, Autumn 2003.

Clancy, Tom. *Clear and Present Danger*. New York: Berkely, 1990.

Engen, Robert. "S.L.A. Marshall and the ratio of fire: history, interpretation and the Canadian experience." *Canadian Military History* 20(4), 2011.

Griffin, W.E.B. *The Corps, Book I: Semper Fi*. New York: Jove, 1986.

Griffin, W.E.B. *The Corps, Book II: Call to Arms*. New York: Jove, 1987.

Grossman, Lt. Col. Dave. *On Killing*. New York: Little, Brown & Company, 2009.

Grossman, Lt. Col. Dave. *On Combat*. Warrior Science Publications, 2008.

MacManus, D, K. Dean, M. Al Bakir, A. C. Iversen, L. Hull, T. Fahy, S. Wessely and N. T. Fear. "Violent behaviour in UK military personnel returning home after deployment." *Psychological Medicine* 42, 2012.

Marshall, S.L.A. *Men Against Fire: The Problem of Battle Command in Future War*. University of Oklahoma Press, 2000.

Monluc, Blais de. *Commentaires et Lettres de Blais de Monluc, Maréchal de France*. Paris: Jules Renouard / Société de l'Histoire de France, 1864.

Pierce, William Luther (as Andrew Macdonald). The Turner Diaries. Hillsboro, WV: National Vanguard Books, 1978.

Richler, Noah. *What We Talk About When We Talk About War*. Fredericton, NB: Goose Lane Editions, 2012.

Rohlfs, Chris. "Does Combat Exposure Make You a More Violent or Criminal Person? Evidence from the Vietnam Draft." *J. Human Resources* 45(2), 2010.

Slotkin, Richard. *Gunfighter Nation: The Myth of the Frontier in Twentieth-Century America*. New York: Atheneum, 1992.

Smoler, Fredric. "The secret of the soldiers who didn't shoot." *American Heritage*, March, 1989.

Spiller, Roger J. "S.L.A. Marshall and the ratio of fire." *Journal of the Royal United Services Institute* 133(4), 1988.

Vinaver, Eugene, ed. *Malory: Works.* Oxford: Oxford University Press, 1977.

Yager, J. "Postcombat violent behavior in psychiatrically maladjusting soldiers." *Archives of General Psychiatry* 33(11), 1976.

Yager, T., R. Laufer, and M. Gallops. "Some Problems Associated With War Experience in Men of the Vietnam Generation." *Archives of General Psychiatry* 41, 1984.

Kingdom of Fear

Catalano, Shannon. "Victimization during household burglary." *US Department of Justice Bureau of Justice Statistics Special Report.* September, 2010.

Eisner, Manuel. "Long-term historical trends in violent crime." *Crime & Justice* 30, 2003.

Francisco, Joycelyn, and Christian Chenier. "A comparison of large urban, small urban and rural crime rates, 2005." *Canadian Centre for Justice Statistics,* 2007.

Glassner, Barry. *The Culture of Fear.* New York: Basic Books, 2009.

Heath, Linda and Kevin Gilbert. "Mass media and fear of crime." *American Behavioral Scientist* 39(4), 1996.

Heath, Linda and John Petraitis. "Television viewing and fear of crime: where is the mean world?" *Basic and Applied Social Psychology* 8, 1987.

Kleck, Gary. *Targeting guns: Firearms and Their Control.* Hawthorne, NY: Aldine de Gruyter, 1997.

Pinker, Steven. *The Better Angels of Our Nature: Why Violence Has Declined.* New York: Viking, 2011.

Postman, Neil. *Amusing Ourselves to Death: Public Discourse in the Age of Show Business.* London: Penguin, 2005.

Thompson, Hunter S. *Fear and Loathing in America: The Brutal Odyssey of an Outlaw Journalist, 1968-1976.* New York: Simon & Schuster, 2000.

Thompson, Hunter S. *Fear and Loathing in Las Vegas.* New York: Vintage, 2008.

Vollmann, William T. *Rising Up and Rising Down: Some Thoughts on Violence, Freedom, and Urgent Means.* New York: Harper-Perennial, 2005.

Warr, Mark. "Fear of Crime in the United States: Avenues for Research and Policy," in *Criminal Justice 2000, Volume 4: Measurement and Analysis of Crime and Justice.* Washington: US Department of Justice Office of Justice Programs, 2000.

Molon Labe

Hofstadter, Richard. "The paranoid style in American politics." *Harper's,* November, 1964.

"Judge orders release of Justin Bourque sentencing exhibits to media." Accessed Dec 5, 2014. http://globalnews.ca/news/1711133/judge-agrees-to-release-of-justin-bourque-exhibits-to-media/.

"'No extra powers' granted to police during G20 summit: Liberals." *The Toronto Star,* June 30, 2010.

"Police admit no five-metre rule existed on security fence law." *The Globe and Mail.* June 29, 2010.

Royal Canadian Mounted Police. Statement Transcript PROS File 2014-646828 (Justin Bourque 2014-06-06). Accessed July 19, 2015, http://www.scribd.com/doc/249312403/Justin-Bourque-RCMP-interview-transcript#scribd

Welch, Robert. *The Blue Book.* The John Birch Society, 1958.

Teotwawki

Ahern, Jerry. *Total War.* New York: Zebra, 1981.

Ahern, Jerry. *The Nightmare Begins.* New York: Zebra, 1981.

Ahern, Jerry. *The Quest.* New York: Zebra, 1981.

Dwyer, Jim, and Christopher Drew. "Fear exceeded crime's reality in New Orleans." *The New York Times,* September 29, 2005.

Kuran, Timur, and Cass R. Sunstein. "Availability cascades and risk regulation." *Stanford Law Review* 51(4), 1999.

Rawles, James Wesley. *How To Survive the End of the World as We Know It.* New York: Plume, 2009.

Sun, Lisa Grow. "Disaster mythology and the law." *Cornell Law Review,* June 2011.

Sun, Lisa Grow. "Disaster mythology and availability cascades." *Duke Environmental Law & Policy Review* 23, 2012.

Tierney, Kathleen, Christine Bevc, and Erica Kulicovsky. "Metaphors matter: disaster myths, media frames, and their consequences in Hurricane Katrina." *Annals of the American Academy* 604, 2006.

Wells, H.G. *The War of the Worlds.* London: William Heinemann, 1898.

Wyndham, John. *The Day of the Triffids.* London: Penguin, 2010.

Something About Our Republic

Baxley, Frances and Matthew Miller. "Parental misperceptions about children and firearms." *Archives of Pediatric Adolescent Medicine* 160, 2006.

Brown, R. Blake. *Arming and Disarming: A History of Gun Control in Canada.* Toronto: University of Toronto Press, 2012.

Carson, Sara. "'Heavy hearts' but business as usual at Ellwood Epps." *The Orillia Packet,* September 8, 2011.

Dahlberg, L.L., R.M. Ikeda and M.J. Kresnow. "Guns in the home and risk of a violent death in the home: findings from a national study." *American Journal of Epidemiology* 160(10), 2004.

Farah, Mirna M., Harold K. Simon, and Arthur L, Kellerman. "Firearms in the home: parental perceptions." *Pediatrics* 104(5), 1999.

Hardy, M.S. "Teaching firearm safety to children: failure of a program." *Journal of Developmental and Behavioral Pediatrics* 23(2), 2002.

Himle, Michael B., Raymond B. Miltenberger, Brian J. Gatheridge and Christopher A.

Flessner. "An evaluation of two procedures for training skills to prevent gun play in children." *Pediatrics* 113(1), 2004.

Himle, Michael B., Raymond B. Miltenberger, Christopher Flessner and Brian Gatheridge. "Teaching safety skills to children to prevent gun play." *Journal of Applied Behavior Analysis* 37(1), 2004.

Jackman, Geoffrey A., Mirna M. Farah, Arthur L. Kellerman, and Harold K. Simon. "Seeing is believing: what do boys do when they find a real gun?" *Pediatrics* 107(6), 2001.

Kellerman, Arthur L., Frederick P. Rivara, Norman B. Rushforth, Joyce G. Banton, Donald T. Reay, Jerry T. Francisco, Ana B. Locci, Janice Prodzinski, Bela B. Hackman and Grant Somes. "Gun ownership as a risk factor for homicide in the home." *New England Journal of Medicine* 329(15), 1993.

Kellerman, Arthur L., Frederick P, Rivara, Grant Somes, Donald T. Reay, Jerry Francisco, Joyce G. Banton, Janice Prodzinski, Corrine Fligner, and Bela B. Hackman. "Suicide in the home in relation to gun ownership." *New England Journal of Medicine* 327(7), 1992.

Kellerman, Arthur L. and Donald T. Reay. "Protection or peril?" *New England Journal of Medicine* 314, 1986.

Lott, John and John E. Whitley. "Safe storage gun laws: accidental deaths, suicides and crime." Yale Law School Program for Studies in Law, Economics and Public Policy Working Paper #237, March 29, 2000.

Ludwig, Jens and Philip J. Cook, *Evaluating Gun Policy: Effects on Crime and Violence.* Washington: Brookings Institution Press, 2003.

Wiebe, D.J. "Homicide and suicide risks associated with firearms in the home: a national case-control study." *Annals of Emergency Medicine* 41(6), 2003.

You'd Have to be Crazy

Brown, R. Blake. *Arming and Disarming: A History of Gun Control in Canada.* Toronto: University of Toronto Press, 2012.

DeVoss, David. "Searching for Gavrilo Princip." *Smithsonian*, August 2000.

Dietz, Park Elliott. "Mass, serial, and sensational homicides." *Bulletin of the New York Academy of Medicine* 62(5), June 1986.

Heer, Jeet. "The line between terrorism and mental illness." Accessed July 19, 2105, http://www.newyorker.com/news/news-desk/line-terrorism-mental-illness

Schulman, Ari N. "What mass killers want—and how to stop them." *The Wall Street Journal*, November 8, 2013.

Kulturkampf

Bartholow, Bruce D., Craig A. Anderson, Nicholas L. Carnagey, and Arlin J. Benjamin, Jr. "Interactive effects of life experience and situational cues on aggression: the weapons priming effect in hunters and nonhunters." *Journal of Experimental Social Psychology* 41, 2005.

Berkowitz, Leonard and Anthony LePage. "Weapons as aggression-eliciting stimuli." *Journal of Personality and Social Psychology* 7(2), 1967.

Kahan, Dan M. and Donald Braman. "The self-defensive cognition of self-defense." *American Criminal Law Review* 45(1), 2008.

Kahan, Dan M. and Donald Braman. "More statistics, less persuasion: a cultural theory of gun-risk perceptions." *University of Pennsylvania Law Review* 151, 2003.

Kahan, Dan M., Donald Braman, John Gastil, Paul Slovic, and C.K. Mertz. "Culture and identity-protective cognition: explaining the 'white male effect' in risk perception." *Journal of Empirical Legal Studies* 4(3), 2007.

Weil, Douglas S. and David Hemenway. "I am the NRA: an analysis of a national random sample of gun owners." *Violence and Victims* 8(4), 1993.

Court Documents

An Uncertain History
Dred Scott v. Sanford, 60 U.S. 393.

An Uncertain History
District of Columbia v. Heller, 554 U.S. 570 (2008).

United States v. Miller, 307 U.S. 174 (1939).

Warren v. District of Columbia, 444 A. 2d 1 - DC: Court of Appeals 1981.

Judged by Twelve
R. v. Montague, 2007 CanLII 51171 (ON SC).

R. v. Montague, 2010 ONCA 141 (CanLII).

R. v. Montague, compiled trial transcripts, Ontario Superior Court.

R. v. Montague, Notice of Application and Constitutional Issue.

R. v. Montague, Taking of expert evidence before the Honourable Justice J. dep Wright on January 4 & 5, 2007, at Thunder Bay, Ontario. Court of Appeal No.CA-48542.

R. v. William Bruce Montague, Reasons on Voir Dire 2007 CanLII 13938 (ON SC).

Blog Posts

Kulturkampf
McKay, Tom. "Who is being shot by their toddlers today? Your Saturday gun fun roundup!" Accessed 19 July, 2015, http://wonkette.com/571732/who-is-being-shot-by-their-toddlers-today.

Wattrick, Jeff. "Hero patriot literally shoots himself in foot at Michigan gun show." Accessed 19 July, 2015, http://wonkette.com/494878/hero-patriot-literally-shoots-himself-in-foot-at-michigan-gun-show

Films

Breakheart Pass. Directed by Tom Gries. 1975. Jerry Gershwin Productions.
Dirty Harry. Directed by Don Siegel. 1971. Warner Brothers.
Death Wish. Directed by Michael Winner. 1974. Paramount Pictures.
Gunfight at the O.K. Corral. Directed by John Sturges. 1957. Paramount Pictures.
Harlan County, USA. Directed by Barbara Kopple. 1976. First Run Features.
High Noon. Directed by Fred Zinneman. 1952. United Artists.
Homesteaders of Paradise Valley. Directed by R.G. Springsteen. 1947. Republic Pictures.
My Darling Clementine. Directed by John Ford. 1946. Twentieth Century Fox.
Raiders of Red Gap. Directed by Sam Newfield. 1943. Producers Releasing.
Romance on the Range. Directed by Joseph Kane. 1942. Republic Pictures.
Shane. Directed by George Stevens. 1953. Paramount Pictures.
The Birth of a Nation. Directed by D.W. Griffith. 1915. David W. Griffith Corp.
The Crooked Trail. Directed by S. Roy Luby. 1936. Supreme Pictures.
The Princess Bride. Directed by Rob Reiner. 1987. Act III Communications.
Tombstone. Directed by George P. Cosmatos & Kevin Jarre. 1993. Buena Vista Pictures.
Under Siege. Directed by Andrew Davis. 1992. Warner Brothers.
Wyatt Earp. Directed by Lawrence Kasdan. 1994. Warner Brothers.

Acknowledgments

Sᴀᴅɪᴇ's ᴛɪʀᴇʟᴇss ᴀɴᴅ ɢʟᴇᴇꜰᴜʟ ᴘᴜʀsᴜɪᴛ ᴏꜰ game birds planted the germ of this thing, although it significantly interfered with the actual work between September and December. No one ought ever neglect a good dog in favour of writing a book. No book will ever jump on you when you come home or wag its tail when you walk into the room. For good or ill, the dumbass book lives forever; the dog lasts only a dog's age. Like most things in life, it's a bad deal. Yet the tail wags on, and it is all too easy to take it for granted.

I thank Dan Wells and the crew at Biblioasis: Grant, Chris, and Kate. Martha Sharpe. Emily Donaldson. Unsung heroes all.

The Ontario Arts Council provided financial assistance.

Without the patient and often thankless support of my wife, Vicky, the manuscript would never have been finished. This I will never take for granted.

A.J. SOMERSET'S WRITING has appeared in magazines throughout the US and Canada. His first novel, *Combat Camera*, received the Metcalf-Rooke Award. He lives in London, Ontario.